War in the American Pacific and East Asia, 1941–1972

AUSA Books

Series Editor: Joseph Craig

War in the American Pacific and East Asia, 1941–1972

Edited by
Hal M. Friedman

UNIVERSITY PRESS OF KENTUCKY

Portions of chapter 5 previously appeared in Hal Friedman, "Arguing over Empire: American Interservice and Interdepartmental Rivalry over Micronesia, 1945–1947," *Journal of Pacific History* 29 (June 1994): 36–48, and Hal Friedman, *Creating an American Lake: United States Imperialism and Strategic Security in the Pacific Basin, 1945–1947* (Westport, CT: Greenwood Press, 2001). Reprinted by permission.

Portions of chapter 6 were previously published in Katherine K. Reist, "The American Military Advising Missions in China, 1945–1949," *Journal of Military History* 77 (October 2013): 1379–1398. Reprinted by permission.

Scholarly publisher for the Commonwealth,
serving Bellarmine University, Berea College, Centre College of Kentucky, Eastern Kentucky University, The Filson Historical Society, Georgetown College, Kentucky Historical Society, Kentucky State University, Morehead State University, Murray State University, Northern Kentucky University, Transylvania University, University of Kentucky, University of Louisville, and Western Kentucky University.

Editorial and Sales Offices: The University Press of Kentucky
663 South Limestone Street, Lexington, Kentucky 40508-4008
www.kentuckypress.com

Library of Congress Cataloging-in-Publication Data

Names: Friedman, Hal M., 1965- editor.
Title: War in the American Pacific and East Asia, 1941-1972 / edited by Hal M. Friedman.
Description: Lexington, Kentucky : The University Press of Kentucky, [2018] | Series: AUSA books | Includes bibliographical references and index.
Identifiers: LCCN 2018027850| ISBN 9780813176550 (alk. paper) | ISBN 9780813176574 | ISBN 9780813176567
Subjects: LCSH: United States—Armed Forces—Pacific Area—History. | United States—Armed Forces—East Asia—History. | United States—Armed Forces—History—20th century.
Classification: LCC UA26.P3 W37 2018 | DDC 355.00973/09044—dc23
LC record available at https://lccn.loc.gov/2018027850

This book is printed on acid-free paper meeting the requirements of the American National Standard for Permanence in Paper for Printed Library Materials.

∞

Manufactured in the United States of America.

Member of the Association of University Presses

We, the editor and contributors,
thank our families for their support,
without which none of our achievements
would be possible.

Contents

Illustrations

Abbreviations

AAC	Army Air Corps
AAF	Army Air Forces
AAG	Army Advisory Group
AAS	Army Air Service
ABC	American Broadcasting Company
ACAN	Army Command and Administrative Network
ACAS	Assistant Chief of Air Staff
ACNO	Assistant Chief of Naval Operations
ACTS	Air Corps Tactical School
AEC	Atomic Energy Commission
AFHRA	Air Force Historical Research Agency
AGF	Army Ground Forces
AP	Associated Press
ARSO	Annual Report of the Chief Signal Officer
ASF	Army Service Forces
AT&T	American Telephone and Telegraph Company
AVG	American Volunteer Group
AWPD	Air War Plans Division
BBC	British Broadcasting Company
BDA	Battle Damage Assessment
BuOrd	U.S. Navy Bureau of Ordnance
CA	Chinese Army
CBS	Columbia Broadcasting System
CCP	Chinese Communist Party
CCS	Combined Chiefs of Staff
CG	Commanding General
CINCAFPAC	Commander-in-Chief, U.S. Army Forces, Pacific
CINCPAC	Commander-in-Chief, U.S. Pacific Command
CINCPACFLT	Commander-in-Chief, U.S. Pacific Fleet
CINCUS	Commander-in-Chief, U.S. Fleet
CMC	Commandant, Marine Corps
CMH	U.S. Army Center of Military History
CNO	Chief of Naval Operations
CO	Commanding Officer

COMGENAIR	Commanding General, Army Air Forces
CSA	Chief of Staff of the Army
DCNO	Deputy Chief of Naval Operations
DDEL	Dwight D. Eisenhower Library
DSM	Distinguished Service Medal
ETO	European Theater of Operations
FCC	Federal Communications Commission
FM	Frequency Modulation
FRUS	*Foreign Relations of the United States*
FSM	Federated States of Micronesia
GAO	Government Accounting Office
GHQ	General Headquarters
GPO	Government Printing Office
GWOT	Global War on Terrorism
HQUSFCT	Headquarters, U.S. Forces, China Theater
HSTL	Harry S. Truman Library
IBM	International Business Machines
ITC	Island Trading Company
JASCO	Joint Assault Signal Company
JCS	Joint Chiefs of Staff
JPS	Joint Staff Planners
JTF	Joint Task Force
JUSMAG	Joint U.S. Military Advisory Group
MAG	Military Advisory Group
MED	Manhattan Engineer District
MG	Military Government
MHI	Military History Institute
MP	Military Police
NA	National Archives
NBC	National Broadcasting Company
NCO	Noncommissioned Officer
NHC	Naval Historical Center
NHHC	Naval History and Heritage Command
NMD	National Ministry of Defense
OA	Operational Archives
OCI	Office of the Coordinator of Information
OPNAV	Office of the Chief of Naval Operations
P&O	Plans and Operations
POA	Pacific Ocean Areas
PTO	Pacific Theater of Operations

PX Post Exchange
RAF Royal Air Force
RCA Radio Corporation of America
RG Record Group
ROC Republic of China
SAC Strategic Air Command
SACO Sino-American Cooperative Organization
SCAP Supreme Commander for the Allied Powers
SCTIL *Signal Corps Technical Information Letter*
SHAEF Supreme Headquarters, Allied Expeditionary Force
SPBC South Pacific Base Command
SWNCC State-War-Navy Coordinating Committee
SWPA Southwest Pacific Area
TTPI Trust Territory of the Pacific Islands
U.N. United Nations
UPI United Press International
USAFC U.S. Army Forces, China
USAFFE U.S. Army Forces, Far East
USCC United States Commercial Company
USFCT U.S. Forces, China Theater
VCNO Vice Chief of Naval Operations
WAC Women's Army Corps
WAMCATS Washington-Alaska Military Cable and Telegraph System
WAR We Are Ready
WHOF White House Official Files

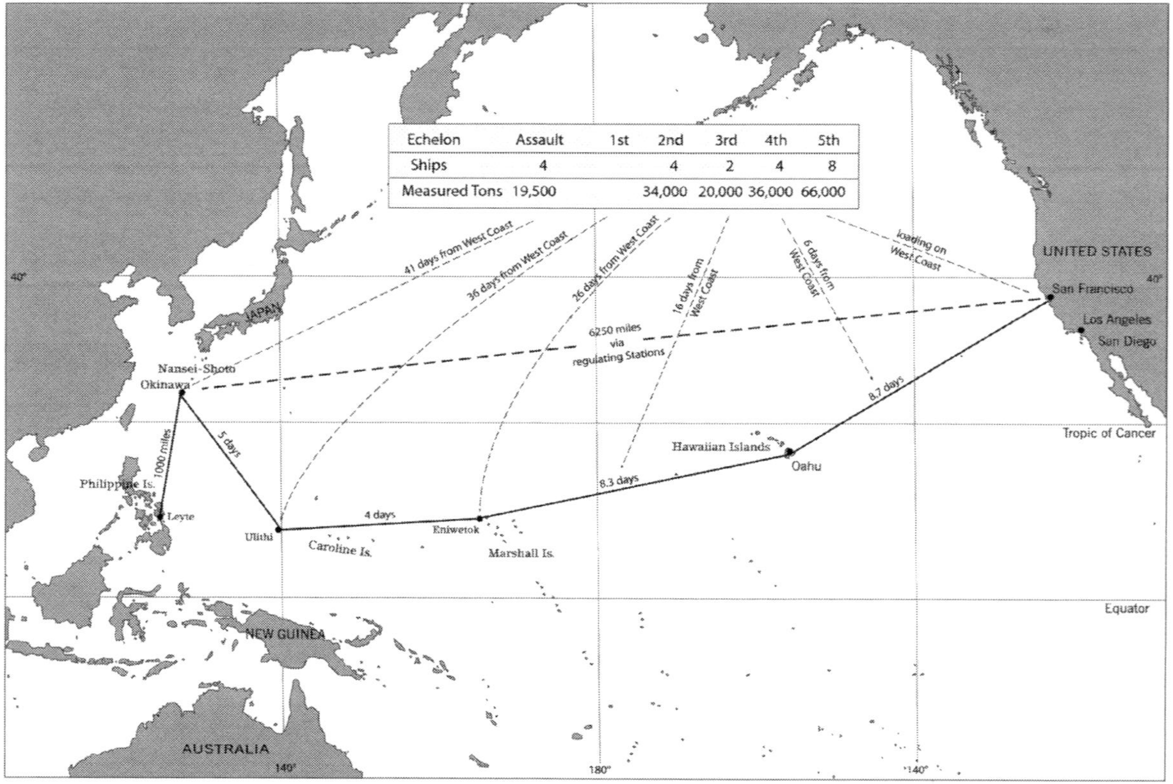

Pacific Basin Distances (Courtesy of the Naval Historical Collection, U.S. Naval War College, Newport, Rhode Island)

Introduction

David J. Ulbrich

This anthology brings together a diverse collection of essays that examine the 1940s as the critical decade in the United States' ascendance in the Pacific. This decade saw the peak of power and the eventual fall of the Japanese Empire, which stood as the greatest single threat to the American presence in the Pacific and East Asia. Following victory in World War II in 1945, the United States assumed the hegemonic role in the region as Japan's defeat left military and political power vacuums in its wake. Other powers, such as France, the United Kingdom, and the Netherlands, saw their prewar influence decline or disappear altogether. The United States rose from the rubble of war to assert its leadership. Without a doubt, Americans actively grasped for hegemony during the 1940s. This process was also a function of other regional competitors being weakened or eliminated, as well as new competitors surfacing to challenge the new superpower.

Americans nevertheless struggled to win the peace or at least maintain stability in the years following their decisive victory in the Pacific War. By decade's end, the Communist victory in China gave that nation strength and posed dangers to American interests, though mostly on the mainland. Revolution and civil war in Southeast Asia grew more visible. The increasingly hostile Soviet Union likewise tried to exert as much influence as possible in the region. The 1940s gave way to several decades of American activism in the Cold War Pacific in response to these challenges.[1]

It is in this context that this anthology's seven essays stand not only as a précis of current scholarship but also as a prospectus for future research. The contributing authors eschew the traditional focus on military operations that has dominated the historiography of the 1940s in the Pacific and East Asia.[2] Instead, the contributors herein venture into areas of race, gender, technology, culture, media, diplomacy, and institutions, all of which add nuance and clarity to the existing literature of World War II and the early Cold War. Some chapters break new ground in their interpretations, while others affirm or revise conventional historical wisdom. Taken as whole, the chapters' threads come together to show that, although the United States may have achieved hegemony in the region by the 1950s, the progression was hardly smooth and sometimes barely planned.

In her chapter on the U.S. Army Signal Corps, Rebecca Raines traces how that branch created a viable radio communications system during World War II. This accomplishment represented the Corps' herculean efforts to overcome the technological challenge of sending wartime messages across the globe as well as such bureaucratic obstacles as austere budgets, disinterested Army officers, and competing radio systems in the prewar years. Surmounting these obstacles fell to a new Signal Corps' Army Command and Administrative Network (ACAN). Raines points out that, over the forty-four months of the conflict, the Army Command and Administrative Network established an effective radio network that made conversations and even conference calls possible between senior leaders in Washington, D.C., and their counterparts nearly 10,000 miles away in the Southwest Pacific Theater. This required ever more advanced technology to be developed, procured, and deployed to Australia, New Guinea, the Philippines, and other bases in the Pacific. Indeed, one can track General Douglas MacArthur's island-hopping campaign from 1942 to 1945 by locating the newest stations built at secured bases and being used in turn to support the next advances. ACAN started with stations in California, Hawaii, and Australia, and then gradually added new ones at Nouméa on Caledonia, Hollandia on New Guinea, Manila in the Philippines, and so on. When needed, the Army utilized Navy ships as communication nodes until a ground-based station could be built. Meanwhile, the tiny prewar Signal Corps expanded to a branch with some 300,000 male and female soldiers and 60,000 civilians. Despite ongoing bureaucratic challenges of coordinating with the Navy's system and environmental challenges of long distances and tropical climates, ACAN's radio network encompassed the globe. It proved instrumental in every operation in the Pacific because it was essential to have effective communications at all levels of leadership. The system was even used by the Allies to negotiate surrender terms with the Japanese in August 1945. Raines adds new details to an often overlooked factor of the American success in the Pacific War.

In the second chapter, Steve Call examines the multiple layers of meaning in media portrayals of American air power in the Pacific War. He points to what he calls the media's didactic roles, which included popularizing the use of aerial bombardment and educating the American public about the war effort, the Japanese enemy, and the nature of war. Movies represented one of the main ways of selling these roles. Wartime audiences were treated to heroic stories of the Flying Tigers in the film of that name as well as the Doolittle Raid in *Thirty Seconds over Tokyo.* Other media venues, such as *The Saturday Evening Post* and *Colliers,* served as platforms to raise public awareness of skip-bombing attacks against Japanese ships and strategic bombardment of targets on land. The United States Army Air Forces (AAF) had its own stars, such as Lieutenant General James "Jimmy" Doolittle and General George Kenney, both of whom became icons of air power on the Pacific. They were the most recent in a line of aviators who captivated the public imagination dating back to World War I. Even so, their exploits had serious competition for the public's attention from the European Theater of Operations (ETO), as well as from the amphibious operations in the Pacific. As Call observes, in November 1943 media coverage of American bombing raids destroying 25 million gallons of Japanese fuel paled in comparison to the invasion of Italy, not to mention the bloody combat raging on Tarawa.

By 1944, the American air campaign gained momentum in a strategic sense with the capture of the Marianas Islands and the arrival of the B-29 bomber. This long-range aircraft flying out the Marianas gave the U.S. Army Air Forces the means of bombarding Japan at will. The momentum can also be seen in the ways in which messages about air power were crafted for public consumption. Strategic bombardment, according to Call, shifted to the use of incendiary ordnance late in the war when Major General Curtis LeMay assumed command of the Twenty-First Bomber Command in the Marianas. The firebombing of Japan and eventually the use of the apex weapon—atomic bombs—not only sealed the Japanese defeat, at least according to the Army Air Forces, but also elevated the AAF to a nearly unassailable level of popularity.

In Chapter 3, Stephen Houseknecht looks to the United States Marine Corps Raiders as a case study in special operations forces whose institutional culture clashed with that of its parent service. Discussion of these elite units is often left to the popular press and memoirists, with little interest from scholars. Yet the Raider Battalions deserve a second look for a variety of reasons. The creation of small, elite cohorts within larger, preexisting military cultures often caused considerable internal tension. In early 1942, the U.S. Marine Corps embarked on this experiment in military elitism with the creation of the Marine Raider Battalions. This foray into the emergent world of special forces was brief and tumultuous, not even lasting until the end of the conflict. The units, especially Evan Carlson's Second Raider Battalion, met with resistance from some elements of the Marine Corps. Among these dissenters was Lieutenant General Thomas Holcomb, Commandant of the Marine Corps (CMC), who saw no need to elevate supposedly elite units like the Raiders above regular Marine Corps combat units. He believed that any Marine could be trained to perform Raiders' missions of reconnaissance and infiltration.[3] Though the operational life-span of the Raider battalions was short, Houseknecht's reconsideration of these units sheds light on the tension between the dominant culture of the U.S. Marine

Corps as a corps d'elite and the emergent, equally elitist subculture of the specialized Raider battalions.

Josh Levy's chapter takes a cultural turn in analyzing the problems facing the U.S. Navy's occupation of one Micronesian island following the American victory over Japan. He uses as his case study the interaction between the Americans and the people of Pohnpei, an island in the East Carolines that had been held by the Japanese during the Pacific War. Levy uses his study of the foodways of the indigenous Pohnpieans as a springboard to analyze Navy policies, gender relations, class distinctions, commercial development, and agricultural production. Although rarely explored in military histories, a study of foodways can lead to several topics relating to the reconstruction of societies and economies in postwar periods. The U.S. Navy assumed control of Pohnpei and tried to Americanize the people's foodways as a means of "dietary colonialism." This, it was hoped, would create a stable system on Pohnpei that in turn could contribute to American security interests in the Western Pacific.

For the most part, however, the U.S. Navy personnel in charge failed to appreciate the place of food in Pohnpei's social and commercial contexts. Food, especially gifts of food, fit into a hierarchy of power relationships between landowners and peasants, and between men and women. Food production and consumption served as symbols of prestige, reward, and even punishment among the islanders. The Americans, who came to Pohnpei in 1945 after liberating it from Japanese control, failed to grasp how and why the Pohnpeians' foodways dictated so much of social and commercial relations. The Americans were also ignorant of how food they imported to the island would undermine hierarchical relations with more democratic notions. Worse still, underlying the intruders' actions was a racial assumption that the Pohnpeians would not easily adapt to an allegedly superior American culture without active pressure to do so. The result was a culture clash, starting with foodways and expanding to other areas of life. Not only did the Pohnpeians dislike the American foods, they also used their own traditional agricultural production and consumption to disrupt the American colonization process. In historicizing diet, Levy demonstrates that the Pohnpeians exercised a remarkable amount of agency.

Hal Friedman's chapter traces the evolution of atomic bomb testing into the postwar years of 1945–1947. He concentrates on the tests of this fearsome weapon at Bikini Atoll in the Pacific. Friedman uses the testing as a touchstone to deal with the United States military as an institution. The motivations for exploding atomic bombs in the air over the atoll and beneath the sea nearby varied greatly among the U.S. Army, the Army Air Forces, the Navy, the State Department, and even the Interior Department. The armed services were vying for control of the Pacific Ocean—styled as the "American lake"—and for significance in the shrinking postwar appropriations. The Army Air Forces wanted to use the tests to validate the atomic bombs as an antiship weapon and a potential weapon in general warfare. The Navy wanted to the use the atomic bomb against enemy shipping but also wanted to demonstrate that that weapon did not make U.S. warships obsolete. The ground warfare proponents in the Army also sought to find a role for its ground units. All three wished to control the media's messages being presented to the American people. Adding to this interservice tension were concerns about increasing already poor relations with the Soviet Union and about possible ecological dangers to Bikini Atoll and its surrounding areas. Friedman disentangles a complex web of interests in drawing two conclusions. He finds that the military's official spin on the Bikini tests provided useful data on the viability of atomic weapons against warships. However, the actual results did not please any of the services. The targeted vessels farther than one-half mile from the aerial atomic explosion took damage but remained afloat. The tests did not change the Navy's strategies, tactics, or organizational structures. For the Army Air Forces' part, the tests did not resolve its conflict with the Navy over the supposed supremacy of land-based or carrier-based aircraft.

Shifting away from the Pacific Ocean onto the Asian mainland, Katherine Reist's chapter reveals how messy China became in the immediate postwar years. The Japanese defeat did not augur much hope for stability and peace for China. Without Japan as a common enemy, hostilities erupted between Chiang Kai-shek's Nationalist forces and Mao Zedong's Communist forces over control of the entire nation. Provincial warlords also vied for local power. Although Americans feared a possible takeover by Mao, they had little hope that Chiang's autocratic government would survive without assistance, such as American combat units deployed to China on occupation duty. The best chance to bring Mao's and Chiang's supporters onto common ground occurred when American President Harry S. Truman sent General of the Army George C. Marshall to China in December 1945. The general's mandate entailed achieving a cease-fire and then establishing a coherent China Army that combined Nationalist and Communist components.

Marshall succeeded in meeting the first part of his mandate, but achieving the second proved difficult in the short term and impossible in the long term. Problems of decentralized control, poor communication, and ineffective transportation plagued Marshall in his work with the opposing sides. Chiang could not solve these problems, and Mao exploited them as weaknesses. Marshall tried to establish Chinese supervisory boards to exert control over the Communist and Nationalist forces, but to no avail. U.S. Army and Navy Advisory Groups also endeavored to help mold a new Chinese military, but again without long-term success. Apart from military structures, neither side in the civil war could agree on what a new Chinese government should look like. For Reist, this latter political point of contention doomed Marshall's work to create a viable Chinese military. No matter the skill and intelligence of Marshall, compromises could not be struck. By the summer of 1946 he realized that failure was certain and finally departed from China in early 1947. Two years later, Mao's forces won the civil war. A Communist regime then assumed political supremacy in mainland China.

In the final chapter, Nicholas Sarantakes takes the volume full circle by returning to media-military relations. His chapter, however, shifts focus to the postwar American military occupation of Okinawa. In the years after the end of the Pacific War, the island of Okinawa remained an important strategic base because it was located only 300 miles to the southwest of Japan. This put Okinawa in striking distance of Formosa (Taiwan after 1949) and in place to play a supporting role elsewhere in East Asia or the Western Pacific. Despite this strategic consideration, the U.S. military occupation could not look like blatant imperialism because Americans had criticized this policy in practice by other nations. Instead, as Sarantakes relates, a creative solution was found that gave Okinawa "residual sovereignty." This bait-and-switch policy translated into ongoing American military administration yet retention by Okinawans of their citizenship.

The American media played an increasingly significant role over time, first by bolstering and later criticizing the arrangement in Okinawa. In the 1940s and early 1950s, the U.S. Military Government (MG) controlled media access on the island and thus dictated the message. However, as the years passed into the 1960s, coverage of the American presence on Okinawa soured. Newspapers and magazines ran stories about American interference in the Okinawan political process, the increase in social problems caused by American personnel stationed on Okinawa, and the constraint of new industrial development on the island. The popular pressure on Okinawa and in the United States slowly gained enough momentum to drive the U.S. Military Government off the island. By the late 1960s, the negative feelings on the island turned into violence in bloody riots. American media outlets brought these scenes to the American people and their elected officials, who in turn spurred the departure of the U.S. Military Government from Okinawa in 1972. Sarantakes concludes that media coverage grew increasingly critical of the American presence on the island, just as media coverage portrayed the American presence elsewhere in the world and especially in Vietnam in a more critical way.

The varying levels of American success revealed in these seven chapters highlight at least two patterns. First was the ability of the U.S. military to overcome obstacles during the Pacific War. This pragmatic process of finding solutions to problems stands as one of the hallmarks of Americans during wartime. Also conspicuous in all of World War II was the incredible industrial capacity of the United States. This adaptability, flexibility, and productivity entailed cooperation—sometimes pushed along and sometimes hindered by internal competition—among America's armed services, civilian leaders, and home-front workers. As the chapters in this volume demonstrate, winning World War II in the Pacific—and in Europe for that matter—required the mobilization of the United States' almost limitless manpower, machines, and media. This is not to say that no setbacks or losses occurred, because there were indeed many hardships in the Pacific Theater of Operations (PTO).

The other pattern can be seen in the postwar years, when the U.S. military could not necessarily construct a viable peace or deal with challenges to that peace. Sometimes, American military or diplomatic policies could not contain threats of communism or the Soviet Union. At other times, U.S. military efforts proved to be too heavy-handed in attempting to win over liberated peoples to the American way of life. In still other cases, efforts to improve military capabilities caused competition, rather than cooperation, within the American military establishment. This volume thus portrays the history of the immediate postwar era as full of mixed results. Regardless, the situations described in this anthology live up to the sobriquet "war by other means."

The contributing authors have demonstrated that American activism and actions in the Pacific and East Asia during the 1940s certainly affected the region in diverse ways. Although the subject is beyond the scope of this volume, American efforts to restructure Japanese society and government into a stable democracy merit great praise as the landmark example of American interventionism.

American activism and actions also helped set the stage for the future American presence during the Cold War and still more recently in the twenty-first century. The Vietnam conflict, for example, stands as the greatest, tragic case study. The American failure in Vietnam occurred because of combined political mistakes and cultural ignorance, not unlike some of the cautionary tales explored by the contributors to this volume.

Indeed, this anthology should appeal to American military personnel and their diplomatic counterparts as the United States military reorients its focus toward the Pacific Ocean in the tense presence and uncertain future. This new strategic emphasis can be seen in such documents as the U.S. Department of Defense's *Sustaining U.S. Global Leadership: Priorities for the 21st Century* (2012) and the nongovernmental, bipartisan Center for Strategic and International Studies' *U.S. Force Posture Strategy in the Asia Pacific Region* (2012).[4]

While there may be differences in degree of strategic, technological, and cultural factors in the Pacific between the 1940s and 2010s, there will probably not be significant differences in kind. American forces will continue to need to project force, maintain communications, utilize advanced weaponry, influence media coverage, and negotiate cultural difference, just as was done in the 1940s. Thus, many lessons of pragmatism during wartime as well as measured restraint and cultural sensitivity in peacetime can be gleaned from these pages.

Notes

I wish to thank Hal Friedman for his invitation to contribute to this volume.

1. See relevant sections in Michael H. Hunt and Steven I. Levine, *Arc of Empire: America's Wars in Asia from the Philippines to Vietnam* (Chapel Hill: University of North Carolina Press, 2012); Hall Gardner, *Averting Global War: Regional Challenges, Overextension, and Options for American Strategy* (London: Palgrave Macmillan, 2007); Odd Arne Westad, *The Global Cold War: Third World Interventions and the Making of Our Times* (New York: Cambridge University Press, 2007); and John Lewis Gaddis, *Strategies of Containment: A Critical Appraisal of American National Security during the Cold War*, rev. ed. (New York: Oxford University Press, 2005).

2. The number of operational histories of the Pacific War is legion, and some noteworthy books are Jeter A. Isely and Philip A. Crowl, *The U.S. Marines and Amphibious War* (Princeton: Princeton University Press, 1951); Gordon W. Prange, *At Dawn We Slept: The Untold Story of Pearl Harbor* (New York: McGraw-Hill, 1980); Richard B. Frank, *Guadalcanal: The Definitive Account of the Landmark Battle* (New York: Random House, 1990); Eric M. Bergerud, *Fire in the Sky: The Air War in the South Pacific* (New York: Basic Books, 2001); Jonathan Parshall and Anthony Tully, *Shattered Story: The Untold Story of the Battle of Midway* (Dulles, VA: Potomac Books, 2005); Steven R. Taafe, *MacArthur's Jungle War: The 1944 New Guinea Campaign* (Lawrence: University Press of Kansas, 2006); and Sharon Tosi Lacy, *Pacific Blitzkrieg: World War II in the Central Pacific* (Denton: University of North Texas Press, 2013).

3. John W. Gordon, "The U.S. Marine Corps and an Experiment in Military Elitism: A Reassessment of the Special Warfare Impetus, 1937–1943," in Robert Love, ed., *Changing Interpretations and New Sources in Naval History: Papers from the Third United States History Symposium* (New York: Garland Publishers, 1980), 362; and David J. Ulbrich, *Preparing for Victory: Thomas Holcomb and the Making of the Modern Marine Corps, 1936–1943* (Annapolis: Naval Institute Press, 2011): 124–125, 143, 152.

4. U.S. Department of Defense, *Sustaining U.S. Global Leadership: Priorities for the 21st Century* (2012), http://www.defense.gov/news/defense_strategic_guidance.pdf; and Center for Strategic and International Studies, *U.S. Force Posture Strategy in the Asia Pacific Region* (2012), http://csis.org/files/publication/120814_FINAL_PACOM_optimized.pdf. The United States is not the only nation showing interest in the Pacific. The most recent Australian Chief of Army History Conference focused on the theme of Armies and Maritime Strategy. For the proceedings of this conference, see http://www.army.gov.au/Our-history/Army-History-Unit/Chief-of-Army-History-Conference/2013-Chief-

of-Army-Conference (all accessed on 28 September 1914). Publishers such as the Naval Institute Press and Routledge are also publishing several books each year dealing with the strategic, technological, and cultural aspects of the Pacific and East Asia.

Bibliography

Primary Sources

Center for Strategic and International Studies. *U.S. Force Posture Strategy in the Asia Pacific Region* (2012), http://csis.org/files/publication/120814_FINAL_PACOM_optimized.pdf.

U.S. Department of Defense. *Sustaining U.S. Global Leadership: Priorities for the 21st Century* (2012). http://www.defense.gov/news/defense_strategic_guidance.pdf.

Secondary Sources

Bergerud, Eric M. *Fire in the Sky: The Air War in the South Pacific.* New York: Basic Books, 2001.

Frank, Richard B. *Guadalcanal: The Definitive Account of the Landmark Battle.* New York: Random House, 1990.

Gaddis, John Lewis. *Strategies of Containment: A Critical Appraisal of American National Security during the Cold War.* Rev. ed. New York: Oxford University Press, 2005.

Gardner, Hall. *Averting Global War: Regional Challenges, Overextension, and Options for American Strategy.* London: Palgrave Macmillan, 2007.

Hunt, Michael H., and Steven I. Levine. *Arc of Empire: America's Wars in Asia from the Philippines to Vietnam.* Chapel Hill: University of North Carolina Press, 2012.

Isely, Jeter A., and Philip A. Crowl. *The U.S. Marines and Amphibious War.* Princeton: Princeton University Press, 1951.

Lacy, Sharon Tosi. *Pacific Blitzkrieg: World War II in the Central Pacific.* Denton: University of North Texas Press, 2013.

Parshall, Jonathan, and Anthony Tully. *Shattered Story: The Untold Story of the Battle of Midway.* Dulles, VA: Potomac Books, 2005.

Prange, Gordon W. *At Dawn We Slept: The Untold Story of Pearl Harbor.* New York: McGraw-Hill, 1980.

Taaffe, Steven R. *MacArthur's Jungle War: The 1944 New Guinea Campaign.* Lawrence: University Press of Kansas, 2006.

Ulbrich, David J. *Preparing for Victory: Thomas Holcomb and the Making of the Modern Marine Corps, 1936–1943.* Annapolis: Naval Institute Press, 2011.

Westad, Odd Arne. *The Global Cold War: Third World Interventions and the Making of Our Times.* New York: Cambridge University Press, 2007.

1

Theater of WAR

The U.S. Army's Command and Administrative Communications Network in the Pacific, 1940–1950

Rebecca Robbins Raines

In February 1939, the Army Signal Corps sought permission to upgrade its radio facilities at Fort Myer, Virginia, a cavalry post strategically located on the hills bordering Arlington National Cemetery.[1] The Signal Corps needed to erect a rhombic antenna that would facilitate communication with Seattle via the War Department's radio net.[2] Reliable communication with the West Coast was becoming increasingly important as international tensions increased in the Far East with Japan's steady expansion of its empire in East Asia.

Colonel George S. Patton Jr., Commanding Officer (CO), 3d Cavalry regiment, opposed the Signal Corps' proposal. Already being hemmed in by suburban development at Fort Myer, Patton did not want to lose any more acreage. He further recommended that the Signal Corps' radio transmission station be removed because he wanted to use the land for barracks and an officers' club. The Signal Corps then attempted to obtain the Navy's permission to erect the antenna on land nearby where the Navy had its own radio station.[3] The problem remained unresolved until 7 January 1941 when Secretary of the Navy Frank Knox officially denied the Army's request. He explained his decision by saying that the "present emergency" made it necessary for the Navy Department to retain the property for its own use.[4] In so doing, he curtailed the Signal Corps' plans to improve its long-distance radio capabilities. The adverse effects of his ruling became evident all too soon—just eleven months later—on 7 December 1941.[5]

On that fateful Sunday morning, the War Department attempted to contact Hawaii by radio with a war warning, but atmospheric disturbances around San Francisco and Honolulu blocked the transmission. The Army then turned to the commercial facilities of Western Union and the Radio Corporation of America (RCA). Somehow, the urgency of the message did not get conveyed, and RCA's office in Honolulu delivered it to Army headquarters at Fort Shafter in a routine manner by motorcycle messenger. The courier arrived while the Japanese bombs were falling. Lieutenant General Walter C. Short, Commanding General (CG), Hawaiian Department, did not receive the decoded message until 1500, long after the attack was over.[6]

With the sudden onset of World War II, the U.S. Army had to vastly expand the scope of its communications capabilities. Operation and management of the Army's worldwide system, eventually known as the Army Command and Administrative Network (ACAN), fell under the aegis of the Signal Corps, the Army's specialized communications branch, first established in 1860. By war's end, the Signal Corps had built a system that spanned the globe. The Army's fixed administrative communications in the Pacific are the focus of this chapter, specifically those in the Southwest Pacific Area (SWPA), where the Army conducted most of its Pacific Basin operations.[7] This essay concentrates on the Army's radio network, as opposed to its wire and cable lines. Despite the importance of the Army's communications system to the war effort, little has been written about it. This chapter is an attempt to shed some light on a long-neglected subject.[8]

Within the military, the Navy had taken the lead in radio matters. Since 1913, the Navy had operated a high-power transmitter in Arlington, and prior to World War I it had begun constructing a chain of stations in the Caribbean and the Pacific to support fleet operations.[9] The Navy had, in fact, sought to gain control over all radio broadcasting. The centralization of radio functions would reduce their vulnerability from ownership by foreign interests. Radio would also break Great Britain's hold over long-distance communications, exercised through its control of the world's cable system. The Navy could point to Britain's successful effort to impose an information blockade against Germany during World War I to illustrate the power that could be wielded by controlling communications.[10]

With the expanding role of the United States in world affairs, the efficacy of international communications assumed increasing significance. Ties between the United States and Asia represented a particularly weak link. Until the Navy opened new overseas radio stations late in the war, connection with East Asia had depended upon just one commercial cable, an extremely vulnerable situation. Because of their political, commercial, and military importance, a joint committee of the State, War, and Navy Departments met in June 1918 to consider ways to improve transpacific communications. Major General George O. Squier, Chief Signal Officer, represented the Army. There were no easy answers: the United States lacked a domestic cable industry that could construct a second cable, and opening additional radio stations also required large amounts of both time and money. Therefore, the nation's strategic communication needs would remain seriously inadequate for the foreseeable future.[11]

During the 1920s, radio broadcasting underwent explosive growth, giving rise to a national broadcasting industry.[12] While the technical aspects of the Army's communications system will not be discussed in detail here, some organizational background concerning its establishment and operation prior to World War II is necessary in order to place into context the transformation that occurred once the nation entered the global conflict.

Despite several attempts, the Navy failed to secure Congressional approval for its consolidation plans. Nevertheless, the Navy continued its pursuit of communications independence. Toward this end, it played a central role in the formation of RCA, created in 1919 to counter competition from foreign companies.[13]

Meanwhile, the Army endeavored to enhance its fledgling domestic radio network through the establishment of the War Department Radio Net in January 1922, using the Navy's system as a model.[14] The radio network enabled the Army's leadership to communicate directly with commanders in the field without going through commercial channels. This strategic network was built in accordance with War Plan White, the Army's contingency plan for dealing with domestic disturbances, part of a series of color-coded plans developed during the interwar period to deal with various hypothetical scenarios.[15]

In March 1923, the War Department consolidated its radio and telegraph offices to form the War Department Message Center under the Chief Signal Officer. The central control station was appropriately designated with the call letters WAR (We Are Ready).[16] It was located at Army Headquarters in the Munitions Building in downtown Washington. From Washington, We Are Ready maintained connections with major military installations around the country, as well as with stations in certain major cities. By 1925, the system consisted of 164 stations. This total included those within the Signal Corps' Alaska Communication System, controlled from Seattle, that served the sprawling northern territory.[17]

At this time, the only other Army radio stations located outside the continental United States were in the nation's overseas territories. By agreement with the Navy in 1927, the Army limited its overseas radio operations to the following communications: with and between its own units wherever located; within the Territory of Alaska; with and between Army vessels except those under naval control; and for radio intelligence operations wherever the Army was operating. The Army was further limited to using transmitters of 10 kilowatts or less.[18] In the event of war, military planners had envisioned that the Navy's radio system would expand globally while the Army's would remain largely confined to the corps areas within the United States.[19]

The Army's austere budgets during the interwar years inhibited growth and improvements in its radio system. Initially equipped with low-frequency, continuous wave sets, technological changes soon rendered this equipment outmoded. Because there was little money to upgrade equipment, transcontinental communication remained difficult: it took a day to send a message from one coast to the other. Messages from Washington destined for the West Coast had to be relayed through several intermediate stations. By 1929, the use of shortwave transmitters and high-frequency amplifiers had largely eliminated this problem, but static remained an obstacle.[20] Static particularly affected overseas transmissions with the significant time differences (thirteen hours between Manila and Washington, for example) and especially the division between daylight and darkness. Thus, careful scheduling was required to find the most effective circuits to use throughout twenty-four hours. The transition from Morse code to voice communications—made possible by improvements in vacuum tubes—coupled with the adoption of frequency modulation (FM) and shortwave transmission, represented the most critical technological leaps during this period. In addition, crystal control enabled more accurate tuning and thus more efficient use of the radio spectrum.[21]

The budgetary constraints also delayed the transition from manual to automatic message transmission. The Signal Corps still relied on manually operated equipment in 1940; radioteletype had not yet come into general usage.[22] The teletypewriters available to the Army required an operator to manually type the message to be sent. At the receiving end, the message was automatically printed out. If it needed to be further relayed, however, an operator at the intermediate station had to type it out again. Despite its ongoing monetary challenges, the Signal Corps undertook efforts in 1940 to upgrade its facilities at all stations—such as the installation of better antennas and wiring. Yet as the war approached, the Army could not even afford to erect protective fencing around its valuable transmitter at Fort Myer.[23]

Shortages of personnel also hindered operations. There were simply not enough men in uniform in the small interwar Army to handle the duties. The prewar Signal Corps of the Regular Army comprised fewer than 300 officers, and most of them had no experience with handling large volumes of message traffic. Moreover, turnover was heavy as men left the Army for better-paying jobs in the private sector. To obtain the qualified personnel needed to operate the system around the clock, the Civil Service Commission inaugurated special recruiting practices for hiring and training civilian radio operators.[24] Without these measures, the system could not have handled the increasing volume of traffic in the months before Pearl Harbor, since during the interwar years, the net had expanded to connect with the nation's telephone, telegraph, and cable companies, and with the growing system of amateur radio operators around the country. From this nucleus, the Signal Corps would form its wartime system.

Since the creation of the Army's radio system, one of its major justifications had been its value as a venue for training new personnel and as a proving ground for testing new methods and equipment. The system was also intended to be expanded in case of emergency—as proved to be the case. The Army established formal connections with radio enthusiasts by setting up the Army Amateur Radio System in 1925. Amateur operators provided a valuable pool of skilled personnel for emergencies. Even so, personnel shortages persisted. Despite their contributions in peacetime, the Federal Communications Commission (FCC) closed some 60,000 amateur stations for the duration of the war in the interest of national security and to provide more space on the broadcast spectrum for military communications.[25]

The Signal Corps had a long-standing record of working successfully with the private sector. The American Telephone and Telegraph Company (AT&T), for example, had provided twelve battalions of trained operators during World War I.[26] With little experience in international communications, the Signal Corps again looked to the civilian world for expertise. Chief among these advisors was David A. Sarnoff of RCA. Sarnoff and other leading industry executives became officers in the Signal Corps Reserve.[27] The Signal Corps had some experience with long-distance telegraphy and underwater cable operations, particularly in the territories of Alaska, the Philippines, the Panama Canal Zone, Hawaii, and Puerto Rico, but nothing on the scale that would be required to meet the worldwide emergency. Even commercial systems were slow and costly, and sending international telegrams was not a common occurrence for the average American before the war.[28]

The Army depended on the private sector not only for advice and personnel, but also for the development and production of communications equipment. The Signal Corps' limited prewar budgets had not allowed for stockpiling items. Even if money had been available, there were few suitable items on the market to be purchased. With no time or money to develop its own specially designed equipment, the Army adapted commercial standard items to its needs. When the available supply fell short, the Signal Corps called upon the amateur radio community for help. The Army also made use of commercial facilities during the critical early months of the war before it could expand to meet wartime requirements.[29]

By July 1942, the Signal Corps had begun to adopt equipment developed by AT&T that could punch, or perforate, a tape that was then fed into a relaying machine for automatic retransmission. The tape relay method represented a considerable improvement over existing procedures, but it still relied upon wires. Among other drawbacks were the large amount of floor space required by the equipment and the need to physically transfer the tapes between machines, but this system was the best available at the time. First used over a circuit between We Are Ready and Governors Island, New York, it constituted the initial link in ACAN's worldwide automatic network.[30]

With the subsequent introduction of radioteletype, using radio waves rather than wire to send messages, the situation improved dramatically. This method enabled the transmission of more than one hundred words per minute—about double that of manual transmission. It worked much like teletype, producing a perforated tape in addition to hard copy. When passed through a transmitting device, radio impulses were generated that corresponded to the perforations. At the receiving end, the message was automatically translated to typed copy. Radioteletype also worked well for the transmission of classified messages, which it coded and decoded automatically. This was an important feature because much of the message traffic was encoded. Radioteletype operation began on the Army's overseas circuits in September 1943. Only with such innovations that enabled operators to easily and rapidly convey vast quantities of information could the Signal Corps meet ACAN's wartime strategic communications needs.[31]

Chief Signal Officer Major General Dawson Olmstead was Chief of the Corps when World War II began.[32] Under his administration, the Army's communications network undertook a vast wartime expansion. To fulfill its vital mission, the manpower of the Signal Corps had to multiply as well. On 7 December 1941, the Corps' strength stood at 3,000 officers and 47,000 enlisted men. By June 1943, the Signal Corps had grown to just over 27,000 officers and 287,000 enlisted men. To that total would be added 60,000 civilian employees.[33] The Corps' budgets underwent a similar explosion. In March 1942, the Signal Corps received its first billion-dollar budget. But even that then-staggering sum would soon prove to be insufficient—by mid-1943 the Signal Corps' budget had quadrupled.[34]

Organizationally, ACAN was placed under the Army Communications Division (later the Army Communications Service) within the Office of the Chief Signal Officer.[35] Two officers headed the Army Communications Service during the war. Colonel Otis K. Sadtler served as Director from 5 August 1941 to 20 February 1942. He was succeeded by Brigadier General Frank E. Stoner, who served for the remainder of the war.[36] Both men had earlier been in charge of the War Department Message Center (renamed the War Department Signal Center in 1942) and had thereby gained valuable experience with handling large amounts of message traffic. As the war progressed, traffic engineering and frequency management would become especially critical issues affecting the efficient handling of the vast loads of information being moved.

In 1942, General George C. Marshall, Army Chief of Staff (CSA), initiated a major reorganization of the War Department and divided the Army into three commands: the Army Ground Forces (AGF); the Services of Supply (later named the Army Service Forces, or ASF); and the Army Air Forces (AAF). Marshall placed the Signal Corps and the Army's other technical services (e.g., Ordnance, Quartermaster, Chemical) under the Services of Supply, commanded by Lieutenant General Brehon B. Somervell, an engineer known for his energy and administrative ability as well as for his prickly personality.[37] Under this arrangement, the Chief Signal Officer had less control over his Branch's operations. Olmstead's rocky relationship with Somervell led to his eventual removal as Chief Signal Officer in June 1943. He was replaced by Major General Harry C. Ingles, an experienced signal officer and a former classmate of Somervell's at West Point.[38]

Although ACAN was a fixed system, it had to be flexible enough to expand to meet the communications requirements generated by the highly mobile warfare conducted during World War II. It also had to be dependable, secure, and swift. As the Commander-in-Chief, President Franklin D. Roosevelt needed to be able to communicate with military leaders at all times, wherever he may be. When traveling around the country, President Roosevelt enjoyed direct access to We Are Ready through a radio station, WTE, located in his private train. The President could also use this station, operated by two enlisted men from We Are Ready, to access the worldwide ACAN. A radioteletype station aboard the Presidential plane, the *Sacred Cow,* was also tied into the system.[39]

The switch from a peacetime to a wartime network brought about a fundamental change in the nature of the network's operations. Before hostilities began, We Are Ready had been in contact with a relatively small number of fixed stations. In 1940, We Are Ready maintained connections with the headquarters of the nine corps areas, with Seattle, and with Wright and Langley airfields in the continental United States. It also operated direct circuits to the Panama Canal Zone, Puerto Rico, and Hawaii. Communication with the Philippines traveled via San Francisco.[40] But a system designed to provide communications during domestic disorders or emergencies was woefully inadequate to meet the needs of a world war. Once hostilities were underway, the Army substituted leased land teletypewriter lines for radio on its domestic network, thus freeing bandwidth for use in the combat theaters.[41]

While tactical communications were obviously indispensable, they actually represented a fairly small percentage of the total wartime communications load. To enable the front to move forward, the Army needed "a virtual AT&T system to carry huge and complex administrative traffic—hospitals, convoys, depots, transportation, press, personnel."[42] During World War II, that need was met by the Army Command and Administrative Network. Once troops moved overseas, ACAN stations changed position as the troops advanced. As ranges became longer, new facilities were necessary. To handle the increased number of circuits, the Signal Corps opened a new receiving facility for We Are Ready in LaPlata, Maryland, about thirty miles southeast of Washington. This station, which became operational at the end of June 1943, served as the common terminus of all overseas radio circuits of the Army Command and Administrative Network and included "probably the greatest concentration of radio antennas ever used to receive radio signals simultaneously from any point on the globe."[43] Early in 1943, We Are Ready itself had moved from downtown Washington into the newly built Pentagon across the Potomac in Virginia. The Message Center in the Munitions Building remained in operation, however, as an auxiliary facility.[44] The Signal Corps' new location on the Pentagon's top floor was state-of-the art for its time. By June 1943, the message center was handling 32,000 messages per day, up from a high of 8,000 a year earlier, all of this before major overseas operations had really begun (other than in North Africa).[45]

Prior to the Pearl Harbor attack, the Panama Canal had been viewed as the most vulnerable spot in the Western Hemisphere. Accordingly, the Signal Corps had shipped its first available radar sets there, rather than to Hawaii where sabotage and subversion were considered greater threats than enemy action. The Canal Zone had also been tied into the War Department's radio network. But Army planners considered a Japanese attack most likely somewhere in East Asia, such as Thailand or the Philippines. Because of the importance of the Panama Canal, Chief Signal Officer Olmstead made an inspection tour of the Canal Zone in early December 1941. Following the Pearl Harbor attack, he remained in Panama for several days to finish his assessment of the needs for men and equipment. Once back in Washington, however, he faced the pressures created by the sudden onset of war.[46]

In Hawaii, construction had begun on an underground command post at Fort Shafter, outside Honolulu, but it had not been completed when the attack came on the morning of 7 December. Fortunately for the United States, the attack did no harm to the radio station or its equipment. Because the cables and switchboards had previously been removed during blasting for the command post, however, landline communications were inoperable. The Signal Corps moved its operations to a new building and quickly restored the switchboards. Miraculously, even the island's wire system had sustained little damage, and interrupted circuits were rapidly repaired.[47]

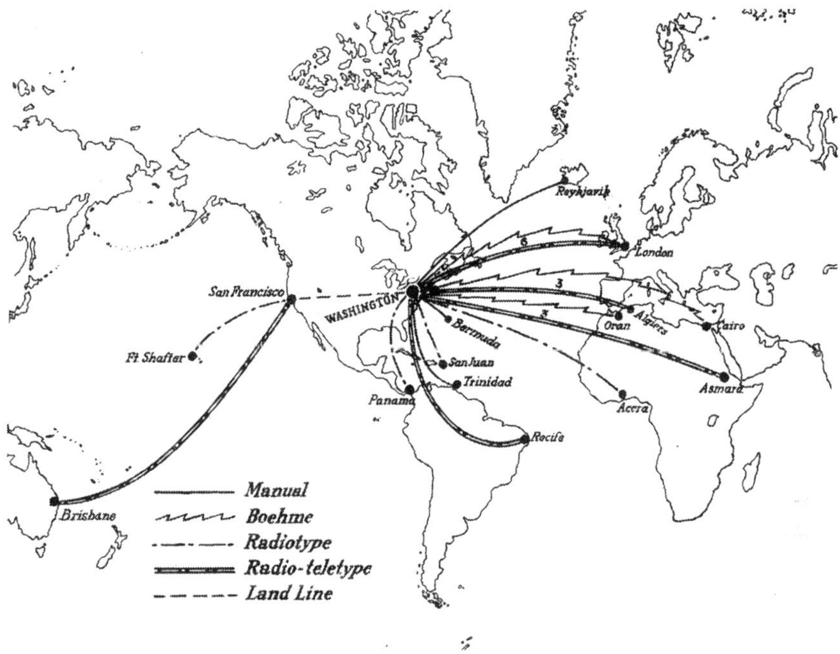

Army Command and Administrative Network Overseas, December 1943 (Green Book Series, *The Signal Corps: The Outcome*, p. 608)

Throughout the ensuing conflict, Honolulu's ACAN station (WTJ) served as a key communications hub for the Pacific Theater of Operations (PTO). Initially, it connected only with Manila, San Francisco, and Washington. Moreover, due to its low power, Honolulu could make direct communication with Washington only under certain atmospheric conditions—usually at night. This was not an acceptable situation for wartime, and the facilities were eventually upgraded to 40 kilowatts. The number of circuits was also increased. By May 1942, the station had circuits to Melbourne (to replace the lost connection to Manila) as well as to islands along the supply route to Australia. Connection had also been made to Nouméa, New Caledonia, where forces were gathering to attack Guadalcanal. At its peak, WTJ handled over 30 million code groups of traffic per month.[48] Honolulu also provided all the fixed station equipment for ACAN throughout the Pacific.[49]

Meanwhile, on the other side of the world, the Army Command and Administrative Network had been extended to meet the needs of hemispheric defense. Shortly before the war started, stations had been opened to the north in Iceland and Greenland and to the southeast in the Caribbean.[50] The establishment of radio connections between the United States and British possessions, such as Bermuda, marked a fundamental change in international communications policy. Previously, all communications with Britain and other members of the Commonwealth had to pass through London. With the exigencies of wartime, the British now agreed to allow direct access, and thus had to adjust to the sudden "American intrusion" into their domain.[51]

The first expansion of the overseas radio network beyond Europe came in April 1942 when the Army opened a circuit to Karachi, in Northwest India (now Pakistan). Next came Accra in West Africa to support the Allied landings in North Africa during November 1942.[52] By mid-1943, the major ACAN stations outside the United States were in London, Algiers, Accra, Cairo, Asmara (Eritrea), Karachi, New Delhi, Brisbane, and Hawaii. From these stations, lesser radio nets and wire lines spread out to meet the needs of local Army installations.[53] To maximize reliability, the Army Command and Administrative Network used an equatorial belt of stations to avoid the polar regions. There was no known method for overcoming the magnetic absorption of signals at the poles or the interruptions caused by atmospheric interference. Thus, the network ran eastward from We Are Ready by way of Asmara around the world and back to San Francisco. Messages then returned to We Are Ready by landline. If trouble developed on the circuits in one direction, messages could be sent the other way to avoid it.[54]

Because the PTO differed significantly from Europe in both terrain and climate, it posed unique communications challenges. Consequently, the nature of warfare in the Pacific differed from that in Europe, and the means of communication reflected that fact. Rather than having to cross long distances over land where wire lines could be strung for tactical, operational, and logistical purposes, only radio or cable could span the watery expanses of the Pacific. Unlike in Europe, troops were not concentrated in large camps but were widely scattered throughout the island chains and archipelagos. Communicators could not depend upon large fixed message centers in urban areas. Most of the islands were small and uninhabited. Each island had to be treated as a separate entity and then linked to the others by radio or by cables. As the fighting advanced, the islands in the rear became bases of operation for successive campaigns.[55]

Even the terrain itself, much of it of volcanic origin or covered with jungle, was inhospitable territory for traditional land-based communications. Because the dense vegetation smothered radio signals, however, wire lines had to be laid. But suitable material for poles could be hard to find. Even when available, poles rotted quickly in the heat or were devoured by termites. Ants, meanwhile, ate the insulation around the cables. Coupled with the difficult terrain was the jungle climate. The hot and humid atmosphere wreaked havoc on all types of equipment, with batteries being particularly susceptible. The dampness corroded the metal while it decomposed the paper containers. Consequently, batteries had to be kept in cold storage until issued. Packing them in discarded ration tins also gave them longer life. Radio sets had to be "tropicalized"—that is, chemically treated against moisture and fungus. The excessive humidity could drive moisture into the tiniest cracks and crevices. The Signal Corps conducted tests in its laboratories in the United States and worked with civilian scientists to determine the best methods of mitigation. The most effective was the application of several coats of lacquer to reduce the absorption of moisture. Other methods included improvising drying ovens for switchboard components. In addition to moisture, the high temperatures and bright tropical sunlight were detrimental to delicate switches and dials. Thus, heavy equipment was kept under cover whenever possible. Added to all of these practical difficulties was the danger posed by enemy troops and booby traps hidden within the lush undergrowth.[56]

The men suffered along with their equipment. The climate itself was debilitating. Tropical illnesses, especially malaria, felled many soldiers, while others suffered from unusual skin disorders and digestive problems. Swamps teemed with leeches and malarial mosquitoes. The presence of other exotic creatures, such as crocodiles and a host of amphibians, made life in the tropics unpleasant as well as unfamiliar.[57]

Logistically, fighting a war in the Pacific presented enormous challenges. Just getting men, supplies, and equipment to the Theater was no small feat. Especially in the beginning, much communications equipment had to be obtained from Australia, some of it manufactured expressly for the American troops. What could not be found locally had to be shipped from Hawaii. Without proper port facilities, items were often damaged during unloading. Depots had to be built from scratch, a task that took several months. Meanwhile, the leapfrogging troops moved on, and the process repeated itself.[58]

The amphibious nature of operations in the Pacific required extensive cooperation between the Army and the Navy. Moreover, the vastness of the PTO necessitated its organization into several operational areas. The Army controlled the Southwest Pacific Area, under the command of General Douglas A. MacArthur. This area included Australia and the islands to the north, such as New Guinea. It also encompassed regions further north and west, especially the Philippines. The rest of the Theater was divided into three areas that were under naval control: the North, Central, and South Pacific Areas, together comprising the Pacific Ocean Areas (POA) under Admiral Chester W. Nimitz.[59]

Joint collaboration extended to communications. The two services sometimes shared equipment and facilities, especially before additional items could reach the Theater. Some consideration was even given to combining Army and

Navy signals to create a joint communications service. In late 1942, General Somervell's office asked Chief Signal Officer Olmstead to investigate the possibility, but the merger never happened.[60] Although differences in policies and procedures inevitably arose, joint communications generally improved as the war progressed.[61] The ACAN station at Nouméa, New Caledonia, for example, was jointly operated, and the Navy helped the Army catch up with a large backlog of messages there. Cooperation required the development of joint radio frequencies and even the organization of new types of units, such as the Joint Assault Signal Company (JASCO), specifically designed to provide communications during joint operations. JASCOs provided the critical links between ships offshore and the troops assaulting the beaches. They also coordinated aerial and naval gunfire.[62]

To supplement their training at the Army's signal schools—which, given the rush to get men into uniform, was barely adequate—newly minted signal operators needed some practical experience before heading into combat. General Somervell wanted only experienced operators at the major overseas stations. Thus, We Are Ready and other stations in the network were called upon to provide "real world" training. We Are Ready provided training primarily for soldiers headed to Europe, while men headed for the Pacific received their preparation at WVY in San Francisco. Eventually, practice circuits connected We Are Ready with the Signal Corps' schools at Fort Monmouth, New Jersey; Camp Crowder, Missouri; and Camp Kohler, California. Officers designated to run overseas message centers also received "postgraduate" training in signal center operations at We Are Ready.[63]

Personnel problems remained vexing throughout the war. Some relief was provided by using members of the Women's Army Corps (WAC). Female soldiers could replace men in such jobs as message center clerks and switchboard operators, releasing the male personnel for other duties. Many members of the Women's Army Corps also performed signal intelligence duties, both at home and overseas.[64] The shortages of trained operators hit especially hard at We Are Ready, where the traffic load increased 800 percent during 1942 and 1943. In a reversal of the situation during the interwar years, many civilian personnel now joined the Army, becoming members of the 17th Signal Service Company, the unit charged with running We Are Ready.[65]

The security of the Army's communications obviously was paramount and warrants a separate study in itself. For protection, the Army depended on the cryptologic work conducted by the Signal Security Agency.[66] During the summer of 1943, the Signal Corps opened the West Coast Traffic Center at San Francisco "to decipher most of the material received from the Central and Southwest Pacific Areas, pertinent matter being transmitted to Washington."[67] It connected with Arlington Hall Station in Virginia, the headquarters for the Army's signal security operations. As action intensified in the Pacific, the increased traffic through the West Coast center necessitated progressive increases in its capacity. In August 1944, the Center began converting from sixteen channels operating at 65 words per minute (wpm) to ten channels operating at 100 wpm. By April 1945, six channels were operating between San Francisco and We Are Ready at 100 wpm.[68]

Increasingly sophisticated technology allowed Allied leaders to communicate between their various headquarters thousands of miles apart. This feat was made possible by such innovations as teleconferencing using equipment known by a cover name, SIGTOT.[69] The conferring parties assembled at the ends of a radioteletype circuit, where an operator tapped out their questions. The equipment provided automatic enciphering and deciphering, ensuring the critical security needed for high-level discussions. The system also produced a written record of the proceedings. A projection screen displayed the text—the iPod of its day. The equipment was versatile enough to work over wire, radio, or cable. With Allied forces deployed all over the world, the ability to hold long-distance meetings via secure teletype marked a significant advantage.[70] Just before the Normandy invasion, General Marshall used SIGTOT to confer with General Dwight D. Eisenhower in Europe, General MacArthur in the Pacific, and Major General John R. Deane, Chief, U.S. Military Mission, Moscow.[71] By V-J Day, SIGTOT facilities were available at nineteen overseas stations, including Brisbane, Guam, Hollandia, Honolulu, Leyte, and Manila in the PTO. The Army Command and Administrative Network also provided SIGTOT for the State Department in Washington; the White House; and the Presidential railroad car, yacht, and plane. General Stoner referred to SIGTOT as "one of the secret weapons of the war."[72] For commanders in the theaters, however, it meant that Washington could now direct matters from across the oceans.

Other cryptographic machines included the SIGABA, developed in conjunction with the Navy, which rapidly enciphered and deciphered written messages. Another device, known as SIGSALY, was a radiotelephone that provided highly secure voice communications. Because of its bulk, about ninety tons, it could not be used in the field. But high-level commanders used SIGSALY to direct troops and equipment. The details of SIGSALY's technical features, which included such pioneering techniques as digital transmission and pulse code modulation, remained classified until 1976.[73]

Unlike Pearl Harbor, the Japanese attack on the Philippines on Monday, 8 December 1941 (7 December in Hawaii) did not come as a complete surprise. The warning message sent by Chief of Staff Marshall from Washington had reached the islands well before hostilities commenced there.[74] News of the

Pearl Harbor attack also arrived before the Japanese planes appeared. General MacArthur, at that time Commanding General, U.S. Army Forces, Far East (USAFFE), had been informed in the early hours of Monday morning. Although its defenses had been strengthened in recent months, the Philippines still lacked adequate numbers of men and equipment. Several radar sets had been shipped from the United States, but only one was completely installed and fully operational by early December.[75] That SCR-270B long-range radar, located at Iba on Luzon's west coast, first detected incoming enemy planes late on Sunday night and radioed the information to Manila. Because of the limitations of the primitive set, the radar operator could not determine the exact number of planes or their altitude, thus making interception difficult.[76] Word of an impending attack reached Clark Field—located north of Manila and the main target of the Japanese—around daybreak, and the news spread with the rising sun. Pilots made preparations and waited for orders to take off. Yet none came from the Army's headquarters in Manila. Hours passed before pilots received permission to begin offensive operations. When the Japanese finally struck Clark Field at 1235 that afternoon—after a delay due to bad weather over Formosa—many American planes were caught on the ground. Clark and Iba airfields received devastating blows that effectively knocked out the Far East Air Force. Among the casualties at Iba was its radar set.[77]

In Manila, General MacArthur had been briefed throughout the day as events unfolded. Although he learned of the attack on Clark shortly after 1300, he did not inform Washington immediately. Moreover, he never offered a satisfactory explanation for how such a disaster could have occurred despite his being forewarned. Matters of blame aside, an apparent breakdown of communications among the various commands involved contributed to the tragic outcome on 8 December.[78]

Without offensive capability and cut off from reinforcement and resupply, the Philippines were doomed. With enemy invasion imminent, MacArthur faced a desperate situation. The available American and Filipino troops could not stop the Japanese advance on Luzon, and MacArthur prepared to withdraw his forces to the Bataan Peninsula, twenty-five miles across Manila Bay. On Christmas Eve 1941, MacArthur moved his headquarters from Manila to the island fortress of Corregidor at the entrance to Manila Bay. In addition to his Chief Signal Officer, Brigadier General Spencer B. Akin, and other staff members, MacArthur was accompanied by his wife and young son.[79]

Meanwhile, Akin's deputy, Colonel Theodore T. Teague, remained behind in Manila to close down the administrative radio network and station WTA. Teague ordered the fixed transmitting equipment and antenna to be blown up to keep them from falling into enemy hands. What could be saved was shipped to

Corregidor, where new facilities were soon built. Teague finished his work just in time; the Japanese entered Manila on 2 January 1942.[80]

On Corregidor, known as the "Gibraltar of the Far East," a vast tunnel complex underneath Malinta Hill became the administrative and operational headquarters for MacArthur and his forces. The tunnel had originally been built for hauling supplies from one end of the island to the other.[81] As Japanese air raids became a common occurrence, the MacArthur family took up residence in the tunnel along with the general's staff and thousands of others, both soldiers and civilians. Though it was crowded, damp, and foul smelling, the tunnel provided protection from the bombs and shells raining down from above. With food in short supply, however, starvation posed a further threat. MacArthur held out hope that relief would arrive, but the damage to the Pacific Fleet, local Japanese force superiority, and the Europe-first strategy being pursued by the Allied leaders precluded that possibility.[82]

Under these extremely adverse conditions, morale presented a major problem. The Japanese exploited the situation by subjecting the Americans to an effective propaganda campaign calculated to make them homesick. In addition to dropping leaflets, each night at 2145 they broadcast a special program over station KZRH in Manila. The Americans, meanwhile, used their radio station on Corregidor, WVDM, to send out "The Voice of Freedom" three times daily. In addition to popular recordings, its programs consisted of news commentaries and items of local interest.[83]

As the situation deteriorated, President Roosevelt ordered MacArthur in late February to move his headquarters to Australia, where he would take command of Allied forces in the Southwest Pacific. After some delay, MacArthur, his family, and select members of his staff departed on 11 March 1942. MacArthur's deputy, Lieutenant General Jonathan M. Wainwright, assumed command of the beleaguered American forces who remained behind. From within the Malinta Tunnel, the last radio station in the Philippines continued in operation. Located under two hundred feet of rock, the station could not maintain direct contact with Hawaii and beyond; it had to depend on the naval radio station on Corregidor. William Gibson, a civilian radio engineer with RCA who took refuge with the soldiers, kept Malinta's hodgepodge of signal equipment working. Despite the adverse conditions, and with hope and supplies running low, the operators on Corregidor maintained their broadcast schedule throughout their ordeal, transmitting a million words a month.[84]

After Bataan fell, the Japanese landed on Corregidor on 5 May 1942, and Wainwright knew that defeat was inevitable. Corporal Irving Strobing sent the last messages from the besieged garrison. As the end drew near, he radioed that the enemy bombardment was "Too much for guys to take." The hopelessness of the situation was clear: "They have got us all around and from the skies."[85] The young soldier from Brooklyn also sent out unauthorized farewells to his family. After making this final broadcast, Strobing and his fellow signal personnel gutted their equipment and destroyed as much of it as possible before the enemy arrived. General Wainwright surrendered the following day. Fifty signal officers and 662 enlisted men, including Colonel Teague and Corporal Strobing, became prisoners of the Japanese.[86]

Following the fall of the Philippines, fugitive American soldiers maintained communications with the outside world by means of a network of portable radio stations that had been secretly spread throughout the islands. These men were assisted by Filipinos and Americans smuggled in afterward by submarine. Some of the stations in this "guerilla network" were powerful enough to establish direct contact with General Headquarters in Australia as well as with San Francisco. The information provided by these clandestine communicators helped pave the way for the eventual liberation of the Philippines.[87]

General MacArthur arrived in Australia on 17 March 1942 and established his new headquarters at Melbourne, which then became the anchor of the Army's communication system serving the South and Southwest Pacific Areas. His Signal Officer, General Akin, was among the group of officers that accompanied him to Australia.[88] Even before MacArthur's arrival, Signal Corps personnel had begun installation of a War Department signal station at Melbourne. The Signal Corps had already opened a radio circuit to the Royal Australian Air Force station near Melbourne in order to coordinate flights and to exchange weather information. This station became the initial entryway for the Army Command and Administrative Network into Australia, and American operators used it temporarily for administrative business. When connections with the Philippines fell silent as the enemy advanced, this station provided a crucial lifeline to the rest of the PTO. With help from the Australian authorities, construction of the new station rapidly reached completion. Through "reverse Lend-Lease," the Australians provided the Americans with necessary equipment and materiel. Ill fortune elsewhere also hastened the process, as items meant for Java and Singapore were diverted by the Dutch and British governments to Australia. Assigned call letters WTJJ, the radio station brought MacArthur's headquarters into better communication with the various posts throughout the PTO, despite its low power of just one kilowatt. The first two months of traffic included the last flow of messages from the besieged Philippines, consisting largely of casualty lists and some operational reports.[89] The Battle of the Coral Sea in May 1942 occurred, however, before the Melbourne station was fully operational. Consequently, there was a delay in the transmission of messages calling for air support during the battle.[90]

With the transfer of MacArthur's headquarters north to Brisbane in July 1942, the Army's communications nerve center moved along with it. The circuits to Sydney, Townsville, and Darwin, in Australia, along with those to Nouméa and Honolulu, originally terminating at Melbourne, were relocated. As American and Australian forces geared up for major operations in the Southwest Pacific during the following months, the web of fixed Army communications extended itself in the wake of the advancing armies. Larger numbers of signal personnel began to arrive in Australia, to include the men of the 52d Signal Battalion. For many months, the radio circuit between Brisbane and San Francisco was the Army's only radio circuit from the Southwest Pacific to the United States.[91]

By June 1943, however, eight ACAN circuits radiated from Brisbane with the addition of circuits to Port Moresby, New Guinea; San Francisco; and New Delhi.[92] The 10-kilowatt circuits to San Francisco and Honolulu, the most powerful transmitters then allowed to the Army, provided direct and dependable communications. As the war progressed, more power was needed, and the transmission strength was further increased to 40 kilowatts.[93] Signal Corps personnel also constructed an alternate telephone land line to connect Brisbane with installations at Sydney, Townsville, and Melbourne. Brisbane remained an important link in the PTO's communications chain, though message traffic dropped off after military operations moved northward.[94]

After months on the defensive following the Pearl Harbor attack, the defeat of the Japanese Navy at Midway in June 1942 proved to be a critical turning point for the Allies, providing them with their first major victory. The Signal Corps' codebreaking operations had much to do with this success, enabling the Allies to learn of the enemy's movements and thus intercept the Japanese Fleet. Intelligence gleaned through these means continued to provide the Allies with a significant advantage as the Pacific campaign advanced.[95]

The war in the Pacific then became a two-pronged offensive: one in the Central Pacific under Admiral Nimitz and the other under General MacArthur in the Southwest Pacific. In August 1942, offensive operations began on the Solomon Islands to the northeast of Australia. Beginning with landings by the Marine Corps on Guadalcanal, the Allies fought to prevent the Japanese from cutting the line of communications between the United States and Australia. The Army joined the ground fighting in October.[96] The worst of it was over by mid-November, but it took two more months of grueling combat for the Allies to finally secure Guadalcanal. The island then became a base for further operations.[97]

While the Marine Corps was battling on Guadalcanal, MacArthur began his offensive operations on New Guinea, the initial stage in what became an island-hopping campaign to take back the Philippines. The Allies moved to stop a Japanese drive toward Port Moresby in the Papua region of southern New Guinea, which both sides recognized as a key strategic point. In September 1942, the Signal Corps opened a circuit to Port Moresby as operations in New Guinea intensified. Port Moresby, on the southeastern coast, was the largest settlement on the mostly undeveloped island and served as the seat of government. Yet, as one Signal Corps veteran remembered, "it was hardly more than a hamlet with a few trading warehouses and one large dock for oceangoing vessels."[98] Despite the conditions, it became the Signal Corps' center of operations on the island. Once the ACAN station could be installed, it received the call letters WVLQ.

New Guinea, the world's second largest island, presented Army communicators with considerable challenges, not least of which was its largely jungle and mountainous terrain. Equally daunting was the very humid climate. During the rainy season, as much as ten inches of rainfall fell daily, making a difficult situation even worse. Meanwhile, the pace of operations on the island continued to escalate. Australian and American forces pursued the enemy across the towering Owen Stanley Mountains—where ranges reached up to 13,000 feet—to the southern tip of the island, where the Japanese had entrenched around Buna on the northeastern coast. It took four months of bitter fighting to dislodge the tenacious Japanese, whose numbers far exceeded the intelligence estimates. Afterward, combat in the PTO slowed for a time, allowing the Allies to prepare for the next phase.[99]

After several months of rest and refitting, MacArthur sent his troops northwestward up the coast of New Guinea. The objectives were the encirclement of the Japanese stronghold of Rabaul on New Britain Island and the establishment of Allied control of the Bismarck Archipelago.[100] While forces under Admiral William F. Halsey fought in the Solomons, MacArthur's men moved toward Finschhafen, an enemy bastion guarding the straits between New Guinea and New Britain. After its capture in October 1943, the Allies became bogged down by pockets of fierce Japanese resistance. Offensive operations resumed in December, and the isolation of Rabaul was completed by March 1944. The following month, the Allies captured Hollandia, a major Japanese air and supply base in northern New Guinea. Using amphibious assaults and aircraft-ferried troops to bypass the enemy and thereby avoid costly ground battles, this operation represented a significant leap forward. Through a series of subsequent such assaults, MacArthur's forces continued to advance up the New Guinea coast toward the Philippines. Although the New Guinea campaign did not officially conclude until 31 December 1944, the heaviest fighting on the island was over by the end of August 1944.[101]

Hollandia became an important staging area for the next phase of operations. A "huge complex of military, naval, and air facilities" was developed there.[102] Consequently, its radio station, WVLH, functioned as a major node in the Army's worldwide chain and became the nucleus of the Pacific ACAN system. It maintained connections to New Delhi and San Francisco as well as with other lesser stations among the Pacific Islands. MacArthur transferred his headquarters to Hollandia in October 1944, and by the end of the year WVLH was handling a million code groups per day.[103] Eventually, Southwest Pacific Area's General Headquarters (GHQ) moved to Leyte, but Hollandia remained an important link in the communications chain until its ACAN station was moved to Manila early in 1945.[104]

From June to September 1944, the signaling equipment at Hollandia received reinforcement from a radio ship that carried transmitters able to reach General Headquarters at Brisbane as well as advanced headquarters at Port Moresby. In a theater characterized by vast expanses of water rather than of land, the Signal Corps came to rely upon vessels equipped with radio to extend its reach. General Akin recognized the value of these communications ships and had much to do with creating and outfitting the Signal Corps' command post fleet. Manned by naval crews with Army communications personnel aboard, these ships represented yet another manifestation of joint cooperation.[105]

Chief Signal Officer Ingles toured the Pacific during 1944 to check on the state of signal operations. He came back favorably impressed with what he had seen. "The relationship between the Army and Navy over there is splendid," he told a press conference. As for the soldiers themselves, "they are confronted with one unusual situation after another, and they display an enormous amount of energy and ingenuity, and also a great deal of humor, in meeting these problems." He described the jungles as "beastly," worse than those he had encountered in South and Central America or the Philippines.[106]

In July 1944, MacArthur met with Roosevelt and Nimitz at Pearl Harbor to discuss Pacific strategy. The President was soon to meet with the Combined Chiefs of Staff (CCS) in Quebec at the Octagon Conference. By September, a SIGTOT system allowed teleconferencing from Hollandia with Washington and points beyond. On 15 September, MacArthur was able to communicate directly from Hollandia with the leaders at Quebec. The combat situation in the Pacific had dramatically improved, with the Allies now in control of both the sea and the air. General Marshall wanted to know if MacArthur could advance the date for attacking Leyte, then planned for December. The Chief of Staff sent an inquiry via SIGTOT to Hollandia and received an affirmative reply.[107] Consequently, the Allied leaders decided to invade the Philippines ahead of schedule—in October. The United States also accepted the British offer to join in the fight against Japan.[108]

General MacArthur made his triumphant return to the Philippines on 20

October 1944 when his forces landed on Leyte. Four Army divisions participated in this assault, making it the largest amphibious operation yet conducted in the Pacific. From a communications truck onshore, MacArthur broadcast his famous words, "I have returned." The message was relayed to his headquarters ship, the cruiser USS *Nashville*, where Signal Corpsmen broadcast it to the Philippine people. Meanwhile, General Akin and his staff were aboard the Signal Corps vessel *Apache*, an old revenue cutter that the Signal Corps had recently refitted for public relations duty. The ship contained a broadcast studio that was encased in rubber to reduce vibrations and provide soundproofing. War correspondents slept in cots on the forecastle. The ship was also mounted with antiaircraft guns for defense. From the *Apache*, signal soldiers recorded and rebroadcast MacArthur's speech so it could be picked up by stations in California and Australia for relay around the world.[109]

The ensuing air-naval Battle of Leyte Gulf effectively shattered the Japanese Fleet, and by late December most of the island had been secured. The *Apache* was one of five ships that comprised the Signal Corps' fleet off Leyte. During the fighting, these vessels frequently came under attack by Japanese bombers. Although the communications ships were damaged, they were never destroyed. During one of these raids, one Signal Corpsman was killed and two were wounded.[110] Typhoons posed a further hazard, and eventually two of the Signal Corps' ships had to return to New Guinea for repairs. MacArthur, now General of the Army, made his headquarters on Leyte, and until equipment could be transferred from Hollandia, the ships provided communications for General Headquarters. From aboard the *Apache*, General Akin resumed his Voice of Freedom broadcasts for thirty minutes each day.[111]

MacArthur's next move was to Luzon, where he landed on 9 January 1945. There his forces faced desperate Japanese defenders who attempted to stall the Allied drive toward their homeland. A mobile communications unit accompanied the Allied commander during the advance to Manila. This equipment enabled General Akin to keep up with the fast-moving MacArthur, who was eager to reenter the city. Among the signal units in the van was the 52d Signal Battalion that had fought its way across the Pacific from Australia. After a bitter month-long battle through the streets of Manila, the U.S. Sixth Army captured the capital in March, and MacArthur established his headquarters at City Hall. Despite having suffered considerable damage, it was still standing.

The Signal Center was set up next door at the former municipal water works and opened for business on 5 March 1945. The old radio station, WTA, which the Japanese had captured three years earlier, resumed operations with its transmitter located at the Manila Country Club. The ACAN installation at Manila steadily grew and improved to become a major hub in the Army's worldwide

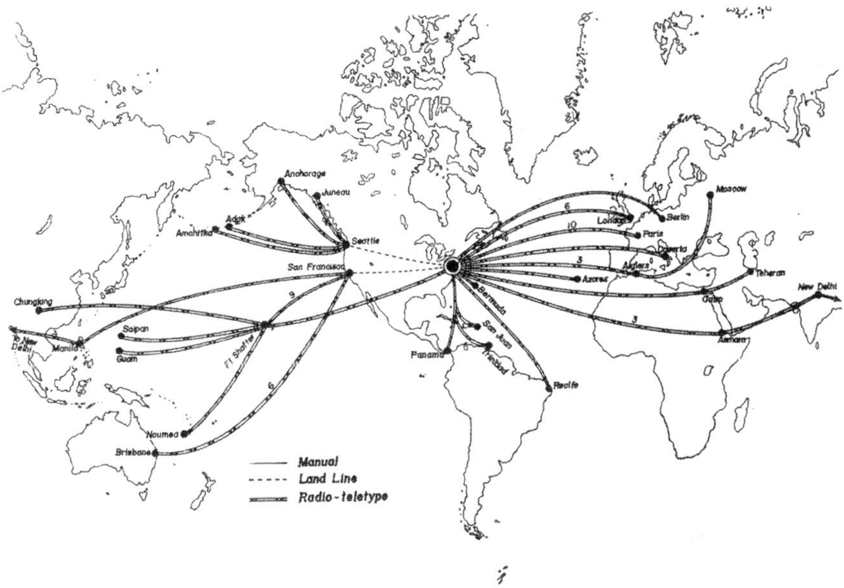

Army Command and Administrative Network Overseas, June 1945 (Green Book Series, *The Signal Corps: The Outcome*, p. 609)

communications network. By 4 April 1945, a SIGTOT conference system had been installed between Manila and Washington. By war's end, a globe-circling chain of radioteleprinter facilities connected Manila with Okinawa, San Francisco, Honolulu, Guam, Nouméa, Finschhafen, Brisbane, Hollandia, Leyte, Calcutta, New Delhi, and Chungking in western China. Over its circuits, a nine-word test message was sent around the world in nine and one-half seconds.[112]

One of the first vessels to enter Manila Bay was a communications ship carrying radio equipment able to reach Brisbane and San Francisco. It was later joined by larger communications barges that carried a complete ACAN-type installation, outfitted with all the facilities of an Army communications station on land. These ships also provided radio telephoto service back to the United States and to Australia, allowing combat photos from the PTO to be received for publication before the accompanying news story could be edited and printed.[113]

As the fighting front advanced toward Japan, the Army Command and Administrative Network moved with it. The Bonins-Volcanoes and Ryukyus were the next chains of islands to see combat, with tenacious battles taking place on Iwo Jima in February and March 1945 and Okinawa between April and June 1945. The following month, the Signal Corps established SIGTOT facilities on both Iwo Jima and Tinian Island.[114] By that point, Germany had surrendered, thus freeing large numbers of Allied personnel and resources for use in the Pacific. Having won control of the Bonins-Volcanoes and the Ryukyus, the Allies were now within easy striking distance of the Japanese home islands.

In addition to supporting combat operations, the Army Command and Administrative Network's facilities provided communications for many of the meetings of the Allied leaders during the course of the war. Often held in remote locations, such as Casablanca, Tehran, and Yalta, these conferences presented a formidable task in terms of communications. The final conference was held at Potsdam, Germany, in July and August 1945. There President Harry S. Truman, who had succeeded Roosevelt after the latter's death in early April, met with his counterparts for the first time. In the so-called Potsdam Declaration, the Allies called upon the Japanese to surrender promptly and unconditionally. Moreover, the Soviet Union reaffirmed its agreement, first announced at Yalta, to join in the war against Japan.[115]

When the Japanese government failed to comply with the demands made at Potsdam, it appeared that an Allied invasion of Japan would be necessary. Under revised command arrangements made by the Joint Chiefs in April, MacArthur received a new title, Supreme Commander for the Allied Powers (SCAP), with control over all ground operations in the Pacific. As such, he would lead the invasion, known as Operation OLYMPIC. As the Signal Corps prepared its communications plan, the dropping of the atomic bombs at Hiroshima and Nagasaki on 6 and 9 August, as well as the entry of the Soviet Union into the war, brought the conflict to a sudden and dramatic conclusion. Japan sued for peace on 10 August, but the fighting did not end immediately.

The Army Command and Administrative Network played a dramatic role in the waning hours of the war in the Pacific. Efforts to establish radio contact with Japan to confirm the terms of surrender proved frustrating and difficult. President Truman announced Japan's surrender to the nation on 14 August—but until the details had been worked out, the war continued. Late in the evening of 14 August (early on the morning of the 15th in the Philippines), General Marshall sent a message via We Are Ready to General MacArthur officially notifying him that the war was over. Marshall instructed MacArthur to proceed with the surrender arrangements.[116]

MacArthur soon composed a message to the Japanese Emperor and the Imperial Command, asking that they begin negotiations with him. Among his stipulations was that business be conducted in English. The ACAN radio operators in Manila made repeated attempts to send this message to Tokyo. Although it was labeled as urgent, they received no reply. Throughout the day, Army transmitters attempted to break in on Japanese stations they could hear operating, but without success. General Stoner in Washington then directed that the message be sent to Japan from stations throughout the world maintained by the

Army, Navy, and other public and private entities. Meanwhile, a second message from MacArthur, directing that all hostilities cease, was transmitted in the same manner. This message contained detailed instructions for sending a delegation to Manila. Tense hours passed as the operators waited for a reply from Japan. As described in a postwar account of the events: "Sweat drenched the shirts of the men laboring in the radio operations room of the Signal Center in oven-hot Manila. They had been at the keys or with the earphones clamped on their heads for ten futile hours. A frantic undercurrent gripped everyone present. There was no drama of the obvious sort, but each man knew that lives were being blotted out for lack of an acknowledgement to the message they were trying to get through."[117]

Finally, after more fruitless attempts, We Are Ready received the first indications that the message was getting through around midnight of the 15th. Monitors heard a Japanese station quoting a portion of MacArthur's first message: an RCA station in San Francisco had made contact with Tokyo. Finally, that afternoon, Manila reported that station WTA was in direct contact with the Japanese. MacArthur received official acknowledgment from Tokyo on the morning of 16 August. Japanese and American operators exchanged messages throughout the morning to work out the surrender arrangements. On 19 August, a Japanese delegation arrived in Manila to make plans for the formal proceedings.[118]

The Signal Corps' next major mission was to provide communications for the surrender ceremony to be held aboard the fast battleship USS *Missouri* in Tokyo Bay. On Sunday morning, 2 September 1945, the official delegations massed on the *Missouri's* deck to witness the formal signing of the surrender documents. Among those present was General Wainwright, recently released from a Japanese prison camp. The surrender proceedings were transmitted via the Army Command and Administrative Network, along with MacArthur's subsequent radio message to the world. "Today the guns are silent," he movingly remarked; "a great tragedy has ended."[119] Photos of the historic event also traveled via the Army Command and Administrative Network and were published in American newspapers within a very short time.[120] Although the *Apache* stood offshore, the ceremony was broadcast over powerful commercial transmitters on land that had somehow remained intact. Meanwhile, an advance signal party had set up operations at the Customs House in Yokohama and entered Tokyo along with General MacArthur on 8 September.[121]

As Supreme Commander for the Allied Powers, MacArthur presided over the occupation of Japan and supervised the rebuilding of that nation. General Akin continued to serve as MacArthur's Chief Signal Officer, overseeing the work performed by signal units who labored to restore Japan's communications infrastructure. MacArthur would not enjoy the services of the Army Command and

Administrative Network, however, as it became a casualty of the peace. The Army instead made use of commercial facilities and took over those of Radio Tokyo.[122]

Because an invasion of Japan had not been necessary, the services of the communications ship *Spindle Eye* were also nearly overcome by events. At the request of MacArthur's headquarters, this special news transmission ship had been outfitted in Seattle to handle voice and telegraph reports on invasion operations. Although the war ended before its conversion could be completed, the *Spindle Eye* proceeded to Japan in mid-September, where it broadcast news of the country's peaceful occupation. It ultimately replaced the venerable *Apache,* which had originally been commissioned in 1891.[123]

Following V-J Day, the Army Command and Administrative Network continued in operation, as the United States still had troops stationed throughout the world. Its facilities were employed for such purposes as communications support for the war crimes trials in Germany, the Philippines, and Japan. As would be expected, traffic volume decreased significantly with peacetime. Concurrently, a steady curtailment of the network's personnel and facilities paralleled the transition from war to peace. In Washington, many of the military employees at We Are Ready exchanged khaki for civilian clothes.[124] While there could be no doubt that the Army Command and Administrative Network had made an invaluable contribution to the Allied victory, its postwar existence was not assured. General Stoner estimated that the Army Command and Administrative Network had sent eight words overseas for every bullet fired by Allied troops. Some 50 million words a day were traveling over its circuits by the end of the war.[125] Without the practically instantaneous communications provided by this network during the conflict, maintenance of coordinated global strategy would have been impossible.[126] Yet it was not enough to save the system in the postwar period. As has been typical at the end of previous major conflicts, the nation and its leaders hurried to return to normalcy. The great war machine was disassembled as the United States Armed Forces quickly demobilized.

Chief Signal Officer Ingles wished to retain the Army Command and Administrative Network and expressed this opinion to General Eisenhower, who had replaced Marshall as Army Chief of Staff in November 1945. Ingles proposed that the Army turn over the Army Command and Administrative Network to a consortium of commercial companies to be operated as a diplomatic and governmental network: only during wartime should the military resume control. Eisenhower did not agree. He believed that the Army Command and Administrative Network should be dismantled and that commercial firms should perform its mission. Eisenhower wanted the Army to focus on maintaining the hard-won peace. Thus, he emphasized the preservation of combat formations over support troops.[127]

Consequently, the Army began divesting itself of its strategic network, losing the opportunity to use the Army Command and Administrative Network as a means of projecting U.S. power in the postwar world and of exercising the nation's global responsibilities.[128] The Army retained stations only at major overseas headquarters. Thus, no ACAN lines remained in East and Southeast Asia, including Korea and Vietnam.[129] The Signal Corps did, however, keep its Alaskan system, which stayed under the Army's control until the 1960s. Despite this significant setback, General Ingles continued to serve as the Army's Chief Signal Officer until 1947. He then became an executive with RCA.[130] His replacement as Chief Signal Officer was now–Major General Akin, who headed the Signal Corps until 1951, when he retired from the Army after forty-one years of service.[131]

General Stoner, who continued to act as Chief, Army Communications Service, until late December 1945, also thought the policy regarding the Army Command and Administrative Network to be shortsighted.[132] In November 1945, he had attended a telecommunications conference held in Bermuda with representatives of government and industry from the United States and the British Commonwealth. Among the seminal agreements reached at this meeting was Britain's abandonment of its prewar monopoly of international communications.[133] General Stoner retired from the Army in 1947 and, like General Ingles, he remained involved with worldwide communications. Prior to retiring, he had taken a leave of absence from the Army to serve as Chairman of the United Nations' (U.N.) Advisory Committee on Telecommunications. After his retirement, he became Chief Communications Engineer for the U.N. Under his direction, the United Nations undertook plans to create an independent worldwide communications system. In designing this system, Stoner hoped to realize his vision for a global network intended for peaceful purposes that was not owned by any one nation. Stoner remained at the U.N. until February 1950, when he retired a second time.[134]

The end of the war certainly did not mean the end of American involvement in the Pacific and East Asia. Although much of the world's attention was now focused on the defense of Europe and the incipient Cold War between the United States and the Soviet Union, trouble was developing on other fronts as well. China fell to the Communists in 1949, complicating matters in East Asia for the United States. Meanwhile, on the Korean Peninsula, long dominated by Japan, the 38th Parallel marked the dividing line between Americans forces occupying the south and Soviets troops stationed in the north. Although the Allies had agreed to eventually grant independence to a unified Korea, the promise was never fulfilled. The Soviets installed a Communist government in North Korea, while in the south a putative republic with an autocratic president took form. Both sets of occupation forces—minus military advisers—withdrew by mid-1949, leaving behind a divided nation. Civil war soon disrupted the fragile peace when North Korean forces invaded South Korea on 25 June 1950. To prevent South Korea's downfall, the United States and other U.N. member nations intervened. General MacArthur again led this effort as Commander-in-Chief, United Nations Command. Because Ingles's and Stoner's advice had not been heeded, the Army again found itself without a telecommunications network in place in that region. The Signal Corps, along with the rest of the Army, had once again been caught unprepared for a major conflict on the other side of the world.

Not until the United States entered the war in Vietnam in the 1960s would the Signal Corps again have a long-distance network to rival the extent of the Army Command and Administrative Network. This time, it would use satellite technology, among other methods, to span the reaches of the Pacific.[135] With the creation of the Defense Communications System in 1960, the Defense Communications Agency became responsible for managing the military's long-haul communications networks. The new defense-level system incorporated the Army Command and Administrative Network—renamed the Strategic Army Communications Network—which the Signal Corps continued to operate. In addition, the succeeding decades have seen an increasing trend toward centralization and joint usability made possible by the adoption of automated systems. Today, the United States Army Network Enterprise Technology Command, for instance, manages the Army's global communications from its headquarters at Fort Huachuca, Arizona.

Appendix: Call Signs of Select ACAN Stations

Southwest Pacific Theater Network

WAR	Washington, D.C.
WTA	Manila (GHQ)
WTE	Mobile for use by the President
WTJ	Fort Shafter, Hawaii (Honolulu)
WTJJ	Melbourne, Australia
WVDM	Fort Mills (Corregidor)
WVJJ	Brisbane, Australia (GHQ)
WVJN	Nouméa, New Caledonia
WVLC	USS *Apache* (later used by *Spindle Eye*)
WVLH	Hollandia, New Guinea (GHQ)
WVLQ	Port Moresby, New Guinea (GHQ)

WVLR	Leyte
WVLT	Lingayen Gulf, the Philippines
WVY	San Francisco, California

Others

WTW	Fort Monmouth, New Jersey
WVA	Washington, D.C. (becomes WAR in 1928)
WVB	Fort Sam Houston, Texas (Eighth Corps Area)
WVC	Fort Leavenworth, Kansas
WVCK	Camp Kohler, California
WVCM	Camp Crowder, Missouri
WVD	Seattle, Washington
WVE	Langley Field, Virginia
WVG	Baltimore (Third Corps Area)
WVJU	Munda, New Georgia
WVL	Panama Canal Zone
WVN	San Juan, Puerto Rico
WVO	Boston (First Corps Area)
WVP	Governors Island, New York (Second Corps Area)
WVQ	Wright Field, Ohio
WVR	Fort McPherson, Georgia (Fourth Corps Area)
WVT	Chicago (Sixth Corps Area)
WVU	Fort Omaha, Nebraska (Seventh Corps Area)
WVY	Presidio of San Francisco (Ninth Corps Area)
WVZ	Fort Hayes, Ohio (Fifth Corps Area)
WXY	Washington, D.C. (becomes WVA, then WAR)

Notes

I would like to acknowledge three individuals from the Historical Resources Branch of the U.S. Army Center of Military History: Frank Shirer, Carrie Sullivan, and James Tobias. They graciously provided me with research materials from that institution's archives, without which this chapter could not have been written. Also essential to this project was the assistance of Steven Rauch and Daniel Brown at the History Office of the U.S. Army Signal Corps, Fort Gordon, Georgia.

1. Fort Myer has a long association with the Signal Corps and is named for the first Chief Signal Officer, Brigadier General Albert J. Myer (1828–1880). On the Signal Corps' transmitter there, see Pauline M. Oakes, "The Army Command and Administrative Communications System, Part 1: War Department Radio Net Thru Fiscal Years

1920–1940," typescript, (Washington, DC: Signal Corps Historical Section, October 1945), 103–107 (hereafter cited as Oakes, "ACAN," Part 1). Copy in the files of the U.S. Army Center of Military History, Washington, DC (hereafter cited as CMH).

2. A rhombic antenna sends out a maximum strength signal in a predetermined direction. Such an antenna was needed to span great distances. See George R. Thompson, Dixie R. Harris, Pauline M. Oakes, and Dulany Terrett, *The Signal Corps: The Test (December 1941 to July 1943)* United States Army in World War II (Washington, DC: Office of the Chief of Military History, Department of the Army, 1957), 114n32.

3. Since 1913, the Navy had operated a high-power radio station in Arlington, Virginia. Its three steel transmitting towers, known as the Three Sisters, were located at the intersection of Columbia Pike and Courthouse Road. At the time, they were the world's second largest man-made structures (the Eiffel Tower was largest). They stood on the site until 1941. For a photograph and brief history, see http://library.arlingtonva.us/departments/libraries.history/librarieshistorybackpages010907.aspx (accessed 12 May 2010).

4. Oakes, "ACAN," Part 1, 107.

5. Dulany Terrett, *The Signal Corps: The Emergency (to December 1941)*, United States Army in World War II (Washington, DC: Office of the Chief of Military History, Department of the Army, 1956), 95–96; Oakes, "ACAN," Part 1, 104–107.

6. Thompson, Harris, et al., *Signal Corps: The Test,* 9–10.

7. The Army Command and Administrative Network represented only part of the Signal Corps' responsibilities. The Army also operated a separate Airways Communications Service and an air warning system. These will not be addressed herein. Tactical signaling is another story in itself. Concomitantly, the Signal Corps continued to run the Army's domestic radio and wire networks, to include those at the mushrooming number of Army camps.

8. Similar studies are needed of Signal Corps communications in the other theaters of the war. The primary source of information on the Army's World War II communications remains the three volumes in the official "Green Book" series, which are frequently cited herein.

9. Jonathan Reed Winkler, *Nexus: Strategic Communications and American Security in World War I* (Cambridge, MA: Harvard University Press, 2008), 64–71. See also Donald R. Headrick, *The Invisible Weapon: Telecommunications and International Politics, 1851–1945* (New York: Oxford University Press, 1991); and Linwood S. Howeth, *History of Communications-Electronics in the United States Navy* (Washington, DC: Government Printing Office, 1963).

10. Jonathan Reed Winker, "Information Warfare in World War I," *Journal of Military History* 73 (July 2009): 845–867. Germany attempted similar attacks on Allied communications, but with less success.

11. Winkler, *Nexus,* 146ff. In fact, a new cable between the United States and Asia would not be laid until 1964. Ibid., 270.

12. See Susan J. Douglas, *Inventing American Broadcasting, 1899–1922* (Baltimore: Johns Hopkins University Press, 1987).

13. Winkler, *Nexus,* 248–258.

14. See Rebecca Robbins Raines, "WAR in Peace: The Establishment of the Army Command and Administrative Communications System, 1920–1941," paper presented at the International Security Studies Conference, Yale University, April 2002. See also Karl G. Larew, "War Department Radio Net," in Christopher Sterling, ed., *Military Communications: From Ancient Times to the 21st Century* (Santa Barbara, CA: ABC Clio, 2008), 505–507.

15. The most famous of these plans was War Plan Orange, which outlined the strategy for a war with Japan. See, e.g., Edward S. Miller, *War Plan Orange: The U.S. Strategy to Defeat Japan, 1897–1945* (Annapolis: Naval Institute Press, 1991). The color plans were superseded by the so-called Rainbow Plans. See Mark S. Watson, *Chief of Staff: Prewar Plans and Preparations,* United States Army in World War II (Washington, DC: Historical Division, U.S. Army, 1950), 87, 103–104. See also Oakes, "ACAN," Part 1, 28; and Clayton D. Laurie and Ronald H. Cole, *The Role of Federal Military Forces in Domestic Disorders, 1875–1945* (Washington, DC: Center of Military History, U.S. Army, 1997), 334.

16. Oakes, "ACAN," Part 1, 7–9 and 100. The War Department had maintained its own telegraph office since the Civil War, separate from that run by the Signal Corps. It operated from the Office of the Chief Clerk. The Signal Corps was unable to get successive call signs beginning with "WA." The net control station was originally assigned call letters WXY, later changed to WVA. The station became We Are Ready on 30 November 1928. Except for We Are Ready and a few other exceptions, the call signs for the Army's administrative radio stations began with the letters "WV." See also Thompson, Harris, et al., *Signal Corps: The Test,* 289n35, and the list of stations in the appendix to this chapter. I have not yet discovered the basis on which the Army assigned call letters to specific stations, other than that they were in general conformance with the parameters set forth by the Federal Communications Commission for military stations.

17. Edward F. French, "War Department Radio Net," *Signal Corps Bulletin* 30 (June 1925): 15. Major (later Colonel) French was Director of the Message Center from 1924 to 1925 and of the War Department Signal Center from 1939 to 1945. Although Alaska was included within the Asiatic-Pacific Theater during World War II, the Signal Corps' work there is not discussed in this chapter.

18. The Joint Army-Navy Board, originally established in 1903, set interservice radio policy. See "Joint Board Policy for Coordination of Radio Activities of the Army and Navy," *Signal Corps Bulletin* 41 (December 1927): 16–19. See also Oakes, "ACAN," Part 1, 132–134. The basic division of responsibility outlined above remained in place until the close of Fiscal Year 1940. The functions of the Joint Board were largely absorbed by the Joint Chiefs of Staff during World War II, and the Joint Board was abolished in 1947. See the administrative history for "Records of Joint Army and Navy Boards and Committees," Record Group (hereafter cited as RG) 225, National Archives II, College Park, Maryland (hereafter cited as NA II), available at www.archives.gov/research/guide-fed-records/groups/225.html (accessed 22 April 2010).

19. Terrett, *Signal Corps: The Emergency,* 57. For administrative purposes, the Army divided the United States into nine geographical corps areas. The radio station at the

headquarters of each corps area served as the control station for the radio network within that area.

20. Oakes, "ACAN," Part 1, 74 and 80–85. The system's technical improvements are discussed in detail in ibid., Chapter 4, 74–99.

21. Ibid., 89–96. For more on the subject of crystal control, see Richard J. Thompson Jr., *Crystal Clear: The Struggle for Reliable Communications Technology in World War II* (Piscataway, NJ: IEEE Press, 2012).

22. Terrett, *Signal Corps: The Emergency,* 57; Oakes, "ACAN," Part 1, 50, 99.

23. Oakes, "ACAN," Part 1, 46, 50, 118–119.

24. Ibid., 49–50.

25. Pauline M. Oakes, "Army Command and Administrative Communications System, Part 2: Signal Corps Domestic Communications Network as Extended to Oversea Terminals Fiscal Year 1940 through 15 August 1945," typescript (Washington, DC: Signal Corps Historical Section, December 1945), 23–24 (hereafter cited as Oakes, "ACAN," Part 2). On the number of stations closed, see Pauline M. Oakes, "Army Command and Administrative Communications System, Part. 3: Signal Corps Domestic Communications Network as Extended to Oversea Terminals during the Period of Demobilization 14 August 1945–31 December 1945," typescript (Washington, DC: Signal Corps Historical Section, March 1946), 55 (hereafter cited as Oakes, "ACAN," Part 3). These studies are also among the manuscript collections at the Center of Military History. The Chief Signal Officer sat on the Board of Wartime Communications, headed by the Chairman of the FCC. The Board established national defense communication priorities and directed the closing of stations and facilities, such as the amateur stations, as necessary. Its membership also included the Director of Naval Communications, the Assistant Secretary of State in Charge of Transportation and Communications, the Assistant Secretary of the Treasury in Charge of Treasury Enforcement Activities, and the Coast Guard Chief of Communications. See description of the records of the Board, RG 259, at the National Archives' website: http://www.archives.gov/research/guide-fed-records/groups/259.html.

26. See A. Lincoln Lavine, *Circuits of Victory* (Garden City, NY: Doubleday, Page, and Co., 1921); M. D. Fagen, ed., *A History of Engineering and Science in the Bell System: The Early Years (1875–1925)* (New York: Bell Telephone Laboratories, 1975); Walter S. Gifford, "The Activities of the Bell System during the World War," *Signal Corps Bulletin* 102 (October–December 1938): 1–9.

27. Sarnoff eventually rose to the rank of Brigadier General in the Signal Corps Reserve. See Kenneth Bilby, *The General: David Sarnoff and the Rise of the Communications Industry* (New York: Harper and Row, 1986).

28. George R. Thompson and Dixie R. Harris, *The Signal Corps: The Outcome (Mid-1943 through 1945),* United States Army in World War II (Washington, DC: Office of the Chief of Military History, U.S. Army, 1966), 581.

29. Oakes, "ACAN," Part 2, 4–6, 24–25. See also Thompson, Harris, et al., *Signal Corps: The Test,* 433.

30. Thompson, Harris, et al., *Signal Corps: The Test,* 219; Oakes, "ACAN," Part 2, 29–30.

31. Oakes, "ACAN," Part 2, 36. A third transmission method, known as radio-type, was developed by the International Business Machines Corporation (IBM). See Thompson, Harris, et al., *Signal Corps: The Test,* 218–222. An extended discussion of the development of the various types of signaling equipment is beyond the scope of this chapter. For more detailed coverage, see Chapters 8 and 9 of Thompson, Harris, et al., *Signal Corps: The Test.* See also Thompson and Harris, *Signal Corps: The Outcome,* Chapters 14 and 15; and "Mechanization of 'WAR,'" *Signal Corps Technical Information Letter* 30 (May 1944): 75–78 (hereafter cited as *SCTIL*). By mid-1944, the total processing time from receipt to transmission of messages at WAR was about nine minutes with an average message totaling around ninety words. See "Mechanization of 'WAR,'" 78. I am grateful to Stephen Rauch and Daniel Brown for digitizing these newsletters, as well as other items, in their archives and making them available to me.

32. Dawson Olmstead graduated from West Point in 1906. He was originally commissioned in the Cavalry, but attended the Signal School at Fort Leavenworth during 1908 and 1909. Following World War I, where he served in the Inspector General's Office of the American Expeditionary Forces in France, he held increasingly responsible Signal Corps–related assignments. Olmstead became the Army's Chief Signal Officer in October 1941. See "Olmstead, Dawson," Biographical Files, CMH.

33. On strength figures see Thompson, Harris, et al., *Signal Corps: The Test,* 23; Thompson and Harris, *Signal Corps: The Outcome,* 511.

34. Thompson, Harris, et al., *Signal Corps: The Test,* 148. By mid-1943, its budget had grown to $5 billion. Thompson and Harris, *Signal Corps: The Outcome,* 3.

35. The Army Communications Division became the Army Communications Service in July 1943. See Thompson, Harris, et al., *Signal Corps: The Test,* 435.

36. Stoner was a native of Vancouver, Washington. He dropped out of West Point in 1917 to join the Army. After serving with the Infantry, he transferred to the Signal Corps in 1926. During the interwar years, he served in a number of Signal Corps assignments, including running the War Department Message Center from 1928 to 1932. He also worked in Seattle at the control center for the Washington-Alaska Military Cable and Telegraph System (WAMCATS)—later known as the Alaska Communication System. While serving at Fort Monmouth in February 1942, at the Signal Corps' Research and Development Center, Stoner received orders to Washington to work in the Office of the Chief Signal Officer. In July 1943, he became the Director of the Army Communications Service. See "Stoner, Frank E.," Biographical Files, CMH.

37. For a brief sketch of Somervell and his earlier career, see John D. Millett, *The Organization and Role of the Army Service Forces,* United States Army in World War II (Washington, DC: Office of the Chief of Military History, Department of the Army, 1954), "Introduction." For a full-length study, see John Kennedy Ohl, *Supplying the Troops: General Somervell and American Logistics in World War II* (DeKalb: Northern Illinois University Press, 1994).

38. Ingles, a native of Nebraska, graduated from West Point in 1914. He served as Deputy Commander, United States Forces in the European Theater, immediately prior

to his assignment as Chief Signal Officer. See "The New Chief Signal Officer," *SCTIL* 20 (July 1943), 5.

39. Thompson, Harris, et al., *Signal Corps: The Test,* 431–432; Oakes, "ACAN," Part 2, 113–114. The *Sacred Cow* was specially fitted for Roosevelt's needs. He used it only once, however, to travel to the Yalta Conference. See http://www.nationalmuseum.af.mil/fact-sheets/factsh eet.asp?id=566 (accessed 26 May 2010).

40. Oakes, "ACAN," Part 1, 50.

41. Oakes, "ACAN," Part 2, 101. The domestic radio network was retained in a standby status as provided for under War Plan White.

42. Major General Francis H. Lanahan Jr., as quoted in Thompson, Harris, et al., *Signal Corps: The Test,* 367. During the war, Lanahan served in the War Plans Division of the Office of the Chief Signal Officer and later as Deputy Chief Signal Officer, Supreme Headquarters, Allied Expeditionary Force (SHAEF). He became Chief Signal Officer, SHAEF, in March 1945 and later commanded Fort Monmouth, New Jersey. See "Lanahan, Francis H., Jr.," Biographical Files, CMH.

43. Oakes, "ACAN," Part 2, 77–82, quotation on 79.

44. U.S. War Department, "Annual Report of the Chief Signal Officer, 1943," 416 (hereafter cited as ARSO with year). Typescript at CMH. See also Steve Vogel, *The Pentagon: A History* (New York: Random House, 2007), 273; Oakes, "ACAN," Part 2, 74–76.

45. Oakes, "ACAN," Part 2, 74–76. During Fiscal Year 1944, the average number climbed to 200,000 messages daily. Ibid., 91.

46. See Watson, *Chief of Staff,* Chapter 15.

47. Donald O. Wagner, "Army Command and Administrative Network, 1941–1945," Part 1: The Pacific, 9, 13. Typescript in possession of CMH (hereafter cited as Wagner, "ACAN, Pacific.") See also Thompson, Harris, et al., *Signal Corps: The Test,* 6–9.

48. Wagner, "ACAN, Pacific," 14–15. Colonel Carroll A. Powell served as Chief Signal Officer, Central Pacific Area, and was stationed in Hawaii throughout the war. See his article "Communications in the Pacific Ocean Areas," *Military Review* 25 (January 1946): 30–34 (statistic from 34).

49. Terrett, *Signal Corps: The Emergency,* 301; Wagner, "ACAN, Pacific," 8–13. By war's end, Honolulu had radio contact with Washington, San Francisco, Brisbane, Nouméa, Kwajalein, Guam, Saipan, Manila, Okinawa, and Chungking. Wagner, "ACAN, Pacific," 12.

50. Terrett, *Signal Corps: The Emergency,* 280–283. See chart in Appendix C in Oakes, "ACAN," Part 2: "Overseas Radio Network—January 1942." At that time, the only stations were at Fort Shafter, Panama, San Juan, Bermuda, and Reykjavik.

51. Headrick, *Invisible Weapon,* 261–262, quotation on 265.

52. Oakes, "ACAN," Part 2, 121–122.

53. Thompson and Harris, *Signal Corps: The Outcome,* 581.

54. Thompson, Harris, et al., *Signal Corps: The Test,* 433.

55. Wagner, "ACAN, Pacific," 18.

56. Oakes, "ACAN," Part 2, 45; Thompson, Harris, et al., *Signal Corps: The Test,* 524–525; "Fungus Growths," *SCTIL* 19 (June 1943): 34; "Equipment Tropicalization," *SCTIL* 36 (November 1944): 21–23; "Signals on Bougainville," *SCTIL* 32 (July 1944): 23–24.

57. For a detailed discussion of the medical problems faced by the Army in the PTO, see Mary Ellen Condon-Rall and Albert E. Cowdrey, *The Medical Department: Army Medical Service in the War against Japan,* United States Army in World War II (Washington, DC: Center of Military History, U.S. Army, 1988).

58. Thompson, Harris, et al., *Signal Corps: The Test,* 303; Thompson and Harris, *Signal Corps: The Outcome,* 265–269.

59. Colonel (later Major General) Francis L. Ankenbrandt was Signal Officer, South Pacific Area. This Area closed out in August 1944 and became the South Pacific Base Command (SPBC). Ankenbrandt then transferred to the Army Air Forces. See Thompson and Harris, *Signal Corps: The Outcome,* 224–225. Colonel Carroll A. Powell was Signal Officer of the Central Pacific Area (see note 48 above). He was promoted to Brigadier General in November 1944. See ibid., 225n65. For the boundaries of each area, see the map in the campaign brochure by Clayton R. Newell, *Central Pacific 1941–1943,* The U.S. Army Campaigns of World War II (Washington, DC: Government Printing Office, 1992) at the following link: http://www.history.army.mil/brochures/72-4/map1.JPG. The Army conducted only limited operations in the North Pacific Area and did not assign a signal officer equivalent to those elsewhere in the PTO. On the war planning for this area, see Louis Morton, *Strategy and Command: The First Two Years,* United States Army in World War II: The War in the Pacific (Washington, DC: Center of Military History, U.S. Army, 1989), Chapter 21.

60. One stumbling block was that the Chief Signal Officer did not have operational control over all Army communications, unlike his naval counterpart, the Director of Naval Communications. Unhappy with his subordination under the Army Service Forces, Olmstead pushed for the placement of the Chief Signal Officer on the War Department General Staff, but without success. Moreover, there were enough differences between Army and Navy signals to make a merger impractical. The Joint Communications Board, on which the Chief Signal Officer sat, functioned as a central directing agency. The Chief Signal Officer also served as President of the Army Communications Board, which reported to the War Department General Staff. See Thompson, Harris, et al., *Signal Corps: The Test,* 550–560.

61. The Allies also had to develop combined communications procedures for working with each other. These were promulgated by the Combined Communications Board. See, for example, Oakes, "ACAN," Part 2, Chapter 10. See also "Combined Procedures," *SCTIL* 35 (October 1944): 13–14.

62. See Thompson and Harris, *Signal Corps: The Outcome,* 209–212. See especially 210n19, 231–233. Joint Assault Signal Companies also served in the European Theater of Operations (ETO). See "How the Navy Uses Signal Corps Equipment," *SCTIL* 32 (July 1944): 15–16, 47.

63. Thompson, Harris, et al., *Signal Corps: The Test,* 442–444; Oakes, "ACAN," Part 2, 65–68; "Combined Training Network," *SCTIL* 36 (November 1944): 16, 20. Fort Monmouth's station received call sign WTW; Camp Crowder, WVCM, and Camp Kohler, WVCK.

64. See Karen Kovach, *Breaking Codes: Breaking Barriers: The WACs of the Signal*

Security Agency, World War II (Fort Belvoir, VA: History Office, Office of the Chief of Staff, U.S. Army Intelligence and Security Command, n.d.). See also Selene H. C. Weise, *The Good Soldier: The Story of a Southwest Pacific Signal Corps WAC* (Shippensburg, PA: Burd Street Press, 1999). Despite the many hardships of working in the Southwest Pacific, where she served as a cryptographer, Weise wrote of her experience: "Our treatment by the Signal Corps was unfailingly professional and dignified and made working with the Signal Corps a joy." See Weise, *The Good Soldier,* 210. For a complete study of the Women's Army Corps, see Mattie E. Treadwell, *The Women's Army Corps,* United States Army in World War II (Washington, DC: Office of the Chief of Military History, Department of the Army, 1954).

65. Oakes, "ACAN," Part 2, 59–60. See also Mary E. Boswell, "The 17th Signal Service Company, a Component of the War Department Signal Center from World War I through World War II." This monograph is among the collections of the Center of Military History.

66. The Signal Security Agency traced its history to the Signal Intelligence Service formed in 1929. Headed by Lieutenant Colonel William F. Friedman prior to the war, this agency succeeded in breaking the Japanese "Purple" diplomatic code. In December 1944, the Signal Corps' security and intelligence activities were transferred to the Military Intelligence Division. In September 1945, these functions were taken over by the newly established Army Security Agency, which later became the National Security Agency. See, e.g., James L. Gilbert and John P. Finnegan, eds., *U.S. Army Signals Intelligence in World War II: A Documentary History* (Washington, DC: Center of Military History, U.S. Army, 1993).

67. Oakes, "ACAN," Part 2, 105–106.

68. Ibid., 106–108.

69. J. V. Boone and R. R. Peterson, *The Start of the Digital Revolution: SIGSALY Secure Digital Voice Communications in World War II* (Fort George G. Meade, MD: Center for Cryptologic History, National Security Agency, 2000), 12n12.

70. Oakes, "ACAN," Part 2, 124.

71. Thompson and Harris, *Signal Corps: The Outcome,* 585–588; Oakes, "ACAN," Part 2, 49–50.

72. Stoner quoted in Thompson and Harris, *Signal Corps: The Outcome,* 586.

73. See David Kahn, *The Codebreakers: The Story of Secret Writing* (New York: Scribner's, 1996), 294–298; Boone and Peterson, *SIGSALY in World War II;* Thompson and Harris, *Signal Corps: The Outcome,* 336–337, 344, 586–588; Oakes, "ACAN," Part 2, Chapter 4. Along with SIGTOT, these systems are the precursors to modern digital communications.

74. When Marshall sent the warning message to General Short in Hawaii, he also relayed it to MacArthur in Manila as well as to commanders in Panama and San Francisco. Thompson and Harris, *Signal Corps: The Outcome,* 10; William H, Bartsch, *December 8, 1941: MacArthur's Pearl Harbor* (College Station: Texas A&M Press, 2003), 257.

75. The operational status of a second radar set on Luzon is a matter of some dispute.

See Bartsch, *MacArthur's Pearl Harbor,* 283, 484n16; and Louis Morton, *The Fall of the Philippines,* United States Army in World War II (Washington, DC: Office of the Chief of Military History, Department of the Army, 1953), 44.

76. Bartsch, *MacArthur's Pearl Harbor,* 299.

77. Thompson, Harris, et al., *Signal Corps: The Test,* 10–15; Morton, *Fall of the Philippines,* 80–88. Bartsch in *MacArthur's Pearl Harbor* provides a detailed narrative of the events before, during, and after the attacks from both the American and Japanese points of view. See Bartsch, *MacArthur's Pearl Harbor,* passim.

78. In the aftermath, Congress did not investigate events in the Philippines as it did those at Pearl Harbor. For a discussion of the various factors that contributed to the disaster at Clark Field, including a breakdown of communications, see Morton, *Fall of the Philippines,* 88–90; Bartsch, *MacArthur's Pearl Harbor,* 262–263, 417–419.

79. D. Clayton James, *The Years of MacArthur, 1941–1945* (Boston: Houghton Mifflin Co., 1975), 23ff. This is the second volume of a trilogy. See also the extensive discussion of events in Morton, *Fall of the Philippines.*

80. Thompson, Harris, et al., *Signal Corps: The Test,* 17–18, 21.

81. The tunnel complex housed a hospital, machine shops, a storehouse, and ammunition magazines.

82. James, *Years of MacArthur, 1941–1945,* 68–76.

83. Morton, *Fall of the Philippines,* 384.

84. James, *Years of MacArthur, 1941*–1945, 98–100; Thompson, Harris, et al., *Signal Corps: The Test,* 117–119.

85. As quoted in "Corregidor's Radio Operated to Bitter End," *Washington Post,* 1 June 1942.

86. Both Oakes and Wagner give Strobing's rank as Sergeant. Oakes, "ACAN," Part 2, 57a; Wagner, "ACAN, Pacific," 47–48. According to Thompson, Harris, et al., *Signal Corps: The Test,* 121n44, Strobing survived the war and became a civil servant. His obituary indicated that he became a national hero when his poignant messages from the doomed garrison were published following the surrender. One oft-quoted transmission read: "We are waiting for God only knows what. How about a chocolate soda?" See "Irving Strobing, Radio Operator on Corregidor, Dies at 77," *New York Times,* 24 July 1997. Teague also survived captivity and retired from the Army in 1949.

87. Wagner, "ACAN, Pacific," 48; Thompson and Harris, *Signal Corps: The Outcome,* 271–275.

88. Akin was a member of the so-called Bataan Gang, the group of officers who served with MacArthur throughout the war and into the postwar period. See James, *Years of MacArthur, 1941–1945,* 100.

89. Prior to the fall of Corregidor, a Signal Corps officer went to Bataan to set up a high-speed radio station for the transmission of such information. See Wagner, "ACAN, Pacific," 22–24; Thompson, Harris, et al., *Signal Corps: The Test,* 116. The sending of casualty messages and personal messages home to soldiers' families comprised yet further aspects of ACAN's services. See Oakes, "ACAN," Part 2, Chapter 9, "Special Services"; and Mary-Louise Melia, "Signal Corps Fixed Communications in World War II:

Special Assignments and Techniques," typescript (Washington, DC: Signal Corps Historical Section, 1945), copy in possession of the Center of Military History.

90. Wagner, "ACAN, Pacific," 23–24; Thompson, Harris, et al., *Signal Corps: The Test*, 112–113.

91. Dayton W. Eddy, "Melbourne to Tokyo: An Article on Communications in the Pacific," 8. Unpublished manuscript in custody of the Office of the Signal Corps Branch Historian, Fort Gordon, Georgia.

92. Wagner, "ACAN, Pacific," 25–26; Thompson, Harris, et al., *Signal Corps: The Test*, 467.

93. Thompson, Harris, et al., *Signal Corps: The Test*, 298.

94. Wagner, "ACAN, Pacific," 25–28.

95. See Edward J. Drea, *MacArthur's Ultra: Codebreaking and the War against Japan, 1942–1945* (Lawrence: University Press of Kansas, 1992). See also Gilbert and Finnegan, eds., *Signals Intelligence in World War II*.

96. The Army's official account of the campaign is that by John Miller Jr., *Guadalcanal: The First Offensive*, United States Army in World War II (Washington, DC: Historical Division, Department of the Army, 1949). The Signal Corps' role is outlined in Thompson, Harris et al., *Signal Corps: The Test*, 476–481.

97. The Guadalcanal campaign officially ended on 21 February 1943. A complete chronology of the major actions in the Pacific cannot be accommodated here. For further reading, the official accounts in the Army's "Green Book" series are highly recommended. Many of them are available online from the U.S. Army Center of Military History's website: http://www.history.army.mil/html/bookshelves/collect/usaww2.html.

98. Eddy, "Melbourne to Tokyo," 6.

99. For a useful summary of the Papuan campaign, see Charles R. Anderson, *Papua*, The U.S. Army Campaigns of World War II (Washington, DC: Government Printing Office, 1992). It is available online at: http://www.history.army.mil/brochures/papua/papua.htm.

100. For more on this campaign see John Miller Jr., *CARTWHEEL: The Reduction of Rabaul*, United States Army in World War II (Washington, DC: Office of the Chief of Military History, U.S. Army, 1959).

101. For a summary of this campaign, see Edward J. Drea, *New Guinea*, The U.S. Army Campaigns of World War II (Washington, DC: Government Printing Office, 1993), available online at: http://www.history.army.mil/brochures/new-guinea/ng.htm.

102. James, *Years of MacArthur, 1941–1945*, 454.

103. Wagner, "ACAN, Pacific," 42ff; Thompson and Harris, *Signal Corps: The Outcome*, 259.

104. Wagner, "ACAN, Pacific," 41.

105. Thompson and Harris, *Signal Corps: The Outcome*, 262–265, 275–288. "Signal Corps CP Fleet," *SCTIL* 44 (July 1945): 1–10. In addition to the transmitter vessels, the Signal Corps also operated several cable ships in the Pacific.

106. "Press Meets Chief Signal Officer," *SCTIL* 29 (April 1944): 5–10.

107. Major General Richard K. Sutherland, MacArthur's Chief of Staff, replied

on MacArthur's behalf. The correspondents could not see each other. James, *Years of MacArthur, 1941–1945*, 526–534.

108. An earlier conference in Quebec had been dubbed QUADRANT. See Wagner, "ACAN, Pacific," 32; Eddy, "Melbourne to Tokyo," 8. See also Thompson and Harris, *Signal Corps: The Outcome*, 270, 589–590.

109. Eddy, "Melbourne to Tokyo," 12. See Thompson and Harris, *Signal Corps: The Outcome*, 276, 278. See also http://offshoreradio.de/fleet/apache.htm (accessed 4 February 2010).

110. William S. Rumbough, "Radio Relay: The War's Great Development in Signal Communications," *Military Review* 26 (May 1946): 11–12; Thompson and Harris, *Signal Corps: The Outcome*, 259–265, 275–280, 283–284; "Radio Relay Equipment in the Philippine Operation," *SCTIL* 43 (June 1945): 1–3, 10.

111. U.S. Army Signal Corps, Southwest Pacific Area, "Seaborne CPs: An Official History of the Southwest Pacific Area Signal Corps' Command Post Fleet (1 January 1945), 18, 27–28. Manuscript in custody of the Office of the Signal Corps Branch Historian, Fort Gordon, Georgia.

112. Wagner, "ACAN, Pacific," 51 and 53.

113. Thompson and Harris, *Signal Corps: The Outcome*, 283. Pictures from the Normandy invasion were the first of operations occurring in another hemisphere to be available for publication at home before the news story could be edited. Oakes, "ACAN," Part 2, 136.

114. Oakes, "ACAN," Part 2, 129.

115. On communications for the VIP conferences, see Thompson and Harris, *Signal Corps: The Outcome*, 588–591. See also Thompson, Harris, et al., *Signal Corps: The Test*, 454; Melia, "Signal Corps: Special Assignments," 40–42.

116. Marshall sent this message at 2325Z (11:25 p.m.). See Oakes, "ACAN," Part 2, 152. See copy of Marshall's message to MacArthur in "Surrender on the Air, an Official Signal Corps History of Message Traffic on the Japanese Capitulation," *Military Review* 26 (May 1946): 31–39. See also ARSO, 1946, 3–4, 472–473; Thompson and Harris, *Signal Corps: The Outcome*, 600–601; James, *Years of MacArthur, 1941–1945*, 776–777.

117. "Surrender on the Air," 33.

118. Oakes, "ACAN," Part 2, 152–153; Thompson and Harris, *Signal Corps: The Outcome*, 600–601; "Surrender on the Air, 31–39; ARSO, 1946, 3–4, 472–473.

119. As quoted in James, *Years of MacArthur, 1941–1945*, 791.

120. Oakes, "ACAN," Part 3, 26.

121. Thompson and Harris, *Signal Corps: The Outcome*, 299–300.

122. Oakes, "ACAN," Part 3, 14–15.

123. Oakes, "ACAN," Part 3, 59–60. See also the following online resources: http://www.offshore-radio.de/fleet/spindleeye.htm and http://www.offshore-radio.de/fleet/apache.htm (both accessed 15 March 2010).

124. See Oakes, "ACAN," Part 3, Chapter 5. Approximately 40 percent of the civilian personnel in 1946 were former enlisted men and women. ARSO, 1946, 487-502.

125. By war's end, the system had the capacity to carry 100 million words a day. Thompson and Harris, *Signal Corps: The Outcome*, 580.

126. Oakes, "ACAN," Part 2, 102.

127. See Eisenhower's letter to Ingles (addressed to "Dear Dad"), dated 4 February 1945 in Louis Galombos, ed., *The Papers of Dwight David Eisenhower* 8 (Baltimore: Johns Hopkins University Press, 1978), 1478 and note 1. See also the quotation from his remarks in a speech to the Army Ordnance Association on 3 June 1946, quoted in Thompson and Harris, *Signal Corps: The Outcome*, 621.

128. For an account of the State Department's attempt to build a global radio network after the war, see Timothy Stoneman, "A Bold New Vision: The VOA Radio Ring and Global Broadcasting in the Early Cold War," *Technology and Culture* 50 (April 2009): 316–344. Stoneman makes no mention of the ACAN, which predated the Voice of America as a global radio network, although ACAN was obviously created for a different purpose.

129. Thompson and Harris, *Signal Corps: The Outcome*, 620–623. Effective 23 August 1947, the War Department Signal Center was redesignated as the Army Command and Administrative Communication Agency. The Army Command and Administrative Network and WAR remained under its control. War Department General Orders 79, 1947; Larew, "Radio Net," 506.

130. "General Harry C. Ingles, Chief Signal Officer, Dies," *Washington Post*, 16 August 1976.

131. "Maj. Gen. Akin, Signal Corps Chief, Retires," *Washington Post*, 11 March 1951.

132. See Thompson and Harris, *Signal Corps: The Outcome*, 620–623; Oakes, "ACAN," Part 3, 52.5.

133. Oakes, "ACAN," Part 3, 27–28.

134. "U.N. Communications Post Goes to Wartime Expert," *New York Times*, 10 April 1947, 12. Stoner expressed his aim in a lecture delivered at the Army Industrial College on 24 September 1945. See Oakes, "ACAN," Part 2, vi-vii. On the system's progress see, e.g., "U.N. World Radio Rushed by Expert," *New York Times*, 9 March 1947; "Big Switchboard Is Planned by U.N.," *New York Times*, 17 December 1947. On plans for the organization of postwar communications and the United Nations' role, see Headrick, *Invisible Weapon*, 267–268. Stoner died in 1966 at age seventy-two. See his obituary, "General Stoner, Signal Officer," *Washington Post*, 29 October 1966.

135. For a detailed history of communications in Vietnam, see John D. Bergen, *Military Communications: A Test for Technology*, United States Army in Vietnam (Washington, DC: Center of Military History, U.S. Army, 1986). As part of the early advisory effort, the Signal Corps opened an ACAN station in Saigon.

Bibliography

Primary Sources

Archives

U.S. Army Center of Military History, Fort Lesley J. McNair, Washington, DC, Biographical Files.

Edited Collections

Eisenhower, Dwight D. *The Papers of Dwight David Eisenhower.* Vol. 8: The Chief of Staff. Ed. Louis Galambos. Baltimore: Johns Hopkins University Press, 1978.

Newsletters

Signal Corps Bulletin
—French, Edward F. "War Department Radio Net." *Signal Corps Bulletin* 30 (June 1925): 13–16.
—"Joint Board Policy for Coordination of Radio Activities of the Army and Navy." *Signal Corps Bulletin* 41 (December 1927): 16–19.
—Gifford, Walter S. "The Activities of the Bell System during the World War." *Signal Corps Bulletin* 102 (October–December 1938): 1–9.
Signal Corps Technical Information Letter (SCTIL)
—"Fungus Growths." *SCTIL* 19 (June 1943): 34.
—"The New Chief Signal Officer." *SCTIL* 20 (July 1943): 5.
—"Press Meets Chief Signal Officer." *SCTIL* 29 (April 1944): 5–10.
—"Mechanization of 'WAR.'" *SCTIL* 30 (May 1944): 75–78.
—"How the Navy Uses Signal Corps Equipment." *SCTIL* 32 (July 1944): 15–16, 47.
—"Signals on Bougainville." *SCTIL* 32 (July 1944): 23–24.
—"Combined Procedures." *SCTIL* 35 (October 1944): 13–14, 38.
—"Combined Training Network." *SCTIL* 36 (November 1944): 16, 20.
—"Equipment Tropicalization." *SCTIL* 36 (November 1944): 21–22.
—"Radio Relay Equipment in the Philippine Operation." *SCTIL* 43 (June 1945): 1–3, 10.
—"Signal Corps CP Fleet." *SCTIL* 44 (July 1945): 1–10.

Professional Journals

Powell, Carroll A. "Communications in the Pacific Ocean Areas." *Military Review* 25 (January 1946): 30–34.

Rumbough, William S. "Radio Relay: The War's Great Development in Signal Communications." *Military Review* 26 (May 1946): 11–12.

"Surrender on the Air, an Official Signal Corps History of Message Traffic on the Japanese Capitulation." *Military Review* 26 (May 1946): 31–39.

Unpublished Works

Boswell, Mary E. "The 17th Signal Service Company, a Component of the War Department Signal Center from World War I through World War II." Typescript. Washington, DC: Signal Corps Historical Section, n.d. Copy in the collections of the U.S. Army Center of Military History, Washington, DC.

Eddy, Dayton W. "Melbourne to Tokyo: An Article on Communications in the Pacific." Copy in the custody of the Office of the Signal Corps Branch Historian, Fort Gordon, Georgia.

Melia, Mary-Louise. "Signal Corps Fixed Communications in World War II: Special Assignments and Techniques." Typescript. Washington, DC: Signal Corps Historical Section, December 1945. Copy in the collections of the U.S. Army Center of Military History, Washington, DC.

Oakes, Pauline M. "The Army Command and Administrative Communications System, Part 1: War Department Radio Net Thru Fiscal Years 1920–1940." Typescript. Washington, DC: Signal Corps Historical Section, October 1945. Copy in the collections of the U.S. Army Center of Military History, Washington, DC.

———. "The Army Command and Administrative Communications System, Part 2: Signal Corps Domestic Communications Network as Extended to Oversea Terminals Fiscal Year 1940 through 15 August 1945." Typescript. Washington, DC: Signal Corps Historical Section, December 1945. Copy in the collections of the U.S. Army Center of Military History, Washington, DC.

———. "The Army Command and Administrative Communications System, Part 3: Signal Corps Domestic Communications Network as Extended to Oversea Terminals during the Period of Demobilization 14 August 1945–31 December 1945." Typescript. Washington, DC: Signal Corps Historical Section, March 1946. Copy in the collections of the U.S. Army Center of Military History, Washington, DC.

U.S. Army Signal Corps, Southwest Pacific Area. "Seaborne CPs: An Official History of the Southwest Pacific Area Signal Corps' Command Post Fleet." 1 January 1945. Copy in the custody of the Office of the Signal Corps Branch Historian, Fort Gordon, Georgia.

U.S. War Department. "Annual Report of the Chief Signal Officer, 1943." Typescript. Copy in the collections of the U.S. Army Center of Military History, Washington, DC.

U.S. War Department. "Annual Report of the Chief Signal Officer, 1946." Typescript. Copy in the collections of the U.S. Army Center of Military History, Washington, DC.

Wagner, Donald O. "Army Command and Administrative Network, 1941–1945, Part 1: The Pacific." Typescript. Washington, DC: Signal Corps Historical Section, n.d. Copy in the collections of the U.S. Army Center of Military History, Washington, DC.

Secondary Sources

Books

Bartsch, William H. *December 8, 1941: MacArthur's Pearl Harbor.* College Station: Texas A&M Press, 2003.

Bilby, Kenneth. *The General: David Sarnoff and the Rise of the Communications Industry.* New York: Harper and Row, 1986.

Douglas, Susan J. *Inventing American Broadcasting, 1899–1922.* Baltimore: Johns Hopkins University Press, 1987.
Drea, Edward J. *MacArthur's Ultra: Codebreaking and the War against Japan, 1942–1945.* Lawrence: University Press of Kansas, 1992.
Fagen, M. D., ed. *A History of Engineering and Science in the Bell System: The Early Years (1875–1925).* New York: Bell Telephone Laboratories, 1975.
Headrick, Donald R. *The Invisible Weapon: Telecommunications and International Politics, 1851–1945.* New York: Oxford University Press, 1991.
James, D. Clayton. *The Years of MacArthur, 1941–1945.* Boston: Houghton Mifflin Co., 1975.
Kahn, David. *The Codebreakers: The Story of Secret Writing.* New York: Scribner's 1996.
Lavine, A. Lincoln. *Circuits of Victory.* Garden City, NY: Doubleday, Page, and Co., 1921.
Miller, Edward S. *War Plan Orange: The U.S. Strategy to Defeat Japan, 1897–1945.* Annapolis: Naval Institute Press, 1991.
Ohl, John Kennedy. *Supplying the Troops: General Somervell and American Logistics in World War II.* DeKalb: Northern Illinois University Press, 1994.
Thompson, Richard J., Jr. *Crystal Clear: The Struggle for Reliable Communications Technology in World War II.* Piscataway, NJ: IEEE Press, 2012.
Vogel, Steve. *The Pentagon: A History.* New York: Random House, 2007.
Weise, Selene H. C. *The Good Soldier: The Story of a Southwest Pacific Signal Corps WAC.* Shippensburg, PA: Burd Street Press, 1999.
Winkler, Jonathan Reed. *Nexus: Strategic Communications and American Security in World War I.* Cambridge, MA: Harvard University Press, 2008.

Official Histories

Anderson, Charles R. *Papua.* The U.S. Army Campaigns of World War II. Washington, DC: Government Printing Office, 1992.
Bergen, John D. *Military Communications: A Test for Technology.* United States Army in Vietnam. Washington, DC: Center of Military History, U.S. Army, 1986.
Boone, J. V., and R. R. Peterson. *The Start of the Digital Revolution: SIGSALY Secure Digital Voice Communications in World War II.* Fort George G. Meade, MD: Center for Cryptologic History, National Security Agency, 2000.
Condon-Rall, Mary Ellen, and Albert E. Cowdrey. *The Medical Department: Army Medical Service in the War against Japan.* United States Army in World War II. Washington, DC: Center of Military History, U.S. Army, 1988.
Drea, Edward. *New Guinea.* The U.S. Army Campaigns of World War II. Washington, DC: Government Printing Office, 1993.
Gilbert, James L., and John P. Finnegan, eds. *U.S. Army Signals Intelligence in World War II: A Documentary History.* Washington, DC: Center of Military History, U.S. Army, 1993.
Howeth, Linwood S. *History of Communications-Electronics in the United States Navy.* Washington, DC: Government Printing Office, 1963.

Kovach, Karen. *Breaking Codes, Breaking Barriers: The WACs of the Signal Security Agency, World War II.* Fort Belvoir, VA: History Office, Office of the Chief of Staff, U.S. Army Intelligence and Security Command, n.d.

Laurie, Clayton D. and Ronald H. Cole. *The Role of Federal Military Forces in Domestic Disorders, 1875–1945.* Washington, DC: Center of Military History, U.S. Army, 1997.

Miller, John, Jr., *CARTWHEEL: The Reduction of Rabaul.* United States Army in World War II. Washington, DC: Office of the Chief of Military History, Department of the Army, 1959.

———. *Guadalcanal: The First Offensive.* United States Army in World War II. Washington, DC: Historical Division, Department of the Army, 1949.

Millett, John D. *The Organization and Role of the Army Service Forces.* United States Army in World War II. Washington, DC: Office of the Chief of Military History, Department of the Army, 1954.

Morton, Louis. *The Fall of the Philippines.* United States Army in World War II. Washington, DC: Office of the Chief of Military History, Department of the Army, 1953.

———. *Strategy and Command: The First Two Years.* United States Army in World War II: The War in the Pacific. Washington, DC: Center of Military History, Department of the Army, 1989.

Newell, Clayton R. *Central Pacific 1941–1943.* The U.S. Army Campaigns of World War II. Washington, DC: Government Printing Office, 1992.

Terrett, Dulany. *The Signal Corps: The Emergency (to December 1941).* United States Army in World War II. Washington, DC: Office of the Chief of Military History, Department of the Army, 1956.

Thompson, George R., Dixie R. Harris, Pauline M. Oakes, and Dulany Terrett. *The Signal Corps: The Test (December 1941 to July 1943).* United States Army in World War II. Washington, DC: Office of the Chief of Military History, Department of the Army, 1957.

Thompson, George R., and Dixie R. Harris. *The Signal Corps: The Outcome (Mid-1943 through 1945).* United States Army in World War II. Washington, DC: Office of the Chief of Military History, Department of the Army, 1966.

Treadwell, Mattie E. *The Women's Army Corps.* United States Army in World War II. Washington, DC: Office of the Chief of Military History, Department of the Army, 1954.

Watson, Mark S. *Chief of Staff: Prewar Plans and Preparations.* United States Army in World War II. Washington, DC: Historical Division, U.S. Army, 1950.

Articles

Larew, Karl G. "War Department Radio Net." In *Military Communications: From Ancient Times to the 21st Century,* ed. Christopher Sterling, pp. 505–507. Santa Barbara, CA: ABC-Clio, 2008.

Stoneman, Timothy. "A Bold New Vision: The VOA Radio Ring and Global Broadcasting in the Early Cold War." *Technology and Culture* 50 (April 2009): 316–344.

Winkler, Jonathan Reed. "Information Warfare in World War I." *Journal of Military History* 73 (July 2009): 845–867.

Conference Papers

Raines, Rebecca Robbins. "WAR in Peace: The Establishment of the Army Command and Administrative Communications System, 1920–1941." Paper presented at the International Security Studies Conference, Yale University, April 2002.

2

Here's Your Air War

Popular Culture Depictions of Land-Based Air Power in the Pacific

Steve Call

The climactic scene of an early World War II movie, *Air Force,* presents a compelling image of land-based American air power in the Pacific, one designed to provide maximum entertainment to the audience, but also one calculated to send a message to the American public about the nature of the Pacific air war. One image played to popular stereotypes of the Japanese as inept warriors. The crew of a lone B-17, the *Mary Ann,* on which the entire film focuses, stumbles upon a Japanese invasion fleet headed for Australia; even though the Japanese also have spotted the B-17 and fired on it, the fleet takes no precautionary measures. No change of course is ordered, no scout planes are launched, no fighter screen is sent aloft. The B-17 crew escapes into the clouds, reports the fleet's location, then loiters waiting for the attack force to arrive; when it does, the Japanese ships are sitting ducks for the American aircraft. Another image presented is one of unbelievable American flexibility and effectiveness. With no warning whatsoever, all American aircraft in the area—Navy, Marine Corps, and Army—immediately launch, rendezvous, and inflict a devastating, coordinated attack. Every bomb or torpedo strikes with near-perfect precision, sinking numerous ships, including one aircraft carrier, and crippling the fleet, thereby winning a stunning victory for America and for air power.[1]

From the dawn of flight, air power quickly became a prominent theme in American popular culture. Movies, novels, poems, songs, and other genres featured airplanes in an exciting new type of warfare. At the very least, the still-new wonders of airplanes and human flight were exciting in any medium, and images of the World War I fighter ace made air power seem to be a romantic and heroic quest for glory. A steady stream of movies such as *Wings, Hell's Angels,* and *Dawn Patrol,* featuring World War I fighter pilots soaring in deadly combat among the clouds, illustrates this point; in fact, *Wings* won the first-ever Best Picture Oscar in 1927. Air power was also a popular theme in written works. Memoirs from such famed aces as Eddie Rickenbacker and Canada's Billy Bishop gave a very personal view of aerial combat, but lesser-known figures added noteworthy contributions. For instance, Cecil Lewis's *Sagittarius Rising* is still considered a classic of the genre, and Beirne Lay's *I Wanted Wings* inspired a movie of the same name. General-interest magazines like *Saturday Evening Post, Life,* and *Reader's Digest* regularly featured articles on military aviation themes and closely followed air power developments. But one significant theme in popular culture during the interwar period presented more ambitious images. Airmen such as Alexander de Seversky, World War I veteran and aeronautical pioneer, and Colonel William "Billy" Mitchell, U.S. Army, used popular culture venues in their attempt to convince government and military leaders, and the American public, that air power had revolutionized warfare. By the eve of World War II, air warfare had become such a staple for popular culture that it was seen as more than just entertaining—it was also meant to educate the public on air power's capabilities. To some it was fascinating, exciting, or heroic; to others it was the face of a revolutionary form of modern warfare.[2]

It is not surprising, therefore, that when war came to America in 1941 air power would continue and, in fact, mushroom as an ever-present theme in American popular culture. The way war came even helped heighten this phenomenon: the attack on Pearl Harbor not only galvanized a divided public opinion and filled the American people with great wrath; the attack also came in the form of air power. Images of the devastation wrought by Japanese airplanes not only riveted America's attention, they gave graphic testimony of the speed and power of attack from the air. Furthermore, as the war played out in the Pacific, air power played a major role in a number of ways, and this provided the venues of popular culture with plenty of grist for their mills. The print media of newspapers and magazines were able to incorporate images of air power early, but others, such as film and books, soon joined in the unfolding drama.

At this point, it is important to clarify the scope of "popular culture" examined in this study and justify that scope. Virtually every medium reported on the war and air power's role in that war. Some media, such as newspapers, news magazines, and war reporting on radio or in newsreels shown in theaters, presented themselves as factual and unbiased reportage; obviously, they were often neither factual nor unbiased, but the genre stressed those expectations. Other media that dealt with air power in the war, such as movies, general-interest magazines, and even comic strips, sought to entertain; thus they were not held to the same strict standards of factuality and impartiality, and their coverage of the air war generally differed in tone and message. Still other media, such as books and memoirs, sought to tell a larger story or presented to the public air power subjects in greater detail. All of these media, too, often lent themselves to a didactic role, instructing the public on the war effort, the enemy, or even the nature of air power. So this study will focus on non-news media of popular culture: movies, general-interest magazines, and books, as well as a comic strip and a radio show based on that comic strip. The goal is to analyze not only what was said, but also images that were embedded in what was said, for these images often conveyed a much different impression than that presented in more formal venues. In this way, we can gain insight into not only what was reported about events in the air battles of the Pacific, but also how the authors and producers hoped to influence the American public in what they thought or felt about the Pacific air war. One other clarification: this study focuses only on material presented during the war itself.[3]

In analyzing that wartime presentation, two larger themes emerge. One is the overall diversity of the Pacific air war; for a number of reasons, one being the "Germany first" focus of America's World War II grand strategy, the war in the Pacific was waged by many different elements in an often widely dispersed manner, and most personnel were forced to operate with limited means. Popular culture found a great deal of excitement in these diverse efforts, and the unequal odds added an additional note of drama, so this chapter will address how a number of those efforts were depicted. Second, there were many reasons why the various aspects of the Pacific air war were depicted as they were in popular culture. Some authors merely wanted to tell a heroic story, whether for patriotic reasons or just because it was heroic and the public clamored for heroes. Other works sought to present a subtly or blatantly biased story; such themes as "America strikes back," or "Treachery avenged," or "Democracy fights Tyranny" were very popular with the public, and air power often gave powerful images to serve those purposes. Finally, some authors and producers were convinced that air power was a revolutionary force and that either World War II should be, or the Pacific air war was, the crucible of that revolution. These authors and producers saw popular culture as a unique venue to present that message, not just to military or political decision makers, but to the American public as well.[4] This study will explore all of these different reasons as a way to gain insight into the messages authors and producers sought to convey.

The attack on Pearl Harbor was a stunning introduction to the Pacific air war, and while more formal venues dissected the how and why, the dominant themes in popular culture emphasized the treachery of, and revenge for, the attack; some media also focused on how the attack proved the superiority of air power over battleships. Several examples of treachery as an explanation for Japan's success can be seen in the 1943 movie *Air Force*. Shortly after the attack on Pearl Harbor, Jack Warner, of the Warner Brothers studio, suggested to then–Lieutenant General Henry "Hap" Arnold, Commanding General, U.S.

Army Air Forces (COMGENAIR), that a movie be produced that would showcase air power, and Arnold embraced the idea eagerly. The result was *Air Force,* a cinematic paean to American air power. It also featured a number of negative Japanese stereotypes throughout, including the idea that Japanese-Americans living on Oahu had acted as saboteurs before, during, and after the attack. The film centers on the exploits of a B-17 crew in the weeks following the Pearl Harbor attack, but it opens with the crew flying into Hickam Air Field on the morning of 7 December in the midst of the attack. They divert to an emergency field, but as the crew tries to repair damage from the landing they are shot at by Japanese-American snipers. They take off and return to Hickam just after the attacks have ended. While there, they are told by ground personnel that a local delivery truck, presumably driven by a Japanese-American, had driven down one row of aircraft parked on the ramp, crashing into the tails of every plane. Later, a local pilot tells of how a similar delivery truck, again presumably driven by a Japanese-American, attempted to block an access road to Hickam Field in order to prevent off-base personnel from joining in the base's defense.[5]

In addition to the film *Air Force*, popular media presented numerous references to American air power paying Japan back in kind for the attack on Pearl Harbor; but two examples stand out. One was a four-part series in the *Saturday Evening Post,* appropriately titled "I Fly for Vengeance," written by Lieutenant Clarence E. Dickinson, U.S. Navy. A scout plane pilot flying ahead of his unnamed aircraft carrier (undoubtedly the *Enterprise*) on its return to Pearl Harbor the morning of 7 December, Dickinson had flown right into the middle of the second Japanese attack, was shot down, and lost his gunner in the attack. Hitchhiking back to Ford Island in a futile attempt to find a plane to fly back into battle, dodging bombs and planes strafing civilian cars, Dickinson would later take part in the Battle of Midway. Throughout his story, he weaves the theme that his primary motivation is to avenge his lost friends and the destruction he witnessed firsthand.[6] The second example is another article from the *Saturday Evening Post*, from July 1944. Bearing another telling title, "We Avenge Pearl Harbor," the author, Eugene Burns, depicts the U.S. Navy's 5 November 1943 attack on the Japanese stronghold of Rabaul as a Pearl Harbor in reverse: this time the Americans inflict a crushing aerial surprise attack on the Japanese naval forces massing there.[7]

The third reaction to Pearl Harbor—that air power had proven its superiority over battleships—was inextricably linked to the interwar debates about the role of air power in America's defenses, as well as wartime efforts to depict air power as a revolutionary force. For that reason, some examples from that interwar debate, or pieces that play off it, are worth noting here. Ironically, six days before the Pearl Harbor attack, *Life* magazine ran a series of photo-essays surveying America's armed forces, along with an article by noted military analyst and commentator Hanson Baldwin, bearing the title "Airpower" and the header "The Experience Gained in This War Shows What It Can Accomplish and What It Can't." In this article, Baldwin flatly states, "So far, *no modern battleship* ever has been sunk by air attack and no battleship, new or old, ever has been sunk by air attack during war"; he then backs the continuing validity of his point by highlighting what battleships are doing to adapt to the threat of air power.[8] In little over a week after those words were published, Japanese aircraft had not only sunk the *Arizona* and other battleships in Pearl Harbor, they had also crippled the British Pacific war effort on 10 December by sinking the battleship *Prince of Wales* and the battle cruiser *Repulse.* In illustrating the obsolescence of Baldwin's words, critics often pointed directly at Pearl Harbor as proof. For example, Army Air Forces Colonel Hugh Knerr, writing in the September 1942 issue of *American Mercury,* mocked "the battleship admirals of our Navy Command—the very men who fought the development of true air power until the smoke cleared from Pearl Harbor." In backing up his words, he quoted Admiral William Veazie Pratt's 11 June 1940 radio address in which Pratt stated (according to Knerr), "A battleship is so heavily armored that when a bomb strikes it, the force of the explosion goes up into the air, and very little damage is done." Similarly, in his 1942 book, *The Fight for Air Power,* William Bradford Huie stated that the fight for air power development "began at the end of the last war [meaning World War I] and ended at Pearl Harbor," where "our enemies demonstrated to the satisfaction of even the blindest that the airplane is the primary offensive weapon of modern warfare."[9]

In the aftermath of the attack on Pearl Harbor, which crippled the U.S. Pacific Fleet, America's Pacific war effort suffered one defeat after another. There was little good news, but air power did provide some solace. The first airmen to lift the American public's spirits were the members of the American Volunteer Group (AVG) in China, better known as the Flying Tigers. China had been fighting the Japanese since the 1931 conquest of Manchuria, but what is sometimes called the Second Sino-Japanese War began in earnest with Japan's 1937 wholesale assault to conquer the rest of China. Badly overmatched in many categories, China appealed for international aid, but little was forthcoming. In 1941, but before the Pearl Harbor attack, the U.S. government gave direct Lend-Lease aid in the form of ninety P-40 Tomahawks—considered obsolete and turned down by the British—and indirect aid by authorizing U.S. Army, Navy, and Marine Corps pilots to volunteer for service in the Chinese Air Force. By autumn of that year, this aid was finally arriving in theater, and the pilots were beginning to train in the unique tactics of Claire L. Chennault, a retired U.S. Army Air Corps (AAC) captain, pilot, and theorist, and the organizer of the AVG.[10]

Chennault had been a gadfly in the Air Corps, but he was also a superb pilot. At the Air Corps Tactical School (ACTS) at Maxwell Field in Alabama, an organization increasingly dominated by strategic bombing theorists, Chennault was one faculty member who advocated defensive air power in the form of pursuit—or fighter—planes, and he devised innovative tactics and formations to shoot down other aircraft, especially bombers. In his postwar insider's account of the development of American strategic bombing doctrine at the Air Corps Tactical School, Brigadier General Haywood Hansell described Chennault as an inflexible personality and a bitter critic of strategic bombing theory in its early stages.[11] But in late 1941, defensive air power was exactly what China needed to save itself from Japan's exploitation of near-total air supremacy, and Chennault and his theories were just what they needed. Still, for his paltry forces to make any dent in Japan's air mastery, Chennault was going to need all the innovative tactics he could conjure up.

The Flying Tigers were still in training when news of the attack on Pearl Harbor came, so even though they had signed up to fight China's air war, they now knew they were fighting America's war as well. The first taste of combat came on 20 December, less than two weeks after Pearl Harbor, and reports of that first action provided a harbinger of things to come. According to one report of that battle, of ten medium bombers intercepted by the P-40s, six were claimed shot down. Near daily engagements followed, but what seemed to be a dramatic climax came on Christmas Day, 1941.[12] In journalist Russell Whelan's wartime account of the Flying Tigers, that first Christmas of the war found many Americans with heavy hearts, low morale, and deep worries for America's ability to catch up from so far behind. News accounts of a dramatic victory won in the skies over Rangoon on Christmas Day hit the American public like a badly needed tonic. On that day, according to Whelan, a total of 108 Japanese aircraft attacked Rangoon—sixty bombers and twenty fighters in the first wave, and twenty bombers and eight fighters in the second. These numbers accentuate a perennial problem for the AVG because they had so little to face so much; thirteen P-40s took to the air, joined by fifteen British Royal Air Force (RAF) fighters. Whelan claimed that the Flying Tigers racked up a tally of twenty-three confirmed kills and eleven more probables; with the RAF kills, Whelan reported, the Japanese lost "at least thirty-six," or a third of their attacking force, while the Americans lost one aircraft and no pilots and the RAF lost five aircraft and pilots.[13]

News accounts of this "stunning victory" flashed around the world, making the Flying Tigers some of the war's earliest heroes, particularly in the United States and China. Reports of more dramatic exploits followed, and virtually every medium of popular culture followed the AVG closely. A host of articles appeared in popular magazines, and Chennault's picture was featured on the cover of both *Time* and *Life* magazines. One such article, for example, appeared in *Reader's Digest,* reprinted from the *American Legion,* and gave eloquent praise not only to the effectiveness of Chennault's tactics, but also to their unique nature. According to the article, the Japanese government threatened to classify AVG pilots as guerrillas instead of combatants if they did not stop using their unorthodox tactics.[14] At least two books published during the war gave detailed coverage of Flying Tiger operations. One, *The Flying Tigers* by Russell Whelan, appeared in 1942 and covered day-to-day operations from the Flying Tigers' inception to 4 July 1942. In that period, Whelan reported that the AVG amassed 286 confirmed kills along with an estimate of "perhaps three hundred other" aircraft that could not be confirmed, while losing only eight pilots in the air and two pilots and a crew chief killed on the ground. At the time of publication, Whelan reported, there were another four pilots listed as missing.[15]

Shortly after Whelan's book came a more personal account from one of the Flying Tigers: Colonel Robert L. Scott's *God Is My Co-Pilot,* published in 1943. In a foreword written by Chennault himself, he praises Scott as a group commander who "scheduled himself as pilot on all possible missions," and who "specialized in the most dangerous" missions.[16] Scott gave the American public an intimate—almost saccharine—view into his own thoughts as he describes his boyhood fascination with fighter planes, his early flying career, and then how he worked his way into the AVG. Besides detailing his own thoughts and actions, though, Scott also gave a tense and thrilling glimpse into the inner day-to-day war of the Flying Tigers. One minute, he helps the reader feel the unbearable tension of pilots waiting in the alert hut, trying to carry on with card games, conversations, or naps, while phone reports from Chennault's warning net come in. Never knowing what reports were irrelevant, the pilots are continually keyed up, knowing that the next time the phone rings it could send them scrambling for their aircraft. At other moments, however, Scott gives some exciting firsthand accounts of the kind of air combat that made the Flying Tigers famous. In one raid on Hanoi, for example, Scott describes how Allied bombers made it to their targets despite heavy Japanese fighter defenses and bombed the Gia Lam Airfield with "very good results" while the P-40s claimed nine "definite" kills and an unstated number of "probables" out of the thirteen Japanese fighters that rose to stop them. All of this was apparently accomplished without suffering so much as a single bullet hole in any of the U.S. aircraft.[17]

The fame and heroics of the Flying Tigers were too good for Hollywood to pass up; but the first movie based on their story, 1942's *Flying Tigers* starring John Wayne, was more an exploitation of their fame than a vehicle for highlighting their exploits. The film featured numerous aerial combat scenes, and one emphasized how the Tigers were often badly outnumbered. When six P-40s encounter eighteen Japanese bombers, one American pilot wisecracks, "Well, whaddaya know; only three-to-one; that won't even wake me up!" That particular air battle results in the death of one Flying Tiger, and as Wayne adds the dead pilot's bundle of "last effects" to a drawer full of other such bundles, he ruefully comments that there wouldn't be so many killed if they did not continually face such overwhelming odds. Nothing was said in the movie, however, of Chennault's unique tactics that helped them succeed against such odds; in fact, Chennault's name is never even mentioned, despite his being virtually synonymous with the Flying Tigers. Most of the action takes place on the ground and revolves around a hot-shot loner pilot who is only interested in the bonus money the volunteers get for each kill, and in stealing Wayne's girl. This sets up numerous scenes where various characters try to impress upon this pilot the importance of teamwork and the higher cause of winning the war, but the same could be said of just about any film during the war. Here again, no mention is made of how Chennault's success and unorthodox tactics were in part based on each aircraft working as part of a larger team. By the end of the film, the hot-shot loner has learned the value of teamwork, and the woman, of course, remains faithful to Wayne.[18] As Michael Paris observed, the film effectively conveyed common propaganda images of American virtue versus Japanese treachery; Paris also points out that this film became a model for later aviation films. But as a depiction of Chennault's unique formula for success or how the Flying Tigers were different from any other heroic group of servicemen, it fails.[19]

Another film depicting the Flying Tigers' operations was a film adaptation of Scott's *God Is My Co-Pilot,* released by Warner Brothers in April 1945. The film is generally faithful to Scott's book; for example, Chennault is a central character and the mastermind behind the unit's operations. As such, it is clear that his genius and vision are the secrets to the Flying Tigers' success. The film also faithfully depicts elements of Scott's story not as well known to the Flying Tiger image. For example, Chennault's pioneer fighter tactics are highlighted and many Japanese pilots are shot out of the skies, but the movie also conveys a point both Scott and Whelan made in their books: that Chennault had outgrown his earlier fighter-pilot-centric theories and denigration of bombers. The highlight of the movie, a bombing raid on Hong Kong, is briefed by Chennault as the great day for which they have all been working so hard; on the next bombing mission, Chennault says it is ushering in a whole new and decisive chapter in the history of the Flying Tigers.[20]

One of the most famous events in the Pacific air war was the bombing raid led by Lieutenant Colonel James Doolittle. Launching sixteen B-25 bombers from the deck of the USS *Hornet,* the United States surprised Japan with a bombing raid on its home islands, and in the process gave the American people one of their first morale boosts of the war. The Doolittle Raiders, as they came to be known, became instant national heroes, and many stories focused on their exploits from various perspectives. Virtually all popular culture media told the tale in some fashion. An early account of the raid and its aftermath came from one of the Raiders as a firsthand memoir. In *Thirty Seconds over Tokyo,* published in 1943, Captain Ted W. Lawson told how he came to be a pilot of one Doolittle's bombers and how the group trained. Lawson also described life aboard the *Hornet* as they steamed toward Japan. He gave a stirring account of the bomb run itself, and then of how his aircraft crash-landed on the Chinese coast and how he was smuggled out of Japanese-held territory and returned to safety. Additionally, he told of the privation of that escape and how he lost a leg in the process. It was a thrilling, yet moving, story that spoke not only of the heroism of the Raiders, but also of the Chinese people, who took great risks to protect, care for, and move not only Lawson, but other Raiders, despite the desperate efforts of the Japanese military to hunt them down. At the same time, though, as one of the Raider pilots, Lawson gives a unique perspective, touching on a number of aspects of this piece of the larger air war.[21]

Surprisingly, Lawson can hardly be considered an air power advocate. He often describes himself as a halfhearted flier and even begins his account by stating that as a result of the raid (perhaps because of his losing a leg, though he does not say this), he is finally getting to do the aeronautical research "which I wanted to do in the first place."[22] Lawson also gives a different depiction of Army Air Forces precision industrial bombing than that which predominated in popular culture. First, he mentions that the famed Norden bombsights were removed from their planes, mainly for security reasons, but also because they would be bombing at low level and, according to Lawson, the Norden bombsight was not "practicable" at low altitude. They were replaced with a makeshift bombsight that Lawson described as "as simple as aiming a rifle."[23] Curiously, Lawson also states that the crews were allowed to pick their own targets and which cities they wished to bomb. Much was made by others throughout the war about strategic bombing crippling the enemy's war production by destroying carefully selected targets; but, perhaps because the Doolittle Raid was more symbolic than tactical, the target lists relied on the preferences of the crews flying the mission.[24] In yet another departure from the "public image" of strategic bombing, Lawson writes that while their main targets would be military and would be struck with 500-pound demolition bombs, the Raiders would also be dropping incendiary bombs. The reason given is chilling, considering later bombing over Japan: the crews were to select an "inflammable section . . . as close as possible to the other targets" in an effort to overwhelm the Tokyo Fire Department. "If you can start seven good fires in Tokyo, they'll never put them out. . . . Seven big scattered fires would be too much for them to cope with."[25]

Lawson describes the takeoff and flight to Tokyo in vivid yet straightforward prose; no romantic or exaggerated hyperbole was employed as was so often the case in popular culture vehicles, especially those dealing with air power. He also describes the bomb run in similarly straightforward language, though a couple of details are worth noting. First, Lawson claims he was able to take one quick look at the first target they struck, a steel smelting plant, and his description conveys an image of total destruction: "the plant seemed to puff out its walls and then subside and dissolve in a black-and-red cloud." The reader is left with the impression that a clearly military target was accurately hit and utterly destroyed. His description of the incendiary strike, however, is an ominous portent of the future. First, they dropped the bomb over a "flimsy area" of the city, and Lawson describes how it would deploy: "[the bomb] would separate and soon as it hit the wind . . . dozens of small fire bombs would molt from it." This hardly conveys the notion of an industrial target being bombed with pinpoint accuracy.[26]

Lawson's own dichotomous characterization of his bombing is itself instructive; it seems to be part of a larger trend concerning political, military, and public views about bombing Japan. In a puzzling postscript to his book, Lawson relates in full the official U.S. communiqué of the raid issued on 20 April 1943, one year after the event. In this communiqué, the War Department emphasized that only military targets—armament plants, dock yards, railroad yards, and oil refineries—were struck, yet the communiqué also mentions the use of incendiary bombs, specifically stating that they were used on the military targets. Lawson also adds his own curious comments in reaction to charges made by the Japanese government about the raid. He calls Japanese claims that the bombers "intentionally bombed non-military targets" a "damned lie" and states that he checked the veracity of this statement by communicating with other bombers' crew members after the raid. One can imagine the War Department failing to mention the intent of the incendiary bombs, but Lawson himself seems to have failed to connect in his own mind that incendiaries aimed at "inflammable sections" and "flimsy areas" to start fires that would rage throughout the city did not constitute the precision bombing of strictly military targets.[27]

The Doolittle Raid not only gave the American people a badly needed morale boost, it also fired their imaginations, and popular culture was quick to exploit that interest. General-interest magazines did not give as much attention as one might have expected, perhaps because the strict news blackout on the raid severely limited details from official sources, thus forcing those media expected to maintain some element of factuality to walk a fine line in their reporting. One famous illustration of the impact of the dearth of details coming from official sources was President Roosevelt's quip, when asked for information, that the raid had been launched from Shangri-La, a reference to the setting of the popular 1933 novel *Lost Horizon*. Still, the *Saturday Evening Post* did run one article, bearing the suggestive title "Rough-on-Japs Doolittle," though it focused more on the man and telling his life story than on the raid.[28] By the time the news blackout was lifted, there were more timely topics for magazine editors to focus on. But the information void did not keep Hollywood from filling in the details with its own imagination. Here the initial theme was to tap into fascination with the raid in any way possible.

The trend to exploit public interest, even if it meant inventing details, is best illustrated by the first of the four films incorporating Doolittle Raid themes, *Bombardier*. Released by RKO Studios in May 1943, barely one month after the official communiqué on the raid, the movie purports to tell the story of how precision bombing won acceptance in the Army Air Forces prior to the attack on Pearl Harbor and how part of that fight was to prove the importance of the bombardier in obtaining the requisite precision. Most of the movie deals with attempts to gain acceptance of the need for highly trained bombardiers and how they are trained, but the climax of the plot involves B-17s launching a daring and risky surprise first raid on the Japanese homeland launched from a Pacific Island identified only as "Island Base." While neither Doolittle nor his raid is mentioned, the parallels, despite the different aircraft and launch site, are clear. In spite of significant obstacles, the bombers leave their targets in shambles and burning. This film also makes one of the most patently ridiculous contributions to the public image of American bombers striking military targets with unerring accuracy: as the bombardier of one of the bombers is setting up for the bomb run, a gunner jokes that he should put a bomb down one of the factory's smokestacks; the bombardier asks which one, and the gunner replies, "the center one." Sure enough, amid the destruction wrought by the bombing, one bomb can be seen dropping down the center smokestack and exploding halfway down.[29]

The second movie, *Destination Tokyo*, also tapped into Doolittle Raid themes, albeit tangentially. Released by Warner Brothers in December 1943, the plot follows a submarine, the *Copperfin*, and its crew as they attempt to sneak into Tokyo Bay and land a shore party to gather military intelligence and weather information for an air raid on Tokyo about to be launched from an unnamed aircraft carrier. Again, Doolittle's name is not used, and the attack is not specifically identified as the Doolittle Raid, but the connections are too plain to be anything but. The movie highlights the critical importance of accurate intelligence for successful bombing, and it showcases the close cooperation of the U.S. Army and the U.S. Navy, as well as the dangers Doolittle's bombers faced in attempting to attack Japan. The depiction of the actual bombing portrays the bombers coming in at high altitude, yet military targets are clearly hit directly and with devastating effect.[30]

The first movie to specifically cover events involving the Doolittle Raid was *The Purple Heart*, which dramatized Japanese treatment of the eight captured Doolittle Raiders. The main plot of this film, released in February 1944, focused on the trial and torture these fliers were subjected to, not as prisoners of war but as war criminals. The notion presented to the American public was that when it came to air warfare, the Japanese would single out airmen who attacked Japan for special cruelty and criminal prosecution. An interesting subplot presents a unique view of the inner workings of the Japanese military structure. When the prosecutor, a Japanese Army general, presents evidence that the Doolittle Raid was launched from an aircraft carrier, the Japanese naval delegation is incensed because this implies that the Japanese Navy had failed to protect Japan from naval attack. The Army-versus-Navy quest to sway the judge on the origins of the attack sets off a bitter internal struggle, where the Japanese generals seem more determined to beat the Japanese Navy than punish the American airmen and the Japanese admiral seems more interested in protecting the reputation of the Navy. The Americans are then subjected to systematic torture by the general in an attempt to extract confessions, not of criminally bombing civilian targets, but to admit that they launched their attack from an aircraft carrier. In fact, the general even offers the crew their freedom if they will just admit to this one detail. The crew refuses, remembering that they had to protect the *Hornet*'s involvement at all costs so it could escape Japanese-dominated waters. As a result of their refusal, they are sentenced to death and march out of the courtroom with resolute faces while the soundtrack plays the Air Corps Song.[31]

Ironically, the last of the wartime films touching on the Doolittle Raid was the only one that attempted to tell the full story; that was the film adaptation of Lawson's *Thirty Seconds over Tokyo.* Two aspects of this movie are worth noting. First, as noted historian of war films Lawrence Suid observed, unlike other war films, *Thirty Seconds over Tokyo* did not need to romanticize its subject or the characters in it—they were already heroic in the eyes of the American moviegoing public. Second, the producers and the military agreed that this film should not single out any one man, but should treat all the Raiders as part of one big team. Here the problem was twofold: first, as the ubiquitous name of the operation would suggest, many saw Doolittle as playing an inordinately large role; second, since the movie would be based on the memoirs of Ted Lawson and was thus presented through his eyes, there would be a natural tendency to put Lawson center stage. The end product succeeded remarkably well in this regard.[32] Also important is the fact that screenwriter Dalton Trumbo interviewed many of the Raiders personally and was allowed to fly aboard a B-25 to familiarize himself with the plane and crew operations.[33] In the end, the film fairly faithfully recreated the straightforward and understated heroism of Lawson's book.

When it came to depicting the nature of the aerial attack, two images stand out. First, when Doolittle, played by Spencer Tracy, briefs the crews on the nature of their raid onboard the *Hornet,* he gives a short speech that echoes themes raised by others concerning the targets they are to strike and the nature of their bombing: "Now let me repeat something I've said previously. You are to bomb the military targets assigned to you and nothing else. Of course, in an operation of this kind you cannot avoid killing civilians because war plants are manned by civilians. If any of you have any moral feelings about this necessary killing, if you feel that you might think of yourself afterwards as a murderer, I want you to drop out. We'll find someone else to take your place, and I promise you that no one will blame you for your feelings." No one declined to go on the mission after this speech. The movie's depiction of Lawson's bomb run reinforces not only the humanitarian nature of Doolittle's sentiments, but also that the bombing was amazingly accurate and effective, and that it was focused solely on military targets. Four targets are struck with four bombs, the first three with demolition bombs, the fourth with incendiaries. In each case, the bomb is aimed with deliberate care, strikes its target precisely, and utterly destroys it. Even the incendiaries disperse within the confines of the target area and set off devastating secondary explosions.[34]

There was one little-known sidelight to the Doolittle Raid. In his book *God Is My Co-Pilot,* Colonel Scott describes a second raid that was supposed to come from unoccupied mainland China and was intended to hit Japan about the same time as Doolittle's Raiders. In fact, it was this raid that got Scott out of the training assignment he was initially slotted for and into the Flying Tigers when he was hand-picked to participate in this mission. According to Scott, twelve B-17 crews and one B-24 crew went through intensive stateside training before heading out in early April 1942 on their long journey to their intended jumping-off point. They spent many days hopping down the South American coast, across the Atlantic to Africa, and thence to Karachi, in British India. Scott never mentions the Doolittle Raid by name, but he says this mission is meant to coincide "with another attack that was coming from the East." After Scott and his colleagues reach Karachi, the fall of Bataan leads to the cancellation of this part of the attack on Japan.[35]

Though the Flying Tigers and the Doolittle Raid were the most famous aspects of the Pacific air war in the American public's consciousness, there were many other air operations being launched throughout the Pacific Theater of Operations (PTO), and those operations received surprisingly regular coverage, especially in the pages of general-interest magazines. From airfields on Pacific

Islands, in New Guinea, and even in India, the public was told that U.S. airmen kept up steady pressure on Japanese operations on land and sea. Two themes predominated in the coverage of these efforts: the great effectiveness of American efforts despite paltry supplies and overwhelming odds, and the contribution to those efforts of good old Yankee ingenuity.

One of the first such magazine articles came from *Collier's* barely a month after Pearl Harbor. In "Blitz over the Philippines," Royal Arch Gunnison explained that the effort to stop the Japanese advance through the Philippines was much more an air war than in Europe or elsewhere in Asia. Considering that Japan was, at that point in the war, still steadily marching forward on all fronts, Gunnison's tone of Japanese "stupidity" and lack of skill countered by "the persistence and skill of American and Filipino flying madmen" is surprising, yet understandable given the atmosphere of racial stereotypes and nationalistic rage—not to mention feelings of impotence—at the time. He also highlighted the courage of American pilots, as with the story of how Lieutenant Colonel Boyd "Buzz" Wagner single-handedly found, bombed, strafed, and then reported on an entire landing force of more than eighty landing barges. Additionally, Gunnison highlighted the sacrifice of American airmen, as when Wagner's wingman, his plane on fire, refused to bail out and instead "drove his blazing plane in a half-mile glide across twenty-five parked Japanese airplanes at Vigan, releasing bombs and machine-gunning all the way."[36]

Another article from later that same year told the story of one B-25 crew flying on a bombing mission out of New Guinea in a raid against the Japanese air base at Lae, located in the Japanese-occupied portion of New Guinea. The author, John Lardner, who accompanied the crew on its mission, describes how air elements of MacArthur's Southwest Pacific command were making small but vital contributions to the Pacific War effort. This article exemplifies themes that run through many of the popular culture images of the American air war against Japan. First, these "seven deadly Americans" are described in extravagant tones of happy-go-lucky youth—All-American boys for whom the war is almost a game and for whom striking back at the Japanese is a great joy. For example, Lardner describes his flight on this bombing mission as "the finest hayride I ever took. It was a voyage of exploration, a voyage of discovery, a fight, a picnic, and a ringside view of the enemy being lathered," but more important to him was that it was "a revelation of how deadly seven young cheerful American men can be." After the bomb run, according to Lardner, the pilot went around the plane "whooping and yelling congratulations to his team," and he hugged the bombardier, whose grin "almost split his face in two." Once again, there is an exaggerated emphasis on American bombing accuracy and effectiveness. The most obvious reflection of this is when the author, watching through the bomb bay, says of the bombs, "they smashed cleanly on the target, all of them." A more subtle celebration of bombing effectiveness is evident throughout the article as Lardner depicts the various crew members working smoothly as a synchronous whole; in this case, the analogy is of a great football team—a common one in popular culture depictions of bomber crews; but another standard image is of the crew working like a well-oiled machine. Whether as a sports team or a fine instrument, such popular depictions of bombing invariably tended to trivialize and dehumanize the process of dropping bombs to kill or destroy.[37]

A series of events happened in the Pacific air war in 1943 that gave popular magazines a lot to cheer about in their pages. The main event was the Battle of the Bismarck Sea, where Americans were told that on 2–4 March every ship of a twenty-two-ship Japanese invasion convoy was sunk by Allied aircraft. The fullest general-interest magazine treatment of this battle came in a 22 May *Saturday Evening Post* article bearing the highly suggestive title "No Survivors." Written by Major H. T. Hastings, one of the pilots who participated in the battle, the article details the action starting from when the convoy was first sighted by a scout plane while dodging a thunderstorm. Describing what followed with another sports metaphor—"a football coach's dream"—Hastings relates how bad weather hampered exploitation of the discovery for three days, but when the weather finally broke, air power immediately seized the opportunity with great effect.[38]

On 2 March, according to Hastings, a squadron of B-17s found a hole in the clouds and sank four of the eight troop transports. Another attack wave that same afternoon sank two more ships. Taking advantage of the constricted waters between the islands of New Guinea and New Britain, a massive dawn attack was planned for the next morning involving B-17s, B-25s, A-20s, P-38s, P-39s, P-40s, and Australian Beaufighters—106 aircraft in all. Hastings described the ensuing battle metaphorically as a "feeding frenzy" as the air fleet sank most of the remaining sixteen ships in less than thirty minutes. Hastings presents what happened next as an exercise in righteous wrath. One of the bombers was badly hit, and as it was going down the crew started bailing out of the stricken plane; "immediately four or five Zeros dived at the men with machine guns blazing. For a moment there was a strange silence over the command set [the radio frequency all the attacking aircraft monitored], and then savage profanity. I think it was this more than anything else that made our boys go out for blood," the author reported. According to Hastings, the Zeros were immediately hunted down, and then the attacking aircraft began strafing life rafts launched from the sinking ships: "We decided no one would get away." To further justify their actions, Hastings added that the commander of the Beaufighters claimed the men in the life rafts were shooting at the aircraft. The air fleet returned to

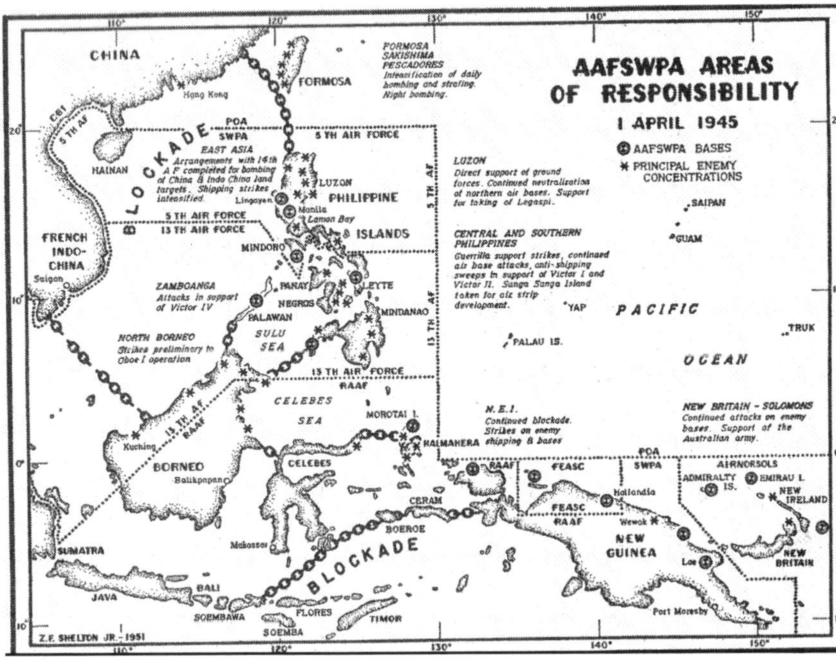

AAFSWPA Areas of Responsibility (from *The United States Army in World War II: The War in the Pacific*, courtesy of the Office of the Chief of Military History, Department of the Army, Washington, DC)

base, refueled, rearmed, and resumed the attack. By the end of the day, Hastings claims, every ship had been sunk except one badly damaged destroyer, but the aircraft also took the time and effort to hunt down and strafe every life raft they could find. The next morning, a B-25 attack reportedly sank the last destroyer.[39]

The interest did not end with Hastings's account of the battle, though, because one of the reasons for the bombers' success against the ships was a new bombing technique known as "skip-bombing." Playing off the "Yankee ingenuity" theme, a flurry of articles appeared in a number of general-interest magazines telling the story of how the technique had been developed and how it came to be accepted in the Southwest Pacific Theater. *Collier's* claimed to present the first full story of how the tactic worked in an article colorfully titled "They Didn't Know What Hit Them." Written by Henry F. Pringle, the article explained how the tactic, more properly known as "minimum altitude bombing," had been developed in the early fall of 1942 at the Army Air Forces Proving Ground at Eglin Field in Florida. Ironically, according to Pringle, the technique was originally meant to be a means of bombing tanks. The reason given for why developers thought it would work well against ships is that normal ship bombing, done from high altitude, is less effective "even with our excellent bombsights." Medium-altitude bombing and torpedo planes were more accurate but more vulnerable to antiaircraft fire and enemy aircraft, in the latter case because the torpedo plane has to remain on a steady course for up to thirty seconds. Skip bombers, on the other hand, come in too low for antiaircraft fire to be effective, and they could take evasive action up to within three seconds of bomb release. The development team had trouble convincing military leadership, so they began briefing it to every official who came through their installation. One such official was Major William Benn, who later joined the staff of Lieutenant General George Kenney, General MacArthur's senior air commander in the Southwest Pacific. Benn told Kenney of the new technique, Kenney was intrigued, and the Battle of the Bismarck Sea was hailed as proof of its effectiveness.[40]

Articles that focused on the development of skip-bombing seem to have caught on with the public, since no fewer than three more articles followed in *Saturday Evening Post, Life,* and *Reader's Digest* during the next year that focused on skip-bombing, especially how it worked, what it looked like, and how U.S. aircraft used it to kill ships. In fact, in one article, "We Skip-Bomb the Japs" in the 4 September 1943 issue of *Saturday Evening Post,* Charles A. Rawlings described how the crew of a lone B-24, having found a Japanese ship lying at anchor in a secluded bay, made several conventional bomb runs on the ship that resulted in all misses, and then used skip-bombing with the last two bombs to score direct hits that sank the ship.[41]

Despite the fact that by mid-1943 there were much bigger combat operations going on in England, North Africa, and across the Pacific, the air operations of small groups scattered from India to tiny Pacific islands received considerable attention in America's general-interest magazines. One reason is that many of the attacks launched by these small groups, each doing little major damage to the enemy, were nonetheless symbolic in nature. Take, for example, the article detailing a bombing raid on Hong Kong, "Hong Kong Home-coming," in the 20 November 1943 edition of *Saturday Evening Post.* The author, Ernest O. Hauser, had lived in Hong Kong until forced out by the war in 1939. He had come to love the city, and so he took great delight in accompanying the bombing raid. In fact, Hauser claimed that "Hong Kong was even lovelier looking when viewed from the vantage point of one of the 14th [Air Force's] B-25 Mitchells, and our lads created some beautiful destruction." According to the author, the destruction was not negligible—twenty-five million gallons of fuel destroyed at the oil refinery they bombed—but it was not on a level with the invasion of Italy then underway. Another intriguing aspect of how the Pacific air war was depicted in popular culture during the war is that the editors of *Saturday Evening Post* deemed this small raid worthy of depiction at all, for as Hauser quotes the bomb squadron commander who led the raid, "You know . . . someday we're going to really fight those Japs. Right now we're just antagonizing them."[42]

Another symbolic series of air raids was detailed in the pages of *Saturday Evening Post* in its 19 February 1944 issue. The Japanese Army and Navy had turned Rabaul, on New Britain Island off of New Guinea, into one of the most important strongholds in the entire South Pacific, and it was the focus of great public attention. In "Strike on Rabaul," Charles A. Rawlings, who had earlier reported on skip-bombing, covered a series of bombing raids seeking to cripple Rabaul's air defenses in anticipation of a ground assault to capture the base. What the public did not know was that these raids were part of "Operation Cartwheel," the Allied campaign to isolate and bypass Rabaul altogether. This article exemplifies another common feature of war reporting in general-interest magazines, one that air power lent itself to quite readily: that of turning even minor details into tense and dramatic moments. In this case, Rawlings heightens the tension by accentuating the weather-imposed delays between the three raids on Rabaul's defenses and how those raids had allowed the Japanese to reinforce their defenses. When the orders finally came down for the third strike, the mood around the air base was, as Rawlings puts it, "battle-taut," and despite the frenetic activity to prepare for the mission, the chaplain had to drag out extra pews for the standing-room-only pre-raid worship services. To complete the theme of delays making this raid especially tough, Rawlings adds that their target was the most heavily defended airfield of the Rabaul complex, and the description of the bombing raid emphasizes the bitter aerial fighting more than other Rawlings pieces. He even highlights one bomber crew, having one engine damaged by a Japanese Zero before the bomb run, continuing to strike the target and limping home despite Zeros pressing attacks from every angle. Rawlings then closes the action with a debate at headquarters on whether—given the intensity of the air battle before, during, and after the bomb run—the bombers' gunners might have shot down as many as twenty Zeroes; as it turned out, according to Rawlings, the bombers' gunners claim to have shot down thirty.[43]

Perhaps more significant to Operation Cartwheel had been the series of bombing raids Rawlings had reported in *Saturday Evening Post* a month earlier. In "Pacific Thriller," Rawlings detailed a series of air raids on the Japanese air base at Wewak aimed at destroying Japanese air power in northern New Guinea that would pave the way for the conquest of the whole island. This article highlights another common theme of popular reporting on the war: American cunning. Rawlings details how General Kenney and his deputy, Major General (later Lieutenant General) Ennis Whitehead, had been watching Japanese air reinforcements at Wewak and other air bases in northern New Guinea and then laid a trap for those forces. While they waited for those reinforcements to reach their peak, according to Rawlings, Kenney and Whitehead focused their air efforts elsewhere, hoping to convince the Japanese that their reinforcement efforts had gone unnoticed. Then, Kenney and Whitehead sprang their trap with a series of bombing raids at those airfields. Rawlings even described the nonstandard bombing attack plan—bombers approaching the target at different altitudes on multiple axes of attack converging over the target simultaneously—which was meant to maximize the surprise and destruction of the raid. Rawlings accompanied one of the bombers on the Wewak raid; in contrast to his "Strike on Rabaul" article, the minor enemy air defenses seem almost a game to the ship's crew. One would gather from this article that the biggest threat the airmen faced was the unpredictable weather patterns over New Guinea. More important were the results reported by Rawlings: of the approximately 300 aircraft massed at the enemy airfields, Kenney's intelligence staff estimated that 175–200 were destroyed by this series of raids.[44]

At this point, it is worth noting the image of George Kenney being created in popular culture at this time. Besides the characterization of Kenney's bold adoption of skip-bombing, which others had scorned—a decision portrayed as paving the way for the stunning victory in the Battle of the Bismarck Sea—and Rawlings's depiction of his craftiness in "Pacific Thriller," Kenney's audacity and innovativeness were the subject of an article in the 8 October 1944 edition of the *New York Times Magazine.* In this article, Frank L. Kluckhohn explained not only Kenney's instrumental role in adapting and applying skip-bombing, but also other tactical innovations, such as putting more machine guns on his bombers. Kluckhohn also illustrated that Kenney was much more than a tactician. He helped redesign bomb fuses used by his command to better adapt them to skip-bombing, and he followed what the author considered an unorthodox method for selecting squadron and group commanders: he chose pilots who could lead and inspire rather than those with the most experience or the most kills.[45]

Kenney's airmen did not monopolize the attention of general-interest magazines. In fact, since there were numerous units operating in isolated locations across the numerous commands engaged in the war against Japan, there seems to have been some attempt to spread the limelight across the entire spectrum. In a two-part piece, for example, Pete Martin reported on the efforts of a unit operating out of India against Japanese forces in Burma. The unit was initially so isolated that its members referred to themselves as a "Detached Detachment," and they operated on such a shoestring that their operations sound reminiscent of the Flying Tigers. The aircraft commanders even took turns as acting squadron commander. Still, according to Martin, they were making a significant contribution. In commenting on the chances of the Allies taking back Burma, Martin quotes one of the lead pilots: "Rangoon . . . hasn't been in fit shape to handle much Jap shipping for months. The docks, railroad yards, oil storage tanks, and refineries are shredded and tattered. . . . The English . . . have been giving the Jap river steamers, barges, and locomotives a going over. The Japs will have trouble even supplying a small airfield."[46]

Coming from the other end of the geographical spectrum was Forrest Davis's "Hale's Handful," a *Saturday Evening Post* article focused on the Seventh Air Force supporting the U.S. Navy's Central Pacific campaign. Naturally feeling a bit out of their element attached to a largely naval operation, the Seventh also felt their efforts were going unnoticed, because when the public thought of Army Air Forces efforts in the PTO they naturally thought of the Flying Tigers and Kenney's command. Still, as Davis illustrates, the B-25s under Major General Willis H. Hale were making contributions as important as any corresponding Army Air Forces unit in the Theater. Covering an area five times the size of the continental United States and operating from airstrips on tiny islands and atolls as the Navy advanced across the Pacific, the B-25 crews faced special fuel and navigation challenges. A slight error in navigation, for instance, could mean they would miss the tiny piece of land serving as their base and have very little fuel remaining to find their way home. Despite these worries, the B-52s played an integral role supporting carrier-borne aircraft in softening up Japanese defenses ahead of amphibious assaults. Davis's article focused on a bombing raid to neutralize Japanese air power at Taroa (not to be confused with Tarawa Island) in advance of the assault on Kwajalein by forces led by Admiral Chester Nimitz, Commander-in-Chief, U.S. Pacific Fleet (CINCPACFLT). Besides emphasizing the effectiveness of their bombing, the article also highlights the vulnerability of the B-25s created by the vast area of open ocean they had to cover and because their P-40 fighter escorts could not accompany them all the way to Taroa. The running battle as Japanese aircraft pursued the bombers on their return trip was fierce; but, aided by the P-40s once the bombers finally got within range, the end result, according to Davis, was no American aircraft lost.[47]

There were numerous other representations of the scattered air operations across the PTO, less specific but still conveying the same message of dogged determination in the face of overwhelming odds. One unique vehicle was Milton Caniff's comic strip *Terry and the Pirates* and the radio program based on it. Running throughout the war, the action was set in China, where the main character, Terry, joined the Army Air Forces, became a pilot, and joined the famed Flying Tigers. In the midst of various side ventures with spies, damsels in distress, and characters getting trapped behind Japanese lines, the strip frequently depicted Chinese military and Army Air Forces operations against the Japanese. For example, through much of June, July, and August 1943 the main action focused on a joint air-ground assault on an island base the Japanese had secretly built.[48] In a literal flight of fancy, the 1943 movie *A Guy Named Joe* imagines an afterlife where good pilots who die in combat are sent back to act as guardian angels for young pilots. That this movie's "pilot's heaven" looks and operates much like the Army Air Forces not only assumed that God was on America's side but also that he appreciated the value of land-based American air power. It also featured a heavenly commander obviously meant to be Billy Mitchell. The plot focuses on a lone-wolf but excellent pilot who died while crashing his crippled plane into a German aircraft carrier and is sent back to help a P-38 pilot who is part of a unit fighting the Japanese in Southeast Asia.[49] It is also worth noting here that in the movie *Air Force* the crew of the *Mary Ann,* once it is driven out of the Philippines, joins up with some unnamed Southwest Pacific operation and participates in a bombing attack on a Japanese convoy reminiscent of the Battle of the Bismarck Sea.[50]

The cumulative effect of all the scattered efforts—though they seemed to the airmen themselves at the time as too small to defeat Japan—was, in the eyes of one journalist, a major impact. In "The Coming Battle for Asia," appearing in the 18 March 1944 edition of *Saturday Evening Post,* Edgar Snow, a *Post* editor, concluded that even with the European war effort poised on an imminent invasion of the continent, the land, sea, and air forces already in place in the PTO were enough to mount major offensive operations on several fronts. In assessing the gains made by all three branches up to that point in the war against Japan, however, he singles out the air war as especially effective: "Our superiority to the enemy now seems established in every branch, but it has most strikingly been demonstrated in the air. Throughout 1943, American planes have scorched the skies of Burma, meeting but negligible opposition. It is now certain that the enemy will never recover the air domination which he held during the conquest. And it is evident that wherever we move in Southeast Asia, Japan will face such tremendous air superiority that she will, in effect, be obliged to fight without air cover."[51]

No discussion of land-based air power in the Pacific would be complete without some treatment of the strategic bombing campaign waged against Japan, but oddly enough there was very little mention of that strategic campaign in popular culture during the war itself. Mostly, this was due to the late and precarious nature of the strategic bombing campaign against Japan. Until the B-29 was developed and all the bugs worked out, the United States did not have a land-based bomber capable of reaching Japan from bases in Allied territory. Even then, the bases closest to Japan were in unoccupied China, the supply lines to those bases were so tenuous it was difficult to keep up a meaningful bombing effort, and the B-29 could then only reach the western parts of Japan from those bases. The first bombing attack on Japan was launched on 14 June 1944, over a week after the Normandy landings in France, but the supply problems kept the scale low and thus results were disappointing. The supply and range problems were solved when the Allies captured the Mariana Islands in the summer of 1944; the Marianas could be easily supplied by sea, and B-29s launched from air bases there could reach nearly any target in Japan. Technical problems still plagued the B-29, however, and with the complexities of setting up new air bases, getting units in place, and preparing for combat, the first mission from the Marianas was not launched until 24 November. The late start of this "main effort" at strategic bombing left little time for reporting. In addition, General Arnold—who kept B-29 forces in China and the Marianas under his direct control—and the on-scene commander of the B-29s in the Marianas, Brigadier General Hansell, were concerned about inflating public expectations, so they did not court publicity until they were sure they had a substantial effort up and running.[52]

As a result, what little coverage of strategic bombing efforts there was in general-interest magazines was either scanty or came at the very end of the war. One *Reader's Digest* editorial—less than one full page—appeared in the August 1944 issue and told how B-29 bases in China had been built with the manual labor of 430,000 Chinese civilians. Another article that appeared in the 25 November 1944 issue of *Saturday Evening Post* focused on the life and career of General Hansell, Commanding General, Twenty-First Bomber Command—which encompassed all B-29s in the Marianas—who was also one of the main architects of the initial strategic bombing campaign against Japan.[53] The only article—actually a series of articles—that focused on the B-29 bombing missions over Japan did not begin until 18 August 1945, after the atomic bombs had been dropped on Hiroshima and Nagasaki. Even then, the author's first installments simply introduced a B-29 crew headed for Guam, and the article covering their first bombing mission over Japan did not appear until 15 September, well after Japan had formally surrendered. Incidentally, this article featured a bombing raid against an industrial target using demolition bombs, even though Curtis LeMay, who had replaced Hansell in January, had by February 1945 switched the bulk of the Army Air Forces bombing missions over Japan to low-level incendiary bombing of Japanese cities.[54]

A more important aspect of the popular culture depiction, however, concerns what was said during the war about how Japan *would* be bombed once the main effort began. This point is especially relevant when compared to how Japan ultimately *was* bombed when the strategic bombing effort reached its full force. That bombing campaign was the center of considerable controversy after the war; and to understand that controversy, as well as why the wartime depiction is relevant, we need to look briefly at America's strategic bombing doctrine at the beginning of the war. The United States entered World War II with strategic bombing as not only the cornerstone of its air strategy, but also a main part of its overall military effort. Moreover, America's approach to strategic bombing was unique and controversial in that it focused on bombing key industries, which was expected to have a magnified—and hopefully crippling—effect on the enemy's war effort. This strategy took shape during the 1930s in the Air Corps Tactical School, and one of its chief theorists was General Hansell. On the eve of war, strategic bombing, in the form of the Air Corps Tactical School approach, was built into overall U.S. war and mobilization planning through the acceptance of an overall American air power blueprint for waging war against Germany and Japan. That blueprint was known as Air War Plans Division Document 1 (AWPD-1). Again, a key figure in writing AWPD-1 and gaining its acceptance by the War Department and the White House was none other than General Hansell.[55]

America's bombing doctrine, however, was unique in that by 1941 most nations were using a blunt-force approach to bombing that focused on creating massive death and destruction by bombing cities. Here the leading prewar theorist had been an Italian air veteran of World War I, General Giulio Douhet. In his landmark book *The Command of the Air*, published in 1921, Douhet argued that by bombing the enemy's cities and civilians, an air force could sow widespread panic, instill political paralysis, and force the enemy to sue for peace.[56] Whether Germany, Japan, or Britain followed Douhet in a strategic sense or whether they bombed their enemies' cities out of vengeance is the subject of great controversy, but many Americans also advocated this approach for U.S. bombing, especially against Japan. In the wake of Pearl Harbor and the rage that ensued, and given the racist notions on both sides between Japan and the United States, many Americans were eager for retribution; and, as the reaction to the Doolittle Raid showed, they were not particular about the form so long as Japan was paid back. Even within the military, many in the U.S. Army and Navy were dubious about the Air Corps Tactical School form of bombing and preferred the blunt-force approach.[57]

As the war dragged on, precision industrial bombing had fewer and fewer supporters. Implementing strategic bombing against Germany had been a long and costly process—costly in material and money, but especially in lives. As the war in Europe turned into a slugfest in the air as well as on the ground, many critics began to doubt that the Air Corps Tactical School theory had delivered on its promises. All of this controversy was reaching its peak as the main phase of America's strategic bombing campaign against Japan was just taking shape. General Hansell, having worked his way up the ranks in the bombing campaign against Germany, was named to lead the campaign against Japan; having been one of the main theorists, architects, and visionaries behind the original Air Corps Tactical School and AWPD-1 visions of strategic bombing, he was determined to make it work against Japan. With all the delays, however, key leaders—some even within the Army Air Forces—had lost patience before he could validate his theories, and in January 1945 he was replaced by Major General LeMay. By February, LeMay switched the main bombing approach to nighttime, low-level firebombing raids against Japan's cities. This proved highly effective in terms of destruction, but it also inflicted massive civilian casualties.[58]

While many of these details appeared in newspapers, little if any made their way into popular culture during the war. But hints of America's dichotomous view toward bombing—some advocating precision industrial bombing, others indiscriminate city bombing—could be seen in popular culture throughout the war, especially when it came to bombing Japan. This facet of how the Pacific air war was depicted might be more revealing than first supposed, because the popular culture images were usually shaped by civilians rather than military leaders or theorists. Thus, this phenomenon very likely reflected public mood even as it helped to shape that mood for greater acceptance of more ruthless measures. We have already seen how Ted Lawson's account of the Doolittle Raid stressed the military nature of the Raiders' primary targets yet also added—with little awareness of the discrepancy—that they were to select "flimsy areas" to drop incendiaries with the expressed intent of creating such large fires so as to overwhelm Tokyo's ability to fight those fires. We have also seen how the movie version of his book mentioned the use of incendiaries while skimming over where they were to be used. Similarly, the movie *The Purple Heart* stressed the injustice of the Japanese claim that the Doolittle Raiders intentionally bombed civilian targets and tried to inflict as many civilian casualties as possible; yet in two critical scenes the pilot of the crew on trial hints at more sinister intentions of future bombing. When talking privately with the Japanese general trying to force them to admit that they flew off an aircraft carrier, the general states that U.S. bombing will be useless against Japan because most of the major buildings are built to withstand earthquakes and thus could take great punishment. The pilot, however, replies, "That makes it tough on the little guys who live in the paper houses, doesn't it, General?" Later, when the crew members are all found guilty and sentenced to death, the pilot tells the court that the coming American bombing raids will burn their cities to the ground.[59] A more direct allusion came shortly after General LeMay switched to incendiary city bombing, when *Collier's* ran a story on how those incendiary bombs had been developed. The text extols the fact that those bombs were being used to burn Japanese homes and entire residential neighborhoods; but if the text wasn't clear enough, the article was accompanied by a graphic drawing of Tokyo engulfed in flames.[60]

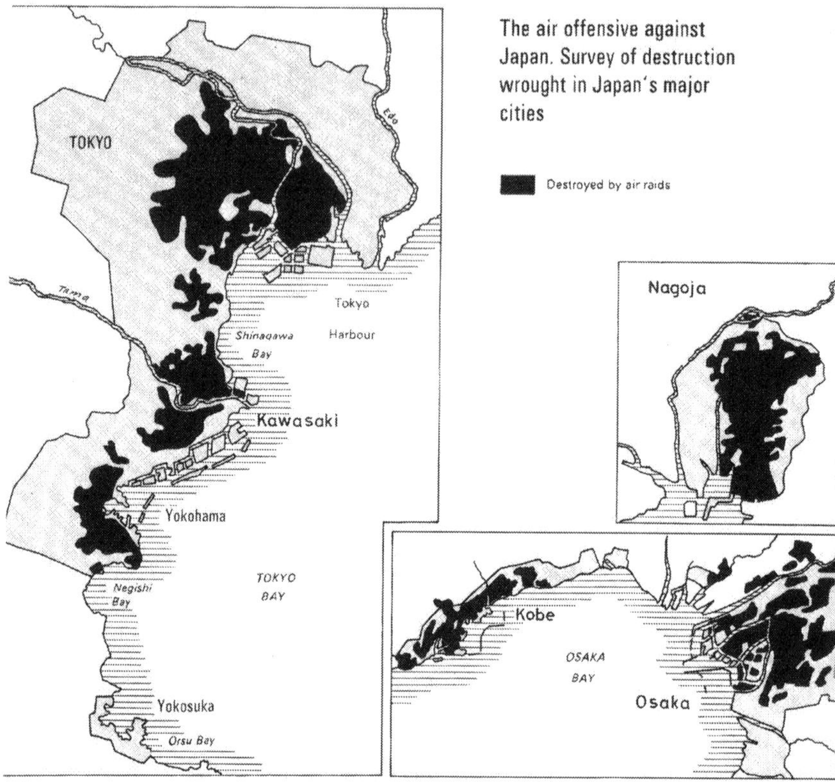

Japanese Cities Destroyed by U.S. Bombing (from *U.S. Military Academy Atlas*, Map 51)

The most influential works in popular culture that reflect this tension between precision bombing and indiscriminate bombing came from the writings of Russian émigré Alexander P. de Seversky and a major movie inspired by his theories. An ace in the Tsarist Navy during World War I, de Seversky emigrated to the United States, where he became a successful aviation pioneer and businessman.

Despite being a businessman, de Seversky's greatest interest was in educating the public on the proper use of air power.[61] He wrote a number of general-interest magazine articles early in the war, even before America entered the conflict, expressing his belief that the war up to 1942 had proven land-based air power to be the only decisive weapon. Gathering his ideas into a book titled *Victory through Air Power*, de Seversky argued that only by industrial bombing along the lines of the Air Corps Tactical School theories could Germany and Japan be defeated without a long, costly, and bloody World War I–style stalemate. If used intelligently, he claimed, bombing could stop Axis war-making potential at its industrial source, paving the way for easy, cheap, and efficient victory.[62]

Buried within this recipe for progressive air power, however, was a much more chilling image. In a chapter titled "Possession or Elimination," de Seversky concluded that air power was only the latest stage in a long progression of increasingly brutal modes of warfare. Further, de Seversky stated that although air power hypothetically allowed a nation to choose between the two extremes of possession or elimination—that is, "whether the purpose is to destroy the enemy or to capture him, whether the prey must be killed or trapped alive"—other factors often forced the nation's decision: "The deeper the civilization and the national pride of a people, the more likely it is to be subjected to the method of extermination, since such a people cannot be reconciled to living the life of the vanquished."[63] According to de Seversky, the process of elimination entails "the elimination of the country as a world factor," where its people are "reduced to impotence beyond easy recovery, through the annihilation of the industrial foundations of their life." In fact, he observes that "the very ease with which a machine-age country can be blasted into chaos from on high is an invitation to the war of annihilation."[64] When it came to Germany and Japan, de Seversky believed that "American strategy must be geared for the war of elimination."[65] Readers were thus left with an image fusing de Seversky's two themes: surgical application of industrial bombing, but used as a means to exterminate the two lethal threats to America's long-term survival.

For a book devoted to military issues, *Victory through Air Power* was surprisingly popular. De Seversky had been publishing articles in popular magazines throughout the interwar and World War II years; and, because he aimed his message at the average American, his work appeared in magazines as diverse as *The Atlantic, Reader's Digest,* and *Ladies' Home Journal.* That level of exposure, plus the fact that it was featured by the Book of the Month Club, helps explain why *Victory through Air Power* was estimated to have reached some 5 million readers. Moreover, a Gallup poll estimated that 20 million Americans were familiar with de Seversky and his theories.[66]

Victory through Air Power got its greatest exposure, however, from a powerful collaboration with Walt Disney. Disney was a self-avowed air power advocate, and when he read *Victory through Air Power* he decided to give de Seversky's theories the audience he felt they deserved. That determination led to a feature-length combination of live action—with de Seversky explaining his ideas—and the kind of colorful animation that had become Disney's hallmark by 1942. The result, also titled *Victory through Air Power,* wedded de Seversky's theories with Disney's vivid imagery.[67] More significantly, the dichotomous images of the Air Corps Tactical School and Douhet were presented with even greater visual—

and potentially subliminal—impact. The sight of waves of high-altitude bombers seeming to rain bombs indiscriminately on the landscape below along with close-ups of each bomb falling unerringly on an industrial or a military target could not help but implant the notion that even when Americans engaged in mass bombing, they did so with near-miraculous accuracy. Adding to these images was that of the massive bombers that de Seversky advocated for bombing Japan from American bases, thus creating an irresistible image that the United States could engage in wholesale bombing and still stick to the antiseptic image of precision industrial bombing.[68]

Another disturbing image came not from de Seversky per se, but from the artists of the Disney Studio, an image with strong racist overtones when considering the gravity of de Seversky's message and the course strategic bombing would later take against Japan. The climax of the film came when it graphically illustrated the effects bombing would have against Germany and Japan. In illustrating the enormity of the military obstacles standing in the way of victory and the grave peril from America's enemies, the illustrators used Germany as an example of the former and Japan as an example of the latter. To show how land-based air power could overcome the enormous military obstacles, Germany's military might was depicted as a spoked wheel shaped like a swastika with its industrial heart pumping out a steady stream of war material to its fighting forces on the wheel's rim. Air power was shown leaping over those ground forces on the front lines and striking efficiently and effectively at the industrial heart. This weakened the German war machine to the point where America's ground forces could easily break through the rim and roll on to victory. When it came to Japan as the embodiment of the grave threat confronting America, Japan was depicted as an octopus anthropomorphized to look sinister, angry, and lurking. First, its tentacles reached out with stabbing daggers toward all its neighbors; then those tentacles wound around more and more territory as the octopus—and the threat—grew and spread. In this scene, American air power was depicted as a bald eagle slashing and clawing not at the tentacles to cut off Japanese forces holding outlying territory, but instead at the head of the beast till it shriveled and finally died. Such a brutal and ultimately fatal solution to the threat posed by Japan must certainly have helped predispose viewers to see the Douhet approach as an appropriate measure to meet the particular threat posed by Japan.[69]

Whether the movie version of *Victory through Air Power* had a demonstrable impact on the average American or altered his or her thinking is hard to ascertain, but it certainly made an impact in official channels. The U.S. Navy and the U.S. Army Air Forces tried to suppress the book version, but there was no suppressing the movie—or who could see it—and it was seen by millions, helping to explain why so many Americans were familiar with de Seversky's theories. None other than Winston Churchill saw the movie and was so taken with it that he insisted that Roosevelt watch it with him at their next summit meeting in August 1943. What impact it had on the two war leaders or the conversations they had concerning it are not recorded in the official record. According to de Seversky, Emperor Hirohito also saw the film during the war, and it troubled him greatly.[70]

Though little of the Douhet image of strategic bombing against Japan made its way into popular culture during the war, it became one of the dominant images after the war. Forgotten, or overshadowed by postwar technical and political realities, were the amazing victories won by plucky airmen against incredible odds. All the efforts of the Flying Tigers faded as the postwar emphasis on nuclear bombing lifted the bomber generals into ascendancy over the fighter pilots. The various scattered units that in the opinion of Edgar Snow had shorn the Japanese Army of its air cover and its logistical support were all relegated to footnotes in the history of the war. Kenney's innovative approach in the Pacific led to his appointment as the initial Commanding General, Strategic Air Command (SAC), seen by many Americans as their first line of defense in the postwar world; but SAC's early shortcomings led to his dismissal in disgrace—another thinking general replaced by General LeMay.[71] In place of the early wartime images from the Pacific air war were the contradictory but fused images of precision industrial bombing, depicted after World War II as having defeated Germany, with the nuclear bombing that was widely seen as having forced Japan to surrender. These fused images became the postwar air power image sold to the public as precision nuclear bombing of industrial targets. De Seversky again tried to explain—and convince—Americans that this was the only "right way" to use air power and that it was the nation's only hope for survival in the Cold War world. In his efforts to make "precision nuclear bombing" seem rational and acceptable, however, he went so far as to argue that nuclear weapons could be delivered with such accuracy that they could paralyze Soviet industrial and military capability while still leaving the Russian people grateful that they had not been targeted.[72] The final stage of the Pacific air war and de Seversky's dichotomous image of air power would become the standard blueprint for land-based air power in the Cold War.

Notes

I wish to thank Hal Friedman first and foremost. Hal's invitation to join this endeavor was greatly appreciated, but his friendly prodding to make the work better and better were just what a dedicated scholar sometimes needs to produce something to be proud of. I also wish to thank the dedicated librarians at the SUNY Broome Community College Library and the George F. Johnson Memorial Library in Endicott, New York. Their help in locating books and magazines from long ago, sometimes on short notice, was instrumental in my work. Finally, I should note that the groundwork for this piece began decades ago with my dissertation. Over the years, the ability to conduct primary research has become easier, but there is still much that needs doing. Although today much research can be done from the comfort of one's own home, thanks to the Internet, this miracle is the result of so many archives, major and minor—including the Smithsonian, the Library of Congress, and the National Archives—digitizing more and more of their vast holdings and making them available for free to scholars and the general public. All who have a chance to facilitate, encourage, or endow this great Herculean process should do everything they can to keep it moving forward. The benefit to learning is tremendous. Viva la Revolucion!

1. Hal B. Wallis, Producer, *Air Force* (Hollywood: Warner Brothers, 1943).

2. Joseph Corn, *The Winged Gospel: America's Romance with Aviation* (New York: Oxford University Press, 2001).

3. For more on the postwar depiction of World War II, see Steve Call, *Selling Air Power: Military Aviation and American Popular Culture after World War II* (College Station: Texas A&M University Press, 2009).

4. The phenomenon of air power advocates using popular culture as a vehicle for their theories and efforts to influence public opinion or advance the cause of air power is a major theme in *Selling Air Power.*

5. Lawrence Howard Suid, ed., *Air Force* (Madison: University of Wisconsin Press, 1983), 14–24; this work is a reprint of the screenplay with an analytical and historical introduction by Suid; Wallis, *Air Force.*

6. Lt. Clarence E. Dickinson, USN, "I Fly for Vengeance," *Saturday Evening Post,* 10 October 1942.

7. Eugene Burnes, "We Avenge Pearl Harbor," *Saturday Evening Post,* 22 July 1944.

8. Hanson W. Baldwin, "Airpower," *Life,* 1 December 1941, 103–104, 106–09; emphasis in original.

9. Colonel Hugh J. Knerr, "Admirals and Air Power," *American Mercury,* September 1942, 283, 284; William Bradford Huie, *The Fight for Air Power* (New York: L. B. Fischer, 1942), 6–7.

10. Russell Whelan, *The Flying Tigers: The Story of the American Volunteer Group* (New York: Viking Press, 1942), esp. Chapters 1–4.

11. Haywood S. Hansell Jr., *The Air Plan That Defeated Hitler* (Atlanta, GA: Higgins-McArthur/Logino and Porter, 1972), 18–22.

12. Whelan, *Flying Tigers,* 50–52.

13. Ibid., 69–75; for the morale boost of this battle, see 7–8. A word should be mentioned of the controversy surrounding the "amazing" results of the Flying Tigers. Air kills claimed by pilots of all nationalities involved in World War II have become a notoriously unreliable source for what today's military calls Battle Damage Assessment (BDA), and the wartime and postwar reports of Flying Tigers exploits bring this issue squarely

to the front. The combination of America's need for any good news in the first year of the war, coupled with news agencies playing willing partners to the U.S. government's propaganda effort—not to mention the problems associated with pilots reporting on their own success—combined to create an almost mythological atmosphere surrounding the Flying Tigers. The legend of the AVG has only grown since the war. As to the difficulty of pilots reporting on their own effectiveness, a common human factor contributes to the problem: humans are inclined to exaggerate the effectiveness of their efforts, even more so during high-stress conditions such as combat, and anyone in the military—on land, sea, or in the air—is prone to this phenomenon. Moreover, in air combat, airmen are often basing their assessment on split-second—or at most a few seconds'—observation of rapidly unfolding events, so the sight of "heavy smoke pouring out of an engine" would seem an obvious indication that the aircraft is doomed even though the pilot did not have the luxury of time to watch the plane plummeting from the sky and crashing. Moreover, in the fluid environment of air battle, multiple observers will see and report the same events, leading to a multiplication of damage reported. One can readily imagine how aircrews might report with absolute certainty far greater results than they actually achieved when two or more pilots or crews are watching the same event from two or more different aircraft. And, in the case of the AVG, there was also an added monetary incentive: they were paid a bonus from the Chinese government for every Japanese plane they shot down. Taken together, there has been much doubt cast upon the reported effectiveness of the Flying Tigers during and since World War II. Arguably the most thorough and objective assessment of the Flying Tigers' impact comes from Daniel Ford and his landmark study, *Flying Tigers: Claire Chennault and the American Volunteer Group*. Published in 1991, Ford had access to extensive records of Allied postwar interrogation of Japanese pilots and air leaders as well as a wealth of postwar memoirs published by Japanese airmen and flying units. Noting a common phenomenon of wartime pilot assessments on both sides—exaggerated claims of enemy planes shot down, yet persuasively accurate reports of losses incurred to one's own forces—Ford offers a compelling corrective to the "mythologization" of the Flying Tigers legacy. For example, in studying the Japanese side of the story, Ford concludes the Japanese lost only ten aircraft on the Christmas raid. For more of Ford's assessment of actual Flying Tigers' kills, see 148, 190, 244, 274–276, 317–318, 369–370, and Appendix I, 387–388. It is worth noting that Ford, while deflating the Flying Tigers' claims to air kills, still gives an insightful report on the psychological impact of the AVG's efforts on Japanese aircrew morale. After having long enjoyed uncontested air supremacy in the skies over China, what damage the Flying Tigers did inflict on the Japanese air forces was enough to send shockwaves and demoralization through the ranks of Japanese airmen confronting the highly effective (though not superhuman) pilots of the AVG. Daniel Ford, *Flying Tigers: Claire Chennault and the American Volunteer Group* (Washington, DC: Smithsonian Institution Press, 1991).

14. William Clemens, "Chennault and His Flying Tigers," *Reader's Digest,* June 1942, 83.

15. Whelan, *Flying Tigers,* 211; see also note 13.

16. Colonel Robert L. Scott, *God Is My Co-Pilot* (New York: Charles Scribner's Sons, 1943), vii–viii.

17. Ibid., 213–215, 237–329. For context on the kill claims, see note 13.

18. Edmund Grainger, Associate Producer, *Flying Tigers* (Hollywood: Republic Pictures, 1942).

19. Michael Paris, *From the Wright Brothers to* Top Gun*: Aviation, Nationalism, and Popular Cinema* (Manchester, UK: Manchester University Press, 1995), 135–136.

20. Robert Buckner, Producer, *God Is My Co-Pilot* (Hollywood: Warner Brothers, 1945).

21. Captain Ted W. Lawson, *Thirty Seconds over Tokyo* (New York: Random House, 1943).

22. Ibid., 5–6, 13, 132, 179, 190; see 3 for quote.

23. Ibid., 26–27.

24. Ibid., 39. For an example of the image of targets being carefully selected for their importance to the war effort, see Brigadier General Edgar P. Sorensen, "We Pick the Targets for Our Bombers," *Saturday Evening Post,* 27 November 1943.

25. Lawson, *Thirty Seconds over Tokyo,* 40.

26. Ibid., 66.

27. For the military nature of targets, see ibid., 193, 194; for the use of incendiary bombs, see 197–198; for Lawson's comments, see 208–210.

28. Lewis B. Funke, "Rough-on-Japs Doolittle," *Saturday Evening Post,* 22 August 1942.

29. Robert Fellows, Producer, *Bombardier* (Hollywood: RKO Radio Pictures, 1943).

30. Jerry Wald, Producer, *Destination Tokyo* (Hollywood: Warner Brothers, 1943).

31. Darryl F. Zanuck, Producer, *The Purple Heart* (Hollywood: Twentieth Century-Fox, 1944).

32. Lawrence H. Suid, *Guts and Glory: Great American War Movies* (Reading, MA: Addison-Wesley Publishing, 1978): 56–57.

33. Ibid., 58.

34. Sam Zimbalist, Producer, *Thirty Seconds over Tokyo* (Hollywood: Metro-Goldwyn-Mayer, 1944).

35. Scott, *God Is My Co-Pilot,* 50–83.

36. Royal Arch Gunnison, "Blitz over the Philippines," *Collier's,* 17 January 1942, 17, 49.

37. John Lardner, "Seven Deadly Young Americans," *Saturday Evening Post,* 14 November 1942, 19, 106.

38. Major H. T. Hastings, "No Survivors," *Saturday Evening Post,* 22 May 1943, 18.

39. Ibid., 18–19, 89. The author's claim that all ships in the convoy were sunk has not stood up to scrutiny either during the war or afterward. As with the kills claimed by and for the Flying Tigers, battle damage assessment by aircrews is notoriously controversial, and the initial claims in the Battle of the Bismarck Sea became more controversial than most. Besides the conscious or unconscious propaganda value, Hastings, or the editors at *Saturday Evening Post,* may also have been looking for the "wow factor" in this article and nothing says "wow!" more than a title like "No Survivors." Added to that was the determination of many airmen, and Army Air Forces leaders, to back up claims of land-based air power's superiority over naval surface and air forces, and the Battle of

the Bismarck Sea offered great support for such claims, since the entire battle to stop the Japanese was an air battle. Even MacArthur's famous ego came into play. Complicating the controversy, however, was the fact that the battle took place over a wide area of ocean and spanned a number of days, during which the Japanese convoy moved in and out of bad weather, which prevented constant surveillance. One result of this complicating factor, for example, is that there is controversy over exactly how many ships were in the convoy throughout the duration of the battle. Official Army Air Forces and Army Historical Office studies during the war—which included the examination of captured Japanese documents—cast doubt on the initial claims; MacArthur's headquarters, however, not only stood by its initial claims but even threatened official action against anyone questioning those claims. After the war, MacArthur remained adamant that the initial claims were accurate. Even postwar interrogation of Japanese officials and examination of Japanese documents failed to definitively resolve the issue. Another complicating factor was that aircrew reports listed some ships as "sinking" while others were reported "in obviously desperate conditions"; were these ships seen slipping below the surface of the waves at any time? How confidently can one assume that a ship seen during an attack in "obviously desperate condition" did indeed later sink? There is a great deal of room for varying interpretations and assumptions. The official history of the U.S. Army Air Forces during World War II assesses the results as follows: "the convoy at no time included more than the original sixteen vessels and of this total, all of the transports, [a service vessel], and four of the destroyers were lost"; it also notes that "the Japanese admit an over-all loss of some 3,000 men and claim that just under 6,000 survived." In a more strategic sense, though, this same official history says of the controversy that "[the] fact that counts is that a major effort to reinforce Lae was turned back with mass destruction inflicted upon an enemy who never thereafter renewed the effort." Wesley Frank Craven and James Lea Cate, eds., *The Army Air Forces in World War II,* vol. 4, *The Pacific: Guadalcanal to Saipan, August 1942 to July 1944* (Chicago: University of Chicago Press, 1948; reprint, Washington, DC: Office of Air Force History, 1983), 146–150.

40. Henry F. Pringle, "They Didn't Know What Hit Them," *Collier's,* 28 August 1943, 14–16, 59.

41. Charles A. Rawlings, "We Skip-Bomb the Japs," *Saturday Evening Post,* 4 September 1943; "Skip-Bombing," *Life,* 15 November 1943; Francis Vivian Drake, "Combat Rehearsal over Florida," *Reader's Digest,* April 1944.

42. Ernest O. Hauser, "Hong Kong Home-coming," *Saturday Evening Post,* 20 November 1943, 22, 95.

43. Charles A. Rawlings, "Strike on Rabaul," *Saturday Evening Post,* 19 February 1944, 24–25, 64, 66. For the kill claims, see note 13.

44. Charles A. Rawlings, "Pacific Thriller," *Saturday Evening Post,* 8 January 1944. Again, for context and perspective on kill claims, see note 13 above.

45. Frank L. Kluckhohn, "'Let's Try It' . . . and Kenney Does," *New York Times Magazine,* 8 October 1944.

46. Pete Martin, "Burma Bomber," *Saturday Evening Post,* 23 and 30 October 1943, quote from Part 2, 88.

47. Forrest Davis, "Hale's Handful," *Saturday Evening Post*, 15 July 1944.

48. Milton Caniff, *The Complete Terry and the Pirates, vol. 5: 1943–1944* (San Diego, CA: IDW Publishing, 2008), 105–135.

49. Everett Riskin, Producer, *A Guy Named Joe* (Hollywood: Metro-Goldwyn-Mayer, 1943).

50. Wallis, *Air Force*, 1943.

51. Edgar Snow, "The Coming Battle for Asia," *Saturday Evening Post*, 18 March 1944, 16.

52. Charles Griffith, *The Quest: Haywood Hansell and American Strategic Bombing in World War II* (Maxwell Air Force Base, AL: Air University Press, 1999), 148–149, 156, 165–167, 171, 176–177.

53. "How 430,000 Chinese Built the B-29 Bases," *Reader's Digest*, August 1944; Sidney Shalett, "This Possum Is Jap Poison," *Saturday Evening Post*, 25 November 1944; Haywood Hansell's nickname was Possum.

54. Richard Tregaskis, "Road to Tokyo: Payoff over Japan," *Saturday Evening Post*, 22 September 1945. The first installments followed the crew as they leave California for Hawaii, proceed on to Guam, and prepare for combat. The weekly installments started with the 18 August issue and concluded coverage of the B-29 efforts with the 22 September issue.

55. For the controversy surrounding U.S. strategic bombing during World War II, see Michael Sherry, *The Rise of American Air Power: The Creation of Armageddon* (New Haven, CT: Yale University Press, 1987); and Conrad C. Crane, *Bombs, Cities, and Civilians: American Airpower Strategy in World War II*, Modern War Studies Series (Lawrence: University Press of Kansas, 1993). For the development of U.S. air power strategy, see Robert T. Finney, *History of the Air Corps Tactical School, 1920–1940* (Maxwell Air Force Base, AL: Research Studies Institute, USAF Historical Division, Air University, 1955; reprint, Washington, DC: Center for Air Force History, 1992); Robert Frank Futrell, *Ideas, Concepts, Doctrine: Basic Thinking in the United States Air Force*, vol. 1, *1907–1960* (Maxwell Air Force Base, AL: Air University, 1971; reprint, Maxwell Air Force Base, AL: Air University Press, 1989); and James C. Gaston, *Planning the American Air War: Four Men and Nine Days in 1941* (Washington, DC: National Defense University Press, 1982).

56. Giulio Douhet, *The Command of the Air*, trans. Dino Ferrari, (New York: Coward-McCann, 1942; reprint, Washington, DC: Office of Air Force History, 1983).

57. See, e.g., John W. Dower, *War without Mercy: Race and Power in the Pacific War* (New York: Pantheon Books, 1986).

58. Sherry, *The Rise of American Air Power;* Crane, *Bombs, Cities, and Civilians;* Dower, *War without Mercy.*

59. Zanuck, *The Purple Heart.*

60. David O. Woodbury, "Tokyo Calling Cards," *Collier's*, 14 April 1945, 44, 58.

61. Phillip S. Meilinger, "Proselytiser and Prophet: Alexander P. de Seversky and American Airpower," in John Gooch, ed., *Airpower: Theory and Practice* (London: Frank Cass and Co., 1995), 9–14.

62. Alexander P. de Seversky, *Victory through Air Power* (New York: Simon and Schuster, 1942); see, e.g., 335–338.

63. Ibid., 101.
64. Ibid., 101–102.
65. Ibid., 120.
66. Meilinger, "Proselytiser," 20.
67. Ibid.
68. Walt Disney, Producer, *Victory through Air Power* (Hollywood: Walt Disney Pictures, 1943).
69. Ibid.
70. Meilinger, "Proselytiser," 19–21.
71. Harry Borowski, *A Hollow Threat: Strategic Air Power and Containment before Korea* (Westport, CT: Greenwood Press, 1982), 183n15.
72. Alexander P. de Seversky, *Air Power: Key to Survival* (New York: Simon and Schuster, 1950), 187–192.

Bibliography

Primary Sources

Magazines

"The Atomic Age." *Life*, 20 August 1945, 32.
Baldwin, Hanson W. "Airpower." *Life*, 1 December 1941, 91–102, 106–109.
———. "The Atom Bomb and Future War." *Life*, 20 August 1945, 17–32.
Burnes, Eugene. "We Avenge Pearl Harbor." *Saturday Evening Post*, 22 July 1944, 18–19, 73–75.
Chase, Stuart. "The Two-Hour War." *The New Republic*, 8 May 1929, 325–327.
Clemens, William. "Chennault and His Flying Tigers." *Reader's Digest*, June 1942, 81–85.
Courtney, W. B. "Air Power—Today and Tomorrow." *Collier's*, 8 September 1945, 11–12, 37; 15 September 1945, 24, 28–30.
Davis, Forrest. "Hale's Handful." *Saturday Evening Post*, 15 July 1944, 28–29, 98–100.
Dickinson, Lt. Clarence E., USN. "I Fly for Vengeance." *Saturday Evening Post*, 10 October 1942, 9–11, 37, 39–40, 42, 44.
Drake, Francis Vivian. "Combat Rehearsal Over Florida." *Reader's Digest*, April 1944, 8–11.
Funke, Lewis B. "Rough-on-Japs Doolittle." *Saturday Evening Post*, 22 August 1942, 20–21, 63–65.
Gayn, Mark. "Terror in Japan." *Collier's*, 16 June 1945, 11–12, 59.
Gunnison, Royal Arch. "Blitz over the Philippines." *Collier's*, 17 January 1942, 17, 49–51.
Hastings, Major H. T. "No Survivors." *Saturday Evening Post*, 22 May 1943, 18–19, 89.
Hauser, Ernest O. "Hong Kong Home-coming." *Saturday Evening Post*, 20 November 1943, 22, 95.
"How 430,000 Chinese Built the B-29 Bases." *Reader's Digest*, August 1944, 74.
Kluckhohn, Frank L. "'Let's Try It' . . . and Kenney Does." *New York Times Magazine*, 8 October 1944, 24–25.

Knerr, Colonel Hugh J. "Admirals and Air Power." *American Mercury,* September 1942, 283–291.

Lardner, John. "Seven Deadly Young Americans." *Saturday Evening Post,* 14 November 1942, 19, 106.

Martin, Pete. "Burma Bomber." *Saturday Evening Post,* 23 and 30 October 1943, 22, 87–89.

Michie, Allan A. "Germany Was Bombed to Defeat." *Reader's Digest,* August 1945, 77–81.

Mitchell, William. "Aëronautical Era." *Saturday Evening Post,* 20 December 1924, 3–4, 99, 101–102.

———. "Aircraft Dominate Seacraft." *Saturday Evening Post,* 24 January 1925, 22–23, 72, 77–78.

———. "Airplanes in National Defense." *Annals of the American Academy of Political and Social Science,* May 1927, 38–42.

———. "American Leadership in Aëronautics." *Saturday Evening Post,* 10 January 1925, 18–19, 148, 153.

———. "Civil and Commercial Aviation." *Saturday Evening Post,* 7 February 1925, 14, 169–170, 173.

———. "How Should We Organize Our National Air Power?" *Saturday Evening Post,* 14 March 1925, 6–7, 214, 216–218.

———. "Look Out Below!" *Collier's,* 21 April 1928, 8–9, 41–42.

Pringle, Henry F. "They Didn't Know What Hit Them." *Collier's,* 28 August 1943, 14–16, 59.

Rawlings, Charles A. "Pacific Thriller." *Saturday Evening Post,* 8 January 1944, 16–17, 80–82.

———. "Strike on Rabaul." *Saturday Evening Post,* 19 February 1944, 24–25, 64, 66.

———. "We Skip-Bomb the Japs." *Saturday Evening Post,* 4 September 1943, 22–23, 65–67.

Royse, M. W. "The Next War in the Air." *The Nation,* 9 May 1923, 537–539; 16 May 1923, 566–568.

Shalett, Sidney. "This Possum Is Jap Poison." *Saturday Evening Post,* 25 November 1944, 17, 94–96.

Sikorsky, Igor. "What Can Aircraft Do in the Next War?" *The Independent,* 7 November 1925, 521–523.

"Skip-Bombing." *Life,* 15 November 1943, 93–99.

Snow, Edgar. "The Coming Battle for Asia." *Saturday Evening Post,* 18 March 1944, 16–17, 95–96.

Sorensen, Brigadier General Edgar P. "We Pick the Targets for Our Bombers." *Saturday Evening Post,* 27 November 1943, 16–17, 95, 97.

Tregaskis, Richard. "Road to Tokyo: Disillusionment in Hawaii." *Saturday Evening Post,* 1 September 1945, 20, 93–94.

———. "Road to Tokyo: The Fine Hand of Mr. Suzuki." *Saturday Evening Post,* 20 October 1945, 18, 111–114.

———. "Road to Tokyo: Guam—This Is It!" *Saturday Evening Post,* 8 September 1945, 22, 91–92.

———. "Road to Tokyo: Have We Given Japan Back to the Japs?" *Saturday Evening Post,* 27 October 1945, 20, 114–116.

———. "Road to Tokyo: I Don't Intend to Ditch." *Saturday Evening Post,* 25 August 1945, 20, 91–92.

———. "Road to Tokyo: The Infantry Never Had It So Tough." *Saturday Evening Post,* 13 October 1945, 20, 106–108.

———. "Road to Tokyo: Payoff over Japan," *Saturday Evening Post,* 22 September 1945, 20, 101–103.

———. "Road to Tokyo: We of the B-29's Say Good-By," *Saturday Evening Post,* 18 August 1945, 17, 86–88.

———. "Road to Tokyo: We Soften the Peace." *Saturday Evening Post,* 6 October 1945, 20, 105–106.

"Victory through Air Power." *Life,* 19 July 1943, 50–52.

"The War Ends." *Life,* 20 August 1945, 25–31.

Woodbury, David O. "Tokyo Calling Cards." *Collier's,* 14 April 1945, 44, 58.

Memoirs and Other Published Primary Sources

Chennault, Claire Lee. *Way of a Fighter: The Memoirs of Claire Lee Chennault.* Ed. Robert Hotz. New York: G. P. Putnam's Sons, 1949.

De Seversky, Alexander P. *Air Power: Key to Survival.* New York: Simon and Schuster, 1950.

———. *Victory through Air Power.* New York: Simon and Schuster, 1942.

Hart, Moss. *Winged Victory: The Air Force Play.* New York: Random House, 1943.

Huie, William Bradford. *The Fight for Air Power.* New York: L. B. Fischer, 1942.

Lawson, Captain Ted W. *Thirty Seconds over Tokyo.* New York: Random House, 1943.

LeMay, Curtis E., and MacKinlay Kantor. *Mission with LeMay: My Story.* Garden City, NY: Doubleday and Co., 1965.

Liddell Hart, B. H. *Paris; or, The Future of War.* New York: E. P. Dutton and Co., 1925.

Mitchell, William. *Skyways: A Book on Modern Aeronautics.* Philadelphia, PA: J. B. Lippincott Co., 1930.

———. *Winged Defense: The Development and Possibilities of Modern Air Power—Economic and Military.* Port Washington, NY: Kennikat Press, 1925, 1971.

Scott, Colonel Robert L. *God Is My Co-Pilot.* New York: Charles Scribner's Sons, 1943.

Whelan, Russell. *The Flying Tigers: The Story of the American Volunteer Group.* New York: Viking Press, 1942.

Films

Buckner, Robert, Producer. *God Is My Co-Pilot.* Hollywood: Warner Brothers, 1945.

Disney, Walt, Producer. *Victory through Air Power.* Hollywood: Walt Disney Pictures, 1943.

Fellows, Robert, Producer. *Bombardier.* Hollywood: RKO Radio Pictures, 1943.
Grainger, Edmund, Associate Producer. *Flying Tigers.* Hollywood: Republic Pictures, 1942.
Riskin, Everett, Producer. *A Guy Named Joe.* Hollywood: Metro-Goldwyn-Mayer, 1943.
Wald, Jerry, Producer. *Destination Tokyo.* Hollywood: Warner Brothers, 1943.
Wallis, Hal B., Producer. *Air Force.* Hollywood: Warner Brothers, 1943.
Zanuck, Darryl F., Producer. *The Purple Heart.* Hollywood: Twentieth Century–Fox, 1944.
Zimbalist, Sam, Producer. *Thirty Seconds over Tokyo.* Hollywood: Metro-Goldwyn-Mayer, 1944.

Secondary Sources

Books

Borowski, Harry R. *A Hollow Threat: Strategic Air Power and Containment before Korea.* Westport, CT: Greenwood Press, 1982.
Call, Steve. *Selling Air Power: Military Aviation and American Popular Culture after World War II.* College Station: Texas A&M University Press, 2009.
Caniff, Milton. *The Complete Terry and the Pirates, vol. 5: 1943–1944.* San Diego, CA: IDW Publishing, 2008.
Coffey, Thomas M. *Iron Eagle: The Turbulent Life of General Curtis LeMay.* New York: Crown Publishers, 1986.
Corn, Joseph J. *The Winged Gospel: America's Romance with Aviation, 1900–1950.* New York: Oxford University Press, 1983.
Crane, Conrad C. *Bombs, Cities, and Civilians: American Airpower Strategy in World War II.* Modern War Studies Series. Lawrence: University Press of Kansas, 1993.
Crouch, Tom D. *A Dream of Wings: Americans and the Airplane, 1875–1905.* New York: W. W. Norton and Co., 1981.
Doherty, Thomas. *Projections of War: Hollywood, American Culture, and World War II.* New York: Columbia University Press, 1993.
Dower, John W. *War without Mercy: Race and Power in the Pacific War.* New York: Pantheon Books, 1986.
Farmer, James H. *Celluloid Wings: The Impact of Movies on Aviation.* Blue Ridge Summit, PA: Tab Books, 1984.
Ford, Daniel. *Flying Tigers: Claire Chennault and the American Volunteer Group.* Washington, DC: Smithsonian Institute Press, 1991.
Goldstein, Laurence. *The Flying Machine and Modern Literature.* Bloomington: Indiana University Press, 1986.
Hansell, Haywood S., Jr. *The Air Plan That Defeated Hitler.* Atlanta, GA: Higgins-McArthur/Longino and Porter, 1972.
Heidenry, John. *Theirs Was the Kingdom: Lila and DeWitt Wallace and the Story of the Reader's Digest.* New York: W. W. Norton and Co., 1993.
Herzstein, Robert E. *Henry R. Luce: A Political Portrait of the Man Who Created the American Century.* New York: Charles Scribner's Sons, 1994.

Hurley, Alfred F. *Billy Mitchell: Crusader for Air Power.* New York: Franklin Watts, 1964.
Kennett, Lee. *A History of Strategic Bombing.* New York: Charles Scribner's Sons, 1982.
MacIsaac, David. *Strategic Bombing in World War Two: The Story of the United States Strategic Bombing Survey.* New York: Garland Publishing, 1976.
McFarland, Stephen L. *America's Pursuit of Precision Bombing, 1910–1945.* Washington, DC: Smithsonian Institution Press, 1995.
Paris, Michael. *From the Wright Brothers to* Top Gun: *Aviation, Nationalism, and Popular Cinema.* Manchester, UK: Manchester University Press, 1995.
Pendo, Stephen. *Aviation in the Cinema.* Metuchen, NJ: Scarecrow Press, 1985.
Schaffer, Ronald. *Wings of Judgement: American Bombing in World War II.* New York: Oxford University Press, 1985.
Sherry, Michael S. *In the Shadow of War.* New Haven, CT: Yale University Press, 1995.
———. *The Rise of American Air Power: The Creation of Armageddon.* New Haven, CT: Yale University Press, 1987.
Shindler, Colin. *Hollywood Goes to War: Films and American Society, 1939–1952.* Boston: Routledge and Kegan Paul, 1979.
Skogsberg, Bertil. *Wings on the Screen: A Pictorial History of Air Movies.* New York: A. S. Barnes and Co., 1981.
Suid, Lawrence Howard, ed. *Air Force.* Madison: University of Wisconsin Press, 1983.
Suid, Lawrence Howard. *Guts and Glory: Great American War Movies.* Reading, MA: Addison-Wesley Publishing Co., 1978.
Wohl, Robert. *A Passion for Wings: Aviation and the Western Imagination, 1908–1918.* New Haven, CT: Yale University Press, 1994.

Official Histories

Craven, Wesley Frank, and James Lea Cate, eds. *The Army Air Forces in World War II.* Chicago: University of Chicago Press, 1948–1958; reprint, Washington, DC: Office of Air Force History, 1983.
Douhet, Giulio. *The Command of the Air.* Trans. Dino Ferrari. New York: Coward McCann, 1942; reprint, Washington, DC: Office of Air Force History, 1983.
Finney, Robert T. *History of the Air Corps Tactical School, 1920–1940.* Maxwell Air Force Base, AL: Research Studies Institute, USAF Historical Division, Air University, 1955; reprint, Washington, DC: Center for Air Force History, 1992.
Futrell, Robert Frank. *Ideas, Concepts, Doctrine: Basic Thinking in the United States Air Force.* Vol. 1, *1907–1960.* Maxwell Air Force Base, AL: Air University, 1971; reprint, Maxwell Air Force Base, AL: Air University Press, 1989.
Gaston, James C. *Planning the American Air War: Four Men and Nine Days in 1941.* Washington, DC: National Defense University Press, 1982.
Greer, Thomas H. *The Development of Air Doctrine in the Army Air Arm, 1917–1941.* Maxwell Air Force Base, AL: USAF Historical Division, Research Studies Institute, Air University, 1955; reprint, Washington, DC: Office of Air Force History, 1985.

Griffith, Charles. *The Quest: Haywood Hansell and American Strategic Bombing in World War II.* Maxwell Air Force Base, AL: Air University Press, 1999.

Articles

Meilinger, Phillip S. "Proselytiser and Prophet: Alexander P. de Seversky and American Airpower." In John Gooch, ed., *Airpower: Theory and Practice.* London: Frank Cass, 1995, 7–35.

Whiteley, John F. "Alexander de Seversky." *Aerospace Historian,* September 1977, 155–157.

3

The U.S. Marine Corps Raiders, 1942–1944

Conflicting Cultures of Elitism

Stephen Houseknecht

The opening salvos of World War II left the Allied Powers reeling under an onslaught of Axis advances. Desperate to cover their strategic weaknesses and bolster flagging morale, they turned to daring hit-and-run raids by specially trained bodies of troops. Some of these groups, such as the British Commandos and the U.S. Army Rangers, feature prominently in the popular memory of World War II, while others are less commonly remembered. Discussion of these elite units is often left to the popular press and memoirists, with little interest from scholars. Yet elite units deserve a second look for a variety of reasons. They often provide an opportunity to examine the cultural dynamics of elitism within military subcultures. The creation of small, elite cohorts within larger, preexisting military cultures often resulted in considerable internal tension. In early 1942, the United States Marine Corps embarked on an "experiment" in military elitism with the creation of the Marine Corps Raider Battalions.[1] The Marine Corps' foray into the emergent world of special forces was brief and tumultuous, not even lasting until the end of the conflict. Though the operational lifespan of the Raider Battalions was short, it does serve as an illustration of the various points of tension inherent in the creation of a new subculture within a strong, preexisting institutional culture. A brief reconsideration of the Raiders' short but distinguished operational history can shed some light on the tension between the dominant culture of the United States Marine Corps as a corps d'elite and the emergent, equally elitist subculture of the specialized Raider Battalions.

Today, the exploits of the Raiders remain largely unknown outside of devotees of Marine Corps history. The scholarly literature on the Raiders is sparse, though they have enjoyed some attention in the realm of popular military history.[2] Serious treatments of the Raiders are usually campaign-based narratives written by Marines, for Marines; the Raiders are also featured to some extent in the campaign histories of Guadalcanal, New Georgia, and Bougainville.[3] To date, little attempt has been made to contextualize the Raiders' experience by linking their operational history with the existent scholarly literature on elite special operations units.[4] As an elite within an elite, the Raiders present a unique situation for the historian. Their emergence as an elite subculture within the larger culture of elitism in the Marine Corps presents an interesting case study of the potential conflicts of elitist cultures in military organizations. The creation of the Raider Battalions and the growth of their own subculture of elitism introduced dissonance into the context of the already elitist culture of the Marine Corps, ultimately leading to the abandonment of the Raider experiment before the end of the war.[5]

Context

The preliminary task of delineating exactly what constitutes a special operations unit is no mere trifle. Special forces units by their very nature defy strict definition, as they necessarily fall outside the normal boundaries of their respective military services. However, the attempt to add qualitative factors to the definition of special operations has produced worthwhile results. Some common identifying factors include small-scale operations, rigorous selection process, special training, high risk, and unorthodox missions. Such units frequently have their special status recognized overtly by way of special insignia, unique uniforms, and higher pay.[6]

One of the inherent difficulties in discussion of such units is the pronounced tendency to conflate "special operations" with "elite." Andrew Hargreaves calls attention to the fact that "most such [special operations] units can be considered elites, but not all elites are specialist formations."[7] Though corps d'elite formations often share similar trappings as special forces, there are significant differences of "status, selection, and size" separating the two types of military bodies.[8] Drawing such distinctions is not pedantic but is crucially important to the study of the Marine Corps Raiders of World War II, a force that essentially amounted to an elite special operations unit housed within a larger corps d'elite. Eliot Cohen has identified one of the key features of a military elite: that it "achieves a reputation—justified or not—for bravura and success."[9] This is an important point to make, for distinguishing among elite units is a highly subjective judgment. When it comes to concepts of elitism, perceptions are often as important as reality, if not more so.

Claims that the Marine Corps constituted a corps d'elite in America's World War II military are often made anecdotally. It was axiomatic: the Marine Corps was America's best, the "First to Fight." Observers frequently noted that "the

Marines simply assumed that they were the world's best fighting men."[10] Historian Allan Millett points out that the Marine Corps had long maintained an elitist image, largely as a result of its small size. Prior experience in World War I "fused the elitist strains of size (which implied selectivity), military discipline, and combat performance. Subsequent wars reinforced this elitist tradition."[11] One of the best attempts to define the processes by which the Marine Corps earned its claims to elitism in the crucible of Pacific combat is by Dennis Showalter, who argues persuasively that the U.S. Marine Corps firmly established itself as a military elite during World War II. His analysis provides a tripartite view of what it means to be an elite unit.[12] Showalter suggests that military elites can be loosely categorized as guardsmen, technicians, and warriors. Guardsmen, the most traditional type of elite unit, are distinguished largely by their selective recruiting, volunteer status, and a general sense of being set apart. Technicians gain recognition as an elite via honing a special set of skills beyond the pale of ordinary service. Showalter's warrior elites combine the selectiveness of the guardsmen and the specialized mission of the technicians, but place primary importance on proven combat ability; once their reputation is earned, these elite units frequently serve as shock troops employed in dire situations.[13] The Marine Corps' status as an all-volunteer force helped bolster its image as guardsmen. The development and perfection of amphibious warfare doctrines during the interwar period and World War II, an especially hazardous method of war fighting, demonstrated the Marines' ability as technicians. But it was their emphasis on the role of individual Marines as riflemen of highest quality, "the men who set the standards of performance on the battlefield," that established their presence as warrior elites.[14]

My study takes Showalter's tripartite standard, as well as his judgment on the Marine Corps' evolution into a warrior elite during the war, as a starting point. The Raiders, I argue, moved along a parallel path, establishing themselves as a subset of warrior elites with their own unique identity and culture. This Raider identity ultimately caused friction with the emergence of the Marine Corps as a warrior elite. Though a full consideration of this cultural conflict is beyond the scope of this chapter, I will here attempt to highlight some of the more prominent aspects of the conflict between the two elitist cultures.

Combat Narrative

The Raider Battalions were not established by the Marine Corps voluntarily. Experience in simulated amphibious assaults had demonstrated the need for a light, fast, and stealthy band of Marines to spearhead amphibious assaults. In the summer of 1941, Major General Holland Smith, commanding general of the

Atlantic Fleet's Amphibious Force, redesignated the First Battalion, Fifth Marines as the First Separate Battalion for such a purpose. Under Lieutenant Colonel Merritt Edson, the First Separate Battalion received specialized training, with an emphasis on stealth landings using rubber boats; however, they remained similar in many aspects to the standard Marine Corps infantry battalion.[15] Special units were not seen as needed in a Corps that already considered itself just as good as the famed British Commandos. Many Marine Corps officers were wary of the term "Commando," for they maintained that the Marines already *were* America's elite amphibious troops, easily the equal of any Commandos.[16] Then–Major General Thomas Holcomb, Commandant of the Marine Corps, believed that "the term 'Marine' was 'sufficient to indicate a man ready for duty at any time, and that the injection of a special name, such as "Commando," would be undesirable and superfluous.'"[17] This opinion was shared by most in the Marine Corps.[18]

At the same time, forces at the highest levels provided the impetus for the Marine Corps to formally create the Raider Battalions. From within the ranks of the Marine Corps, Major Evans F. Carlson, an enigmatic Marine Corps veteran of multiple China tours and a personal friend of President Franklin Roosevelt, advocated for creating a unit modeled after the Chinese guerrillas.[19] His ideas acquired a powerful follower in the person of Marine Corps Reserve Captain James Roosevelt, the President's son, who wrote directly to General Holcomb in support of the idea.[20]

In December 1941, President Roosevelt, further encouraged to develop a special "commando" unit by British Prime Minister Winston Churchill, was presented with a proposal by William Donovan. Donovan, Director, Office of the Coordinator of Information (OCI), had made a formal proposal for a "guerrilla corps, independent and separate from the Army and Navy."[21] Of course, such a commando unit would be commanded by Donovan, who wanted a Brigadier General's commission in the Marine Corps. The idea of having a non–Marine Corps officer placed in charge of a Marine Corps unit was anathema to that service's officer corps. However, President Roosevelt and Secretary of the Navy Frank Knox liked the commando concept. Admiral Ernest King, Commander-in-Chief of the U.S. Fleet, therefore made it clear to General Holcomb that the Marine Corps was to furnish such units, with or without Donovan.[22] In the face of such high-level pressure, and sure that the forced acceptance of Donovan would be "the worst slap in the face the Marine Corps was ever given," Holcomb improvised.[23] Edson's First Separate Battalion would be converted to the First Marine Raider Battalion on February 16, 1942; the Second Raider Battalion, under Carlson and James Roosevelt, was formed later that month in California.

From their initial days, the Raider Battalions began building the Raider mystique, quickly establishing themselves as premier special operations units.

But even more than their special-mission purpose, the Raiders were set apart by their natural evolution into a distinctly elite force, advancing rapidly from guardsmen to technicians and finally earning the coveted status of warrior elites. The high standards for acceptance as a Raider contributed heavily to their guardsman persona. In order to ensure that only the most highly motivated Marines remained in his battalion, Edson made every member of the battalion either re-volunteer for continued service as a Raider or else be granted a transfer, no questions asked.[24] Edson wanted only the highest quality of personnel to replenish his ranks. He petitioned for the transfer of officers who were "younger, more active and aggressive . . . well grounded in infantry tactics" and who were "above average ability for their rank."[25] He was not above invoking the Raiders' favor with high command either, frankly explaining that Admiral King "has directed these two battalions be organized and trained for active operations at the earliest possible date. As a result, the Commandant has directed that we be given priority on personnel and equipment over other units in the Corps."[26] Edson's assembly of a hand-picked team resulted in "the most eminently qualified and experienced [officer corps] ever assembled in one Marine battalion."[27]

In California, Evans Carlson had an even freer hand in selecting his Second Raiders and seized the opportunity to shape a fighting unit that was "uniquely Carlson's creation."[28] Carlson and James Roosevelt personally interviewed every volunteer, accepting only those whose temperaments and skills matched what Carlson was seeking. The rumor quickly started in the Second Marine Division that Carlson was searching for "the *crème de la crème*, the Marine of the Marines," for his new "rugged, suicide" outfit.[29] Prospective Raiders were questioned thoroughly, and given no illusions as to what they were signing up for: "I promise you nothing but hardships and danger. . . . When we get to battle, we ask no mercy, we give none."[30] Carlson proudly explained to President Roosevelt, "We have combed 6000 men to secure the 600 which comprise this organization."[31]

The emphasis on stringent selection standards and reliance on volunteers helped make the Raiders distinct from the beginning. The guardsman aura surrounding the Raiders encouraged many eager Marines to try out for selection. Private Lee Minier, upon being accepted into the First Raiders, explained his decision to his mother:

> I volunteered for service with the 1st Marine Raider Battalion and was accepted. This outfit corresponds to the British Commandos and also is a spearhead for landing parties. We operate from destroyers and land in rubber boats. . . . I only hope this outfit is as good as they say it is. They call it a suicide outfit. But I notice a lot of Marines try to get

> into it. One of the requirements is that you must volunteer and are not asked to join and must realize what you are asking for . . .[32]

By relying on volunteers and hand-picked personnel taken from the ranks of the Marine Corps, which according to Showalter had achieved recognizable guardsmen status by the 1940s, the Raiders guaranteed that they would be going into battle with the proverbial cream of the crop.

The specialized training these Marines received to perform raids and other special warfare missions clearly established the Raiders as emergent technician elites. Though the methods of Edson and Carlson differed widely, both shared the emphasis on mastery of a highly specialized mission. Physical fitness was a top priority in both Raider Battalions, with a heavy emphasis on endurance and speed on long hikes over rough terrain.[33] From the outset, the Raiders had to prepare for a variety of potential missions, including reconnaissance, diversions, raids, flank attacks, or even full landings in support of conventional troops. Their forte was specialized insertion methods, allowing them to strike quickly, quietly, and with complete surprise. To assure the element of surprise meant that the Raiders had to master stealth landings; their training emphasized night operations with rubber boats, eventually perfecting their methods to the point where they could disembark, land, and move toward their objectives without verbal commands. The entire structure of the Raider Battalions was designed around the operating capacity of fast high-speed transports (destroyers converted to serve as fast troop transports), and with the understanding that even more unconventional platforms—to include submarines—could be used to insert the Raiders to their mission areas.[34] In contrast to Edson's more conventional ideas, Carlson envisioned his Raiders as a guerrilla force and focused his training agenda on "operations for a protracted period behind enemy lines."[35] The Raiders' perfection of specialty crafts, such as the fast-strike raid, guerrilla operations, and stealth insertions, demonstrates their accession to the technician elite as put forth by Showalter. Additionally, their honing of a particularly demanding form of amphibious assault, already hazardous enough, made the Raiders a highly specialized subset of technician elites.

In Showalter's approach, the warrior elites earn their status through "proved or potential superiority as fighters."[36] The Raiders had ample potential from the start, but they earned their warrior status on the island jungles of the Southwest Pacific, fighting in several desperate campaigns from August 1942 to January 1944.[37] The First Marine Raider Battalion served a prominent role in the Guadalcanal campaign, America's first land offensive against the Japanese.

On 7 August 1942, the First Raiders wrested control of the island of Tulagi from some 350 Japanese naval special landing troops. The Raiders rose to the

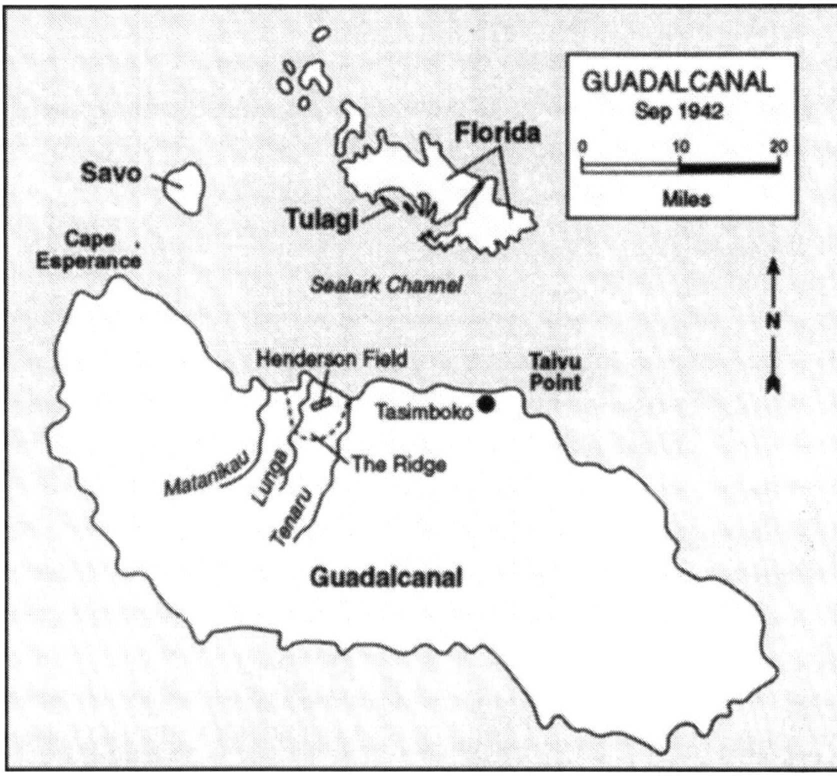

Guadalcanal, September 1942 (Courtesy of Jon T. Hoffman, *From Makin to Bougainville: Marine Raiders in the Pacific War*, Washington, DC: Marine Corps Historical Center, 1995)

challenge with their characteristic aggressiveness. By the end of 8 August, the island of Tulagi was declared secure; in neutralizing 347 Japanese defenders, the Raiders had suffered 38 of their own killed, with another 55 wounded. The Raiders then moved to the main island of Guadalcanal to assist Major General Alexander Vandegrift's First Marine Division with the defense of Henderson Field. The Raiders were tasked with defending an open ridge to the south of the airfield, a ridge thereafter known as Edson's Ridge. For two nights (13 and 14 September), Japanese Major General Kiyotake Kawaguchi's veteran Thirty-Fifth Infantry Brigade attacked the Raider positions. The Raiders successfully held the ridge against Japanese assault on both nights, repelling the enemy with small arms fire, grenades, and frequently with hand-to-hand fighting. The Raiders lost 135 of their own—including 59 dead—defending the ridge, but they had decimated the Japanese brigade, killing more than 700 attackers and permanently

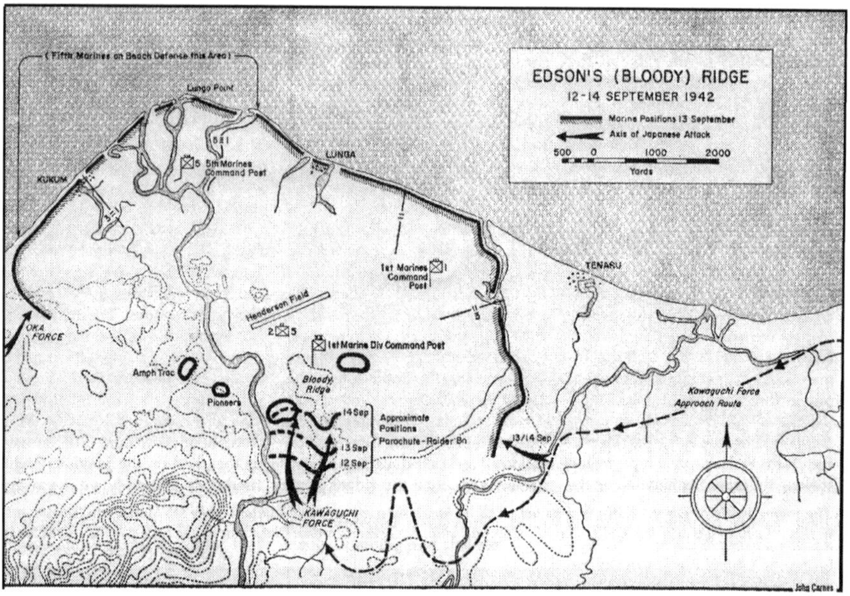

Edson's (Bloody) Ridge, 12–14 September 1942 (Courtesy of Henry I. Shaw Jr., *First Offensive: The Marine Campaign for Guadalcanal* (Washington, DC: Marine Corps Historical Center, 1992)

thwarting Kawaguchi's attempts to recapture the airfield. When they departed Guadalcanal on 13 October, the First Raider Battalion registered only one quarter effective strength—some two hundred Raiders—but they had cemented their status as warrior elites.

Carlson's Second Raiders earned plenty of accolades of their own, including one of the most daring raids by any American force during the war. In the first submarine-borne raid in American history, two companies of the Second Raiders, some 220 men, raided the Japanese installation on Makin Atoll on 17 August 1942. In addition to gathering intelligence, Carlson's raid diverted Japanese attention from the American offensive in the Solomons. After landing unseen, the Raiders engaged the Japanese garrison in a heavy firefight. Despite setbacks, including a tense night spent virtually stranded on the island, the Raiders were able to destroy the garrison, the island's radio station, and several seaplanes. Rough surf threatened to maroon the Raiders permanently, but on the second night the Raiders were able to reach the submarines. Tragically, nine Raiders were left ashore in the confusion surrounding the extraction. These Raiders were later captured by the Japanese and executed; their fate was not known until after the war.[38]

Carlson's Raiders then moved to Guadalcanal, where they landed at Aola Bay to the east of Vandegrift's Henderson Field perimeter. Carlson proceeded to lead his Raiders on a month-long patrol behind enemy lines, guided by indigenous peoples and engaging the Japanese in true guerrilla fashion. The Second Raiders operated independently, surviving on supplies provided via airdrops and their indigenous guides. The Second Raiders had been specifically prepared for such a mission, and they performed as Carlson had promised. During their patrol, the Raiders engaged the Japanese on numerous occasions, gathering vital intelligence for the First Marine Division and disrupting Japanese movements. The Raiders killed 488 Japanese before finally returning to the American perimeter on 4 December. A total of sixteen Raiders were killed in action, with another eighteen wounded.[39]

The success of the First and Second Raider Battalions during the latter half of 1942 brought them considerable attention, leading General Holcomb to authorize the creation of two new Raider Battalions in the fall of 1942: the Third Raider Battalion under Lieutenant Colonel Harry Liversedge, and the Fourth Raider Battalion under Major James Roosevelt. The Raiders entered the second year of their existence without their namesake commanders. Edson had been promoted to command the Fifth Marines on Guadalcanal shortly after the defense of Edson's Ridge; command of the First Raiders passed to Edson's Executive Officer, Lieutenant Colonel Samuel Griffith. Carlson was hospitalized due to malaria in spring 1943 but soon thereafter was assigned to the Second Marine Division in its assault on Tarawa. He was replaced by Lieutenant Colonel Alan Shapely, a tough and thoroughly orthodox veteran who had misgivings about the Raider concept. The expansion of the Raiders and concurrent command changes brought about philosophy changes as well. The Raiders increasingly served as "a highly trained, lightly equipped force using conventional tactics to accomplish special missions or to fill in for a line battalion."[40] This represented a move away from the special operations role the Raiders were originally designed to fill as they evolved into a light infantry role. The Raiders often served as shock troops in situations where a warrior elite was needed to rise to the challenge of the day. The subtle transformation of the Raiders' mission was not unique to them or to the Marine Corps. Indeed, scholars of early special operations units have noted that almost without exception, special operations units—both American and British—underwent similar distortions of their original mission in the later years of the war.[41] The Marine Corps, however, already served as naval shock troops, meaning that the Raiders were quickly losing their distinctiveness.

All four of the Raider Battalions served with distinction in the New Georgia and Bougainville campaigns of 1943, helping the Allies climb the ladder toward the ultimate goal of Rabaul on New Britain. In June 1943, the Fourth Raider

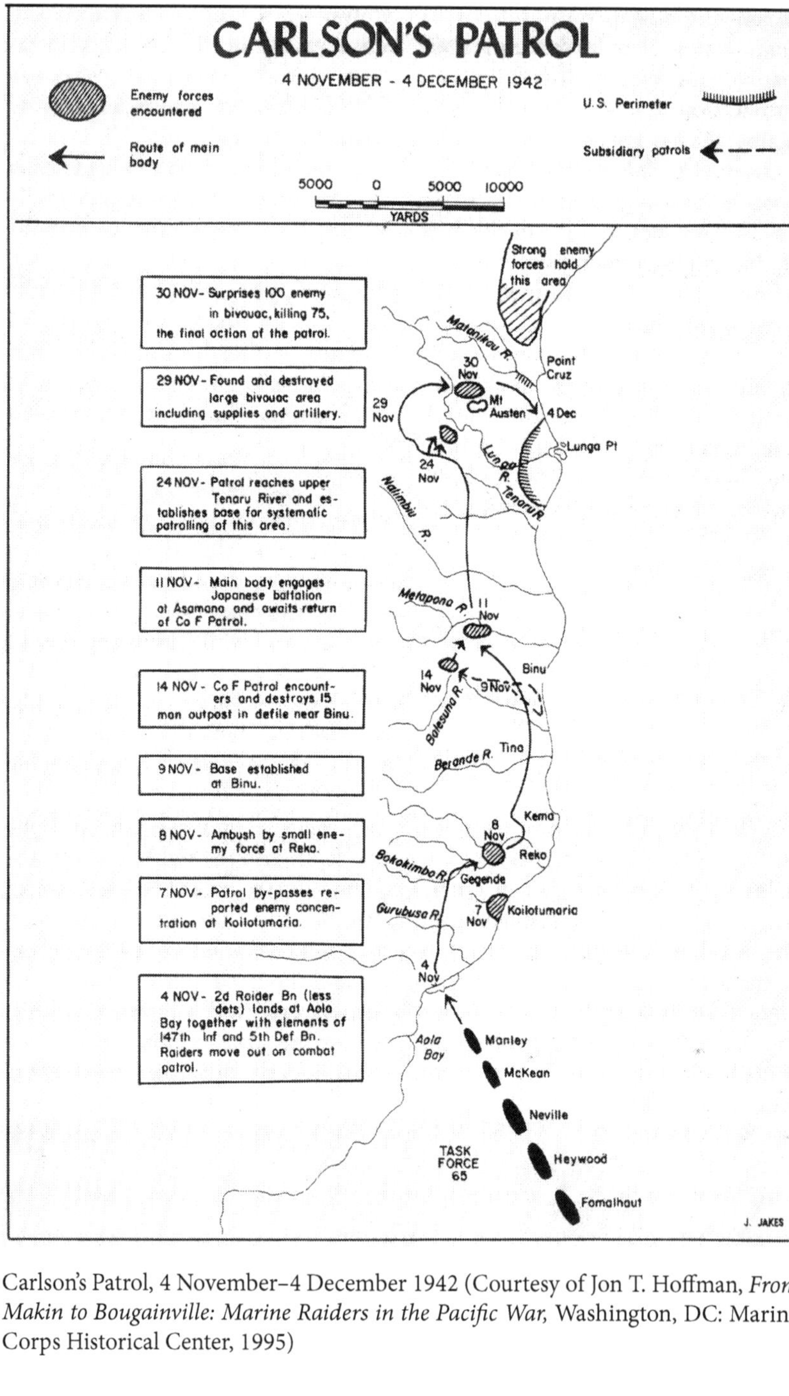

Carlson's Patrol, 4 November–4 December 1942 (Courtesy of Jon T. Hoffman, *From Makin to Bougainville: Marine Raiders in the Pacific War*, Washington, DC: Marine Corps Historical Center, 1995)

Battalion executed a forced march through swampy jungles previously considered impenetrable and was able to surprise and defeat the Japanese garrison at Viru Harbor on New Georgia. In July, the First Raiders duplicated that success on the north side of the island at Enogai Inlet. However, the limitations of the lightly armed Raider battalions were shown when the First and Fourth Raiders attacked nearby Bairoko Harbor. Lacking the element of surprise and faced with a well-prepared enemy behind substantial fortifications, the Raiders were forced back with heavy losses. The failure at Bairoko was a symptom both of the changing nature of the Pacific War and of the inherent limitations of special purpose troops. At the same time the Raiders were laying claim to their status as a subsct of warrior elites, they were drifting ever further afield from their original role as lightly armed, highly mobile troops. In November 1943, the Second and Third Raider Battalions served in the invasion of Bougainville. The Bougainville operation has been considered the "beginning of the end for the Raider organization," as the Raiders served essentially as standard Marine Corps infantry battalions throughout the campaign.[42]

On 1 February 1944, the Raider experiment came to an end. The four Raider Battalions were officially disbanded, and their personnel were used to re-form the Fourth Marines, the original unit having been forced into captivity at Bataan and Corregidor in the early days of the war. Thus, the earliest American foray into special forces in World War II did not even last the duration of the war, despite the accolades for their successes. The Fourth Marines, whose core cadre of former Raiders provided excellent leadership for incoming recruits, would go on to fight in some of the most brutal campaigns of the late war, including Guam and Okinawa, and would serve in the postwar occupation of Japan.[43] The pragmatic reasons behind the decision to disband the Raiders are straightforward. By 1944, the situation in the Central Pacific had changed substantially. The Allies were on the offensive across the Pacific, and with an ever-increasing array of firepower being brought to every campaign, the need for small hit-and-run units was dramatically lessened. Repeated Allied victories lessened the need for colorful commando outfits to bolster flagging morale. Furthermore, as they learned firsthand at Bairoko, using lightly armed Raiders for the siege warfare of the later Pacific War was akin to using "wide receivers as linemen just because a moment had arrived in the war where finesse was not needed."[44] The Raider Battalions, as originally constructed, were neither equipped nor intended to fight in a war of attrition.[45]

Analysis

The history of the Raiders, brief though it was, is worth a closer look for the commentary it can provide on the potential for conflict between subcultures, specifically when both subcultures emphasize narratives of exceptionalism and elitism. In the Raider experience of 1942–1944, it would seem that the two cultures shared an uncomfortable coexistence at the best of times. The end of the Raiders—indeed, the whole Raider experience—generated much emotion, ranging from devotion by former Raiders to resentment to jealousy by many in the larger body of the Marine Corps. As in any study of cultural forces, there are many interrelated themes that could be traced. However, three areas stand out as major points of contention between the subculture of the Raiders and the culture of the Marine Corps: perceptions of favoritism, biased publicity, and the implicit threat of disunity.

The seeds of jealousy against the Raiders were sown in their early days when the Raiders enjoyed favored status in almost every area. One of the foremost complaints leveled against the Raiders, as has been true of many other special operations units, was their co-opting of prime personnel at a time when they were desperately needed.[46] General Vandegrift recalled the difficulties caused to the fledgling First Marine Division in March 1942 when "Merritt Edson, armed with appropriate orders, arrived to comb our units for officers and men deemed suitable for his First Raider Battalion. . . . Edson's levy against our division, coming at such a critical time, annoyed the devil out of me, but there wasn't one earthly thing I could do about it."[47] The preferential treatment in personnel selection accorded to the Raiders in the opening months of the war hurt more than the pride of other unit commanders, as it compounded the already acute shortages of personnel faced throughout the Corps in the early days of the war.

Major General Charles Price faced a similar predicament when Evans Carlson began recruiting Raiders out of the already depleted ranks of Price's newly formed Second Marine Division. Price could do little except complain that "this commando business is a hobby with high authorities in our nation and Capt. James R. is the Executive of the Bn. [battalion]."[48] In this, he expressed an impression of Presidential favoritism that was commonly held among Marine Corps officers. The Second Raiders found that "having the President's son as our executive officer was a big help in procuring special arms and equipment," including the coveted and scarce M-1 Garand rifle.[49] As a whole, the Raider Battalions were armed with a disproportionate number of automatic weapons at a time when these weapons were in high demand throughout the Marine Corps. The Raiders also enjoyed "priority on equipment," frequently requesting and receiving items far afield of standard Marine Corps equipment—including customized uniforms, helmets, and footgear.[50] Edson's First Raiders were also not shy about custom-ordering weapons and equipment, including Boys antitank rifles specially ordered from Canada.[51] All four of the Raider Battalions enjoyed preferential selection of weapons and numerous items completely unique to the Raiders, including occasional weapons of personal choice and the famous Raider stiletto.[52] The almost unlimited access to specialized weapons and gear certainly made an impression throughout the rest of the Marine Corps, resulting in outlandish rumors—one officer matter-of-factly repeated a rumor that "As you know, Carlson had bows and arrows"—and widespread derision for the Raiders and their "Boy Scout equipment."[53]

Another area where the Raiders certainly seemed to receive preferential treatment was in publicity. The Raiders, similar to the British Commandos early in the war, served to bolster morale on the home front. Stories of their combat exploits were eagerly consumed by Americans desperate for any break from the dismal news of 1941–1942. The first official mention of the Raiders came in the Navy Department's press release on the Makin Island raid, which painted the Raiders as only a few degrees removed from supermen.[54] Such images were eagerly seized upon by the press.[55] In a time when special forces units and the British-Canadian commando raid on Dieppe dominated national headlines in America, Carlson's raid on Makin Atoll gave the press the opportunity to glamorize some American commandos.[56] The Makin raid generated a flurry of publicity, including feature spots and several front-page stories in the *New York Times* during the latter months of 1942. The fact that the President's son took part in the action garnered much attention.[57] The initial *New York Times* article boasted "Foe Belted on Isle . . . Atoll Is Left a Shambles," citing eighty enemy dead and few Raider losses.[58] A subsequent front-page story further enhanced the Raider image by embellishing the report. Now, "there were about 200 Japanese marines on the island," but by the time Carlson's Raiders were through, "there was not a Japanese to be found alive."[59]

The desperate actions of Edson's First Raiders made for their share of good copy as well, particularly their seizure of Tulagi and defense of Edson's Ridge.[60] However, nothing attracted public attention quite like Carlson and his Raiders. The media reveled in tales of Carlson's Raiders, whom they labeled "The Roughest and Toughest."[61] The *Saturday Evening Post* ran a two-part series on the Makin raid by Lieutenant Wilfred LeFrancois of the Second Raiders.[62] LeFrancois's account was so popular that it provided the inspiration for a Hollywood film. With General Holcomb's permission, Carlson himself served as an advisor to the film and heartily approved of the final release.[63] Starring popular leading man Randolph Scott as "Colonel Thorwald," a fictionalized Carlson figure, the movie *Gung Ho!* served as an excellent wartime morale booster, complete with a patriotic monologue from Scott.[64] Certainly not one of the better films to come out of wartime Hollywood, it was nevertheless favorably received at the time, with one critic writing that "the settings are true and the fighting on the island is as hot and lurid as any that we've seen."[65]

The Raiders status as media darlings did not sit well with many other Marines, men who were often living and fighting under the same conditions as the Raiders. The resentment became especially acute towards Carlson's battalion. Carlson's highly unorthodox methodology and his flair for publicity raised suspicions that he was building a personality cult, to the detriment of the Marine Corps at large.[66] Even some Raiders themselves realized that so much publicity was potentially unhealthy for the cohesion of the Marine Corps. As former First Raider Lee Minier noted, "There was too much publicity and false and exaggerated stories and movies being published about the Raiders . . . the Marine Corps doesn't like that sort of thing."[67] Though Minier had no way of knowing it, his analysis mirrored the Commandant's own thoughts on the Raiders.

During World War II, the Marine Corps carefully cultivated its image as America's aggressive, amphibious shock troops wresting control of the Pacific from Japan. However, the coverage of the Raiders tended to elevate their status as Raiders at the expense of the Marine Corps.[68] The idea of the press exalting select groups of Marines over the rest of the Corps did not sit well with Marine Corps leaders. Even before the Raiders had proven themselves in combat, they had been publicly equated with the British Commandos.[69] Such elevation of the Raiders as the proverbial cream of the crop in the public eye persisted in spite of General Holcomb's repeated insistence that "the United States already has a large and growing Commando force—the United States Marine Corps."[70] Holcomb was sincerely concerned that the glamour of the Raiders, with their special equipment and methods, and their abundance of flamboyant personalities, would come at the cost of the good image of the Marine Corps in its entirety.

His fears were not unfounded. In December 1943, *Fortune* magazine featured a thirteen-page article, "The Psychiatric Toll of Warfare," exploring the frequency of mental breakdown of troops in prolonged combat.[71] The author asserts that "psychiatrically, the American Dunkerque [*sic*] was Guadalcanal."[72] The tone and language employed in the article leaves a distinct impression of Vandegrift's First Marine Division as generally hapless, tired, and beyond hope of victory. They were allegedly prone to such psychological symptoms as "headaches, lower thresholds to sharp noises, periods of amnesia, of panic, psychosomatic complaints, generalized or limited tremors, functional palsies."[73] The supposedly weary, neurosis-prone Marine infantry contrasted rather unfavorably with Carlson's Raiders, who "were sent into battle psychologically prepared" and only suffered "one case of traumatic war neurosis" during their month-long trek behind enemy lines on Guadalcanal.[74] After praising Carlson and his methodology in glowing terms, the author upbraids the Marine Corps' leadership: "Despite the successes of Carlson's methods, no steps have since been taken to use them elsewhere in the Marine Corps, or in any other unit of the armed forces for that matter."[75] Taken as a whole, the article reflected badly on the Marine Corps, as it diminished the capability of the battle-tested veterans of Guadalcanal in order to extol the merits of the Raiders' psychological training. This, of course, did not sit well at all with the Commandant, who questioned the validity of the sources listed in an initial draft of the article.[76] Holcomb's complaints did elicit a response from the executive editor of *Fortune,* Albert L. Furth, but the final copy of the article appeared in the December issue without substantially incorporating Holcomb's objections.[77] It is impossible to escape the article's generally negative impression of Vandegrift's Marines when such phrases as "group neurosis," "lost hope," "expendable—doomed . . . tired—bone tired," were employed to describe them.[78] Meanwhile, Carlson comes across as a sort of modern George Washington, benevolent and wise, able to inspire his Raiders against overwhelming odds with his "proven qualities of leadership and with his respect for the dignity of man."[79]

The *Fortune* magazine incident serves as an example in the public press of the potential for discord that came along with the establishment of small, elite bands within a group that already operated as an elite. In the Raider Battalions, shaped as they were by their special operations designation, the ideal of elitism flourished as they rapidly moved along the path from guardsmen to technicians and finally to warrior elites. However, the evolution of the Raiders into a de facto elite of the elite threatened the unity of spirit that was essential to the "narrative of Marine Corps exceptionalism."[80] Former Raider officer Oscar Peatross proudly asserted many years later that the Raiders "became the 'greatest' because great leaders such as Edson, Carlson, Liversedge, Roosevelt, and many others nurtured in these men a spirit far transcending that implied by *esprit de corps*—a *gung ho* spirit, as it eventually came to be called, that inspired individuals to accept as standard a level of performance that elsewhere would have been termed 'outstanding' and marked them as unique among Marines."[81]

This emergence of a small but powerful subculture within the Marine Corps that asserted its own exceptionalism threatened to divide loyalties within an organization that depended on the power of its own culture far more than the larger military branches. As historian Aaron O'Connell aptly points out, Marine Corps culture was defined largely by a combination of potent narratives of Marine exceptionalism and rigorous policing of the boundaries between those who were and were not Marines. Marines, says O'Connell, "imagined themselves as a small and loyal tribe of warriors who were outnumbered, disrespected, and persecuted . . . [who] drew regularly on the language of religion, practices of extreme discipline, and intricately scripted rituals to mark themselves as different, separate, and superior to every other organization around them."[82] The Raiders, however, may have posed a tacit threat to the unity of

Marine Corps culture by injecting the possibility of divided loyalties. To have a small group of hand-picked personnel groomed to be the best warriors within an organization of proud warriors was perceived as an implicit questioning of Marine Corps exceptionalism.

Furthermore, singling out a group of warriors that was more elite and exalted than the remainder of the group undermined the efforts of the Marine Corps to instill the pride and esprit de corps throughout the service—which despite its wartime expansion, remained quite small compared to the other military institutions. The potential division of loyalties that was carried with the Raiders' special operations designation became a refrain of the critics of the Raider experiment, as evidenced by the opinions of many senior Marine Corps officers. Lieutenant Colonel Shapely, Carlson's replacement as commander of the Second Raiders, expressed a criticism commonly leveled against the Raiders: "a [Marine infantry] battalion or a regiment could do anything that a Raider battalion or Raider regiment could do. And further, you don't have a Marine Corps within the Marine Corps. The Marine Corps is too small for this."[83] Said Major General (later full General) Gerald Thomas, a future assistant CMC, "I don't believe that an outfit as good as the Marine Corps needs to build special organizations [i.e., Raiders]. Shock troops and special organizations are the device of declining power. When they can't build real formations, they start in and grab all the good men and put them in one outfit so they got somebody they know can fight. It's a losing game."[84] Major General Omar Pfeiffer expressed the concern felt by many in the Corps' leadership: "My thoughts were that we wanted to train every Marine to believe that he was *an elite;* and to have *an elite of the elite* was carrying things too far. To have [created more Raider battalions] would have emasculated orthodox fighting units."[85] Then–Lieutenant Colonel Lewis Puller, who would become arguably the most iconic Marine of all time, put it even more bluntly. When asked by Holcomb to weigh in on the Raider Battalions, Puller replied: "Nothing special about them, sir. They're just ordinary Marines, when they're good. No better than our good men in the ranks. There's too much guff about them, I mean too much Hollywood stuff. It isn't good for the Raiders, and it's mighty bad for the regular Marines. . . . The Raider idea should be abandoned."[86] Such was the mentality among many officers in positions of influence outside of the Raiders. The presence of such cultural tensions does not nullify the pragmatic rationales for abandoning the Raider experiment in early 1944, but these tensions certainly colored the judgment of many within the Marine Corps' leadership.

Though their initial existence was brief, barely two years total, the dynamics involved in their creation, their combat experiences, and their decline make the Raiders one of the more intriguing features of the Pacific War. While the Raiders shared similar frustrations with other emergent elite units of World War II, they offer a unique case of an elite subgroup within a larger elite institution. Viewing the Raiders in light of their impact on the larger culture of the Marine Corps lends a fresh insight into some of the institutional turmoil that accompanied the Marine Corps' earliest foray into the world of special forces. Though the experiment did not bring about the dramatic results its champions had hoped for, the Raiders nonetheless contributed more than their share to the American war effort in the Pacific and firmly established their place in the annals of Marine Corps history. But even more than their strategic, operational, and tactical significance, their dramatic entrance and quiet exit from the stage present a glimpse into the complex cultural dynamics attendant to the use of elite, special operations units within a larger military establishment.

Notes

This chapter would not have been possible without the support of numerous people. First and foremost, Hal Friedman encouraged me to pursue my interest in writing on the Marine Corps and helped me develop a background in the historiography of the Pacific War. Without Hal's early encouragement, guidance, and patience with extended deadlines, this would not have been possible. Thanks also to Dr. W. Robert Miller for introducing me to Hal. Dr. William Garrett Piston offered unflagging support throughout the research and writing process. Many others offered encouragement and guidance along the way. Dr. Rich DiNardo of the Marine Corps Command and Staff College helped me tremendously with advice on archival research and suggestions for studying military elites. David Ulbrich offered helpful comments on an early version of this project, and pointed me toward the best treatments of Evans F. Carlson. Annette Amerman was supremely helpful during my visit to the Historical Reference Branch, Marine Corps History Division. Martha Robertson and James Ginther of the Archives and Special Collections, Alfred M. Gray Research Center, both went above and beyond in their efforts to help me locate material. I am also grateful to Shannon Conlon and Deborah Williams at the Meyer Library, Missouri State University, and to Joy Boyer and Deborah Buesking at the Kendrick Library, Evangel University, for their assistance. Thanks also to the organizers of the 2014 Midwest Popular and American Culture Association Conference, at which an early version of this chapter was presented.

1. John W. Gordon, "The U.S. Marine Corps and an Experiment in Military Elitism: A Reassessment of the Special Warfare Impetus, 1937–1943," in Robert Love, ed., *Changing Interpretations and New Sources in Naval History: Papers from the Third United States History Symposium* (New York: Garland Publishers, 1980), 362.

2. As examples, see Edwin P. Hoyt, *The Marine Raiders* (New York: Pocket Books, 1989); and George W. Smith, *The Do-or-Die Men: The 1st Marine Raider Battalion at Guadalcanal* (New York: Pocket Books, 2003).

3. Some of the best scholarly treatments on the Raiders include Jon Hoffman, *From*

Makin to Bougainville: Marine Raiders in the Pacific War (Washington, DC: Marine Corps Historical Center, 1995); Joseph Alexander, *Edson's Raiders: The 1st Marine Raider Battalion in World War II* (Annapolis: Naval Institute Press, 2001); Hoffman, *Once a Legend: "Red Mike" Edson of the Marine Raiders* (Novato, CA: Presidio, 1994); John Wukovits, *American Commando: Evans Carlson, His WWII Marine Raiders, and America's First Special Forces Mission* (New York: NAL Caliber, 2009); and Davis Tyre Lovelady, "The Marine Corps' Third and Fourth Raider Battalions during World War II." (master's thesis, Texas Technological University, May 2002). Oscar Peatross's *Bless 'Em All: The Raider Marines of World War II* (Irvine, CA: ReView Publications, 1995) is also a valuable source, as it blends firsthand knowledge and considerable research, though it was not written to formal academic standards.

4. Andrew Hargreaves, *Special Operations in World War II: British and American Irregular Warfare* (Norman: University of Oklahoma Press, 2013) is a notable exception, though the Raiders do not figure prominently in his analysis. See also John Gordon's "U.S. Marine Corps and an Experiment in Military Elitism."

5. For more detailed discussion of the cultural tensions introduced by the Raider Battalions, see Stephen Houseknecht, "The Elite of the Elites—The U.S. Marine Raider Battalions, 1942–1944: A Case Study in Elite Military Organizations" (master's thesis, Missouri State University, 2015), 5.

6. See Colin Gray, *Explorations in Strategy* (Westport, CT: Praeger, 1996), James Kiras, *Special Operations and Strategy: From World War II to the War on Terrorism* (New York: Routledge, 2006); and Bernd Horn, "'Love 'Em or Hate 'Em': Learning to Live with Elites," *Canadian Military Journal* 8, no. 4 (Winter 2007–2008): 32–43.

7. Hargreaves, *Special Operations in World War II*, 6.

8. Kiras, *Special Operations and Strategy*, 6.

9. Eliot Cohen, *Commandos and Politicians* (Cambridge, MA: Center for International Affairs, Harvard University, 1978), 17.

10. Robert Sherrod, *Tarawa: The Story of a Battle* (New York: Duell, Sloan and Pearce, 1944), 35.

11. Allan Millett, *Semper Fidelis: The History of the United States Marine Corps*, rev. ed. (New York: Free Press, 1991), xvii.

12. Dennis Showalter, "The Evolution of the U.S. Marine Corps into a Military Elite in the Twentieth Century," *Marine Corps Gazette* 63 (November 1979): 44–58.

13. Ibid., 45–46.

14. Ibid., 54.

15. See Alexander, *Edson's Raiders*, 3–25; and Hoffman, *From Makin to Bougainville*, 1–5.

16. See "Gen. Holcomb Likens Marines to Commandos: Says Rigorous Training of Corps Prepares Men for Daring Amphibious Raids," *New York Herald Tribune*, 24 February 1942, attached to letter from G. A. Percy to Edson, 25 February 1942, Merritt Austin Edson Papers, Manuscript Division, Library of Congress, Washington, DC (hereafter cited as Edson Papers).

17. Joel Thacker, "The Marine Raiders in World War II," 2, Edson Papers; Alexander, *Edson's Raiders*, 27.

18. See David J. Ulbrich, *Preparing for Victory: Thomas Holcomb and the Making of the Modern Marine Corps, 1936–1943* (Annapolis: Naval Institute Press, 2011), 124–125; and Charles Updegraph, *Special Marine Corps Units of World War II* (Washington, DC: Headquarters, U.S. Marine Corps, History and Museums Division, 1977), 1–3.

19. The best portrait of Carlson is provided by Phyllis Zimmerman's "Military Missionary: The Riddle Wrapped in a Mystery inside an Enigma That Was Evans F. Carlson," in Randy Balano and Craig Symonds, eds., *New Interpretations in Naval History: Selected Papers from the Fourteenth Naval History Symposium* (Annapolis: Naval Institute Press, 2001), 251–263.

20. Updegraph, *Special Marine Corps Units of World War II*, 1.

21. Donovan to Franklin D. Roosevelt, 22 December 1941, facsimile reproduced in Robert Mattingly, *Herringbone Cloak—GI Dagger: Marines of the OSS* (Washington, DC: Headquarters, U.S. Marine Corps, History and Museums Division, 1989), Appendix B, 236.

22. King to Holcomb, 8 January 1942, facsimile reproduced in ibid., 237.

23. Holcomb to Samuel W. Meek, 19 January 1942, facsimile reproduced in ibid., 254. See also Millett, *Semper Fidelis*, 346–347.

24. Alexander, *Edson's Raiders*, 32.

25. Edson to Smith, 17 February 1942, "Personal Correspondence, 1940–1942," Box 4, Edson Papers.

26. Edson to Cates, 2 March 1942, "Col Edson Personal Letters (1 of 3)," Box 4, Edson Papers.

27. Peatross, *Bless 'Em All*, 11.

28. Holcomb to Price, 4 February 1942, "Correspondence, General, Jan–Feb 1942," Box 4, Thomas Holcomb Collection (hereafter cited as Holcomb Collection), Marine Corps Archives and Special Collections, Gray Research Center, Quantico, Virginia (hereafter cited as MCUA); Peatross, *Bless 'Em All*, 13.

29. Michael Blankfort, *The Big Yankee* (Boston, MA: Little, Brown and Co., 1947), 9; see also Peatross, *Bless 'Em All*, 13.

30. Carlson, quoted in Blankfort, *Big Yankee*, 12.

31. Carlson to Franklin D. Roosevelt, 2 March 1942, "Correspondence," Box 1, Evans Fordyce Carlson, Reference Branch, History Division, Quantico, Virginia.

32. Lee Minier to Jolette Minier, 23 February 1942, "Letters—Jan–Mar 1942," Lee N. Minier Collection (hereafter cited as Minier Collection), MCUA.

33. See Edson to M. L. Dawson, 21 January 1942, "Col. Edson Personal Letters (1 of 3)," Box 4, Edson Papers. W. P. McCahill, unpublished press release, 14 March 1942, "Personal Correspondence, 1940–1942," Box 4, Edson Papers, gives details as to the strenuous nature of physical training in Edson's battalion. Lee Minier describes the physical training in the First Raiders in Minier to Jolette Minier, 7 March 1942, "Letters—Jan–Mar 1942," Minier Collection, MCUA. John Apergis, a former First Raider who transferred into Carlson's Second Raiders, also described the strenuous physical training schedule of the Second Raiders in a letter to Edson: John Apergis to Edson, 19 February 1942, "Col. Edson Personal Letters (1 of 3)," Box 4, Edson Papers.

34. Edson to Smith, "Recommended Organization for a Battalion Embarked on Destroyer Transport," 8 February 1942, First Raider Battalion Unit File, MCUA.

35. Carlson to Holcomb, "General Information," 27 January 1943, Raiders: Second Marine Raider Battalion, Reference Branch, History Division, Quantico, Virginia.

36. Showalter, "Evolution of the U.S. Marine Corps," 46.

37. The following narrative is based on the above-mentioned Raider histories, as well as the authoritative works on the Solomon Islands campaigns: Richard B. Frank, *Guadalcanal: The Definitive Account of the Landmark Battle* (New York: Penguin Books, 1989); Brian Altobello, *Into the Shadows Furious: The Brutal Battle for New Georgia* (Novato, CA: Presidio, 2000); and Harry Gailey, *Bougainville, 1943–1945: The Forgotten Campaign* (Lexington: University Press of Kentucky, 1991).

38. The tragic story of these Raiders, as well as of the belated investigation to identify their remains, can be found in Tripp Wiles, *Forgotten Raiders of '42: The Fate of the Marines Left Behind on Makin* (Washington, DC: Potomac Books, 2007).

39. Hoffman, *From Makin to Bougainville*, 25.

40. Ibid.; see also Houseknecht, "Elite of the Elites," 147.

41. See Hargreaves, *Special Operations in World War II*, 187–192, and Colin Gray, *Explorations in Strategy*, 167: "In World War II, both the British and the U.S. armies, for example, focused on the elite combat capabilities rather than the special qualities of their raiding forces . . . elite-special forces units often find themselves assigned desperate jobs suitable to their warrior virtues, though not to their numbers, their firepower, or their ability to absorb high casualties."

42. Peatross, *Bless 'Em All*, 237.

43. See Kenneth Condit and Edwin Turnbladh, *Hold High the Torch: A History of the 4th Marines* (Washington, DC: Headquarters, U.S. Marine Corps, Historical Branch, 1960).

44. Peatross, *Bless 'Em All*, 237.

45. Millett, *Semper Fidelis*, 393, 404–406; Alexander, *Edson's Raiders*, 300–307; Hoffman, *From Makin to Bougainville*, 39–40.

46. The view that special units drain the best and brightest personnel away from the general service branches of a military organization was common throughout both the American and British militaries, as reflected by Field Marshal William Slim's admonition that "the result of these methods was undoubtedly to lower the quality of the rest of the army, especially of the infantry, not only by skimming the cream off it, but by encouraging the idea that certain of the normal operations of war were so difficult that only specially equipped *corps d'elite* could be expected to undertake them." Field Marshal Sir William Slim, *Defeat into Victory* (New York: David McKay Co., 1961), 455.

47. Alexander A. Vandegrift and Robert Asprey, *Once a Marine: The Memoirs of General A. A. Vandegrift, as Told to Robert Asprey* (New York: W. W. Norton Co., 1964), 100.

48. Price to Edson, 17 February 1942, "M. A. Edson 1940–42 Lt. Col.," Box 4, Edson Papers.

49. Peatross, *Bless 'Em All*, 15–16; Charles L. Banks, Oral History Interview Transcript, MCUA, 17.

50. John Apergis to Edson, 19 February 1942, "Col. Edson Personal Letters (1 of 3)," Box 4, Edson Papers.

51. E. M. Ransford to Edson, 20 March 1942, "Col. Edson Personal Letters (1 of 3)," Box 4, Edson Papers.

52. See R. G. Rosenquist, Martin J. Sexton, and Robert A. Buerlein, *Our Kind of War: The Illustrated Saga of the U.S. Marine Raiders of World War II* (Richmond, VA: American Historical Foundation, 1990), 163–185, for more details on the armament of the Raiders.

53. Victor H. Krulak, Oral History Interview Transcript, MCUA, 72; Alan Shapely, Oral History Interview Transcript, MCUA, 74.

54. Navy Department Press Release, 25 August 1942, "Reports of Raider Expedition," Box 2: October 1942–1984, Evans F. Carlson (hereafter cited as Carlson Collection), MCUA.

55. See "Marine Corps 'Raider' Battalions Employed in Solomons Offensive," *New York Times*, 26 August 1942.

56. See "Army Forms 2 Air-Borne Divisions and U.S.-Canadian 'Commandos,'" *New York Times*, 7 August 1942; "Raid Heroes Sing on Return Home" and "U.S. Rangers in Dieppe Raid Were Pupils of Commandos," *New York Times*, 20 August 1942; and "Dieppe Raid Assessed," *New York Times*, 21 August 1942.

57. See, e.g., "White House Hails Raid," *New York Times*, 22 August 1942; "President Rejects Japanese Gift Flag," *New York Times*, 18 September 1942.

58. "Foe Belted on Isle," *New York Times*, 22 August 1942.

59. Robert Trumbull, "Marines Wiped Out Japanese on Makin Isle in Hot Fighting," *New York Times*, 28 August 1942.

60. Charles Hurd, "Marines on Tulagi," *New York Times*, 11 August 1942; Robert C. Miller, "Tulagi Won in 48 Hours; T.N.T. Buried Foes in Caves," *New York Times*, 29 August 1942; Hanson W. Baldwin, "Solomons Action Develops Into Battle for South Pacific," *New York Times*, 27 September 1942; and William McKennan and Sidney Whipple, "The Battle of Bloody Hill," *Saturday Evening Post*, 20 February 1943.

61. F. Tillman Durdin, "The Roughest and Toughest," *New York Times Magazine*, 8 November 1942.

62. Wilfred LeFrancois, "We Mopped Up Makin Island," Parts I and II, *Saturday Evening Post*, 4 December 1943 and 11 December 1943.

63. Holcomb to Carlson, "Correspondence—3 July 1943 Memorandums," Box 1: 1927–Aug. 1942, Carlson Collection; Matthew Bernstein, *Walter Wanger: Hollywood Independent* (Berkeley: University of California Press, 1994), 192.

64. Bernstein, *Walter Wanger*, 192.

65. Bosley Crowther, "'*Gung Ho!*' a Lurid Action Film about the Makin Island Raid, with Randolph Scott, Opens at the Criterion Theatre," *New York Times*, 22 January 1944.

66. Carlson fashioned his battalion on his signature "gung ho" method, a combination of his native Yankee individualism, the New Deal optimism and liberalism of his hero Franklin D. Roosevelt, and the egalitarianism he observed among the Chinese Communists in prewar China. For more on this unique Marine, see Zimmerman's "Military Missionary" and Wukovits's *American Commando*, passim.

67. Minier to Jolette Minier, 20 February 1944, "Letters—January–March 1944," Minier Collection, MCUA.

68. Ulbrich, *Preparing for Victory*, 124.

69. A. J. Drexel Biddle to Edson, 2 March 1942, "Col. Edson Personal Letters (1 of 3)," Box 4, Edson Papers.

70. "Gen. Holcomb Likens Marines to Commandos," newspaper clipping, "Col. Edson Personal Letters (1 of 3)," Box 4, Edson Papers.

71. "The Psychiatric Toll of Warfare," *Fortune* 28, no. 6 (December 1943).

72. Ibid., 278.

73. Ibid.

74. Ibid., 280.

75. Ibid.

76. See Mia M. Fritsch to Holcomb, 25 October 1943, "Aug–Oct 1943," Box 6, Holcomb Collection, MCUA.

77. Albert L. Furth to Holcomb, 9 November 1943, "Correspondence—Other," Box 1: 1927–Aug. 1942, Carlson Collection, MCUA.

78. "Psychiatric Toll," 278.

79. Ibid., 282.

80. Aaron O'Connell, "'A Harsh and Spiritual Unity': A New Look at Culture and Battle in the Marine Corps' Pacific War," *International Journal of Naval History* 7, no. 3 (December 2008): 3.

81. Peatross, *Bless 'Em All*, 295.

82. Aaron O'Connell, *Underdogs: The Making of the Modern Marine Corps* (Cambridge, MA: Harvard University Press, 2012): 6. O'Connell offers the best cultural history of the Marine Corps thus far, capturing the nature and effects of the narratives of Marine Corps exceptionalism. As he puts it, "Running through nearly every artifact of Marine Corps culture in this era were regular, almost compulsive affirmations of the Marines' inherent superiority over everyone else, coupled with a wariness of outsiders that bordered on paranoia." Ibid.

83. Shapley, Oral History Interview Transcript, MCUA, 82.

84. Gerald C. Thomas, Oral History Interview Transcript, MCUA, 235.

85. Omar T. Pfeiffer, Oral History Interview Transcript, MCUA, 194 (emphasis in original).

86. Quoted in Burke Davis, *Marine! The Life of Chesty Puller* (New York: Bantam Books, 1962), 162.

Bibliography

Primary Sources

Archives

Library of Congress, Manuscript Division, Washington, DC
Merritt Austin Edson Papers

Marine Corps University, History Division, Quantico, Virginia
Reference Branch Files
Evans Fordyce Carlson
Raiders: Second Marine Raider Battalion
Marine Corps University, Archives and Special Collections, Gray Research Center, Quantico, Virginia
Evans F. Carlson Collection
First Raider Battalion Unit File
Thomas Holcomb Collection
Lee N. Minier Collection
Oral History Interview Transcripts
Charles L. Banks
Victor H. Krulak
Omar T. Pfeiffer
Alan Shapely
Gerald C. Thomas

Magazines

Durdin, F. Tillman. "The Roughest and Toughest." *New York Times Magazine,* 8 November 1942.

LeFrancois, Wilfred. "We Mopped Up Makin Island: Part I." *Saturday Evening Post,* 4 December 1943.

———. "We Mopped Up Makin Island: Part II." *Saturday Evening Post,* 11 December 1943.

McKennan, William, and Sidney Whipple. "The Battle of Bloody Hill." *Saturday Evening Post,* 20 February 1943.

"The Psychiatric Toll of Warfare." *Fortune* 28, no. 6 (December 1943).

Memoirs and Other Published Primary Sources

Mattingly, Robert. *Herringbone Cloak—GI Dagger: Marines of the OSS.* Appendix B, 236–301. Washington, DC: Headquarters, U.S. Marine Corps, History and Museums Division, 1989.

Sherrod, Robert. *Tarawa: The Story of a Battle.* New York: Duell, Sloan and Pearce, 1944.

Vandegrift, Alexander A., and Robert Asprey. *Once a Marine: The Memoirs of General A. A. Vandegrift, as Told to Robert Asprey.* New York: W. W. Norton Co., 1964.

Secondary Sources

Theses

Houseknecht, Stephen. "The Elite of the Elites—The U.S. Marine Raider Battalions, 1942–1944: A Case Study in Elite Military Organizations." Master's thesis, Missouri State University, 2015.

Lovelady, Davis Tyre. "The Marine Corps' Third and Fourth Raider Battalions during World War II." Master's thesis, Texas Technological University, May 2002.

Books

Alexander, Joseph. *Edson's Raiders: The 1st Marine Raider Battalion in World War II.* Annapolis: Naval Institute Press, 2001.

Altobello, Brian. *Into the Shadows Furious: The Brutal Battle for New Georgia.* Novato, CA: Presidio, 2000.

Bernstein, Matthew. *Walter Wanger: Hollywood Independent.* Berkeley: University of California Press, 1994.

Blankfort, Michael. *The Big Yankee.* Boston: Little, Brown and Co., 1947.

Cohen, Eliot. *Commandos and Politicians.* Cambridge, MA: Center for International Affairs, Harvard University, 1978.

Davis, Burke. *Marine! The Life of Chesty Puller.* New York: Bantam Books, 1962.

Frank, Richard B. *Guadalcanal: The Definitive Account of the Landmark Battle.* New York: Penguin Books, 1989.

Gailey, Harry. *Bougainville, 1943–1945: The Forgotten Campaign.* Lexington: University Press of Kentucky, 1991.

Gray, Colin. *Explorations in Strategy.* Westport, CT: Praeger, 1996.

Hargreaves, Andrew. *Special Operations in World War II: British and American Irregular Warfare.* Norman: University of Oklahoma Press, 2013.

Hoffman, Jon. *Once a Legend: "Red Mike" Edson of the Marine Raiders.* Novato, CA: Presidio, 1994.

Hoyt, Edwin P. *The Marine Raiders.* New York: Pocket Books, 1989.

Kiras, James. *Special Operations and Strategy: From World War II to the War on Terrorism.* New York: Routledge, 2006.

Millett, Allan R. *Semper Fidelis: The History of the United States Marine Corps.* Rev. ed. New York: Free Press, 1991.

O'Connell, Aaron. *Underdogs: The Making of the Modern Marine Corps.* Cambridge, MA: Harvard University Press, 2012.

Peatross, Oscar. *Bless 'Em All: The Raider Marines of World War II.* Irvine, CA: ReView Publications, 1995.

Rosenquist, R. G., Martin J. Sexton, and Robert A. Buerlein. *Our Kind of War: The Illustrated Saga of the U.S. Marine Raiders of World War II.* Richmond, VA: American Historical Foundation, 1990.

Slim, Field Marshal Sir William. *Defeat into Victory.* New York: David McKay Co., 1961.

Smith, George W. *The Do-or-Die Men: The 1st Marine Raider Battalion at Guadalcanal.* New York: Pocket Books, 2003.

Ulbrich, David J. *Preparing for Victory: Thomas Holcomb and the Making of the Modern Marine Corps, 1936–1943.* Annapolis: Naval Institute Press, 2011.

Wiles, Tripp. *Forgotten Raiders of '42: The Fate of the Marine Left Behind on Makin.* Washington, DC: Potomac Books, 2007.

Wukovits, John. *American Commando: Evans Carlson, His WWII Marine Raiders, and America's First Special Forces Mission.* New York: NAL Caliber, 2009.

Official Histories

Condit, Kenneth, and Edwin Turnbladh. *Hold High the Torch: A History of the 4th Marines.* Washington, DC: Headquarters, U.S. Marine Corps, Historical Branch, 1960.

Hoffman, Jon. *From Makin to Bougainville: Marine Raiders in the Pacific War.* Washington, DC: Marine Corps Historical Center, 1995.

Updegraph, Charles. *Special Marine Corps Units of World War II.* Washington, DC: Headquarters, U.S. Marine Corps, History and Museums Division, 1977.

Articles

Gordon, John W. "The U.S. Marine Corps and an Experiment in Military Elitism: A Reassessment of the Special Warfare Impetus, 1937–1943." In Robert Love, ed., *Changing Interpretations and New Sources in Naval History: Papers from the Third United States Naval Academy History Symposium,* 362–373. New York: Garland Publishers, 1980.

Horn, Bernd. "'Love 'Em or Hate 'Em': Learning to Live with Elites." *Canadian Military Journal* 8, no. 4 (Winter 2007–2008): 32–43.

O'Connell, Aaron. "'A Harsh and Spiritual Unity': A New Look at Culture and Battle in the Marine Corps' Pacific War." *International Journal of Naval History* 7, no. 3 (December 2008): 1–60.

Showalter, Dennis. "The Evolution of the U.S. Marine Corps into a Military Elite in the Twentieth Century." *Marine Corps Gazette* 63 (November 1979): 44–58.

Zimmerman, Phyllis. "Military Missionary: The Riddle Wrapped in a Mystery inside an Enigma that Was Evans F. Carlson." In Randy Balano and Craig Symonds, eds., *New Interpretations in Naval History: Selected Papers from the Fourteenth Naval History Symposium,* 251–264. Annapolis: Naval Institute Press, 2001.

4

Yams, Rice, and Soda

Food and the U.S. Navy on Pohnpei, 1945–1951

Josh Levy

In the fall of 1945, the bombs over Japan's Western Pacific territory had fallen silent, but the food war continued. On Pohnpei, a high volcanic island 1,600 miles to the southeast of Guam, a small contingent of American sailors took charge of nearly 7,800 Japanese military personnel and 6,000 Japanese civilians. All of them, both military and civilians, would be repatriated to Japan before Christmas. But in the meantime, as these two militaries shared Pohnpei with its population of more than 5,000 islanders, soldiers and sailors quietly feuded over a subject whose history in the Pacific ran deep: the meaning of a gift of food. Pohnpei was spared a direct land invasion during the war, but it had seen daily aerial bombings and punishing food shortages. Once the battles were lost, American planes swapped their bombs for airdrops of tobacco, chocolate, and candy. But Pohnpei's Japanese military command refused to surrender its pride, ordering hungry soldiers to gather up the boxes and deliver them to headquarters for safekeeping.[1]

Over the next several months, as a small contingent of American sailors took charge of operations on the island, military personnel from both sides clashed and commiserated over food. Japanese and Americans offered one another the understanding that comes with shared experience, as when American officers congratulated Japanese civilian officials for their discipline and skill in managing Pohnpei's food stores during the war.[2] But Japanese soldiers also loftily refused American offers of California rice, condiments, and canned foods, citing their "Bushido spirit" and leaving American sailors to complain about having to eat it themselves. When some of that rice ended up in the hands of islanders instead, soldiers like Takehiko Akita accepted it gratefully, seeing in the regifted rice a sign that the affinity between colonizer and colonized so heralded in Japan's nationalist rhetoric was still intact after the trauma of war.[3] Even after Pohnpei's last Japanese residents crossed over its reef, food retained this pivotal role in framing the island's military governance. Pohnpeians continued to use food as a tool to define their political relationships and social identities as they had for centuries, and swiftly drew American military personnel into the logic of their own food politics.

Oral histories of Pacific Islanders who lived through World War II and its aftermath are replete with memories of food: the hunger and deprivation of wartime, the forced agricultural labor, and the revelatory liberation of a full plate after the guns finally fell silent.[4] The image of Americans bearing food so abundant that, in the Marshalls, it cast them as "the parallel of traditional conquerors writ large" is pervasive in written histories of the war as well.[5] An early historical account penned by an American in 1947, for instance, confidently predicted that islanders' "full stomachs and healthy bodies" had laid the foundation for America's future administrative success.[6] But on bypassed islands like Pohnpei the story was never quite so clear-cut, if indeed it was anywhere.

American personnel landed peacefully and relatively quietly on Pohnpei, arriving in small numbers and without the supplies that accompanied them to Kwajalein, Peleliu, or the sites of Melanesia's "cargo cults." Thus, Pohnpei offers an opportunity to consider military gifts of food on an island where gifts were few and often contested, where American sailors imbued food and nutrition with their own anxieties over race and modernity, and where military planners moved to assert control over imports in hopes of shielding the region from subversive foreign influence. Pohnpeians and American sailors encountered one another through food throughout the Navy's awkward transition from military occupier to civil administrator, and the six years of this transition were as critical in setting the stage for the region's future governance as were the dramatic land invasions that laid different foundations elsewhere.

Prehistories of Food and Power

Pohnpei's system of traditional leadership has its origins in the early eighteenth century, when a warrior named Isokelekel overthrew the island's ruling dynasty and split it into paramount chiefdoms (*wehi*). By the late nineteenth century, Pohnpei was divided into five of these *wehi,* each of them autonomous from the others and ruled by two parallel lines of titled chiefs. The *nahnmwarki,* head of the first line, owned all of the land in his *wehi* and everything it produced.[7] He entrusted this land to chiefs of local sections (*kousapw*), who in turn entrusted it to common people. In practice, commoners rarely had their farmsteads confiscated. But they did mark their gratitude for the use of their land and the *nahnmwarki's* divine ability to make it productive with an elaborate complex of tribute feasting. Relationships between the people, their chiefs, and their land were thus

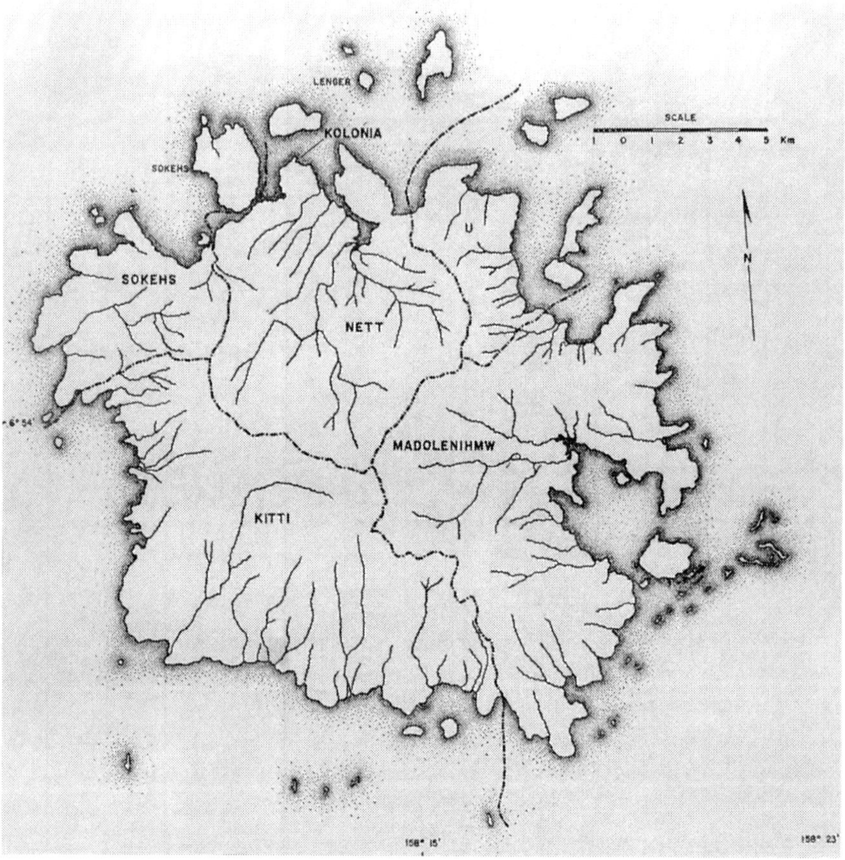

The Five *Wehi* (Paramount Chiefdoms) of Pohnpei, with Kolonia Town at the Island's North (Saul Riesenberg, *Native Polity of Ponape*, Smithsonian Institution, 1968)

formalized through highly ritualized feasts known as *kamadipw.* These feasts were the island's most critical venues for recognizing and conferring the traditional titles that constituted the lifeblood of Pohnpeian social identities.

Titles could be granted in appreciation for *tautik* (little work), typically short bursts of action such as bravery in battle. They could also be had for *taulap* (great work), which included "direct labor and all expressions of obedience, etiquette, and deference."[8] As traditional warfare waned and then ceased under German and Japanese rule, *taulap* became the more viable route to prestige. Its most visible manifestation was as *nohpwei,* the offering of the first fruits of the harvest to the *nahnmwarki.* First-fruits offerings that demonstrated exceptional agricultural skill could then result in the presentation of a title. The value of prestige crops like yams or pit breadfruit was so powerful as to make the daily consumption of those crops unworkable for ambitious Pohnpeians. Some families even went hungry with harvestable high-status crops growing on their farms.[9] Thus, a separate subsistence economy emerged alongside the island's prestige economy, in which families relied on lower-status crops like bananas or fresh breadfruit for daily consumption. Men and women participated in each of these economies, performing "equivalent, complementary, and interdependent" roles.[10]

A commercial economy also gathered influence on the island beginning in the 1830s, when Pohnpei was incorporated into the Pacific whaling trade. Just as *nahnmwarkis* exercised certain rights over the island's crops, they now asserted control over its trade goods as well. At first, the most popular trade items were firearms, metal tools, and cloth, and the flow of food was mostly outward, toward hungry sailors. But when the copra trade reached the island in the 1870s, imported foods began to cross Pohnpei's reef more regularly.[11] Most of those foods entered the subsistence economy, freeing up land and labor for prestige competition. But the pigs left behind by traders and whalers swiftly attained a prominent role in the prestige economy, becoming a constant companion to the families who raised them and a fixture of the *kamadipw*.[12]

Colonial regimes recognized that the land and its products laid the foundation for the power of Pohnpei's traditional leaders and adopted various strategies to undercut their influence. After the strategy of direct military confrontation under the island's Spanish occupation (1886–1898) failed, the German regime (1898–1914) pursued a transformative package of land reforms instead. Those reforms suddenly became viable when German military forces defeated a rebellion in the *wehi* of Sokehs in 1911. By 1912, traditional leaders had agreed to strip *nahnmwarkis* of their ability to evict commoners from their land. They also agreed to deed land to individual families, reduce the number of "unproductive feasts," and institute a shift from matrilineal to patrilineal inheritance. Most of the 1912 reforms garnered enough popular support to keep traditional leaders from demanding their repeal, even under Japanese rule (1914–1945).[13] But *nahnmwarkis* did lean more heavily on their ability to award titles to maintain their influence, and traditional titles maintained their centrality within Pohnpeian society.[14]

Whereas Spain aimed to assert military control over Pohnpei and Germany sought to transform it into a center for copra production, or at least a permanent home for outer islanders, whose atolls they hoped to convert into plantations, Japan embarked on a full-scale program of settler colonization. By the end of the 1930s an influx of settlers from Japan, Okinawa, and Korea had surpassed Pohnpei's indigenous population. Those settlers built towns and established businesses that offered new moneymaking opportunities for the islanders and spurred a rapid expansion of the island's commercial economy. Pohnpeians and the growing communities of resident outer islanders now had access to a wide range of products imported from Japan and sold in local stores. High-status Pohnpeians, including Henry and Oliver Nanpei, the patriarch and scion of the island's wealthiest family, adopted some of these foreign goods, thereby heightening the prestige value of certain imports.[15] Even so, none of the imported foods upon which Japanese settlers became so "curiously and obsessively dependent" were welcomed into the island's prestige economy in the way pigs had once been.[16]

While Japan increased the number of allowable tribute feasts on the island, it consistently worked to sideline traditional leaders. It replaced troublesome chiefs with government loyalists, appointed Japanese officials to rural areas and outer islands, and struck at *nahnmwarkis'* access to land. The deepest cut was the regime's seizure of the land in each *wehi* not previously apportioned to individual families during the German land reform, and unrest over the ownership of the remainder of the *wehi* persisted well into the island's American occupation (1945–1979).[17] Once the Pacific War arrived in earnest, however, challenges to Pohnpei's food and political systems mounted. With an influx of Japanese military personnel, imports reduced to a trickle; and once regular American bombings started in 1943, islanders found themselves subject to seizures of food and land and were pressed into labor for war preparations. Tribute and feasting were banned outright, and in many cases chiefs could offer their people little more than moral support.[18] It was into this thicket of meaning that American sailors arrived in 1945, looking healthy and well-nourished and bearing gifts of food.

Naval Economies on Pohnpei

The three to four dozen American sailors detached to Pohnpei carried with them a vague but potent rhetoric of liberation, a bundle of racialized assumptions about the Pacific, and an official policy rooted in anxiety over Micronesia's role in the emerging Cold War world. Pohnpeians took American pronouncements of freedom seriously, returning to their farms to reinvigorate the island's subsistence and prestige economies and refusing any government work orders that lacked a clear long-term benefit to their communities. Meanwhile, the American personnel they encountered were reading them through a powerful haze of literary, artistic, and filmic representations of Oceania. Sailors regarded the islands either as stepping-stones to the East or, in the words of one observer, as "ends-of-the-earth, cultural limit-cases unencumbered by notions of sin, antitheses to the industrial worlds of economic and political modernity," and they frequently compared islanders to the racial minorities already familiar to them.[19]

Official policy seemed to build on these assumptions, calling for a program of "cultural security" intended to reconstruct Japan's war-ravaged island territory as a culturally isolated, strategic buffer zone politically and culturally coupled to the United States and assisting in defense against hostile powers to the west. Thus, as Hal Friedman suggests, islanders' racial composition, political leanings, cultural values, language use, consumer habits, and food preferences took on an unlikely geopolitical urgency.[20]

Sailors swiftly erected a small base at the heart of the devastated Japanese settlement at Kolonia Town and began to rid the island of all visible Japanese influence. Some 6,000 civilians and 7,800 military personnel were repatriated to Japan by the end of 1945, splitting apart families and leaving Kolonia a virtual ghost town. The Navy removed all of the island's yen from circulation, allowing Pohnpeians to exchange their cash for dollars at unfavorable rates and erasing a great deal of Pohnpeian wealth in the process.[21] Sailors destroyed leftover Japanese ammunition and encouraged Pohnpeians to dismantle Japanese buildings for construction supplies. The Navy closed the territory to foreign merchants and laborers, dramatically restricting the flow of imports.[22] Meanwhile, the "gratuitous issues" of food and other supplies so visible elsewhere were few are far between on Pohnpei. Shortages mounted, moneymaking opportunities were few, and the island's store shelves sat bare for much of 1945 and 1946 as military planners warned against the danger of "spoiling" islanders with too much generosity.[23]

At times, naval officers deepened tensions by lobbing attacks at traditional leaders, treating Pohnpeians as a conquered population, and appearing stingy in their interactions with islanders. Accounts of various slights circulated through the island: officials publicly urging Pohnpeians not to "waste" their food in feast presentations; administrators who meted out arbitrary punishments for minor offenses; and the repeated snubbing of Oliver Nanpei by Lieutenant Joseph Louchheim, who anthropologist John Embree asserted was "by far the worst specimen of military government officer it has been my misfortune to meet."[24] Enlisted men, meanwhile, stirred controversy as they strolled about shirtless or drunk, used obscene language, and pursued sexual liaisons with local women.[25] Anthropologist Edward Hall suggested that some of these conflicts stemmed from military culture, whereby "old military men" found themselves more at ease with enemy soldiers than civilian allies.[26] Some of these tensions eased over time, as American operations grew more established and, in 1947, the territory transitioned from military government to civil administration under the authority of the Trust Territory of the Pacific Islands (TTPI). American personnel then promoted some form of self-government more explicitly, at least to the extent that American strategic interests were unimpeded.

Even so, generosity remained a centrally important attribute of leadership on Pohnpei, and one the American regime repeatedly failed to model. Joseph Iriarte, an influential traditional leader from the *wehi* of Nett, argued in 1947 that American parsimoniousness was damaging the regime's standing on Pohnpei. Germany had once treated traditional leaders to lavish feasts on the Kaiser's birthday and relaxed drinking restrictions during the festivities, a pattern Japan later replicated in its own festivals. Yet Americans not only attempted to ban feasting altogether but repeatedly breached Pohnpeian etiquette in smaller ways, as when the regime sold hot dogs during sporting events rather than giving them away. Iriarte believed Pohnpeians were taking note of these small affronts and contrasting them with the military's generosity on other islands, judging the Americans less favorably than their previous colonizers as a result.[27]

Of course American personnel were aware that Pohnpeians preferred to receive goods for free, at least on symbolic occasions. But in the midst of the military's postwar demobilization, Americans envisioned themselves as hands-off caretakers tasked with restoring the islands to basic self-sufficiency, and doing so as economically as possible. When the United States Commercial Company (USCC) entered Pohnpei in 1945, officials charged it with promoting self-sufficiency, preventing dependence on imported goods, and shielding islanders from exploitation by foreign economic interests.[28] The USCC aimed to move from giveaways to the sale of trade goods as swiftly as practicable. But imported goods were believed to possess powers of their own, such as to inculcate islanders with the modern economic values American personnel assumed they lacked and to impress them with the quality of American products. Still, in its first years on Pohnpei, the USCC managed only to clean and replant the old Japanese agricultural station, make a few purchases of local produce for use in the Navy mess, and open a single retail store.[29] An anthropologist who visited the store in 1946 found a meager selection of goods and noted that they were illogically priced and of low quality.[30]

Where the Navy's faith in American capitalism most clashed with its paternalism was in its insistence that Pohnpeians should only be able to purchase basic necessities from island stores. Committed to rebuilding a stripped-down version of the island's moribund commercial economy and yet suspicious of islanders' ability to be truly modern, officials warned against introducing an "overdose of civilization" to the region.[31] The Navy happily included American staple foods in its standardized inventory lists. Yet officials also waxed poetic over the corrupting but ultimately unstoppable ability of products like Coca-Cola to "change native life."[32] One American doctor expressed horror that USCC stores on Saipan were selling Pepsi, insisting that, "there is no doubt that some of the natives, if not most of them, will purchase Pepsi-Cola instead of food."[33]

An anthropologist visiting Yap in 1946 likewise complained of the "arbitrary and vicarious" cancellations of orders made by Yapese customers, and of the USCC staffers who abruptly asserted, "Natives don't need goods."[34]

Better-connected Pohnpeians found ways to circumvent these restrictions, which often appeared to stem from American anxieties over the "evils" of foreign rule. Rear Admiral Carleton Wright, Deputy High Commissioner of the TTPI, for instance, declared in 1947 that more intensively colonized islands like Guam had become "at best only a poor imitation of the Anglo-Saxon and Hispanic civilizations." He therefore enjoined the United States to pursue a slow-paced, limited program of reform in the Trust Territory, with imports strictly limited to basic necessities.[35] Accordingly, in 1948, therefore, Joseph Iriarte was forced to write to anthropologist Saul Riesenberg for a shipment of seeds, as Western-style vegetables were no longer available anywhere on the island.[36] Over the next several years, Riesenberg sent Iriarte a steady stream of gifts from the United States, including children's clothes and blankets, catalogs, books, and other items.[37] Other Pohnpeians relied on mail-order catalogs to circumvent import restrictions, and by the end of the 1940s the Trust Territory saw $300,000 in imports from catalog orders alone.[38]

As the regime worked to erase non-American foreign influences from Pohnpei and maintain its control over imports, the enduring demand for Japanese goods on the island rankled. Prior to the war, rice was among the imports best integrated into Pohnpei's subsistence economy, and rice consumption was vital to maintaining the ethnic and national identities of its Japanese settlers.[39] The Navy did not object to including rice on its inventory lists, but did insist on sourcing the rice from the United States. An official in the Island Trading Company (ITC), which took over USCC operations in the Trust Territory in 1947, praised the "high standards demanded by the Navy" in purchasing, but blamed local resistance to American rice on islanders themselves. "The natives," he claimed, "have never been used to anything superior to a grade equivalent to about a US #4 (Choice) . . . consequently the high price demanded for Navy rice was not understood and the quality never appreciated."[40] Yet the island's minor consumer revolt spoke for itself: unhappy customers meant bad business.

By 1948, the Navy was forced to concede that islanders had the right to decide their own purchases, rice included, and to recognize that Micronesia's blood ties to Japan would not be severed by government action.[41] By 1950, with Pohnpei's commercial economy still far smaller than its prewar state but finally at equilibrium, the ITC was sourcing more than 20 percent of its imports from Japan.[42] The following year, when the Navy handed over control of the Trust Territory to the Interior Department, the ITC had so abandoned the cultural security approach as to secure an import partnership with NBK, the Japanese firm that had held a near-monopoly on the territory's prewar trade.[43] Still, islanders agitated for greater access to Japanese goods well into the 1950s. Enerico Mallarme of Nett, for example, petitioned the United Nations to open "free trading channels between Japan and the Trust Territory" in 1953, arguing subversively that the widespread poverty of American-controlled Pohnpei made cheaper Japanese goods indispensable.[44] Nevertheless, cultural security had had its effects, having reshaped the TTPI's racial composition, reshuffled its economic infrastructure, and left a lasting first impression of American rule that would prove difficult to shake.

Health, Modernity, and the Pohnpeian Body

As with its economic development programs, the Navy's health-care initiatives were primarily restorative. Americans aimed to reconstruct islander bodies to a state untouched by the malnutrition and infectious disease that so marked Pohnpei's wartime suffering. Once fighting stopped and the island was made food secure, naval doctors focused almost entirely on infectious disease and gave little thought to conditions that became visible only decades later: diabetes, hypertension, heart disease, and obesity. But doctors and military personnel alike were concerned with modernity's impacts on islander bodies, and with the consequences too close an association with islanders and their environment might have on their own. As Donald Rubinstein suggests, postwar American health policy was grounded in the assumption that islanders were "inherently soft populations, vulnerable to the diseases of the Europeans, and doomed because of a psychological inability to adapt to contact with a superior civilization."[45] But Americans were nearly as concerned for themselves, both for the illnesses they feared might result from their time in the islands and, to a lesser degree, for the consequences of their own consumption of canned and processed foods.

Pohnpei's first hospital was built in 1922, under Japanese rule. A staff of doctors, nurses, and pharmacists had set out to combat depopulation, supposedly the most critical issue facing islanders at the time. Health officials urged Pohnpeians to part with traditional practices they judged unclean and transition to a modern, Japanese lifestyle.[46] The Japanese regime therefore enforced a raft of sanitation regulations, built model homes for Pohnpeians to imitate, and pressured islanders to wear Western-style clothing.[47] As Pohnpei's Japanese and Okinawan populations grew, however, the island's health-care infrastructure increasingly became oriented toward serving settlers. Islanders still received medical treatment, but the regime now worked primarily to protect settlers from Pohnpeian disease. During wartime, priorities shifted toward providing soldiers with basic medical care, and islanders' health-care needs were largely ignored.[48]

Meanwhile, the U.S. Navy was directing its health officials in the Pacific to "protect military personnel by care of the health and well-being of the civilian population."[49] The Navy was particularly concerned with infectious disease and parasites in the islands, and attributed both to Micronesia's "primitive" sanitation conditions. One report warned of intestinal diseases resulting from "unhygienic water supplies, primitive sewage disposal, contaminated soil, and the generally low plane of personal hygiene" and cautioned military personnel to regard all meats, fruits, and vegetables as unsafe without an American-supervised inspection, "especially those handled by natives."[50] But once the war was won, American personnel began to assert that "beneficent" American rule, economic development, health care, and education would eliminate unsanitary living spaces from the islands and restore islander health.[51] Thus, the Navy enforced its own set of sanitation regulations, promising to make the "continued improvement of health and sanitation" a central goal of its administration.[52]

The first U.S. Navy doctors to reach Pohnpei encountered a population in a poor state of health. By 1946, Pohnpeians were receiving 2,000 to 3,000 free medical treatments per month, with the island's population standing at just over 5,000.[53] But medical personnel repeatedly misattributed the war's deleterious effects on community health to Pohnpeian cultural practices. Dr. Elmer Alpert, for instance, asserted with little evidence that "it is obvious that the basic foods of the Micronesian natives—in quantities now available and ordinarily consumed—are deficient in practically every nutritional factor studied."[54] Alpert's remedies mainly involved imports: increased consumption of high-protein foods like fish, poultry, meat, eggs, and milk; substituting brown rice for white rice and enriched flour for white flour; substituting cola and candy for citrus juice; and making a more "intelligent use" of healthy local foods like leafy vegetables. Alpert concluded that economic development, rather than foods like breadfruit or fish that had long stood Pohnpeians in good stead, was the key to improved health.[55]

Trust Territory leadership believed that healthy diets were the inevitable outgrowth of economic development, and therefore not a matter worthy of serious consideration on their own. Thus, the TTPI's 1949 annual report assured readers that "store foods" were already filling whatever nutritional gaps existed among consumers.[56] When in 1951 a University of Hawai'i nutritionist named Mary Murai produced a damning study on declining nutritional standards in the Marshall Islands, Navy historian Commander Dorothy Richard shot back that Murai's work was "pessimistic." If islander diets still "left much to be desired according to American standards," Richard argued, the issue could simply be resolved through economic growth and education.[57] Murai's study was still a target for Interior officials nearly a decade later. High Commissioner Delmas Nucker argued in 1958 that Murai's findings were irrelevant because "it does not appear the same energy demands exist in Micronesia" as in the United States, an apparent reference to the long-standing foreign trope of islander laziness.[58]

On the one hand, administrative resistance to nutrition-centered interventions stemmed from practical considerations: limited funding that hamstrung official action, nearly static commercial economies that reduced the flow of imports, and trading companies that were unwilling to swim against the current of consumer demand. But complicated American relationships with imported foods played a role as well. Canned and processed foods seemed to function for many Americans as a metaphor for their own presence in the islands: preconditions for modernity that might cripple what was most precious in island life, harbingers of self-sufficiency that drew the region ever closer to foreign economic and political powers, and pervasive reminders that American home life could almost be reconstituted abroad, but not quite. Thus, while many of the Americans on Pohnpei relied almost entirely on imported foods, just as some Japanese settlers had, neither the military personnel of the 1940s nor the Interior Department staffers who replaced them in the 1950s were entirely satisfied with the simulacrum of home that appeared on their plates.

When Saul Riesenberg visited Pohnpei's mess hall in 1947, he was stunned when cooks served him canned pineapple, writing in his diary, "officers say they never have native fruits or vegetables; say cooks find it much easier to open cans."[59] A visitor the following year reported that sailors on the island typically consumed meats like beef and pork, fish, potatoes, rice, and canned fruits and vegetables, and that only a few enlisted men ate local foods.[60] Officially, the Navy stood by this canned food, arguing that the provisions it provided American sailors and hired islander laborers was "exceptional in quality and quantity."[61] But, in practice, imported foods of all kinds took a long and sometimes unreliable journey to arrive in Pohnpei's kitchens and did not always weather the trip safely. A sailor stationed at Kwajalein during the war recalled worms in his oatmeal, insects baked into his bread, and greenish dehydrated potatoes. After a few months, his swollen, aching arm and leg joints caused him to suspect malnutrition, while Marshallese whose diets incorporated local foods appeared perfectly healthy.[62] American complaints over the quality and variety of imported foods continued well into the 1960s, though rarely with such dramatic health impacts.

Once the immediate health crises of wartime had subsided in the Trust Territory, American officials largely put the project of reconstructing islander health to bed. The regime maintained only a small health service to accommodate routine procedures in the islands until the 1960s. But as health officials and military personnel concurrently embraced and withdrew from the food they imported, they revealed the double bind of their presence in islands they understood to be paradisiacal, in need of American development, and untenable in the face of sustained contact with the modern world. In addition, as they struggled over their part in advancing what Captain Walter Karig called "tin-can civilization" in his confused meditations on the Navy's nuclear testing in the Marshalls, Pohnpei's traditional leaders took advantage of the opportunity to advance their own fortunes.[63]

Reassessing Chieftainship

Keith Camacho has argued that Micronesia's postwar era presented islanders with an opportunity to reassess their relationships with the United States and Japan.[64] But Pohnpei's postwar reconstruction also offered an opportunity for Pohnpeians to reassess their relationships with their traditional leaders. Weakened by the trials of war, chiefs took advantage of the power vacuum the Navy created on their island to reassert their authority. Initially, cultural security policies had inadvertently enhanced that authority. Fewer stores meant less accessible imports, which enabled elites to reassert control over the flow of goods to commoners. In the *wehi* of Kitti, for instance, a single store replaced nine prewar Japanese shops, and Lieutenant Robert Halvorsen warned dramatically of a "clique" that had become so powerful that "unless you get down on your knees you cannot eat."[65] But while some naval officials worked to reduce chiefly power, others preferred to delegate authority to islanders in an attempt to build up democratic institutions they hoped could incorporate outer islanders previously excluded from traditional governance. Ultimately, however, it was islanders who shepherded traditional leadership into the postwar era, and islanders who formulated the interdependent relationships between chiefs and secular politicians that defined the island's governance for the balance of the century.

Among the most visible players in Pohnpei's early postwar power struggles was Oliver Nanpei, a minor titleholder in the *wehi* of Kitti and the island's wealthiest man.[66] Educated at Oahu's Kamehameha School, Nanpei was worldly, connected, and ambitious. Whereas some American officials declared Pohnpei's chiefly system undemocratic, Nanpei insisted on maintaining traditional hierarchies and boosting his position within them.[67] In the disruption that came with the war's end, Nanpei repeatedly clashed with the regime over the disposition of abandoned Japanese goods and the distribution of American military stocks. In one incident, Nanpei exercised his prerogative as chief to claim three Japanese boats. Naval officials stripped him of two of these and required him to rent the third, which repeatedly broke down afterward.[68] In another incident, officials initiated a distribution of clothing and cigarettes. Nanpei insisted that the items should be distributed on the basis of rank in a manner that enabled chiefs to accrue the social capital that came with gift giving, and complained that the Navy was "giving to low class people who had no position in Ponape society."[69]

Nanpei's lobbying earned him some enemies among the naval leadership. But he did enjoy respect among islanders, and particularly those who were longtime allies of his family: Protestants, Mortlockese, and the people of Kitti among them. Taking a stroll around Sokehs Island in December 1945 after another humiliation by Lieutenant Louchheim, Nanpei brought along a servant to collect the gifts of bananas and other items islanders presented to him along the way.[70] Nanpei's influence outside his home *wehi* nearly led to his appointment as the island's "Supreme Representative" a few years later, a short-lived position that resembled the island-wide role Nanpei's father had once envisioned for himself. Still, in campaigning for the job, Nanpei also revealed the limits of Pohnpei's tolerance for his ambition.

During the campaign, Nanpei scrupulously worked to build goodwill, using personal funds to pay down a portion of Kitti's municipal debt and sponsoring athletic games there.[71] But he seems particularly to have targeted his longtime rival Max Iriarte, who probably desired the position as well but declined to pursue it publicly. The campaign inflamed tensions between the two men and their followers, partly because Navy officials encouraged Nanpei to pursue a vigorous American style of electioneering that was entirely at odds with the island's political norms. Nanpei's campaigning proved so destructive that Iriarte recalled being laughed at in public, shamed by opponents who walked past his Kolonia office bearing gifts of kava and pigs for Nanpei rather than him, and driven nearly to tears as he asked those gathered at community meetings "to abandon these practices which are not good for us."[72] The situation provoked so much division that the Navy was forced to eliminate the position of all-island chief altogether, if not to repudiate its strategy of seeking to resolve conflicts through a public airing of grievances.

As Pohnpeians considered the proper role for their traditional leaders under American rule, the influence of feasting surged. But feasts also increasingly reflected the growing interconnectedness between the island's prestige and commercial economies, continuing a trend that had begun in the nineteenth century and accelerated under Japanese rule. One of Riesenberg's "semiacculturated informants" determined that given his low title, first-fruits offerings represented an economic loss, and he therefore withdrew from tribute feasting altogether. Another man suggested that since he had inherited his land from his mother rather than from the *nahnmwarki,* he no longer felt obligated to engage in tribute.[73] A small minority of commoners now purchased the yams they offered their chiefs, while a few traditional leaders sold the yams they received.[74] Yet in spite of the eagerness of some foreigners to sound the death knell for the island's feasting complex, feasts on Pohnpei evolved without diminishing, maintaining their consequence in island life and continuing to bolster the influence of traditional leaders.[75]

Even so, determining the proper relationship between traditional leaders and the democratic institutions the Navy wished to build proved complex. The island saw a popular backlash against the appointment of chiefs as magistrates in 1947 and the appearance and dissolution of the Office of Supreme Representative. In 1950, Pohnpeians reached a tentative agreement on a unicameral legislature. At the insistence of the district's American governor, that agreement was abruptly modified to a bicameral legislature incorporating outer islanders and Kosraeans.[76] By the 1960s and 1970s, the Ponape district legislature had emerged as a real political force, largely without the direct participation of chiefs. But because *nahnmwarkis* had been elevated from day-to-day politicking and were distanced from colonial rulers, their influence persisted, still rooted in the island's thriving prestige economy.[77] In the meantime, a younger generation of leaders, many of them educated in the United States, pursued political office and ultimately independence for their island. And as those leaders bridged Pohnpeian and American political norms, they embraced the symbolism of gift giving and of paying their respects to traditional governance in the furtherance of their political agendas.

Subsequent decades muted and transformed the food wars that lingered on Pohnpei after American sailors departed the island in 1951. While warring armies no longer feuded over the politics of feeding and memories of wartime grew distant, gifts of food retained their centrality in Pohnpeian political life. And smaller food struggles multiplied: an explosion in the cash economy during the 1960s and 1970s that ballooned imports while promoting sedentary lifestyles at work and home; fears of sovereignty lost to overdependence on imported goods in the midst of the Trust Territory's independence negotiations; and an ongoing struggle against lifestyle-related diseases that reaches into the present day.

Pohnpei's short-lived American Navy occupation came and went long before these struggles played out. Yet the island's initial encounters with an American Navy not quite able to make sense of its role within Micronesian food politics proved just as indelible as the explosions of generosity that followed sailors to other islands. And, in fact, in later years the Navy was never far from sight. Military rations appeared in unexpected places for decades, from school lunches to typhoon relief packages to official meetings.[78] Seabees surfaced intermittently to complete construction projects, and Pohnpeians themselves increasingly enlisted for military service. Still, even when the Navy's presence seemed far out of view, the histories of the negotiations over food that had so shaped Pohnpei's postwar reconstruction remained, deeply embedded not only in the region's politics but also in the bodies of those who lived there. As American rule and American money swelled Pohnpei's commercial economy beginning in the 1960s those histories resurfaced, layered amid a century of colonial rule and manifesting with growing frequency in the form of pain: from diabetes, hypertension, cardiovascular disease, and obesity.

Notes

I thank Fred Hoxie, Vince Diaz, Tina DeLisle, David Hanlon, Kristin Hoganson, Martin Manalansan, and Fran Hezel for their insights and encouragement. Thanks also to the wonderful archivists at the University of Hawai'i Pacific Collection, the Bishop Museum Library, the College of Micronesia-FSM, the Micronesian Area Research Center, and the National Anthropological Archives.

1. While Pohnpei's military command adamantly refused to be fed by enemy soldiers, group leader Takehiko Akita recalled his disgust at the callousness of preventing hungry troops from eating. On the one occasion he encountered airdropped American food, he advised the soldiers under his command to use it as they pleased, but to keep the incident a secret. Takehiko Akita, *War Diaries from Pohnpei: Unsinkable Ship on the Pacific* [Ponapetō Senki: Nankai no Fuchinkan]. (Tokyo: Kobunsha, 1981), 146–147.

2. Kozo Tokumi, "Memory of Pohnpei" [Ponapetō no Omoide], in *Memories of the South Seas* [Omoide no Nanyō Guntō]. (Tokyo: Nan'yō Guntō Kyōkai, 1965), 188–189.

3. Akita, *War Diaries,* 149–151, 169.

4. See, for instance, Lin Poyer, "Dimensions of Hunger in Wartime Chuuk Lagoon, 1943–1945." *Food and Foodways* 12, no. 2 (2004): 137–164.

5. Lin Poyer, Suzanne Falgout, and Lawrence Carucci, *The Typhoon of War: Micronesian Experiences of the Pacific War* (Honolulu: University of Hawaii Press, 2001), 245.

6. *History of the Islands,* n.d., Pacific Collection, University of Hawai'i at Manoa, 50.

7. David Hanlon, *Upon a Stone Altar: A History of the Island of Pohnpei to 1890* (Honolulu: University of Hawaii Press, 1988), 39.

8. Akitoshi Shimizu, "Chiefdom and the Spatial Classification of the Life-World: Everyday Life, Subsistence, and the Political System on Ponape," in Machiko Aoyagi, ed., *Islanders and Their Outside World* (Tokyo: Committee for Micronesian Research, St. Paul's [Rikkyo] University, 1982), 160; Hanlon, *Upon a Stone Altar,* 70.

9. William R. Bascom, "Ponapean Prestige Economy," *Southwestern Journal of Anthropology* 4, no. 2 (1948): 212.

10. Kimberlee Sterritt Kihleng, "Women in Exchange: Negotiated Relations, Practice, and the Constitution of Female Power in Processes of Cultural Reproduction and

Change in Pohnpei, Micronesia," (Ph.D. diss., University of Hawaii at Manoa, 1996), 74.

11. In 1874, Adolph Capelle established Pohnpei's first copra trading station on Lenger Island in the northern lagoon as a representative of the Godeffroy Company. Paul Hambruch. *Ponape, vol. 1: History, Geography, Language and Natives,* trans. Elizabeth A. Murphy and Ruth E. Runeborg, 1983, 40-II.

12. Hanlon, *Upon a Stone Altar,* 71, 76; William R. Bascom, *Ponape: A Pacific Economy in Transition,* vol. 22, Anthropological Records (Berkeley: University of California Press, 1965), 12, 54.

13. Hanlon, *Upon a Stone Altar,* 206; Francis X. Hezel, *Strangers in Their Own Land: A Century of Colonial Rule in the Caroline and Marshall Islands.* (Honolulu: University of Hawaii Press, 1995), 133–134, 143.

14. Glenn Petersen, *One Man Cannot Rule a Thousand: Fission in a Ponapean Chiefdom* (Ann Arbor: University of Michigan Press, 1982), 23; Saul Riesenberg, *The Native Polity of Ponape* (Washington, DC: Smithsonian Institution Press, 1968), 39.

15. Saul Riesenberg, Diary, 22 July 1947, Folder 2, Box 2, Saul Riesenberg Papers (hereafter cited as SRP), Pacific Collection, University of Hawai'i at Manoa, Honolulu, Hawai'i; John F. Embree, *Field Report on Trip to Micronesia, December 14, 1945–January 5, 1946* (Pacific Collection, University of Hawai'i at Manoa, 1946), 72.

16. Mark R. Peattie, *Nan'yo: The Rise and Fall of the Japanese in Micronesia, 1885–1945* (Honolulu: University of Hawaii Press, 1988), 205.

17. The Constitution of the Federated States of Micronesia, of which Pohnpei is now a part, was ratified in 1979. The nation's relationship with the United States was formalized under the Compact of Free Association in 1986.

18. Poyer, *Typhoon of War,* 212–213.

19. Paul Lyons, *American Pacificism: Oceania in the U.S. Imagination* (New York: Routledge, 2006), 24.

20. Hal M. Friedman, *Creating an American Lake: United States Imperialism and Strategic Security in the Pacific Basin, 1945–1947* (Westport, CT: Greenwood Press, 2001), 95, 117.

21. Pohnpeians received 22 percent of the value of the yen they surrendered in 1946. Bascom, *Ponape,* 15.

22. Ibid., 49; Friedman, *Creating an American Lake,* 95.

23. Dorothy E. Richard, *United States Naval Administration of the Trust Territory of the Pacific Islands,* vol. 1 (Washington, DC: Office of the Chief of Naval Operations, 1957), 381; Bascom, *Ponape,* 53.

24. Embree, *Field Report,* 64, 87, 91

25. Bascom, *Ponape,* 16.

26. Edward Hall, "Military Government in Truk," *Human Organization* (Summer 1950): 26.

27. Iriarte's strategy of playing colonial powers against one another in service of contemporary political argument was a staple of Pohnpeian strategies for "talking back" to their colonizers, each of which was keen to be received more favorably than

their predecessors. Riesenberg Diary, 13–30 December, 18 December 1947, Folder 8, Box 3, SRP.

28. Richard, *United States Naval Administration,* vol. 2, 516. On the intersection between colonial rule and economic development in Micronesia, see David Hanlon, *Remaking Micronesia: Discourses over Development in a Pacific Territory, 1944–1982* (Honolulu: University of Hawaii Press, 1998).

29. Hezel, *Strangers in Their Own Land,* 266; Bascom, *Ponape,* 53.

30. Bascom writes, "On Ponape, as in other parts of the area, prices were apparently unrelated to any conceivable factor; they were not consistent with the quality of the goods or with their purchase price, nor were they comparable to previous prices for the same items, and they certainly had no relation to Ponapean purchasing power. A carton of cigarettes, usually mouldy or watersoaked, cost two and a half days' wages; and a can of meat and vegetable stew cost more than a day's wages." Bascom, *Ponape,* 53.

31. Hezel, *Strangers in Their Own Land,* 262, 270.

32. These particular officials were stationed in the Marshalls, where the Navy's presence was more visible. Embree, *Field Report,* 10.

33. Elmer Alpert, "Nutrition and Dietary Patterns of Micronesia," October 1946, Trust Territory Archives (hereafter cited as TTA), University of Hawai'i at Manoa, Reel 414, 16.

34. John Useem, *Notes on Yap (and Ulithi)* (Pacific Collection, University of Hawai'i at Manoa, 1946), 20.

35. Carleton H. Wright, "Let's Not Civilize These Happy People," *Saturday Evening Post* 3 May 1947, 23, 149–150.

36. Joseph Iriarte, Letter to Saul Riesenberg, 23 July 1948. Folder 69, Box 7, SRP.

37. Riesenberg, Letter to Joseph Iriarte, 4 August 1949 Folder 69, Box 7, SRP; Riesenberg. Letter to Joseph Iriarte, 4 May 1950, Folder 69, Box 7, SRP.

38. Hanlon, *Remaking Micronesia,* 62.

39. See: Emiko Ohnuki-Tierney, *Rice as Self: Japanese Identities through Time.* (Princeton: Princeton University Press, 1993).

40. John Spivey, "History of the Island Trading Company of Micronesia," TTA, Reel 118, 34–35.

41. Ibid., 35.

42. Navy Department, *Report on the Administration of the Trust Territory of the Pacific Islands for the Period June 1, 1949 to June 30, 1950* (Washington, DC: Navy Department, 1950), 72.

43. Spivey, "History of the Island Trading Company," 1–2, 4, 6; Appendix C, 3.

44. "Petitions to United Nations Visiting Mission, March 4–6, 1953, from citizens of Ponape District," John L. Fischer and Ann K. Fischer Papers, Smithsonian National Anthropological Archives, Suitland, Maryland, Series 3 Ponape, Box 10, Notes 1953, 2.

45. Donald H. Rubinstein, "Staking Ground: Medical Anthropology, Health, and Medical Services in Micronesia," in Robert C. Kiste and Mac Marshall, eds., *American Anthropology in Micronesia: An Assessment* (Honolulu: University of Hawaii Press, 1999), 331.

46. For an account of a prewar Japanese doctor intent on "rescuing the Kanakas of Yap from the sad fate of total extinction," see Tadao Yanaihara, *Pacific Islands under Japanese Mandate* (Shanghai: Kelly and Walsh, 1939), 250.

47. Willard Price, *Pacific Adventure* (New York: John Day, 1936), 138.

48. Peattie, *Nan'yo,* 88–90.

49. Richard, *United States Naval Administration,* vol. 1, 7.

50. American castaways were advised to be less picky. A 1942 informational booklet offered techniques for preparing and eating local foods as well as "native" cooking techniques, and it assured military personnel that "any food eaten by the natives can be eaten by you, with perhaps a slightly lower degree of enjoyment." U.S. Navy Department, Bureau of Medicine and Surgery, *Compilation on the Diseases of Naval Importance in Micronesia, including the Identification and Distribution of Arthropods of Medical Importance* (Washington, DC, 1944), 6, 16; "Castaway's Baedeker to the South Seas," 1942, Reel 622, TTA, 40.

51. See Peabody Museum of American Archaeology and Ethnology, *The Micronesians of Yap and Their Depopulation; Report of the Peabody Museum Expedition to Yap Island, Micronesia, 1947–1948* (Cambridge, MA: Peabody Museum, Harvard University, 1949); United States Senate, "Joint Resolution Authorizing the President to Approve the Trusteeship Agreement for the Trust Territory of the Pacific Islands," *Hearing before the Committee on Foreign Relations, on S.J. Res. 143,* 80th Congress, 1st Session, 7 July 1947 (Washington, DC: Government Printing Office, 1947), 7, 10.

52. Richard, *United States Naval Administration,* vol. 2, 517. Similar language was included in the Trusteeship Agreement of 1947. See ibid., vol. 3, 1132.

53. About half of these treatments were for yaws. Gonorrhea was also prevalent at this time. Virtually no treatments for lifestyle-related diseases like diabetes and hypertension appear in the records during the 1940s or 1950s. Bascom, *Ponape,* 57.

54. Alpert made these assertions without scales to weigh his subjects, translators to interpret their dietary histories or neurological examinations, and laboratory equipment to analyze the nutritional values of island foods. Alpert, "Nutrition and Dietary Patterns," 3, 21.

55. Ibid., 22–23.

56. Navy Department, *Report on the Administration of the Trust Territory of the Pacific Islands for the Period July 1, 1948 to July 30, 1949* (Washington, DC: Navy Department, 1949), 57.

57. Richard, *United States Naval Administration,* vol. 3, 943–945; Mary Murai, *Nutrition Study in Micronesia* (Washington, DC: National Academy of Sciences, 1954), 9.

58. High Commissioner to Distad Ponape, "Addition of Enriched Rice and Flour to Micronesian Diet," 14 May 1958, Robert Gibson Papers, Pacific Collection, University of Hawaii (hereafter RGP), Box 7, Folder 93, 1–2.

59. Riesenberg Diary, 11 July 1947, Box 2, Folder 2, SRP.

60. Charles Al Bailey, *An Epidemic of Eosinophilic Meningitis, a Previously Undescribed Disease, Occurring on Ponape, Eastern Carolines* (Bethesda, MD: Naval Medical Research Institute, National Naval Medical Center, 1948), 16.

61. Navy Department, *Handbook of the Trust Territory of the Pacific Islands* (Washington DC: Navy Department, 1948), 153–154.

62. Bruce Muench, *Spam Cans, Rice Balls, and Pearls: Snippets of Memory from World War II* (Austin, TX: Turnkey Press, 2002), 64–65.

63. Walter Karig, *The Fortunate Islands: A Pacific Interlude* (New York: Rinehart and Co., 1948), 226.

64. Keith Camacho, *Cultures of Commemoration: The Politics of War, Memory, and History in the Mariana Islands* (Honolulu: University of Hawai'i Press, 2011), 60.

65. Robert Halvorsen, "Political Conditions in Ponape," 2–3 December 1946, Correspondence Individual, Halvorsen, Box 6, Folder 61, SRP, 7; "Halvorsen Visits Ponape," *Ponape-per,* 15 December 1961, 2.

66. Riesenberg, *Native Polity of Ponape,* 30.

67. Embree, *Field Report,* 64–65, 88.

68. Ibid., 64–65, 71.

69. The specific objection in the first instance was that the clothing and cigarettes were to go to people who had worked for the Navy, but poor record keeping resulted in a sloppy distribution. Ibid., 65, 69, 88, 89.

70. Ibid., 65, 69, 88.

71. John Fischer, "Informant: Peli," 11 August 1950, D26S1, John L. Fischer Papers (hereafter cited as JFP), Bishop Museum Library, Honolulu, Hawai'i.

72. Noting the poor fit between American-style elections and behind-the-scenes Pohnpeian politicking, Fischer wrote that one Pohnpeian involved in this dispute told him, "You Americans can have an election and forget about it until the next election. We Ponapeans can not." Another suggested that the election had opened up a rift so deep that in past years it could only have been settled by war, and that some of those involved had actually proposed turning to violence. John Fischer, "Titles, etc. Makis, copy of 10/xi/50. 12/xi," JFP, 548; Political Affairs Officer to Civil Administrator, "Present and Potential Political Development of Ponapean Society," JFP, 564.

73. Riesenberg, *Native Polity of Ponape,* 78.

74. Saul Riesenberg, Journals, Net, 5 January, 8 January, and 30 December 1947, Folder 9, Box 3, SRP; John Fischer, "Informant: Kurekohr. Complaints about Feasts and Titles," 19 December 1950, JFP, 6.

75. For a later study on the enduring centrality of Pohnpei's traditional leadership system, see: Petersen, *One Man Cannot Rule a Thousand.*

76. Hezel, *Strangers in Their Own Land,* 28.

77. Glenn Petersen, "Ponape's Body Politic: Island and Nation," *Pacific Studies* 8, no. 1 (1984): 177.

78. See, e.g., Francis B. Mahoney, Memorandum to Donald Heron, 31 August 1956, Folder 72, Box 6, RGP, Hawai'i, 3; "Gunners Knot Rides Out Typhoon," *Micronesian Reporter,* November–December 1957, 13; "The Wind: Typhoon Ophelia Passes over Breadth of Micronesia Leaving Disaster and Sorrow," *Micronesian Reporter,* March–April 1958, 7; Theodore Henning, *Buritis in Paradise* (New York: Greenwich Book Publishers, 1961), 133–134; E. J. Kahn Jr., *A Reporter in Micronesia* (New York: W. W. Norton and Co., 1966), 183.

Bibliography

Primary Sources

Archives

Bishop Museum Archives, Bishop Museum Library, Honolulu, Hawai'i
John L. Fischer Papers
Smithsonian National Anthropological Archives, Suitland, Maryland
John L. Fischer and Ann K. Fischer Papers
University of Hawai'i at Manoa, Honolulu, Hawai'i
Trust Territory Archives, Hamilton Library
Robert Gibson Papers, Pacific Collection
Saul Riesenberg Papers, Pacific Collection

Congressional Records

United States Senate. "Joint Resolution Authorizing the President to Approve the Trusteeship Agreement for the Trust Territory of the Pacific Islands," *Hearing before the Committee on Foreign Relations, on S.J. Res. 143*, 80th Congress, 1st Session, 7 July 1947. Washington, DC: Government Printing Office, 1947.

Contemporary Sources

Bailey, Charles Al. *An Epidemic of Eosinophilic Meningitis, a Previously Undescribed Disease, Occurring on Ponape, Eastern Carolines.* Bethesda, MD: Naval Medical Research Institute, National Naval Medical Center, 1948.

Embree, John F. *Field Report on Trip to Micronesia, December 14, 1945–January 5, 1946.* Pacific Collection, University of Hawai'i at Manoa, 1946.

Hambruch, Paul. *Ponape, vol. 1: History, Geography, Language and Natives*, trans. Elizabeth A. Murphy and Ruth E. Runeborg. Pacific Collection, University of Hawai'i at Manoa, 1983.

Henning, Theodore. *Buritis in Paradise.* New York: Greenwich Book Publishers, 1961.

History of the Islands, Pacific Collection, University of Hawai'i at Manoa, n.d.

Karig, Walter. *The Fortunate Islands: A Pacific Interlude.* New York: Rinehart and Co., 1948.

Peabody Museum of American Archaeology and Ethnology. *The Micronesians of Yap and Their Depopulation; Report of the Peabody Museum Expedition to Yap Island, Micronesia, 1947–1948.* Cambridge, MA: Peabody Museum, Harvard University, 1949.

Price, Willard. *Pacific Adventure.* New York: John Day, 1936.

Useem, John. *Notes on Yap (and Ulithi)*. Pacific Collection, University of Hawai'i at Manoa, 1946.

Yanaihara, Tadao. *Pacific Islands under Japanese Mandate.* Shanghai: Kelly and Walsh, 1939.

Government Documents

U.S. Navy Department. *Handbook of the Trust Territory of the Pacific Islands.* Washington, DC: Navy Department, 1948.

———. *Report on the Administration of the Trust Territory of the Pacific Islands for the Period July 1, 1948 to July 30, 1949.* Washington, DC: Navy Department, 1949.

———. *Report on the Administration of the Trust Territory of the Pacific Islands for the Period June 1, 1949 to June 30, 1950.* Washington, DC: Navy Department, 1950.

U.S. Navy Department. Bureau of Medicine and Surgery. *Compilation on the Diseases of Naval Importance in Micronesia, including the Identification and Distribution of Arthropods of Medical Importance.* Navmed 211. Washington, DC: Navy Department, 1944.

Periodicals

Micronesian Monthly/Micronesian Reporter

—"Gunners Knot Rides Out Typhoon." *Micronesian Reporter,* November–December 1957, 12–13, 27.

—"The Wind: Typhoon Ophelia Passes over Breadth of Micronesia Leaving Disaster and Sorrow." *Micronesian Reporter,* March–April 1958, 4–9.

Ponape-per

—"Halvorsen Visits Ponape." *Ponape-per,* 15 December 1961, 2.

Saturday Evening Post

—Wright, Carleton H. "Let's Not Civilize These Happy People." *Saturday Evening Post* 3 May 1947, 23, 149–150.

Secondary Sources

Dissertations

Kihleng, Kimberlee Sterritt. "Women in Exchange: Negotiated Relations, Practice, and the Constitution of Female Power in Processes of Cultural Reproduction and Change in Pohnpei, Micronesia." PhD diss., University of Hawaii at Manoa, 1996.

Books

Akita, Takehiko. *War Diaries from Pohnpei: Unsinkable Ship on the Pacific.* [Ponapetō Senki: Nankai no Fuchinkan]. Tokyo: Kobunsha, 1981.

Bascom, William R. *Ponape: A Pacific Economy in Transition*, vol. 22, Anthropological Records. Berkeley: University of California Press, 1965.

Camacho, Keith L. *Cultures of Commemoration: The Politics of War, Memory, and History in the Mariana Islands*. Honolulu: University of Hawaii Press, 2011.

Friedman, Hal M. *Creating an American Lake: United States Imperialism and Strategic Security in the Pacific Basin, 1945–1947*. Westport, CT: Greenwood Press, 2001.

Hanlon, David. *Remaking Micronesia: Discourses over Development in a Pacific Territory, 1944–1982*. Honolulu: University of Hawaii Press, 1998.

———. *Upon a Stone Altar: A History of the Island of Pohnpei to 1890*. Honolulu: University of Hawaii Press, 1988.

Hezel, Francis X. *Strangers in Their Own Land: A Century of Colonial Rule in the Caroline and Marshall Islands*. Honolulu: University of Hawaii Press, 1995.

Kahn, E. J., Jr. *A Reporter in Micronesia*. New York: W. W. Norton and Co., 1966.

Lyons, Paul. *American Pacificism: Oceania in the U.S. Imagination*. New York: Routledge, 2006.

Muench, Bruce. *Spam Cans, Rice Balls, and Pearls: Snippets of Memory from World War II*. Austin, TX: Turnkey Press, 2002.

Murai, Mary. *Nutrition Study in Micronesia*. Washington, DC: National Academy of Sciences, 1954.

Ohnuki-Tierney, Emiko. *Rice as Self: Japanese Identities through Time*. Princeton: Princeton University Press, 1993.

Peattie, Mark R. *Nan'yo: The Rise and Fall of the Japanese in Micronesia, 1885–1945*. Honolulu: University of Hawaii Press, 1988.

Petersen, Glenn. *One Man Cannot Rule a Thousand: Fission in a Ponapean Chiefdom*. Ann Arbor: University of Michigan Press, 1982.

Poyer, Lin, Suzanne Falgout, and Lawrence Carucci. *The Typhoon of War: Micronesian Experiences of the Pacific War*. Honolulu: University of Hawaii Press, 2001.

Riesenberg, Saul. *The Native Polity of Ponape*. Washington, DC: Smithsonian Institution Press, 1968.

Official Histories

Richard, Dorothy E. *United States Naval Administration of the Trust Territory of the Pacific Islands*. Vols. 1–3. Washington, DC: Office of the Chief of Naval Operations, 1957.

Articles and Book Chapters

Bascom, William R. "Ponapean Prestige Economy." *Southwestern Journal of Anthropology* 4, no. 2 (1948): 211–221.

Hall, Edward. "Military Government in Truk." *Human Organization*, Summer 1950: 25–30.

Petersen, Glenn. "Ponape's Body Politic: Island and Nation," *Pacific Studies* 8, no. 1 (1984): 112–136.

Poyer, Lin. "Dimensions of Hunger in Wartime Chuuk Lagoon, 1943–1945." *Food and Foodways* 12, no. 2 (2004): 137–164.

Rubinstein, Donald H. "Staking Ground: Medical Anthropology, Health and Medical Services in Micronesia." In Robert C. Kiste and Mac Marshall, eds., *American Anthropology in Micronesia: An Assessment* (Honolulu: University of Hawaii Press, 1999), 327–359.

Shimizu, Akitoshi. "Chiefdom and the Spatial Classification of the Life-World: Everyday Life, Subsistence and the Political System on Ponape," in Machiko Aoyagi, ed., *Islanders and Their Outside World.* Tokyo: Committee for Micronesian Research, St. Paul's (Rikkyo) University, 1982, 153–215.

Tokumi, Kozo. "Memory of Pohnpei" [Ponapetō no Omoide]. In *Memories of the South Seas* [Omoide no Nanyō Guntō]. Tokyo: Nan'yō Guntō Kyōkai, 1965, 176–202.

5

Arguing over A-Bombs

Interservice Rivalry and the Atomic Bomb Tests at Bikini Atoll, September 1945–June 1947

Hal M. Friedman

Between 1945 and 1947, the United States sought an imperial solution to its security problems in the Pacific Basin. Faced with fears of a future Pearl Harbor–style attack by a potentially resurgent Japan, and facing an even more realistic confrontation with the Soviet Union, American policymakers, planners, and strategic thinkers saw the creation of an "American lake" in the postwar Pacific as the best means by which to guarantee U.S. security interests vis-à-vis East Asia. In particular, they saw a need to blanket the Pacific with mobile American military force, as well as fortified bases at selected sites, while attempting to Americanize Micronesia and as many other areas of the region as possible. The problem with creating an American lake in the postwar Pacific, however, had to do with differences of opinion among the Executive Branch Departments that had responsibilities in the area. The War, Navy, State, and Interior Departments all agreed with one another, as well as with the Office of the President and Congress, on the efficacy of creating an American lake in the postwar Pacific Basin. However, these departments and agencies all disagreed, often vehemently, with one another on how to carry out these national security measures. So, while the final goal of creating an American lake in the postwar Pacific was a rough strategic consensus between these Executive Branch Departments, the means by which to carry out the Americanization and defense of the region led to significant interdepartmental and sometimes even intradepartmental bickering and rivalry. As will be seen, one of the primary arenas for the interservice rivalry between the Army and the Navy was the atomic bomb tests carried out at Bikini Atoll in the Marshall Islands in July 1946.

The Context

Interservice rivalry had been a reality of American defense policymaking since the earliest days of military aviation. Before that, there had been informal agreements between the Army and Navy about the division of defense responsibilities. Before the invention of the airplane, for instance, it had been largely understood that the Navy was responsible for defending American interests on the high seas and that the Army was primarily responsible for the defense of the nation itself and its overseas territories.[1] The development of military aviation in the early twentieth century, however, changed this situation. In fact, it can be said that since the 1920s, interservice debates on the roles and missions revolving around the military use of the airplane had become a staple of American defense policymaking. In essence, the potential of the airplane as a military weapon largely dissolved the neat line separating roles and missions and cast doubt on the Navy's ability to continue as the nation's first line of defense.[2] That neat line was further dissolved in the early 1920s when forces under Brigadier General William Mitchell, Assistant Chief, U.S. Army Air Service (AAS), carried out aerial bombing experiments against old U.S. Navy and ex–Imperial German Navy battleships off the Virginia Capes. The resultant controversy over the conditions of those tests given the lack of simulation of realistic combat scenarios further heightened the interservice rivalry that would be at the center of the Bikini Atoll tests. With the attack on Pearl Harbor, the revolutionary advances in weaponry during World War II, and the shortened response time to surprise attacks, this doubt among the Navy's critics about its future capabilities greatly intensified and put the Navy on the defensive in postwar Congressional hearings over future defense policy.[3]

Interservice rivalry over strategy, roles, and missions was further motivated by increased competition over declining defense budgets after the end of World War II. Convinced that high military expenditures and large Federal deficits were not conducive to a healthy political economy, the Truman Administration was determined to balance the Federal budget by curtailing military expenditures. In fact, from the summer of 1945 to the summer of 1947, the military services were reduced from a budgetary authorization of over $80 billion to one of $14.5 billion. Strategy, roles, and missions determined a service's budget. If a particular service was perceived as the nation's first line of defense, then the major budgetary appropriations would fall to that service. However, if a service was relegated to minor roles, that service would be denied the lion's share of the postwar defense budget. Not surprisingly, almost every defense issue at this time—including debates over the roles of advanced weapons—became an arena for interservice rivalry over strategies, roles, and missions.[4]

The Call for and Preparation for the Tests

The Pacific Basin especially became an arena of postwar interservice rivalry in 1946 when atomic bomb tests were proposed at Bikini Atoll in the Marshall Islands against selected American, German, and Japanese naval vessels, first an air strike by B-29s of the Army Air Force's 509th Composite Bomb Group and then an underwater burst in the Bikini Lagoon. The tests were first thought of by scientists at Los Alamos Laboratory in New Mexico in 1944, who wanted to see tests conducted against Japanese fleet concentrations.[5] By 1944, however, much of the Japanese Fleet had been sunk and the idea did not surface again until September 1945, when Senator Brien McMahon of Connecticut, Chairman of the Senate Special Committee on Atomic Energy, proposed that a test against surviving Japanese warships be conducted. The tests were enthusiastically endorsed by the Army Air Forces as a way to demonstrate the superiority of land-based atomic air power. Thereafter, the Navy also supported the idea and broadened the proposal to include American and German warships as a way to illustrate that atomic bombs had not made warships or navies obsolete.[6]

One of the earliest calls for a test also came from General of the Army Douglas MacArthur, who was at the time Commander-in-Chief, U.S. Army Forces, Pacific (CINCAFPAC) as well as Supreme Commander for the Allied Powers (SCAP) in Japan. In October 1945, MacArthur asserted to General of the Army George Marshall, Chief of Staff of the Army (CSA), that studies done of the annihilation inflicted on Hiroshima and Nagasaki indicated the atomic bomb's destructive effects on ground targets and personnel. MacArthur thought that the bomb would "revolutionize" military thought regarding the composition and character of ground forces. He also cited scientists who had predicted the same type of impact on forces afloat. Further citing the relative uselessness of the remnant Japanese Fleet for anything else but as atomic bomb test targets, MacArthur called for test shots that would assist the United States in determining the part played by naval forces in the future.[7]

In regard to the idea of testing atomic weapons on naval vessels, it is not surprising to find the military services quickly beginning preparations soon after Senator McMahon made his initial proposal. One Office of the Chief of Naval Operations (OPNAV) document from as early as October 1945 discusses General of the Army Henry Arnold's proposal that the Joint Chiefs of Staff (JCS) determine which Japanese warships would be suitable for testing with conventional bombs, atomic bombs, guided missiles, and "other" possible weaponry. More specifically, Arnold suggested that General MacArthur, as Supreme Commander of the Allied Powers in Japan, inventory surviving Japanese naval vessels and that the State Department be advised about these matters. Arnold further suggested that at least seven vessels of heavy cruiser type or larger be used in the tests. In this same document, Fleet Admiral Ernest King, Chief of Naval Operations (CNO), also detailed to a subordinate command the responsi-

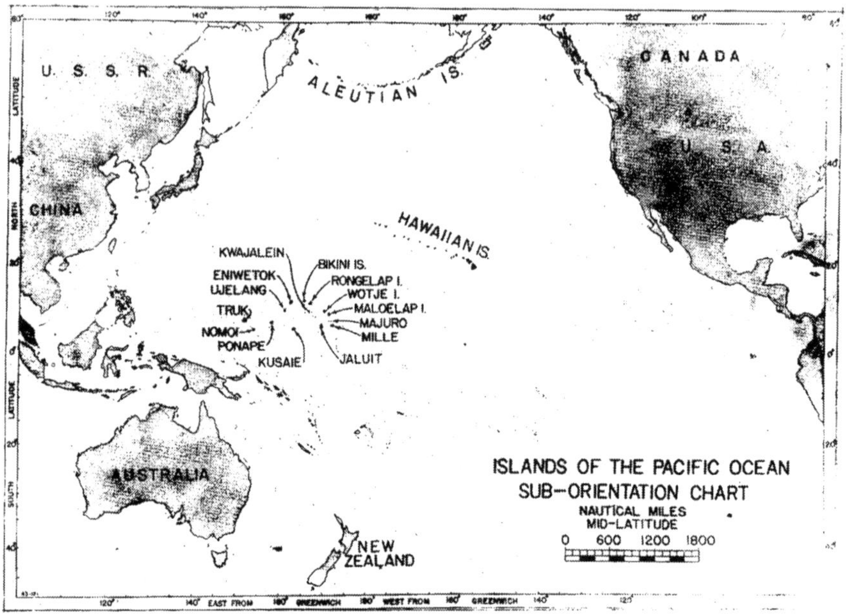

Islands of the Pacific Ocean: Sub-Orientation Chart (Courtesy of the Naval Historical Collection, U.S. Naval War College)

bility to find out which Japanese warships would be suitable for testing and what would be necessary to make them ready for use as targets.[8]

Given the serious (or petty) nature of the interservice rivalry revolving around the tests, it is important to understand that great stress was made by the various parties about the purposes of the tests. Therefore, in December 1945, Vice Admiral William Blandy, Deputy Chief of Naval Operations (DCNO), Special Weapons, made clear the Navy's exact perspective on the tests in testimony before the Senate Special Committee on Atomic Energy. Blandy first stated that at the present time it was "anyone's" conjecture as to how atomic weaponry would be used for naval purposes. He was, however, quick to answer questions about the estimated life expectancy of surface ships in light of atomic weapons.[9] Blandy claimed, for instance, that it was a fallacy to assume that a weapon or weapons platform became obsolete once a newer weapon could destroy it. According to Blandy, the older weapon or platform was not obsolete until its function could be replaced. He used the aircraft carrier in the Pacific War as his example. Asserting that no other kind of platform could replace the aircraft carrier at the time, Blandy pointed out that damaged or destroyed carriers were repaired or replaced, not classified as obsolete.[10] Blandy was willing to admit that at some future time it might be possible to transport men, supplies, and resources by means other than over the surface of the oceans. However, he argued that until that time came, surface transportation would remain vital to the economy and the defense of the nation and that, therefore, the Navy had to defend the nation's access to those oceans. In other words, Blandy countered the Army Air Forces argument that military aviation transportation could somehow replace surface naval transportation. Blandy, in fact, was not willing to concede much to the atomic bomb. Moreover, the Senators were in concurrence with Blandy that surface ships not being able to resist atomic bombs did not make navies obsolete. In return, Blandy was in concurrence with the Senators that civilian scientists had to help judge the effects of the tests so that military officers with vested interests did not dominate the analyses.[11]

The tests were approved by President Harry S. Truman in early January 1946. It had been decided by the Joint Chiefs that the tests would be conducted by a joint task force, designated Joint Task Force One (JTF One), under the command of Admiral Blandy. JTF One would be under Joint Chiefs control, with administrative support from the Commander-in-Chief, U.S. Pacific Fleet—at this time Admiral Raymond Spruance—and General MacArthur as Commander-in-Chief, U.S. Army Forces, Pacific. In addition, JTF One would have full support from War and Navy Department agencies such as the Manhattan Engineer District (MED), the Army command that oversaw the wartime development of the atomic bomb. It was also outlined that Admiral Blandy would have the authority to deal directly with interested agencies and that the operation would have an unclassified code name of "Operation Crossroads." It was further stated that the probable location of the tests would be Bikini Atoll in the Marshall Islands, since the Atoll was very lightly populated and therefore the population could supposedly be easily relocated. It was also assumed that Bikini had natural facilities that were key to successful tests. It was additionally assumed that Bikini had been relatively untouched by the war and was far from any major American population centers. Finally, it was estimated that the first test would be an airdrop that would be conducted in mid-May 1946.[12]

Early Army Air Forces perspectives on public perceptions of the tests were seen in a memo in late January 1946. Major General Lauris Norstad, Army Air Forces Assistant Chief of Air Staff (ACAS), Plans, noted that the Joint Chiefs of Staff had determined the need for an advisory board to study and interpret the results of the tests for strategic purposes. The Joint Chiefs called for equal representation on this board from the Army, the Navy, the Manhattan Engineer District, and the civilian community. The evaluation board was to consist of two civilians; two Army officers, of whom one had to be an Army Air Forces officer; two Navy officers, one of whom had to be a naval aviator; and one civilian from the Manhattan Engineer District. The Army Air Forces determined that it was "manifestly in the best interest of the Army Air Forces that its representation be an officer of established professional reputation and one known to possess broad vision and progressive views." Not surprisingly, the Army Air Forces leadership recommended that General Arnold represent the Army Air Forces as soon as he retired from the Army.[13]

In a memo by Arnold at the same time, the Army Air Forces Commanding General (CG) agreed to the need for the tests but did not want the Joint Chiefs to justify the operation solely to determine future naval design and tactics. Since he considered the bomb such a "powerful aerial weapon," Arnold wanted it tested for its general implications for future warfare, not just naval warfare. Moreover, he did not entirely agree with the idea that the Joint Task Force Commander had to be a naval officer. The experimental nature of the bomb and the significant role of the scientific community in its development meant, to him, that Army Service Forces (ASF) Major General Leslie Groves, Commanding General, Manhattan Engineer District, could just as easily be the Task Force Commander.[14] Arnold reiterated that he thought the atomic bomb was primarily an aerial weapon, that it to date was only deliverable by long-range aircraft, and therefore it was of "vital interest" to the Army Air Forces. He particularly wanted General MacArthur to have a say in the selection of the Task Force Commander. Arnold thought that MacArthur already had a staff comprised of air, ground, and naval officers who were capable of carrying out the logistical and operational aspects of these tests. Further, Arnold argued that it was "highly probable" that the tests would take place in an area under MacArthur's jurisdiction. Therefore, "the designation of a man of his stature would aid immeasurably in accomplishing a very important objective, namely" confidence in and acceptance of the results by the many factions and services— scientific and political—which had "legitimate and vital interests" in consequent decisions.[15]

Countering the assertion that Operation Crossroads was a strictly naval operation, Admiral Blandy pointed out in subsequent Congressional testimony that the JTF One Deputy Task Force Commander for Aviation, Major General William Kepner, was an Army Air Forces officer; that an Army Ground Forces officer, Major General Anthony McAuliffe, was assigned as JTF One Ground Forces Adviser; that Blandy had a number of both Army and Navy officers as Assistant Chiefs of Staff; and that there were civilian scientists assigned from the Manhattan Engineer District. Moreover, Blandy pointed out to the Senate Special Committee on Atomic Energy that JTF One's Evaluation Board was similarly composed of civilian scientists as well as both Army and Navy officers.[16] However, it should also be realized that the information the Senators were being given about various aspects of the operation was at times sanitized. For instance, at one point Blandy discussed the force composition of JTF One, part of which was a squadron of Navy destroyers. Blandy focused on the destroyer squadron's role of cordoning off the test range so as to keep ships out of danger, especially waters contaminated with radiation. Yet Blandy never mentioned that while safety was probably one objective,[17] first and foremost the destroyer squadron was there to prevent any type of espionage into a test range employing the most highly sensitive weapon the United States had ever developed. At the least, that kind of selective communication brings into question the completeness of Blandy's assertions and many of the other statements about the tests that were made by senior military officials and officers.[18]

Blandy, for instance, tried to de-emphasize newspaper stories that the tests were a case of U.S. saber rattling against the Soviet Union or some sort of competition between the Army and Navy, even though the tests were exactly the latter to a great degree. Testifying before the same Senate Committee in late January 1946, Blandy also spoke about the need to balance the amount and type of information that the public received with the needs of American national security and secrecy. He also went to great lengths, however, to assert that this was a joint military operation between the services, not a Navy operation or one dominated by the Army Air Forces.[19] Blandy was willing to admit that the primary mission of the Task Force was to determine the impact of atomic weapons on naval vessels for purposes of planning the future of American naval power. However, secondary purposes also included atomic bombing practice for the Army Air Forces, as well as an opportunity for the Army Ground Forces to determine the effect of the bombs on ground equipment.[20] At times, however, there were subtle contradictions or omissions in the testimonials and reports. For example, Blandy stressed toward the end of his testimony that the test was a scientific experiment and not a contest between the armed forces. Of course, the latter contradicts more internal documentation being cited in this chapter and it de-emphasizes the military nature of the tests Blandy spoke about at the beginning of his testimony. Certainly, science and the military security of the United States were not mutually exclusive, but Blandy's later emphasis on science instead of the future of American naval and air power again tries to deny what the tests were really all about.[21]

This focus on the tests as an arena of interservice rivalry, however, is not to say that agreement between the services did not exist at all. In fact, in early February 1946, the Army and Navy agreed on conditions for admitting foreign observers to the tests. There had been debate between the Army and Navy on the one hand and the State Department on the other about reconciling security with the need to demonstrate U.S. openness about the atomic bomb. By this time, the Army and Navy both agreed that two observers from each of the eleven foreign member nations on the United Nation's Commission on Atomic Energy should be allowed to attend the test. The exception to this number of observers was Great Britain, which had requested a larger number. Secretary of War Robert Patterson and Secretary of the Navy James Forrestal agreed to refer the matter of special consideration for the U.K. to the Joint Chiefs of Staff.[22] Patterson and Forrestal also agreed that news-service representatives from each of these nations should be invited, but they wanted a minimum number of news agencies and representatives involved. In fact, they wanted to leave that determination up to Admiral Blandy in consultation with General Groves after those two officers coordinated with the Army's and Navy's respective public relations agencies. It was thought that if further accommodations could be made, the number of U.S. observers and press representatives could be increased, but Patterson and Forrestal were also leaving that determination up to the Joint Chiefs. Finally, Patterson and Forrestal agreed that for reasons of security, foreign observers and press representatives should be transported on ships other than those carrying any American military personnel, observers, or scientists.[23]

The tests again came up for discussion in mid-February 1946, this time between President Truman, Secretary Forrestal, and Fleet Admiral William Leahy, Chief of Staff to the Commander-in-Chief of the Army and Navy. Forrestal recorded in his diary that Truman wanted a commission appointed to oversee the bomb tests in order to meet criticisms that the tests were under military control and might be "rigged." Truman was apparently referring to a letter from Secretary of Commerce Henry Wallace to that effect.[24] In the same conversation, Leahy took the occasion to criticize the McMahon Bill, legislation that would have given the development of atomic energy and weapons to a civilian commission. Leahy took this as a sign of great mistrust by Congress toward the armed services. Truman answered that he understood McMahon was out to get publicity for himself, but Truman also thought that as President he still had to go the route of a civilian commission as a way to meet "all of the crackpot criticisms and that not only would it need to be objective but we had to convince the public it was objective."[25]

There was also a great deal of concern when it came to public relations in terms of the ecological and environmental effects of the test shots. In early March 1946, Assistant Secretary of the Navy for Air John Sullivan telephoned Admiral Blandy to find out if Blandy had something in writing from the Department of the Interior about the bombs not permanently damaging the fish in the Marshall Islands. In fact, there were rumors in the air and complaints from one member of the House of Representatives that the test shots might ruin the salmon industry as far away as Washington State![26] Blandy had written confirmation from

Interior that no harm would be done to the U.S. fishing industry. In addition to wanting a copy of the documentation from Interior, however, Sullivan also wanted Blandy to be aware that there were concerns that the atomic explosions might damage the ocean floor in some way. In particular, in order to "have the Navy's interest protected in some sort of assurance," Sullivan wanted reports from leading geologists that the explosions would not damage the Earth's crust or cause some similar type of damage.[27] Blandy assured Sullivan that he would get such reports in writing and get copies to Sullivan, even though he had been trying to allay public concern with the press for some time. Sullivan surmised that the explosions would, in fact, cause some "general change in the earth's formation in part of the world" but that "if it's in the record before this happens then you won't get blamed for every thundershower we have the rest of the year." Of course, what Sullivan should have added is that he would not take such blame either.[28] The conversation then proceeded to the safety of the Bikini population, which had been removed to Rongerik Atoll. Sullivan wanted to be sure that the people would be safe there. He also wanted to know why they had not been evacuated to Eniwetok, which was further to the west. Blandy assured Sullivan that Rongerik was safer because Eniwetok was in the general direction of wind and water movement. Sullivan asked if Blandy was satisfied that the Bikini population was safe in Rongerik, but the transcript ends without an answer.[29]

Concern about public perceptions of the tests came up later in the month when Navy Captain Fitzhugh Lee, JTF One Public Information Officer, gave even more detailed suggestions to Blandy about "proper" indoctrination of press representatives. Lee began by asserting how important it was to indoctrinate the press since they had such a special mission of conveying Operation Crossroads to the public. Accordingly, it was necessary to ensure that the gentlemen of the press were "men of integrity and ability." Lee went on to assert that these men should be present when Blandy's staff briefed the President's Commission and the Joint Chiefs of Staff Evaluation Board about the tests. However, it was to be clear that the press representatives would only be present for the declassified aspects of the briefing and that the entire briefing was to be off the record.[30] Lee also suggested that a radio program be scheduled for the day before the first test, a program in which Patterson, Forrestal, Fleet Admiral Chester Nimitz (now Chief of Naval Operations), General of the Army Dwight Eisenhower (now Army Chief of Staff), General Carl Spaatz (now Commanding General, Army Air Forces), and Blandy would all talk about the purpose of Operation Crossroads. Lee guaranteed that there would be coverage on all four national networks, and he thought that the program should be well publicized. He also believed that the texts of the remarks "should be very carefully prepared with the view to impressing on the American public (and the world) the correct facts concerning the tests and preventing hasty, incorrect, and possibly harmful, conclusions."[31]

Lee further spoke to the need to have the press members visit one or two target ships and Bikini Atoll before the test. It was recommended that a "very careful schedule" be planned for the press and the observers, and that Admiral Blandy and his senior staff go far in making last-minute presentations to the press and observers about the purpose of the tests.[32] Finally, Lee spoke to the need to ensure that the press and observers have some sort of physical view of Bikini Lagoon for two or three days after the tests, but before they would actually be allowed onto the island. Lee was concerned that the press and observers not think the military was altering the test sites or "fixing" things in any way. Lee thought that such scene alteration was really not possible, but that the press and public might suspect something was being done. Therefore, Lee recommended that the press and observer ships be permitted to cruise close aboard the windward rim of the Atoll—though outside of the Lagoon—as soon as was "feasible" after the first wave of test ships entered the Lagoon. Lee thought that this would "permit them to get a general bird's-eye view of the scene, which should be satisfactory." Lee concluded by asking Blandy for approval of these suggestions and stating that if these suggestions wound up being infeasible at the time, the matter could be explained then.[33]

Later in the month, there was also clarification about which commands had authorization to release information about the tests when a message was sent from the War Department to MacArthur concerning public relations releases about Operation Crossroads. Though it is unclear if MacArthur's command had been issuing statements on the impending tests, the document made it clear that Admiral Blandy's command would be solely charged with responsibility for publicity regarding the tests and that Blandy's command was directed to emphasize in all of its communications the "true scope, importance, joint nature and impartiality of tests." MacArthur was therefore asked to refrain from issuing separate press statements or other publicity concerning the tests. Any issuances MacArthur's command might desire were to be directed to Blandy's headquarters.[34]

Memoranda from the Office of the Chief of Naval Operations also indicate how important the Navy took these tests in determining future roles, missions, force levels, budgets, and public perceptions of each service. In late March 1946, Rear Admiral Matthias Gardner, head of OPNAV's Strategic Plans Section, sent a memo to Vice Admiral Forrest Sherman, Deputy Chief of Naval Operations for Operations. In the memo, Gardner discussed the negative possibility—from a Navy public relations perspective—if the Japanese battleship *Nagato* and light cruiser *Sakawa* survived the atomic bomb blasts of Operation Crossroads. If these ships survived the bomb blasts, Gardner surmised that these vessels would be on their "last legs." He therefore assumed that the Army Air Forces would "pounce" on such an opportunity to sink a "mighty vessel" like the *Nagato* and that such a sinking would make a good press release for the Army Air Forces. Gardner suggested to Sherman, therefore, that the Navy, in order to "forestall such a possibility . . . should have plans of our own."[35] Attached to the memo for Sherman's signature was another memo from Sherman to Rear Admiral Jerauld Wright, head of OPNAV's Operational Readiness Section. Sherman, like Gardner, thought that the *Nagato* and *Sakawa* would be destroyed by the tests. If the ships were not destroyed, however, in order to eliminate the possibility of an Army Air Forces public relations coup, Sherman wanted Wright's comments on directives to Admiral John Towers, Spruance's successor as Commander-in-Chief, Pacific Fleet, to "sink them promptly by such means as you believe will be beneficial from the point of view of any experiments which may be pending and for which they would be a suitable target."[36] This memo, in fact, is somewhat consistent with authority given to the Secretary of the Navy by the Senate. Senate Report 1238 gave Forrestal the discretion to either sink the test vessels if they were so damaged as to be unseaworthy or salvage them if they were useful for other testing or experimentation purposes.[37] However, it is doubtful that the Senate meant its authority to be stretched as far as Sherman and his officers were doing.

There was also some talk of postponing the tests because of an increasingly tense diplomatic situation with the Soviet Union. Forrestal strongly resisted any idea of postponing the tests because of the large number of personnel involved and the problem of organizing military personnel and civilian scientists again after an initial postponement. In a related manner of public relations, Forrestal also wanted the first test to occur about 15 May, with members of Congress who were part of the President's Evaluation Commission being invited to that test. In addition, he thought that the second test should take place about 1 July and have sixty members of Congress present.[38] It should also be made clear, however, that not everyone was in favor of holding the tests in the first place. In late March, Representative Herman Kopplemann of Connecticut sent Truman a note applauding the President's decision to postpone the tests because of criticism from Congress and scientists about the cost of the tests and their reception by other nations, such as the Soviet Union. Moreover, Kopplemann told Truman that he thought the majority of the American people would approve of the decision. Kopplemann also thought that canceling the Bikini "demonstration" outright would help alleviate any suspicions that the USSR was harboring about the United States.[39] Further, Kopplemann told Truman that the United States had to be firm in its determination that world peace would not be endangered by any actions taken by any nation. Since Kopplemann also thought that all international issues should be deliberated at the United Nations, he expressed gratitude that Truman postponed an "exhibition" that might have aggravated tension and suspicion. He concluded the letter by telling Truman how proud he was of the President's decision.[40] Truman returned a note two days later, thanking Kopplemann for the expression of approval, though in reality the President had merely postponed the tests until July so as to accommodate other members of Congress who wanted to observe the tests without disrupting business on Capitol Hill.[41]

Concern for written documentation by the concerned parties about the importance of the tests may also have been the reason for another report issued in late March 1946 by the Senate Naval Affairs Committee that reiterated the purposes of the tests and their strategic need. According to the report, the tests were necessary in order to explore the effects of the atomic bomb on naval vessels, especially in terms of ship design, tactical formations at sea, anchoring distances in port, the number and location of operating bases and repair yards, and the strategic disposition of ships. Stated again were the secondary purposes of testing the effect of the bomb on aircraft—both airborne drones and grounded planes—and military ground equipment. The report went on to assert that the tests were absolutely necessary because without any guarantee that atomic weapons would be eliminated from other nations' arsenals, the United States could not be expected to operate "in the dark" concerning the effects and use of these weapons.[42] However, there continued to be some Congressional concern about the tests, especially about the necessity, the expense, and the need, in some cases, to prevent postponement. To alleviate this concern, Forrestal sent a letter to Senator David Walsh of Massachusetts, Chairman, Senate Naval Affairs Committee, in late March in which the Secretary of the Navy placed the failure to test the atomic bomb in terms of the United States potentially suffering a future disaster "worse than Pearl Harbor." The need to determine tactical formations at sea and anchoring formations in port was again stressed, as was strategy in light of arms control failures to "eliminate" the bomb.[43] In addition, Senator Walsh apparently had to be convinced that the sums obtainable from the surplus scrap and sale of the warships was much less than the information that could be obtained from atomic bomb tests. Forrestal even admitted to the Senator that he had had initial doubt about the value of the tests, but claimed that Fleet Admiral Nimitz and Vice Admiral Blandy had convinced him that the tests were essential for the future of American naval strategy and naval architecture. Forrestal concluded the letter by urging Walsh that House Joint Resolution 307—the legislation that would authorize the tests—be passed.[44]

On the same day, Walsh was sent another letter from Bradley Dewey, a member of the President's Evaluation Commission and Vice Chairman, Joint

Chiefs of Staff Evaluation Board. Dewey talked specifically about the need to "outlaw war" rather than postpone the test or even consider the test as an aggressive move on the part of the United States. Dewey—in words that could have matched that of a Navy public relations officer—wanted Walsh and other American leaders to be more forthright that the tests were actually defensive in nature. He also wanted it asserted that if the United States could not eliminate the weapon it would have to test it and prepare for its use, and that the alternative would be some sort of unilateral disarmament, something unthinkable if war were not outlawed.[45]

Apparently, criticism and doubt on the part of Congress, the press, and the public was significant enough for Admiral Blandy to issue a memo on the subject to all JTF One personnel. Blandy first stated that a key to the success of Operation Crossroads was continued public confidence that the tests were being conducted in "impartial" ways and that this impartiality and the joint nature of the tests was fully subscribed to by the public and press.[46] Blandy went on to assert that the public must not obtain the "erroneous" impression that the sole purpose of the tests was the effect of atomic explosives on naval vessels. He wanted all personnel to strive to ensure that the public and the press understood that these were sincerely "joint" operations between the Army and the Navy, that neither service was out to "prove" or "disprove" anything, and that information for the elimination of one military service or the other was not the goal. He ended the memo with a call for all JTF One personnel to work toward bettering public understanding that the tests were about science, not interservice politics.[47]

Concern about media coverage, however, was again apparent in a late April 1946 memo dealing with the plans for a conference with Operation Crossroads press representatives. Blandy received the memo from Captain Lee, now head of Operation Crossroads Public Information Section. For security reasons, Lee wanted to ensure that reporters "thoroughly understood" that the press conference was to be "off the record" and could not be used as a "springboard" for news stories. Lee also wanted to ensure that press representatives knew the information they were receiving was privileged and that it was meant only for persons who were going to report on the tests. Finally, Lee further wanted to ensure that the press representatives understood that the information they were receiving was only needed for "the best and most authentic background from the lips of those who have the most authority to speak on the subject."[48]

Concern for the Navy's public relations—this time on the part of a member of Congress—again came out in early May 1946 in a conversation between Captain Edmund Taylor, aide to the Secretary of the Navy, and Representative Willis Robertson of Virginia. In regard to recent public relations events about the tests, Representative Roberts thought the Navy had gotten good publicity out of certain pictures and newsreels. However, Roberts was also concerned about getting a "very fine" newspaperman from Virginia to cover the atomic bomb tests.[49] Robertson specifically wanted Louis Spilman from Waynesboro News, Virginia, to cover Operation Crossroads. Spilman was a member of the Virginia Press Association, and Robertson wanted him on the assignment because no one from Virginia or from a small newspaper had apparently been selected to cover Operation Crossroads. Robertson thought Spilman would be perfect, since "this boy had a son in the Marines who fought on Iwo Jima and all through the Pacific campaign and he is strong for the Navy and he a good reporter and he means a lot to me." Captain Taylor told Representative Robertson that he thought the reporters had all been selected. When Robertson related that not all had been chosen, Taylor assured him that he would see what he could do. Robertson reiterated Spilman's value to the Navy because he was "a splendid man, and he is strong for the Navy. I wouldn't recommend him if he wasn't."[50]

This concern for both security and image was again evident in a letter from Blandy to Forrestal the same month. Blandy was discussing the need to allow members of the media access to the tests but without sacrificing control over the whole process. Blandy reiterated to Forrestal that the Joint Chiefs of Staff had vested Blandy with the authority to control all publicity concerning Operation Crossroads. He stated that carefully controlled movements and procedures for the "proper indoctrination" of the press had been developed. Blandy also stated that all photographs would be reviewed for security but that the press would be allowed to write without censorship. In Blandy's opinion, this could be allowed because movements would be so controlled that the reporters "will not be exposed to information which they should not use for publication."[51] Blandy also told Forrestal that there were about 200 newsmen accredited and that some of the reporters wanted to travel to the Marshall Islands with the high-ranking officials and officers. In Blandy's opinion, however, these reporters should not be allowed to proceed to the Marshalls with the high-ranking officials since "the interests of harmony with existing plans and adequate control of security" might be compromised.[52] From a security perspective, Blandy's concerns were legitimate, and there would obviously have to have been some sort of security screening of the bomb tests since the weapon was so new, powerful, and potentially vital to U.S. national interests. Interestingly, Blandy dealt with this problem not by censoring the reporters per se, but by allowing them to write without censorship about what they had seen yet highly limiting their freedom of movement. Again, this might have been done for legitimate security reasons, but it also might have been done because of fear of negative reporting about the armed services in general and the Navy in particular.

Disagreements between the services about the effects of the bomb on American defense policymaking continued to be apparent just before the tests took place. In a Columbia Broadcasting System (CBS) program in late May 1946 from the JTF One flagship, the USS *Mount McKinley,* Admiral Blandy talked about Operation Crossroads being an experiment intended to keep a peace-loving America strong in a troubled world. He then asserted, however, that the bomb "may represent a turning point in the strategy of warfare." In the same broadcast, General George Kenney, now Commanding General, Strategic Air Command (SAC), stated most clearly at the end of the interview that the United States should do everything it can to protect itself in the atomic age. However, he also explicitly stated that "the atomic bomb has revolutionized our whole concept of defense. There just isn't any adequate defense against atomic attack."[53] Also late in May, Admiral Nimitz emphasized the need for the tests in testimony before Congress. Nimitz was asked by Senator John Overton of Louisiana, Chairman, Senate Subcommittee on Appropriations, about the effectiveness of battleships in atomic warfare. Nimitz answered that the battleships were the "toughest" ships the Navy had and that he expected them to have "greater" resistance to atomic attack than any other type of ship. Still, Nimitz thought that the Bikini tests would give some indication of just what that resistant capacity might be. According to Nimitz, this was one reason that significant numbers of German and Japanese surface ships had, to date, not been disposed of.[54]

The Tests and the Aftermath

Conducted in July 1946, the tests illustrated that warships were very vulnerable to atomic air power, but the results were otherwise indecisive. In fact, the results were so indecisive that the Navy continued to argue that it could survive an atomic war at sea. Nor did the tests change the Navy's low opinion of precision strategic bombing, since the B-29 that dropped the bomb had done so miles off the target. At the same time, however, the very destructiveness of the weapons was made quite clear, and this demonstration allowed the Army Air Forces to continue its claim that in a real war the fleet would have been destroyed.[55] The rivalry was so serious between the services, and that rivalry was so potentially damaging to the credibility of the tests, that President Truman had the President's Evaluation Committee, noted above and chaired by Senator Carl Hatch of New Mexico, witness and report on the tests. Unfortunately, the committee's report only gave additional evidence for each service to argue its case.[56]

For example, Hatch's committee was quick to point out the destructiveness of the bomb, the danger to ships and personnel in any kind of sudden or surprise attack, and the probable effects of radiation. All of this, no doubt, was seen by the Army Air Forces as confirmation of its claims. At the same time, however,

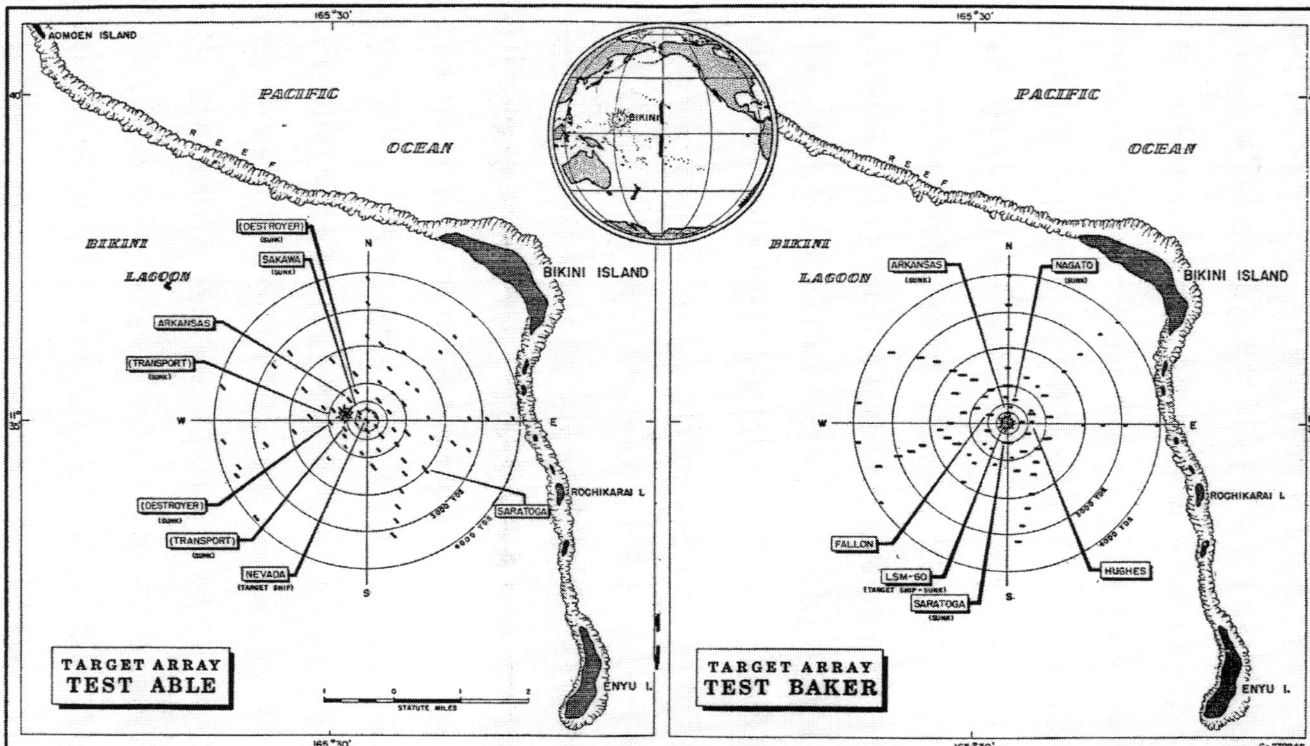

Target Arrays: Tests Able and Baker (War Department *Intelligence Review,* 29 August 1946, Courtesy of the Air Force Historical Research Agency)

Beginning of Test Baker (from *The Manhattan Project: An Interactive History*, courtesy of the Office of History and Heritage Resources, U.S. Department of Energy)

the report gave the Navy some hope. The committee suggested, for instance, that redesigning ships and allowing for greater spacing intervals between ships in formation would offer the protection needed against atomic attack.[57] While these suggestions did not appear to downplay the destructiveness of the bomb, they were the same suggestions offered by the Navy's leadership before, during, and after the tests as evidence that navies were not made obsolete by atomic air power. In fact, there was even a general feeling of nonchalance about the bomb, since a relatively small number of ships were sunk by the test shots.[58]

Even after the tests took place, official reports also continued to emphasize the various purposes of the tests but downplayed any type of interservice rivalry. This perspective can be seen in a statement by Blandy to JTF One in late August 1946. Pointing out that Tests Able and Baker had been completed and that individuals and units were being detached from JTF One, Blandy also told his men that JTF One personnel would be called upon to express their opinions about the tests and that they were free to do so. However, he wanted them to understand that their remarks were to be guided by the principles laid out in the public information policies being used by the Joint Task Force. He encouraged his men to provide descriptions of a "general" nature but not to disclose factual data that was any more detailed than the information provided by the President's Evaluation Commission and the Joint Chiefs of Staff Evaluation Board. Additional facts known to JTF One personnel because of their association with the Task Force "should only be made public if it is positively known that such publication does not prejudice the security interests of the United States. In case of doubt they should be referred to Commander Joint Task Force One."[59]

Given all of the factors involved, it is not surprising that the results of the tests continued to be inconclusive. For instance, one War Department message to key Army commanders in the Pacific included a report by the Joint Chiefs of Staff Atomic Test Evaluation Board that found that naval vessels operating within about one mile of the aerial bomb burst would become inoperative, if not from bomb damage then from massive crew casualties. While the Board found that ships that were more than half a mile from the burst had no "obvious" damage, its report included significant detail on radioactivity in the air and water around the Bikini Lagoon after both the air and subsurface bursts, and it again emphasized crew casualties as a factor in naval atomic operations.[60] The Board then asserted that it thought JTF One set a pattern for close, effective cooperation between the armed services and civilian scientists as well as providing valuable training for personnel in joint operations! In spite of its findings about certain destruction to ships and personnel within a one-mile radius of an atomic bomb blast, however, the Board was still not willing to offer a final analysis of all of the bomb's effects. Instead, it called for more research into the effects of the bomb, though it also claimed that the tests were sufficient for the Army and Navy to begin redesigning Army ground equipment and Navy vessels to meet the atomic threat. It also recommended that the services begin rethinking strategy and tactics, and it called for the continued production of atomic material, weapons, and research as long as the weapons had not been internationally outlawed and as long as other countries threatened the United States. To the Board, even though the tests did not answer all of the questions about atomic weaponry, they answered enough to assert that the atomic age equated the nation's best defense with that of effective, offensive strength.[61]

In addition to disagreement about the lessons learned from the first two test shots, there continued to be disagreement about the need for a third test. In August 1946, Admiral DeWitt Ramsey, Vice Chief of Naval Operations (VCNO), sent a top secret dispatch to Blandy stating that General Groves had made public statements claiming that the first test shot demonstrated that a "properly placed" atomic air burst could destroy any capital ship. Groves was also reported to have said that the second subsurface shot did the same, and that therefore the third test that the Navy wanted was unnecessary. Groves was additionally reported to have said that the Los Alamos Laboratory would not have the personnel for a

USS *Independence* after Test Able: Damaged, but Still Afloat (Courtesy of the Naval Historical Center, Department of the Navy)

third test shot and that the expense and effort was not needed.[62] Blandy returned an answer to Nimitz a few days later, saying that he did not agree with Groves that the purpose of the test was to find out if a Nagasaki-type bomb could sink a capital ship. Blandy found such a question "oversimplified" and he asserted that the real test was the range at which radiation and degrees of damage dictated ships to be redesigned and spaced differently in port and at sea. Blandy also found Groves's statement about Los Alamos personnel not being available for a third test to be "disturbing" because it pointed out U.S. strategic vulnerability if a few civilian scientists and technicians at the Laboratory were the only personnel able to assemble the bombs. Nor did Blandy think Groves should have been making these statements since authority over the bomb was about to transfer from the Army to the new U.S. Atomic Energy Commission (AEC). In addition, Blandy thought Groves had negated the Navy's role in the entire bomb assembly process, in spite of the key role played in the wartime development of the bomb by Rear Admiral William Parsons, Assistant Chief of Naval Operations (ACNO) for Special Weapons and JTF One Deputy Task Force Commander for Technical Direction. Blandy thought that if the third test was canceled "it should be over the protest of the Navy. Otherwise the Navy will be essentially accused of dodging 'the most decisive test.'" Truman, however, must have followed Joint Chiefs of Staff recommendations not to hold a third test since Walter Millis, in his editorial commentary in *The Forrestal Diaries,* mentions a "postponement" by the President without any objections from his advisers.[63]

Focus on a good public facade was also apparent in an early September 1946 message from Blandy to his JTF One subordinates. Most of the three-page document detailed the kinds of photographs and films that were being produced about Operation Crossroads as well as the procedures by which those media could be reproduced or released to various parties. Blandy reiterated his charge from the Joint Chiefs, however, that he was to ensure that all publicity on the Operation emphasize the "true scope, importance, joint nature and impartiality of these tests." Accordingly, he ordered that no public releases of any material were to be made without permission from him. This included JTF One control over all paintings and drawings. These media were all to remain under control of Joint Task Force One until its dissolution. At that time, paintings were to be divided between the branches of the armed services "on the basis of primary interest in subject matter." These media could be loaned for exhibitions and could be reproduced, but all credit had to go to Joint Task Force One.[64]

Concern with press coverage could again be seen in a postmortem report in November 1946. In his section of the report to the Joint Chiefs of Staff, General Kepner asserted that in spite of all of the effort by Blandy and his staff, Operation Crossroads publicity created the impression that the tests were a naval activity rather than a joint service effort. Kepner argued that the bombs were tested on naval vessels and that the news of the tests was reported from aboard ship. In addition, he noted the location of the tests and the fact that Blandy and most of his principal officers were naval officers. To Kepner, this all added up to the public notion that the Bikini tests were naval tests.[65] Kepner also complained that housing the Task Force Headquarters in the Navy Building in Washington, D.C., allowing early conferences to be dominated by naval officers, and even permitting naval officers to give occasional "unauthorized" releases of information also added to this public misperception. Kepner further pointed out news headlines such as "Navy Atom Bomb Tests" as evidence for the need for greater centralized control of public relations and information in the future in order to make "perfectly balanced" and "objective reporting" the norm for joint operations. In particular, Kepner thought that future joint operations public relations releases should be "controlled through a committee composed of representatives of the interested services. By this method, the interests of all concerned would be fostered and protected and differences reconciled." Kepner thought that "deadlocked issues" could be settled by the Task Force Commander.[66]

Kepner noted other "lessons" from the tests as well. He pointed out that the

Vice Admiral and Mrs. Blandy (wearing a hat that resembles a mushroom cloud) Cut the Atomic Cake, Celebrating Operation Crossroads (Wikipedia)

tests were highly valuable, even indispensable, from a joint organization and training perspective, and he thought that histories and reports on Operation Crossroads would be important references for the future. However, to "insure balance and true perspective, it is desirable that each of the participating services contribute qualified personnel to collaborate in the preparation of reports and histories."[67] In addition, he did not think he had been "promptly furnished" with all of the important communications that were pertinent to his office. In particular, he had a problem with Navy procedures of correspondence distribution, and he thought that in the future both a Navy Flag Secretary and an Army Adjutant General should be employed with some sort of compromise between service administrative organizations. He further reported that this problem extended to the use of call signs and other predominantly Navy communications procedures.[68]

In the JTF One report on Operation Crossroads to the Joint Chiefs of Staff, Admiral Blandy reached several more conclusions about the press coverage of the event. His recommendations discussed the importance of the coverage in dispelling "fantasies" and "public misperceptions" that would have "handicapped" the "intelligent" development of the United States military. More specifically, if public "mistrust" had not been "cleared up" by effective press coverage of the tests, he thought that "requests for military and naval appropriations in the future might well have been suspect in the public mind."[69] Blandy also talked about the waste of having Army and Navy nonparticipating observers on hand, since he claimed these observers could have gained as much information from effective still photographs and motion pictures of the tests as they did from personal observation. While Blandy discussed the absolute necessity of having the maximum amount of printed information for the press, he also thought that both civilian American and foreign nonparticipating observers could have learned more from the photos and films. Probably angling for more positive press coverage, Blandy then suggested that instead of having foreign technical observers on hand, more foreign press should have been invited. Similarly, representation by members of Congress was seen as key, and he thought it "unfortunate that more members of Congress could not have witnessed this outstanding example of perfect integration of the Army, Navy and Air Force."[70]

At this time, Blandy also published an article in the journal *Army Ordnance*, which further reiterated the Navy position that the bomb had not changed very much in terms of naval strategy, tactics, or organization. After stating the purposes of the tests, Blandy noted that great care had been taken in organizing the tests around admittedly "competitive" interests. Explaining why Bikini was selected and describing the actual test shots themselves, Blandy then wrote about how the test results were "less than expected."[71] He admitted that the second, subsurface shot was more powerful and destructive, but contended that dire predictions about Bikini Atoll becoming "Nothing Atoll" or "No Atoll At All" did not come true. He even asserted at one point that "nothing" at all happened there. According to Blandy, at Bikini after the tests, the "palm trees waved in the wind, and the beer was flowing at the bars soon after the first test." Blandy did not discount the "awesome" destructiveness of the weapon, but he stated that the solution was again to discover the proper changes in ship design and tactical formations so that defenses against the bomb could be integrated into current American defense policy.[72]

About this time, Forrestal made statements to the House Subcommittee on Appropriations about the atomic bomb as well, also focusing on the idea that it was not the revolutionary weapon that would end "mighty battles" at sea. In an even more detailed statement than Blandy's article, Forrestal claimed that what really made the atomic bomb strikes on Hiroshima and Nagasaki so effective was that Japan by August 1945 was already defeated at sea, industrially, and in the air. Moreover, Forrestal was quick to point out that long before the atomic strikes, B-29 attacks on Japan greatly benefited from having bases in the Marianas and the Bonins-Volcanoes,[73] bases that were taken with a combination of air, land, and sea power. While Forrestal claimed not to want to detract from the credit due the land-based bomber crews that had delivered the atomic bombs, he wanted the Subcommittee to understand that atomic strikes against an "undefeated" major power would be an entirely different kind of operation than those undertaken in August 1945. Moreover, he wanted the House Subcommittee to know that major technical improvements were needed before warfare across the oceans became atomic and "push button."[74] In further testimony, Forrestal claimed the Bikini tests indicated that the "intolerable immediate vicinity" for atomic blast effect on naval vessels was "something less" than 1,000 yards and that a safe range for personnel would depend on the amount of shielding with which they were provided. While Forrestal owned up to the great vulnerability of naval bases and facilities to atomic strikes, he argued that the test results showed that a mobile fleet at sea would make a "remarkably" poor target. Discounting conclusions based on "unproved" theories or "assumptions" about future discoveries, Forrestal reiterated that in the coming generation the importance of the sea to American national life and the ability of the U.S. Navy to operate on those seas would remain paramount.[75]

A final controversy also illustrates the seriousness with which Operation Crossroads could be taken in a context of interservice rivalry. In mid-May 1947, Captain William Smedberg, Aide to the Secretary of the Navy, recommended to Forrestal a list of naval personnel to be awarded decorations and medals for their part in Operation Crossroads. According to Smedberg, now–Under Secretary Sullivan had recommended approval, as did Fleet Admiral Nimitz. Smedberg reminded Forrestal that the Joint Chiefs of Staff had agreed to a "liberal" awarding of decorations for personnel involved in Operation Crossroads but that the Navy had adhered to a more "restricted custom" of presenting awards. Smedberg thought, however, that the result of this policy was to make the Navy, in comparison with the Army, "miserly" when it came to awarding decorations to its own personnel. Smedberg went on in detail that the Navy "had six times the number of personnel in this operation that Army had and yet the Army is receiving four and a half times the number of awards the Navy is. We have refused to prostitute our awards to bring them into conformity with the lavish handouts of the Army." Smedberg continued that it was his personal opinion that the awards were not in any way warranted except for a few people at the top who were responsible for planning and conducting Operation Crossroads.

Officers and men carrying out their assigned duties were engaged in operations like fleet maneuvers, fleet problems, target practice, "or any other job for which they were being paid."[76]

Nearly a month later, Captain Charles Buchanan, Aide to the Secretary of the Navy, brought the same problem up to Forrestal. He reminded Forrestal that the Army had recommended that General Kepner's award of a Distinguished Service Medal (DSM) be downgraded to a Legion of Merit. Admiral Ramsey, Vice Chief of Naval Operations, in consultation with Under Secretary Sullivan and Rear Admiral Robert Hayler, Senior Member of the Board of Decorations and Medals in the Executive Office of the Secretary of the Navy, decided that the Navy should reduce the award to Admiral Parsons, now OPNAV Director of Atomic Defense, to the same while holding out "strongly" for the Distinguished Service Medal to Admiral Blandy. According to Buchanan, Hayler and the Board recommended that the other awards remain as they were.[77]

Buchanan then told Forrestal that he personally did not think the Navy had to "back down" on Admiral Parsons's award just because the Army had done so with General Kepner. In contradiction to all of the public statements that had been made about the Operation thus far, Buchanan reminded Forrestal that Operation Crossroads had been a naval operation with six times as many naval personnel as the Army and therefore "it was entirely fitting that the Navy should have two Distinguished Service Medal's with none for the Army." Buchanan also told Forrestal that he had discussed the matter with Parsons. According to Buchanan, Parsons "emphatically" thought that Blandy should receive the only Distinguished Service Medal and that he would not want the medal unless Kepner received one since they worked on the same level. Parsons also told Buchanan that he would not want to receive a Distinguished Service Medal unless Rear Admiral Thorvald Solberg was likewise decorated. Solberg had been the Director, Ship Material, during Operation Crossroads and was now Naval Member, Military Liaison Committee, on the U.S. Atomic Energy Commission. Buchanan stated that both Blandy and Parsons praised Solberg's work in the highest terms and that Parsons thought Solberg deserved a Distinguished Service Medal even more than he did, even though Solberg reported to Parsons during Operation Crossroads. Given all of this background, Buchanan recommended that Admiral Blandy be the only recipient of the medal. Two days later, Forrestal approved all of the decorations and awards put forth by the Board, including the recommendations that Blandy be awarded the Distinguished Service Medal and Parsons be awarded the Legion of Merit.[78]

The rivalry between the two services over the Bikini Atoll tests was an example of the larger rivalry over roles, missions, and budgets that was endemic to U.S.

defense policy in the years following World War II. The tests became embroiled in this larger conflict because of the perception that they could be employed by each service to argue its case for the lion's share of resources and attention in the postwar world. In this context, each service, the Joint Chiefs of Staff, and President Truman's Cabinet officers went to great lengths to try to assure the press and public that the tests were not "rigged." In the same context, it is not surprising that Operation Crossroads became an arena for interservice rivalry between the Army and Navy in a much more highly American-controlled Pacific Basin. What is interesting, however, is the fact that the test results were so inconclusive. In regard to settling the dispute between the services over the efficacy of land-based versus carrier-based airpower, the tests simply did not provide enough evidence for either service to argue conclusively that its particular defense policy should be relied on exclusively. Instead, each service was able to marshal enough evidence to continue to foster doubt about the other's capability and therefore to continue to fuel the debate between the Army and Navy as to which branch should lead in peace and war.

Notes

1. Still, there were disagreements even over this rather simple formula. For example, there was no clear jurisdiction over coastal defense; see Kenneth Hamburger, "The Technology, Doctrine, and Politics of U.S. Coast Defense, 1880–1945," (Ph.D. diss., Duke University, 1986); and Michael Unsworth, "Coast Defense: Roles, Missions, and War Plan Orange," paper delivered to the 59th Annual Meeting of the Society for Military History, Fredericksburg, Virginia, 10 April 1992. In addition, there were problems over jurisdiction when it came to the defense of some overseas territories such as the Philippine Islands; see Brian Linn, *Guardians of Empire: The U.S. Army and the Pacific, 1902–1940* (Chapel Hill: University of North Carolina Press, 1997).

2. The famous court-martial of then-Colonel William Mitchell was just one instance in a long and bitter interwar debate over roles, missions, and budgets between the War Department and the Navy Department in the interwar period. For a detailed account of these controversies, see Vincent Davis, *The Admiral's Lobby* (Chapel Hill: University of North Carolina Press, 1967), 48–86; see also Jeffrey Underwood, *The Wings of Democracy: The Influence of Air Power on the Roosevelt Administration, 1933–1941* (College Station: Texas A&M University Press, 1991), 6–26.

3. For the controversies over the 1921 Army Air Service bombing tests, see Thomas Wildenberg, *Billy Mitchell's War with the Navy: The Interwar Rivalry over Air Power* (Annapolis: Naval Institute Press, 2013), 43–94. For an overview of defense unification and the post–World War II debate over roles and missions, see Vincent Davis, *Postwar Defense Policy and the U.S. Navy, 1943–1946* (Chapel Hill: University of North Carolina Press, 1966); and Paolo Coletta, *The United States Navy and Defense Unification, 1947–1953* (Newark: University of Delaware Press, 1981).

4. Russell Weigley, *The American Way of War: A History of United States Military Strategy and Policy* (Bloomington: Indiana University Press, 1973), 368; and Allan Millett and Peter Maslowski, *For the Common Defense: A Military History of the United States of America* (New York: Free Press, 1994), 478.

5. William Shurcliff, *Bombs at Bikini: The Official Report of Operation Crossroads* (New York: William H. Wise and Co., 1947), 9.

6. Ibid., 10–11. See also the *New York Times,* 16 September 1947, Section IV, 6; Forrestal to Representative Carl Vinson, 8 September 1945, Box 89, Day Files, Papers of James Forrestal, Seeley Mudd Library, Princeton University, Princeton, New Jersey; Joseph Alsop and Stewart Alsop, "Atomic Bomb Tests Must First Overcome Inter-Service Rivalry," 10 February 1946, Box 61, Papers of the Office of the President, Institute Archives and Special Collections, Massachusetts Institute of Technology Libraries, Cambridge, Massachusetts; Bureau of Ships and Bureau of Ordnance to the Chief of Naval Operations, 16 October 1945, attached to Joint Staff Planners (JPS) 770/5, Box 169, Record Group (hereafter cited as RG) 218, National Archives (hereafter NA) II; Colonel Harry A. Toulmin, Jr., "Is Bikini a Fair Test?," as told to Douglas Ingalls, *Flying* (1946), 17, 84–86; *New York Times,* 16 November 1945, 1; also, Admiral Arthur Radford to Admiral D. Ramsay, Memorandum, 24 January 1946, Official Correspondence of the Deputy Chief of Naval Operations (Air), 7 January 1946–5 March 1947; and Admiral William Purnell to Major General Leslie Groves, Draft of Memorandum, 1945, Records of Guided Missiles and Atomic Energy Divisions, Records of the Office of the Chief of Naval Operations, Operational Archives, Naval Historical Center (now the Naval History and Heritage Command [NHHC]), Washington Navy Yard, Washington, DC [Records of the Office of the Chief of Naval Operations is now RG 38 at NA II, College Park, Maryland]; all found in Lloyd Graybar, "The 1946 Atomic Bomb Tests: Atomic Diplomacy or Bureaucratic Infighting?" *Journal of American History* 72 (March 1986): 892.

7. MacArthur to Marshall, 11 October 1945, RG 9: Collections of Messages, CINCAFPAC, General (hereafter cited as Radiograms), Douglas MacArthur Memorial Archives and Library, Norfolk, Virginia (hereafter cited as MacArthur Memorial Archives).

8. Top Secret Dispatch from King, 9 October 1945, Folder D-3, Dispositions Japanese Ships, Box 161, Strategic Plans Division Records (hereafter cited as Strategic Plans), RG 38, NA II.

9. Blandy to the Senate Special Committee on Atomic Energy, 14 December 1945, *Hearings before the Special Committee on Atomic Energy,* United States Senate, 79th Congress, 1st Session, 392.

10. Ibid., 393–395.

11. Ibid., 394–395.

12. Joint Chiefs of Staff to Fleet Admiral Chester Nimitz, Chief of Naval Operations; General of the Army Dwight Eisenhower, Chief of Staff, United States Army; Major General Leslie Groves, Commanding General, Manhattan Engineer District; Admiral Raymond Spruance, Commander-in-Chief, U.S. Pacific Fleet; and General of the Army Douglas MacArthur, Commander-in-Chief, U.S. Army Forces, Pacific; 12 January 1946,

RG 9: Radiograms, Blue Binders, Plans & Operations (hereafter cited as P&O) File, MacArthur Memorial Archives. According to the Navy's official history of Trust Territory Pacific Island administration, the Joint Chiefs of Staff chose Bikini Atoll in late January as the test site and Admiral Blandy was ordered to effect the evacuation of the Bikini people by mid-March 1946. Bikini was apparently chosen because it met the JCS requirement that the location be at least 500 miles from all sea and air routes and have steady directional winds for "better control" of the atomic cloud. What then followed was a tragic case of Great Power imperialism and cultural arrogance in which the United States removed the Bikini Islanders from their ancestral home and proceeded to try to settle them at other locations in the Pacific. None of these attempts were very successful, the Bikini Islanders have since sued the U.S. for damages throughout the years, and the whole matter turned into a public relations disaster for the United States. In particular, this incident fueled the criticism about Pacific Island naval civil administration that came from individuals such as former Secretary of the Interior Harold Ickes. For the Navy's official view that the Navy did its best with the Bikinians, see Naval Reserve Commander Dorothy Richard, *United States Naval Administration in the Trust Territory of the Pacific Islands,* Vol. 3 (Washington, DC: Office of the Chief of Naval Operations, 1957), 507–555. For a more accurate perspective written from declassified Navy documents, see Jonathan Weisgall, *Operation Crossroads: The Atomic Tests at Bikini Atoll* (Annapolis: Naval Institute Press, 1994), 30–33, 104–115, 161–162, 218–219, and 308–316. For Ickes's criticisms, see Harold Ickes, "Man to Man," *Washington Star,* 26 September 1947, as cited in Richard, *United States Naval Administration,* Vol. 3, 524.

13. Norstad to Arnold, "Memorandum for the Commanding General, Army Air Forces, Subj: Army Air Force Representation on the Evaluation Board of the Atomic Bomb Test," 22 January 1946, Folder Atomic Bomb Projects, Box 20, Papers of Lauris Norstad, Dwight D. Eisenhower Library, Abilene, Kansas (hereafter cited as Norstad Papers, DDEL).

14. "Attached Memorandum by the Commanding General, Army Air Forces, Joint Chiefs of Staff Tests of the Effects of Atomic Explosives," undated, Folder Atomic Bomb Projects, Box 20, Norstad Papers, DDEL.

15. Ibid.

16. Testimony by Blandy, 24 January 1946, *Hearings before the Special Committee on Atomic Energy,* United States Senate, 79th Congress, 1st Session, 453–454.

17. Ibid., 454, 457, 459.

18. Ibid.

19. Ibid., 453.

20. Ibid., 454.

21. Ibid., 459.

22. "Memorandum by the Secretaries of War and the Navy," 4 February 1946, Appendix "A" to State-War-Navy Coordinating Committee (hereafter cited as SWNCC) 248/3, *State-War-Navy Coordinating Committee Policy Files, 1944–1947* (Wilmington, DE: Scholarly Resources, 1977), microfilm. For the debate between the military and the State Department, see SWNCC 248, Press and Foreign Observers at Atomic Bomb Tests,

4 February 1946, *State-War-Navy Coordinating Committee Policy Files,* microfilm. See also Minutes of the 33rd Meeting, 21 January 1946, *State-War-Navy Coordinating Committee Policy Files,* microfilm.

23. "Minutes of the 33rd Meeting," 21 January 1946, *State-War-Navy Coordinating Committee Policy Files,* microfilm.

24. Forrestal, "Atomic Bomb Tests," 13 February 1946, Papers of James Forrestal, *The Forrestal Diaries, 1944–1949* (Washington, DC: NPPSO-Naval District Washington Microfilm Section, 1973–1979) (hereafter cited as *Forrestal Diaries*).

25. Ibid.

26. "Telephone Conversation between Sullivan and Blandy," 4 March 1946, Folder 1, United Nations Organization, Box 12, Papers of John L. Sullivan, Harry S. Truman Library, Independence, Missouri (hereafter cited as Sullivan Papers, HSTL), 1.

27. Ibid., 2.

28. Ibid.

29. Ibid., 2–3.

30. Lee to Blandy, 18 March 1946, "Memo: Suggested Steps to Insure Proper Public Information Coverage of CROSSROADS," Folder 39–1–37, Box 72, Record Group 80, General Records of the Office of the Secretary of the Navy (hereafter cited as RG 80), NA II, 1.

31. Ibid.

32. Ibid., 2.

33. Ibid., 2.

34. Eisenhower to MacArthur, 22 March 1946, RG 9: Radiograms, Blue Binders, Atomic Energy Commission, MacArthur Memorial Archives.

35. Gardner to Sherman, Memorandum for OP-03, Destruction of *Nagato* and *Sakawa,* 25 March 1946, Folder D-3, Box 161, Strategic Plans, RG 38, NA II; see also Sherman to Wright, Memorandum for OP-34, 25 March 1946, Folder D-3, Box 161, Strategic Plans, RG 38, NA II.

36. Gardner to Sherman, "Memorandum for OP-03, Destruction of *Nagato* and *Sakawa,*" 25 March 1946, as well as Sherman to Wright, "Memorandum for OP-34," both dated 25 March 1946 and found in Folder D-3, Box 161, Strategic Plans, RG 38, NA II.

37. Senate Report No. 1238, *Authorizing the Use of Naval Vessels to Determine the Effect of Atomic Weapons upon Such Vessels,* 5 March 1946, United States Senate, 79th Congress, 2nd Session, 6.

38. Forrestal, "Atomic Bomb Tests," 21 March 1946, *Forrestal Diaries.*

39. Kopplemann to Truman, 23 March 1946, Folder OF 85-P, United Nations Security Council, Box 573, White House Official Files (hereafter cited as WHOF), HSTL.

40. Ibid.

41. Truman to Kopplemann, 25 March 1946, Folder OF 85-P, United Nations Security Council, Box 573, WHOF, HSTL.

42. Senate Report, *Authorizing the Use of Naval Vessels to Determine the Effect of Atomic Weapons upon Such Vessels,* 24 March 1946, United States Senate, 79th Congress, 2nd Session, 1 and 4.

43. Forrestal to Walsh, 29 March 1946, Folder 39–1-37, Box 72, RG 80, NA II, 1.

44. Ibid., 1–2.

45. Dewey to Walsh, 2 April 1946, Folder 39–1-37, Box 72, RG 80, NA II.

46. Memo from Blandy, "Subj: Publicity Regarding Operation CROSSROADS," 2 April 1946, Folder 39–1-37, Box 72, RG 80, NA II.

47. Ibid.

48. Lee to Blandy, 17 April 1946, Papers of William Kepner (hereafter cited as Kepner Papers), 168.6005–160, Air Force Historical Research Agency, Maxwell Air Force Base, Montgomery, Alabama (hereafter cited as AFHRA), 2.

49. "Telephone Conversation between Taylor and Robertson," 7 May 1946, Folder 39–1-37, Box 72, RG 80, NA II.

50. Ibid.

51. Blandy to Forrestal, no date, Folder 39–1-37, Box 72, RG 80, NA II. Though there was no date on this letter, it was filed with other materials from May 1946.

52. Ibid.

53. Columbia Broadcasting System show "Operation Crossroads," 28 May 1946, Folder Operation Crossroads, Box 407, Papers of Harold Ickes, Manuscript Division, Library of Congress, Washington, DC (hereafter cited as Ickes Papers), 1 and 6.

54. Nimitz to the Subcommittee, 30 May 1946, *Hearings before the Subcommittee of the Committee on Appropriations,* United States Senate, Navy Department Appropriation Bill for 1947, 79th Congress, 2nd Session, 8, 13–14.

55. JCS 1691/10, 29 December 1947, Combined Chiefs of Staff (hereafter cited as CCS) 471.6 (10–16–45), Section 9, Part 2 and Section 3, "Effects on Ships," JCS, Bikini Evaluation Report, "The Atomic Bomb as a Military Weapon" as well as Vice Admiral W. H. P. Blandy, "Bikini: Guidepost to the Future," *Sea Power* 6 (1946), 7–9; both sources cited in David Rosenberg, "American Postwar American Air Doctrine and Organization: The Navy Experience," in Alfred Hurley and Robert Ehrhart, eds., *Air Power and Warfare: The Proceedings of the 8th Military History Symposium* (Washington, DC: Office of Air Force History, 1979), 248–249; see also Lloyd Graybar and Ruth Graybar, "America Faces the Atomic Age: 1946," *Air University Review* 35 (January–February 1984): 72, 73, 75.

56. Hatch, 29 July 1946, Folder 39–1-37, Box 72, RG 80, NA II.

57. Ibid.

58. For the view about nonchalance, see Graybar and Graybar, "America Faces the Atomic Age," 72–73; Lloyd Graybar, "Bikini Revisited," *Military Affairs* 80 (October 1980): 121; James Farrell, "The Crossroads of Bikini," *Journal of American Culture* 10 (Summer 1987): 55–66; Paul Boyer, *By The Bomb's Early Light: American Thought and Culture at the Dawn of the Atomic Age* (New York: Pantheon Books, 1985), 22, 152, 293; and Weisgall, *Operation Crossroads,* 192–205.

59. Blandy to JTF One, 27 August 1946, Folder 39–1-37, Box 72, RG 80, NA II.

60. War Department Message to Commanding General, 1st Army et al., 2 August 1946, RG 9: Radiograms, Blue Binders, Atomic Energy Commission, MacArthur Memorial Archives, 1, 2, 4, 5.

61. Ibid., 5–8; see also Beecher to Forrestal, Memorandum for the Secretary, 31 July 1946, Folder 39–1–37, Box 72, RG 80, NA II.

62. Ramsey to Blandy, 14 August 1946, Folder O-1 (Operations—Future), Box 163, Strategic Plans, RG 38, NA II.

63. Blandy to Nimitz, 17 August 1946, Folder O-1, (Operations—Future), Box 163, Strategic Plans, RG 38, NA II, 1–3; see also Walter Millis, ed., *The Forrestal Diaries* (New York: Viking Press, 1951), 203.

64. Blandy to JTF One, 5 September 1946, Folder 39–1–37, Box 72, RG 80, NA II.

65. Blandy, *Operational Report on Atomic Bomb Tests Able and Baker (Operation Crossroads) Conducted at Bikini Atoll, Marshall Islands on 1 July 1946 and 25 July 1946,* vol. 1 (Washington, DC: XRD-206, NTIS Document No. A473986, Department of the Navy, 1946), II(B)3–II(B)4, http://www.dtic.mil/docs/citations/AD0473986

66. Ibid., II(B)4–II(B)5.

67. Ibid., II(B)6.

68. Ibid., II(B)6–II(B)7.

69. Ibid., II(A)2–II(A)3, http://www.dtic.mil/docs/citations/AD0473986

70. Ibid., VII(Q)14, http://www.dtic.mil/docs/citations/AD0473986

71. W. H. P. Blandy, "Operation Crossroads: The Story of the Air and Underwater Tests of the Atomic Bomb at Bikini," *Army Ordnance* 31 (January–February 1947): 341–342.

72. Ibid., 343. For an account that relates from primary sources how much more powerful and dangerous the bomb's effect was than originally anticipated, see Weisgall, *Operation Crossroads,* 182–245.

73. Forrestal to the House Subcommittee on Appropriations, Navy Department Appropriation Bill for 1948, *Hearings before the Subcommittee of the Committee on Appropriations, House of Representatives,* 80th Congress, 1st Session, 21 January 1947, 25–26.

74. Ibid., 26.

75. Ibid.

76. Smedberg to Forrestal, 17 May 1947, Folder 69–5-21, Box 118, RG 80, NA II.

77. Buchanan to Forrestal, 10 June 1947, Folder 69–5-21, Box 118, RG 80, NA II.

78. Ibid., and Forrestal to the Board of Decorations and Medals, 12 June 1947, Folder 69–5-21, Box 118, RG 80, NA II.

Bibliography

Primary Sources

Archives

Air Force Historical Research Agency, Maxwell Air Force Base, Montgomery, Alabama
Papers of William Kepner, 168.6005-160

Division Records
Record Group 80, General Records of the Office of the Secretary of the Navy
Douglas MacArthur Memorial Archives and Library, Norfolk, Virginia
Record Group 9, Commander-in-Chief, US Army Forces Pacific Collections of Messages (Radiograms)
Blue Binders, Plans and Operations File
Dwight D. Eisenhower Library, Abilene, Kansas
Papers of Lauris Norstad
Harry S. Truman Library, Independence, Missouri
Papers of John L. Sullivan
White House Official Files
Library of Congress, Washington, DC, Manuscript Division
Papers of Harold Ickes
National Archives II, College Park, Maryland
Record Group 38, Records of the Office of the Chief of Naval Operations, Strategic Plans
Naval History and Heritage Command, Washington Navy Yard, Washington, DC
Operational Report on Atomic Bomb Tests Able and Baker (Operation Crossroads) Conducted at Bikini Atoll, Marshall Islands on 1 July 1946 and 25 July 1946, vol. 1 (Washington, DC: XRD-206, NTIS Document No. A473986, Department of the Navy, 1946); also available at http://www.dtic.mil/docs/citations/AD0473986

Congressional Records

U.S. House of Representatives. House Subcommittee on Appropriations, Navy Department Appropriation Bill for 1948. *Hearings before the Subcommittee of the Committee on Appropriations*. 80th Congress, 1st Session

U.S. Senate. *Hearings before the Special Committee on Atomic Energy*. 79th Congress, 1st Session

———. *Hearings before the Subcommittee of the Committee on Appropriations*, Navy Department Appropriation Bill for 1947. 79th Congress, 2nd Session

———. Senate Report No. 1238, *Authorizing the Use of Naval Vessels to Determine the Effect of Atomic Weapons upon Such Vessels*, 5 March 1946. 79th Congress, 2nd Session

Edited Collections

Millis, Walter, ed. *The Forrestal Diaries*. New York: Viking Press, 1951.

Microfilm

Papers of James Forrestal. *The Forrestal Diaries, 1944–1949*. Washington, DC: NPPSO-Naval District Washington Microfilm Section, 1973–1979.

State-War-Navy Coordinating Committee Policy Files, 1944–1947. Wilmington, DE: Scholarly Resources, 1977.

Published Sources

Blandy, W. H. P. "Operation Crossroads: The Story of the Air and Underwater Tests of The Atomic Bomb at Bikini." *Army Ordnance* 31 (January–February 1947): 341–343.

Secondary Sources

Dissertations

Hamburger, Kenneth. "The Technology, Doctrine, and Politics of U.S. Coast Defense, 1880–1945." Ph.D. diss., Duke University, 1986.

Books

Boyer, Paul. *By the Bomb's Early Light: American Thought and Culture at the Dawn of the Atomic Age.* New York: Pantheon Books, 1985.

Coletta, Paolo. *The United States Navy and Defense Unification, 1947–1953.* Newark: University of Delaware Press, 1981.

Davis, Vincent. *Postwar Defense Policy and the U.S. Navy, 1943–1946.* Chapel Hill: University of North Carolina Press, 1966.

———. *The Admiral's Lobby.* Chapel Hill: University of North Carolina Press, 1967.

Linn, Brian. *Guardians of Empire: The U.S. Army and the Pacific, 1902–1940.* Chapel Hill: University of North Carolina Press, 1997.

Millett, Allan, and Peter Maslowski. *For the Common Defense: A Military History of the United States of America.* New York: Free Press, 1994.

Shurcliff, William. *Bombs at Bikini: The Official Report of Operation Crossroads.* New York: William H. Wise and Co., 1947.

Underwood, Jeffrey. *The Wings of Democracy: The Influence of Air Power on the Roosevelt Administration, 1933–1941.* College Station: Texas A&M University Press, 1991.

Weigley, Russell. *The American Way of War: A History of United States Military Strategy and Policy.* Bloomington: Indiana University Press, 1973.

Weisgall, Jonathan. *Operation Crossroads: The Atomic Tests at Bikini Atoll.* Annapolis: Naval Institute Press, 1994.

Wildenberg, Thomas. *Billy Mitchell's War with the Navy: The Interwar Rivalry over Air Power.* Annapolis: Naval Institute Press, 2013.

Official Histories

Richard, Commander Dorothy, USNR. *United States Naval Administration in the Trust Territory of the Pacific Islands,* Vols. 1–3. Washington, DC: Office of the Chief of Naval Operations, 1957.

Articles

Farrell, James. "The Crossroads of Bikini," *Journal of American Culture* 10 (Summer 1987): 55–66.

Graybar, Lloyd. "Bikini Revisited," *Military Affairs* 80 (October 1980): 121.

———. "The 1946 Atomic Bomb Tests: Atomic Diplomacy or Bureaucratic Infighting?" *Journal of American History* 72 (March 1986): 892.

Graybar, Lloyd, and Ruth Graybar. "America Faces the Atomic Age: 1946," *Air University Review* 35 (January–February 1984): 72, 73, 75.

Rosenberg, David. "American Postwar American Air Doctrine and Organization: The Navy Experience," in Alfred Hurley and Robert Ehrhart, eds., *Air Power and Warfare: The Proceedings of the 8th Military History Symposium.* Washington, DC: Office of Air Force History, 1979.

Conference Papers

Unsworth, Michael. "Coast Defense: Roles, Missions, and War Plan Orange." Paper delivered to the Fifty-Ninth Annual Meeting of the Society for Military History, Fredericksburg, Virginia, 10 April 1992.

6

Training a National Army in Time of Civil War

The American Military Advisory Mission to China, 1945–1949

Katherine K. Reist

The American training mission continued wartime efforts to create a modern professional force for the Nationalist (or Guomindang) Government of the Republic of China, which was recognized by most other countries. Negotiations for unification and an integrated government and military of the Chinese Communist and other small parties with the Nationalists were undertaken. The American goal of a unified democratic China, able to protect its borders, seemed possible. The role of the military would be a successful element in achieving this goal.

The importance of the U.S. Military Advisory Missions in China was subsumed in the debate over the responsibility for the Chinese Communist victory. American policy in the postwar period was ambivalent and divided in its aspects and goals. Thus, little more than mentions of the program are found in the literature under the broader discussions of the Stilwell mission, the Marshall mission, Wedemeyer's experiences, or Cold War relations in Asia. One exception is an article in the *Journal of Military History*.[1]

When the war against Japan ended in August 1945, the major players were, for the most part, unready to immediately begin the transition to peace. The Chinese government was established in Chungking, in the country's west; the Communists were expanding in the north and central areas. Warlord armies, of only expedient loyalty, and puppet troops, encompassing those who had worked with the Japanese-dominated local governments, were able to maneuver in many provinces. In addition, two million plus Japanese troops, for the most part in the eastern cities, the north, and the northeast, provided a potential threat if not immediately repatriated.[2] Under these circumstances, China was not prepared for an immediate transition to peace. The Soviets, under the Yalta Agreement, reinforced by a treaty with the Nationalist Government, occupied Manchuria and part of adjoining North China.[3] The American Headquarters, U.S. Forces, China Theater was also located in Chungking, and with the end of the war, many stationed there anticipated a return to the United States. Japan had surrendered; but the uncertainty that all of its military forces, particularly those in Manchuria, would obey such an order complicated the transition to peace. For United States policymakers, the reality that the balance of power in Asia had been upset and reconfigured meant that new policies would have to be crafted to meet the volatile situation.

Prewar American planning focused on the Philippines. War Plan YELLOW was an evacuation operation for Americans from China in the event of an antiforeign military threat from the Chinese. Most of the American forces in China were reassigned prior to the attack on Pearl Harbor. One exception was the stationing of the American Volunteer Group, the Flying Tigers, serving with the Chinese Air Force. In 1943, the Sino-American Cooperative Organization operating along the coastal areas of China under Captain Milton E. Miles, USN, and Tai Li, head of the Investigations and Statistics Bureau of the Nationalist Government, scouted possible landing sites in South China for American forces to be supported by a large guerrilla force operating in the area.[4] Taiwan was also considered as a staging area for the invasion of Japan. Events in the Pacific, as well as a poor showing of the Nationalist forces against the Japanese Ichigo campaign in 1944, obviated the need for a landing site in China.

The Chinese situation, politically and militarily, was complex. Although in theory a united effort against the Japanese had been agreed to during the war, neither the Guomindang nor the Chinese Communist Party, given their recent history of civil war, was able to cooperate in any meaningful manner. Geographical separation was one factor, although the Guomindang maintained troops around the Communist areas in the north and the Chinese Communist Party had taken advantage of the war situation to organize areas and troops in the center and south. The Americans had a military aid mission to the Chinese under Lend-Lease and other programs during the war. The isolation of the Chinese political organizations limited the ability of the Americans to deliver supplies. The majority of the supplies went to the recognized Nationalist Government, although an observer group, the Dixie Mission, was stationed in Yan'an with the Communists. The Americans had trained some Chinese divisions to fight the Japanese, and aid and training for a Chinese Air Force had also been part of the package.[5] In the areas not controlled by either of the above forces, warlord and puppet governments and military organizations worked for their own goals. Areas of China were controlled directly by Japanese forces and their civilian counterparts, who were to be disarmed and repatriated. The presence of Soviet forces in the northeast further complicated an already complex military and political arena.

For the United States, a defeated and demilitarized Japan left Asia unstable. In the era of increasing disagreement and tension in relations with the Soviets, a strong democratic country, to offset the appeal of Communism in disorganized, underdeveloped areas as Japanese forces were withdrawn, seemed the way to reestablish a balance of power in the area. The obvious choice for the State Department was China. China had been a wartime ally, recognized by President Franklin D. Roosevelt as one of the "Big Four" at the Cairo Conference.[6] In the early years of the war, the exploits of the Flying Tigers seemed to be one of the few areas where the Americans were hitting back at the Japanese. The American-educated Madame Chiang Kai-shek (Jiang Jieshi) had been given a warm welcome in the United States, and China had been given extensive coverage in many of the Henry Luce publications. The American branch of the Chamber of Commerce in China, along with many religious organizations, also had strong interests in China, which tended to reinforce a rather romantic view of the country in the eyes of the American public.

Some in the American government hoped to use prewar and wartime contacts and relations with China as a springboard to helping the Chinese government to create a strong, unified national government that would offset both the vacuum left by the Japanese defeat and the armed presence of the Soviet Union in China. The Soviets had a treaty with the Nationalists, an ability to aid the Communists, and a strong military presence extending into the northern part of Korea.[7] They were obviously in a position to affect the direction of postwar events in China. Therefore, American policy needed to offset the Soviet advantages, denying them a major role in influencing developments.

The immediate need from the Chinese government's perspective was to reestablish control over China and its territories (Taiwan and other islands) and disarm the Japanese troops still on Chinese soil. Both missions had to be carried out before the Communists could obtain Japanese weapons through the demobilization of these troops and establish control over more Chinese territory. Therefore, the Guomindang requested American air and sealift support in moving government military forces to Manchuria and North China, especially to the major cities, with some American forces holding these territories until Nationalist forces could take control. President Chiang Kai-shek requested five American divisions to occupy northern and eastern China.[8] The Americans were able to send the First and Sixth Marine Divisions for occupation duty, and elements of the Seventh Fleet to move Chinese Nationalist troops, in addition to those that were airlifted for immediate control.

China: Administrative Divisions (Courtesy of CIA.gov)

The Chinese Communist Party recognized the right of the established government to reoccupy territory, but wished to be recognized for its wartime efforts and included in the process. The Guomindang, however, ordered that the Japanese forces not surrender to the Communists and to maintain their weapons and civil order until relieved by the Nationalist Government's forces. Thus, a race for weapons and territory accelerated. The Soviets helped and hindered both groups. The Americans recognized the problems that the imminent civil war would cause for China as well as for their own policies. The Americans also tried to convince both the Nationalists and the Communists that China's interests would not be served by division, war, and further expenditures for war when a massive rebuilding of Chinese infrastructure and industry should be a major priority. U.S. Ambassador to China Patrick Hurley attempted to negotiate a cease-fire and settlement in the fall of 1945, but without sustainable results.

President Harry S. Truman decided to send General of the Army George C. Marshall to China to try to negotiate a cease-fire and to encourage the formation of a unified, democratic government and military. Marshall had served in China in the 1920s, and had, as Army Chief of Staff during the war, been aware of some of the problems there as a result of the reports of General Joseph Stilwell and Lieutenant General Albert Wedemeyer, the successive Commanding Generals of U.S. Forces in China. Marshall arrived as President Truman's Special Ambassador to China in December 1945, having retired from the Army in November. The resignation of Ambassador Hurley occurred in November as well. Marshall attempted, through a marathon series of meetings, to assess the political, economic, and military situations by contacting the major groups with political and/or military organizations. To prevent an undermining of his ability to influence the various players, but in particular by the Chinese government, Truman had given to Marshall control over economic aid and assistance, including supervising the heads of the Treasury Department, the Secretary of War, the Secretary of the Navy, the Maritime Commission, the Shipping Administration, and the Export Bank, none of whom was to negotiate with the Chinese except through the State Department with Marshall's approval.[9]

Initially greeted with enthusiasm by the various parties, Marshall tried to be neutral, facilitating the negotiations toward the desired goals. He was able to arrange a cease-fire agreement between the Guomindang and the Chinese Communist Party, and a promise to appoint members to a Political Consultative Conference from the Nationalists, the Communists, and the Democratic League who would write a constitution for a broadly representative national government. In addition, a preliminary agreement on reorganizing and restructuring a national military had been achieved. The problems, of course, were in the particulars of the agreements and their implementation.

The cease-fire agreement focused on the clashes, in North China in particular and Manchuria peripherally, between the Communists and the Nationalists. Each had control of territory, particularly as the Soviets withdrew, by May 1946. The Guomindang took control of the cities; the Chinese Communist Party organized much of the countryside. Each party, and each party army, was positioning itself for maximum benefit when either a cease-fire or a civil war began. Rail lines, as well as communications, had been cut. Poor roads made reinforcement and resupply difficult. Local commanders frequently took unauthorized actions, to the detriment of agreements. Local peasants were less than satisfied since the war had ended, yet no stability had been achieved.

Marshall's answer was to set up an Executive Headquarters in Peiping (now Beijing), where the Executive Committee was comprised, initially, of Marshall, General Zhou Enlai of the Chinese Communist Party, and General Chang Chun of the Guomindang.[10] Under them were to be field teams, again each comprised of a three-man unit, with one Nationalist member, one Communist member, and an American, who acted as chair. The teams would investigate allegations of infractions of the cease-fire, with unanimous agreements on decisions required. No decisions would be made if one party failed to send a representative.[11] If the nascent civil war in the north could be settled, with temporary control of territory agreed upon, the reestablishment of road, rail, and telegraphic communication could occur. With the north more or less stable, other problems, such as negotiations towards a unified government, could be addressed more easily.

Although the Executive Headquarters, after much argument, was also permitted to send teams to Manchuria—and in time fielded approximately twenty-three teams (all told), which actively investigated numerous violations or alleged violations—little progress of a permanent nature was accomplished.[12] Agreements were made for the repair of telegraph and rail lines, as well as the pullback of units, with a "neutral zone" separating them, but the agreements rarely held, if they were even implemented in the first place. One American commented that although both party representatives made speeches, and could often discuss problems with some candor, neither had authority to accomplish more than that.[13] Needless to say, the cease-fire did not hold; when Marshall left China on 11 March for a short trip to the United States to argue for aid to China based on the early political and military agreements, both sides exploited his absence to expand their territory, with numerous armed clashes. Marshall returned to China on 17 April. Although another cease-fire was negotiated in June with many of the same terms as the original, it fared no better. Neither party trusted the other, as each thought that it was capable of winning a military conflict against the other. Each made some effort with Marshall's plan, at least at the higher levels, but skeptics on both sides, for their own reasons, managed to persuade their leaders to negotiate only as long as some advantage from the negotiations was perceived. The Guomindang wanted continued aid, both monetary and military, but with the minimum of restrictions or reforms. The Chinese Communists wanted official standing as a party, with representatives under the new constitution, and a recognized role in the national military establishment. Yet the manner in which each was to accomplish its goals could not be reconciled.

The initial political agreement, which followed in many ways previous attempts at reconciliation, was to end the period of tutelage, which had been recommended by Sun Yatsen, the first President of the Republic of China (ROC), as a transition period to democracy. This period would be dominated by the Guomindang Party. Such a government had been in place essentially since 1927. The next step was to convene a National Assembly and write a constitution for a democratic government in China. To aid in the implementation of this next step, Marshall facilitated an agreement for a Political Consultative Conference where representatives from the Nationalists, the Communists, the Democratic League, the Youth Party, and non-party-affiliated groups could meet and work out an agreed political agenda, including the formation of a coalition government, the convoking of an elected National Assembly, and the writing of a constitution.

The Political Consultative Conference was to have thirty-eight members, with eight from the Guomindang, seven representing the Chinese Communist Party, nine from the Democratic League, five members of the Youth Party, and nine non-party-affiliated members.[14] The powers of the organization were not defined, although expectations were high. With a political settlement, other problems of immediate concern, most of them of a social and/or economic character, could be addressed. The press had requested that the sessions be open; all groups except the Nationalists agreed.[15] The expectation was that the Constitutional Convention could be elected by May. Marshall tried to convince the various parties that a timely agreement was necessary since delays allowed the Soviets more opportunity to hinder China's recovery from the war and U.S. forces would soon leave the country.

Initially, there were proposals to abolish the Supreme National Defense Council and to have the government be independent of the Central Executive Committee of the Guomindang. A multiparty Council of State was to be formed, which would operate according to parliamentary principles. The cabinet ministers were also to represent various parties, and checks on the powers of appointment and the emergency powers of the President were to be emplaced. The Constitution would contain a charter of civil rights.[16] Since both major parties had compromised their original positions, Marshall remained to try to shepherd the process from agreement to implementation.

At first, Chiang Kai-shek announced that rights to be guaranteed included rights to speech, assembly, and association, with equal legal status for all parties; that elections would be held; and that political prisoners would be released.[17] The National Assembly was scheduled to meet on 5 May 1946. The Guomindang hoped to hold elections soon thereafter in order to guarantee a political process dominated by the Nationalists. Others wanted the elections first, and initially at the village level, then the district and national levels. The Draft Constitution reflected the Nationalist Party's wishes: a strong executive with few checks on his power by an elected National Assembly. The latter was to meet one month every three years, and had no power over the budget. Civil liberties were severely restricted.[18] Opposition parties demanded revisions.

The major points of disagreement between the Nationalists and the Communists reflected their views of political and military power; each, of course, had a party government that did not share meaningful aspects of power with others. The Guomindang wanted the Chinese Communists to surrender its troops prior to the establishment of a constitutional government. The Communists insisted that it could not trust the Nationalist Government, and therefore the troops would be integrated into a national army only after a constitutional government with Chinese Communist participation was established. The Nationalists, as reflected above, wanted a strong presidential system; the Communists favored a strong cabinet system. The Guomindang wanted a strongly centralized government; the Communists would give more power to the legislature and the provinces to offset the Guomindang domination of the executive. The Political Consultative Conference had been assigned no enforcement capability; basically, it operated as an argument for continuous American aid or as a means to buy time for military preparations.[19]

These disagreements only strengthened the extremists in each party, who argued that the only solution was military and that Marshall had delayed their certain victory. Vocal members of each organization also believed that only after a few months of fighting could meaningful negotiations be undertaken. If the seriousness of each position could be demonstrated to the other militarily, then a settlement on its terms would be achieved. Continued jostling for territorial position, increasing mistrust, and increasing disillusionment with the Americans ensued. Because the United States proclaimed its neutrality in China's political affairs while it continued to support monetarily and militarily the established government, American credibility was questioned. Marshall did suspend aid for eight months in the fall of 1946 to attempt to prove to the Chinese government that American support was not automatic, but Congressional pressure led to the resumption of aid without change in the established order in China.[20] Marshall began to position himself to return to the United States.

While the issues of implementing a cease-fire through the Executive Headquarters teams and the formation of a broadly based constitutional government were under discussion, a third area, that of a reorganized and modernized national army, was of equal concern. In order to facilitate a representative government, a unified and reorganized military had also to be negotiated. This area was one in which Marshall felt his expertise was of particular value. If a national military could be agreed upon, surely the conditions for both a cease-fire and a political agreement could be implemented. The Americans had experience with training Chinese forces in the war against Japan. Both air and ground elements had received training and equipment through aid and advisory programs. For Marshall, the reorganization of the ground forces had first priority since most of China's military were ground forces. The core of the Guomindang modernized forces were the thirty-nine divisions of the ALPHA Forces, units that had received American training and organization. Some American training manuals had been translated into Chinese, which could be employed for the purpose of further modernization. Major problems related to the organization and command of the various forces, some in only nominal control by the Guomindang, and some in actual or potential opposition. To create a modern force, one that China could afford as it recovered from the war, meant a demobilization of some units and a unification of those remaining into a single national entity.

Chiang Kai-shek had requested the formation of the U.S. Military Advisory Mission in September 1945.[21] The Americans had agreed, particularly after the Nationalist leader had pointed out that the Soviets and British had also offered their assistance, a point he would frequently raise when problems with the Americans arose.[22] Many disagreements relating to the attempts to integrate party armies ensued; the puppet, warlord, and other forces—usually described as "bandit," and some of which included Japanese—were to be gradually demobilized according to a timetable. Issues were raised as to the social and economic effect of so many unemployed officers and men in a country recovering from a fifteen-year war. While it was assumed that the majority of the enlisted forces could be employed in farming, fishing, or otherwise on the land, the officers, with their status and privileges, posed a bigger problem. Suggestions for employment in police and border forces as rail guards or other paramilitary organizations were made, but such a transition would be difficult at best.[23] The Chinese Communist Party was also reluctant to demobilize its officers. The stated reason was that when Chinese Communist officers returned to their homes in Nationalist-controlled territory, they were murdered by government forces.

By the time Marshall arrived in China, attempts to turn some of the American forces in China into an advisory group—for both ground (including air) and naval forces—were underway. Marshall had negotiated a plan for the reorganization of ground forces in China in February 1946.[24] It was a very complex arrangement. The government forces, inclusively, numbered approximately three million men. The Communist forces, including irregular and militia elements, were composed of approximately two million. Therefore, both groups had to demobilize some of their strength and reorganize the rest. The goal was a national army of sixty divisions, fifty of them Guomindang and ten Communist. These forces would be trained and equipped by the Americans.[25] The plans included an elaborate timetable as to the reduction of forces and their composition. The country was divided into ten military districts, each of which was to have a training center. The army units stationed there were to be variously composed of Nationalist and Communist divisions, generally in a three-division unit. In some areas, such as South China, only Guomindang troops would be assigned; in others, one or two of the divisions would be Communist. These units would report to the Minister of War.[26] The timetable for demobilization was a major problem, as neither force wished to be placed in a weakened position until some of the outstanding political problems were negotiated.

Training would be conducted at a series of schools set up according to the American system, with the first priority being the training of instructors for subsequent classes. Sites for the schools would have to be located; support in terms of housing, medical facilities, and supplies would have to be established; equipment for training the various forces would have to be acquired; and manuals would have to be created or translated. Additionally, some officers would be selected and sent for training at various military schools in the United States. A series of combined military committees or other organizations would have to be established as part of the overall reorganization to coordinate American and Chinese efforts. These efforts for the Americans would be organized through the Army Advisory Group (AAG) and the Naval Advisory Group Survey Board, which were in existence, or with similar organizations that were to be created.

Several immediate concerns were expressed by both sides. One was the continual flow of American supplies for training purposes, particularly as Lend-Lease legislation expired in June 1946.[27] American surplus supplies in Asia and the Pacific provided an opportunity for the Chinese to acquire equipment at relatively low cost. Further aid for rebuilding and modernizing the country and the military was frequently requested. Control over the supplies delivered was an issue, particularly under the terms of the military agreement. An initial plan to establish a twelve-week basic course for both the Nationalists and the Communists was proposed.[28] The Communist forces, however, were initially reluctant to join a retraining program until many months after it was to be established. Marshall believed that their reluctance stemmed from the lack of formal training and organization for most of the Communist forces. He proposed a six-week initial program for the Communists in territory they controlled at Kalgan in order to allow them to acquire a minimal ability in marching and formations, which would relieve their fear of embarrassment before the Nationalist elements in the joint training effort.[29] Initial approval for this proposal was granted. However, when supplies for this program arrived in Shanghai, permission to ship them to the north was never obtained.[30]

Problems in the acceptance of American plans occurred since supplies were not shared, nor did there seem any prospect that they would be. Nor, as fighting continued between the contending forces, could Communist criticism and disillusionment with American efforts be refuted without an enforceable political settlement. In addition, popular discontent among those who did not support the established government was evident, especially within the intellectual community. This discontent was reflected in several publications, particularly in their editorials. By the summer, Marshall was convinced that his mission had failed. He remained in China as promises of change were made but never implemented. One of the key problems was that Marshall saw his role as a mediator, while Chiang saw his role as a facilitator in an anti-communist alliance.[31] Marshall requested his recall in October 1946 and left for the United States in January 1947.

Nonetheless, the American advisory missions were underway in China and were continued by the Chinese government. Requirements for American participation in an advisory program were spelled out in unmistakable terms for the Chinese parties. American combat troops would not be sent to China. The American advisers would not instruct or advise on tactics, nor accompany troops in the field. Neither would they have control over distribution of supplies.[32] They were there to train instructors for the schools, set up a modernized military organization, and offer advice as to training. They were not to get involved in political matters, nor work in direct contact with Chinese forces in the field. Americans were ordered not to comment on aspects of Chinese practices or personnel. Initially, there was even a stipulation that American arms were not to be used in any civil war.[33] Chiang had stated requirements as well: that no possibility of differing viewpoints on the above conditions were to be placed before him for resolution and that some method be adopted to ensure that duplication or overlap of functions be avoided by the various groups in China.[34]

For the Americans, having decided on the parameters of their advisory mission, the number of personnel required, the conditions under which they would serve, and their chain of command in country had to be agreed upon. In September 1945, a Joint Chiefs of Staff memo outlined a proposal for a military mission consisting of 3,880 personnel, with guaranteed rights and concessions to be negotiated by the State Department. The Americans would serve a two-year tour in this assignment, and it was estimated that the mission would take five or six years. The State Department, however, decided that the Joint Chiefs of Staff memo's conditions were too similar to the unequal treaty rights only recently abrogated and that the number proposed could be perceived as an attempt to dominate China, not to assist the country.[35] A small-scale advisory mission was approved by January 1946 under the war powers of the President.[36] Therefore, in February 1946, President Truman directed Secretary of State James Byrnes to negotiate with the Chinese government for the U.S. Military Advisory Mission, and that Secretary of War Robert P. Patterson and Secretary of the Navy James V. Forrestal should jointly establish such a mission.[37]

American planning for the military advisory group could be organized traditionally in one of two ways: first, similar to missions to Latin America, individuals would retain their rank and status, but be employed by the local government and responsible to it; second, people would be sent as units and responsible to the American government.[38] Marshall favored the second approach under the Ambassador. A variation of this form was adopted.

In order to take advantage of the American military personnel in China at the end of the war, a transition in organization and function was undertaken in order to keep experienced Americans in the country. Replacements would be necessary once a permanent mission was established. Therefore, U.S. Forces, China Theater in Chungking and the Chinese Combat Command in Kunming were dissolved by December 1945, to be replaced by the Nanking Liaison Group in 1946, which was reconfigured as the Nanking Headquarters Command that same year. By October 1946, the Army Advisory Group was formally recognized, later to be incorporated in a Joint U.S. Military Advisory Group (JUSMAG) in 1948. The American Observer Group was withdrawn from Yan'an in March 1947.[39]

The Army Advisory Group was organized by General Wedemeyer prior to his return to the United States. The Naval Advisory Survey Board was also functioning as it turned over to the Chinese some ships and naval craft from the U.S. inventory and trained the Chinese in their use and maintenance. A naval school system was also instituted. The Air Advisory Group was part of the Army Group. Its training and schools were built on the existing bases and training programs from the war. In August 1946, Congress authorized the Naval Advisory Group, which was formally activated in September.[40] The Army mission would not be formally approved by Congress for eighteen months. The AAG was left for that period in an anomalous status. It continued to operate, however, and together these groups comprised the Military Advisory Group (MAG), China.

The reconfiguration of the Chinese chain of command was also necessary. While Chiang Kai-shek was the head of the government, and of the Guomindang and military, the rest of the chain of command and responsibility was less than clear, or when evident, followed. Since Chiang valued loyalty over all other characteristics, he frequently interfered with promotions and operations. Naturally, those who felt themselves part of his inner trusted group appealed directly to him in many matters. Subordinates often did not feel compelled to follow their superiors' orders.[41] Americans observed that there seemed to be no pattern of assigning functions. They saw the Chinese organization as "cumbersome, unwieldy, and lacking proper coordination."[42] Obviously, this construct was far from a modern organization, which the Americans hoped to create under civilian, but not Nationalist, control. Efforts were made to establish a clearer military organization for the Chinese. The first priority was the National Ministry of Defense, which was established from the National Military Council of the Guomindang, beginning in June 1946; the transition, however, was still underway one year later.[43]

The mission of the Ministry of National Defense was to defend China, with a capability to expand from peacetime to wartime requirements. Its organization was to be relatively simple so as to allow the response to the Chief of Staff's orders to be both rapid and supervised. Authority would also be delegated to the Supreme General Staff. The Regional Army Commanders, under the reorganization plan, would report to the Ministry. The Commander-in-Chief had the power to appoint and relieve subordinates.[44] American advice would be available to this organization and to its Chief of Staff, Secretariat, and Planning Staffs through Combined Chiefs of Staff—including the American Navy and Army Chiefs of the Advisory Mission, a Combined Secretariat, an American Joint Secretariat, and a Combined Planning Staff—with the Joint Planning Staff. In addition, a Joint Advisory Council, comprised of the Chief of the Naval Advisory Group and the Chiefs of the Army Advisory Group (including the Air Chief), would be available to advise the Chinese President.[45] This Council was authorized by President Truman in May 1946.

By May 1946, the Chinese government had specified some of the training areas to be undertaken by the Americans. These included: personnel and administration, intelligence, plans and operations, the service of supply and procurement, organization and training, the Adjutant General's Office, the Judge Advocate General's Office, the Provost Marshal's Office, the Special Services Office, the Chemical Warfare Service, the Corps of Engineers, the Finance Department, the Medical Corps, the Transportation Corps, the Public Information Office, the Civil Affairs Office, the Reserve Affairs Office, the Manpower Board, the Budget Office, and the Inspector General's Office.[46] These areas obviously paralleled component American organizations, but the Chinese tendency to overstaff positions and overlap functions did not bode well for a timely adaptation to this system. Indeed, many organizational plans were written, translated, and sent back for amendment on a regular basis.

For the Americans to staff such positions as have already been detailed, a large number of senior field grade officers and senior enlisted personnel would be needed. Both combat experience and specific expertise were required, especially as the entire training mission for the Army and its Air Corps (until 1948, when a separate Air Force component became part of the Joint U.S. Military Advisory Group) numbered somewhere around 750 people, of whom 242 were Air Corps. The Naval component, including naval and marine personnel, numbered approximately three hundred.[47] In addition, schools for motor maintenance for both ground vehicles and aircraft engines, signal communications, radio operations, maintenance and repair, and similar needs would add to the burden of those assigned to the mission.[48] Further training was to be undertaken at staff military academies, which awarded a bachelor of science degree; reserve officer training corps programs; service schools; a war college; a command and general staff school; an army industrial college; and branch schools.[49] Instructors would have to be carefully chosen for their teaching ability as well as their professional skills.

Also by May 1946, plans to train a group of Chinese Army officers in the United States had been approved. Approximately 325 officers ranging in rank from captain to colonel were to be screened first by the Chinese and then by the Americans for suitability—that is, for health, language proficiency, and education.[50] The school system in China was to begin on a small scale, emphasizing quality and based on the previous training conducted during the war. Selection of Chinese officers and noncommissioned officers to be trained as instructors also had to be expedited. Many arguments over eligibility and/or subsequent promotions occurred. Many Chinese did not wish to be trained as instructors or so assigned. Civilians from nearby universities were utilized initially, but their lack of military knowledge and values proved to be less than desirable.[51] Still, by September 1947, a standard operating procedure for preparing U.S. manuals in the Chinese language had received limited approval from the Ministry of National Defense.[52]

In planning for the operations of the Military Advisory Group, the preparation of studies of the mission as well as the organization and functions for all major elements of the Ministry of National Defense was undertaken. Then, an explanation to all the agencies concerned had to be made. Advice and assistance for the supervision of schools was established. Included in the latter were the supervision of personnel, procurement, and supply systems; the training of inductees; the training of the reorganized field forces; training for the operation and maintenance of telecommunications systems; the training and operation of an air force weather system; and training for the care, operations, and maintenance of aircraft and naval craft.[53] The latter elements, while not part of the formal Army mission, still came under Army and/or joint planning concerns.

By the end of June 1947, every advisory section met almost daily with corresponding sections of the Ministry of National Defense. The average number of weekly contacts was estimated at 230; to June of that year, forty-one formal studies had been done on the reorganization of the Chinese Armed Forces. The Armed Forces Medical Center in Shanghai had also been established.[54] The normal problems with bureaucracy were more than doubled by the need for translations, and for the approval of individuals in a system that had retained persons more comfortable with a different organization. Frequently, the senior officers simply wished for continued supplies, but not for formal changes; junior officers appeared to be more amenable to change. Many senior officers were not convinced that the American system, which they acknowledged had won the war with Japan, could be adapted successfully in China. Differences in history, psychology, and tradition were noted. Each detail of a proposed change was carefully reviewed. Up to that point, for much of the twentieth century the Chinese had attempted to replace traditional political, social, and economic systems with Western-influenced ones. Some modifications had proved necessary to these systems as they had been understood and applied in China. So, too, would be the case for these military reforms. The Americans were not the first foreign military advisers in China; therefore, the Chinese wished to take those elements that were useful for their own and modify or reject the rest. Yet to change the system while fighting a war made anything more than discussion of systematic change difficult. Any military reverses could be blamed by commanders on unsuitable American methods. Most Chinese officers remained skeptical of proposed changes. There was some complaint that the Americans treated the Chinese as teachers did school students, with understandable resentment.

Americans, then, were involved with advising the President and the Advisers Office of the Ministry of National Defense and its support staff. The Americans were also involved with aiding in the establishment of a school system, with the training of the initial instructors, and with advice on the curricula once the schools were established. The Americans advised in other capacities as well. In addition to active duty military personnel, civilian staff were also employed—both American and Chinese. This mission would have been sufficiently complex in a time of peace. Instead, these responsibilities had to be carried out in a time of political and economic instability, most particularly a civil war. The uncontrolled inflation rate in China also made the lives of Americans sent there difficult. Much of the housing—where existent—was inadequate, and the high cost and shortage of building materials and construction limited the ability to improve the situation. There was a need for more housing, offices, storage space, and permanent hospital facilities. Food was occasionally scarce, water was frequently unhealthy, and even tea was occasionally unsafe. Creature comforts such as beer, wine, or soft drinks were also lacking.[55] Adaptations, in other words, were necessary for the Americans.

Training a professional force was difficult. Problems occurred with language, as no exact equivalent could be found for some terms; organization by American standards did not seem to mesh with the military mind-set or political beliefs of many of the Chinese, nor did the need for a single chain of command. Personal relationships were an important means of appointment and promotion in China. The problems of recruitment were also difficult to overcome. Many times, new recruits were sent immediately to the field without much formal training.[56] It was assumed that they were to learn on the battlefield. In addition, the wealthy could still buy their sons out of military service. Demobilization of the Nationalist Army had also been delayed or disguised. Frequently, two understrength units would be combined without any essential reduction in forces.[57] Even this cosmetic approach was resisted since one of the commanders would have to lose his independent command and privileges. A party domination still existed politically and, therefore, also militarily under whatever name the reorganization had assigned.

The civil war often meant that a school or other facility had to be relocated just when it had begun to function. Then, once again a site would have to be found and bargained for, repairs had to be planned, and, with luck, somewhat carried out. Students then had to be moved, instructors persuaded to remain with the school, and an interrupted curriculum reestablished. These changes were difficult to handle with any speed or efficiency. Initial estimates as to a timetable for the first graduates of the reorganized military—with the first officer and noncommissioned officer classes going into the field, with the first graduates of the Command and General Staff school being assigned to staffs, and a possibility of combined operations ready to be realized—were six years.[58] However, under existing conditions, this estimate was optimistic. Training at all ground force centers was to begin by 10 April 1948,[59] with the number of recruits decided and immediately sent to the nearest center. At the centers, recruits were screened for health problems. Eye and heart conditions were frequent causes for dismissal, as was the presence of communicable disease such as tuberculosis. In addition, some recruits were found to be illiterate and therefore unacceptable. In one group of 192 prospective candidates, only 107 were accepted for these reasons.[60] Nevertheless, the training of instructors at the Ground Force Center at Tangshan had begun by February 1947.[61]

By 1948, the Joint U.S. Military Advisory Group China had been authorized. Its mission was to assist the development of the Chinese Nationalist Armed Forces. Training programs for naval and marine forces, as well as air force and ground personnel, were continued. Coast Guard personnel were also assigned. However, the military advisers—other than those of the U.S. Army—believed that their missions were vastly overshadowed by the latter. Since the majority of China's military were ground forces, the Army Advisory Group seemed to dominate those assigned to coordinate with the Ministry of National Defense and with the President.[62] The Army advisers were aware that their advice to the Chinese Commander-in-Chief was only informal and confidential, and could therefore be easily ignored.[63] As their mission was defined as support for the Nationalists, why should the government or the military commanders carry out reforms when supplies were guaranteed? The Nationalists underestimated the revulsion which many Americans felt at the blatant corruption in the established system. Chiang believed that the Americans would support his anti-communist efforts under all conditions. Further, he believed that the rising tensions between the United States and the Soviet Union would result in a war that would secure for China the same protection and status as had been the case in the war with Japan.

The Army advisers had developed the Ground Forces Headquarters into an organization capable of operating in a reportedly "barely satisfactory" manner. The Ground Force School and the operations of the Artillery and Infantry Schools and Ground Force College were deemed to be fairly efficient. A system of training centers had been established—though only the one on Taiwan had produced satisfactory results—and improvement in the established Chinese Military Academies had been achieved.[64] Thousands of officers had been exposed to American ideas, doctrines, and methods of instruction. Yet the results of such exposure would not be known for several years under ideal circumstances, and progress was not accomplished with the average ground force division. More than anticipated by the Americans, the conditions imposed by the continuing civil war, coupled with the deteriorating economic conditions (which translated into lack of supplies, equipment, and housing), meant that not much in the way of actual reform of more than surface elements could occur. In addition, the lack of a positive "command presence," and at least passive, if not active, resistance to changes recommended, hampered the American efforts.[65] The absence until 1948 of a Chief of Chinese Ground Forces at the Ground Forces Headquarters also affected decision making at that level and for the Ground Forces subordinates. Staffs, when organized, were not utilized, as a reluctance to delegate authority was prevalent at all levels of command.[66]

There were reports that the Training Center at Canton had trained one division, which was rated "average" by Chinese standards but found to be "unsatisfactory" by the Americans. The school at Nanking produced a core of trained people for other institutions and individual replacements for divisions engaged in battle.[67] However, the limitations of funds for training meant that many of the units south of the Yangtze were unable to be retrained. For some of the centers, orders were evaded: that is, no training took place except on paper. For example, at Canton, a center to train cadres was established in December

1947. The Chinese staff was assigned over a period of two to three months. By May, little had been accomplished; when the Americans were permitted to inspect the facilities, they were found to be completely unsuitable for the project. The Center then moved in June and July.[68] American advisers arranged the preliminary course in August 1948. It was judged to be successful since nineteen American instructors were employed. But the school could not regularly operate until November as the three divisions concerned failed to send their people to be trained.[69] Many discussions were held, but the lack of a unified command structure hampered progress. When conditions in the government's military situation became critical in October 1948, the government recognized the need for change and requested further assistance and direct American military involvement.[70]

Reports from the field in 1948 noted that progress had been made since 1946, even though the scope of activities had expanded. There were Army Advisory Teams in Nanking, Shanghai, Peiping (Beijing), Hankow, Hangchow, Chengtu, Canton, and Formosa (Taiwan).[71] Critical problems were identified as being the lack of transport and trained aircraft maintenance personnel. Poor road conditions in China outside of the cities, coupled with the difficulty of movement in some areas due to the effects of the civil war, meant a heavy reliance on transport aircraft. Other areas that needed improvement were in the Ground Forces replacement system, with a need to increase combat strength in some units. Many units had a paper strength, on which resources were allocated, but which in reality were undermanned at some level. The supply system also required some simplification, with individuals having industrial experience needed as well. Additionally, requirements for more training for maneuver and firepower of the Nationalist Army and their coordination were reported. One memo from the Chief of the American Army Group to a Chinese lieutenant general stated that due to limitations of American personnel, it was not possible to give advice and assistance to commanders in the field, nor would operational advice be given to them during the civil war.[72] Attempts by the Chinese at various levels to bring the Americans into operational matters were continuous.

The political and military situation in China in 1948 made the position of some of the Advisory Teams precarious. Every problem seemed to be affected by the military situation. Approximately 70 percent of the Chinese budget went to the military, thereby postponing needed infrastructure rebuilding, particularly of the railroads and utilities. No reforms therefore could be undertaken, and there was little apparent planning for them. Unless political stability based on a sound economy was quickly established, the work of the Advisory Teams would be wasted. Chiang was isolated from the political and economic realities. He believed that he could not act except in the interests of China. He did not see that many intellectuals had lost faith in his leadership, as had many in the business community. His party-dominated government was dominated by him; he controlled the party, the military, and the government. Yet the party itself was not united. An American attaché had identified a number of cliques, political and military, each with its own loyalties, needs for position, and power in the various political and military establishments. The political cliques included the CC clique, the Political Science clique, the K'ung Sung (T. V. Soong) organization, the Chu-Chia-Hua, the Sun Fo, the Elders, the Brain Trustees, Madame Chiang, the GMD Leftists, the University, the Youth Party, and the Democratic Socialists. The military cliques were the Central Government, the Japanese Trained Officers, the Hoying Chun, the Baoding, the Whampoa, the Revenue Guards, the Non-Central Government, the Northwest, the Shansi-Suiyuan, the Northeast, the Kwangsi, the Local, the Szechuan-Sikang, the Kwantung, the Yunnan, the Muslim Army, and the Inner Mongolian Army.[73] Balancing these factions was a major preoccupation for Chiang to remain in power. Little time was available to him for other issues.

Military problems identified by the Americans in the first half of 1948 included the tendency of Chiang to interfere at the strategic and tactical levels in field operations from behind the lines, usually from the capital.[74] One observer described Chiang sending essential supply planes to a friend in an area not at that time critical while commanders in the northeast under attack in an area critical to the control of China were starved of the supplies they requested.[75] The low caliber of ranking officers in terms of integrity or professional skills was also noted. Failure to organize an adequate program for military government and to replace the military with civilian institutions was a major problem in Chiang's military campaigns. Along with the inadequacies of the supply system, there was an imbalance between the resources available in manpower and materials and where they were needed to be deployed. But the principal cause of Nationalist reverses was poor overall training and operational control, and poor support of the commanders. Even with a planning process of six months for an operation, orders for its implementation were sometimes ignored, with the excuse that the relevant unit was unready.[76] One problem was that commanders had no assurance that ammunition and equipment expended would be replenished. Status was sometimes considered when it came to the control of supplies, not their effective usage. Many planners' tactics were not adapted to the actual conditions of war. They had no theoretical basis for fighting a war in which many campaigns against them were conducted guerrilla-style.

A report to the Joint Advisory Staff in 1948 identified further Guomindang problems. The memorandum reported that too many government troops were in garrison, with piecemeal defense of cities undertaken by them. No practical plan had been made to deal with the mobile warfare of the Communists. Apparently, the defending forces engaged in the maximum expenditure of munitions from behind the walls in order to demonstrate their military prowess, but no direct engagements occurred. Also, no separation of military and civil rule was evident in many places. It was suggested that the local leaders avoid ostentation and using their forces for personal interests.[77] Many of the problems with the government's prosecution of the conflict were due to this traditional mindset still prevailing in the Guomindang from the top down. Little could be done by the few American-trained Chinese officers and men who, without support, could not change the system. Chiang obviously believed, with reason, that the Americans would support him without his having to change the system in other than cosmetic ways. He wanted their aid, not their advice, unless it was tactical, and the American mission forbade giving such advice.

A report of the achievements of the Ground Division to June 1948 included the setting up of a military organization, to be supported by the various schools' graduates, intended to translate various field and technical service manuals, and to select personnel for training. Many hours of conferences had been needed to achieve this result.[78] Also, the equipment for the defunct Kalgan training project and for the Executive Headquarters was disposed of by the Army Advisory Group. The Executive Headquarters had been officially deactivated on 6 February 1947. In fact, it had effectively ended before Marshall left in January. Many courses in English had been conducted for those selected for the American schools. In addition, the initiation, preparation, and some implementation of Mission, Organization, and Function papers had been achieved.

Although the report made many mentions of various schools moving and training plans done, the results of the expenditure of resources, time, and effort by the Americans could be summarized in a few words. In March 1947, the Artillery School had enrolled its twelfth class, with no graduates, while the Coast Defense School had opened in February, but also had no graduates. For the Infantry School, the first Basic Class was held in September of 1947, with an emphasis on weapons; plans to assist the Airborne School had not been implemented. Plans to move the Infantry School at Tangshan to Hsuchow had not been undertaken, as the site assigned was not adequate. For the Armor School, preparations for lesson plans for one hundred plus interim instructors who had graduated from the Cavalry Course were to begin in October.[79]

By December 1948, plans to withdraw American dependents were made due to the deteriorating military and political conditions. Preliminary steps for the reduction and/or suspension of the Joint U.S. Military Advisory Group had been planned, although advisory roles for those at the top levels continued. In the face of Communist military action, the Headquarters was moved to Shanghai in November 1948, and then to Japan in January 1949. The Joint U.S. Military Advisory Group formally ceased operations on 3 March 1949.[80]

The American effort in China to reorganize and train a modern professional army was a mission that encompassed many problems. That it was attempted during a civil war only added to its difficulties. Aside from the problems of reorganization undertaken during a military conflict, and the problems of language and culture, the political reality in China seemed to be absent from much of the planning process. Americans were trying to adapt a system that worked well for them. An element of idealism, which encouraged the thinking that this successful system would work for others without massive modification, was divorced from the actual conditions in Chinese society, which required more immediate rather than long-term training, and in the field. Americans were further isolated by the limitations of their mission. Their lack of information was not surprising, given that many members of the Nationalist General Staff had no access to meaningful data, and might not have shared it in any event. Even the ALPHA Forces, trained during the war, had not been fully trained or equipped by the end of it. Chiang wanted aid, not advice. He wanted the appearance of the American system, but not the reality, which would have necessitated the sharing of power. He offered to some Americans an empty rank and status, but no ability to change his power base. He, or his officials, continuously attempted to increase American responsibility and participation in his military efforts; these attempts were strongly resisted by the Americans. Since he was unwilling, or unable, to change a personal military for a professional one, subordinates saw no advantage in embracing changes in any meaningful way. Plans had assumed a political stability, which was lacking. Plans also assumed that American training standards would be given the time needed to achieve their slow transformation. This assumption proved impractical. Political pressure on both sides kept the mission active until it was threatened by the Communist advances.

The Military Advisory Group China was an investment in the modernization of the Nationalist Army, needed in the postwar world in order to unify and protect a (projected) democratic government. Begun during the war, the training mission envisioned a unified professional army supported by a recovering economy. In the process a reduced force would be trained and equipped by the Americans, an organized chain of command would be developed, and a structure for a modern force would be created. Some of the problems in this transformation were anticipated; others were discounted or ignored. But the Marshall and Advisory missions, with continuing economic and military aid, illustrated the American commitment to a goal they were confident of achieving, at least to some degree.

China had experienced conflicts between warlords, civil war, war against Japan, and then further civil war. The same leaders who had engaged in the first civil conflict were still in power in the second. Their basic goals and attitudes had not changed. They shared a very bitter history; each retained a party government and military as well as a memory of the previous encounters. To introduce to one group, albeit the larger and officially recognized one, a new system of military organization while it was engaged in combat was not practical. The actual and symbolic help of the American mission was meant to serve this purpose. Marshall's plans had been militarily practical, but they were not implemented for political reasons. Further plans had been accepted, but the command system and structure had not changed significantly, remaining personal in nature. Nor had changes to government or economic structure been achieved. Given these conditions, the attempt to train a professional national army (or even a Nationalist Army) failed.

Notes

I would like to thank the archivists at the National Archives (College Park and San Francisco) and at the U.S. Army Military History Institute for their help with document searches and sources. I would also like to thank the various commentators who read conference papers on the subject and offered constructive criticisms.

1. Katherine K. Reist, "The American Military Advising Missions in China, 1945–1949," *Journal of Military History* 77 (October 2013): 1379–1398.

2. Jonathan D. Spence, *The Search for Modern China* (New York: W. W. Norton and Co., 1990), 485.

3. Rana Mitter, *Forgotten Ally: China's World War II, 1937–1945* (New York: Houghton Mifflin Harcourt, 2013), 353, 365.

4. Maochun Yu, *OSS in China: Prelude to the Cold War* (Annapolis: Naval Institute Press, 1996), 67–69.

5. Shamseer Rahman, "United States Economic and Military Assistance Policy toward China and Its Immediate Aftermath," (Ph.D. diss., University of Kansas, 1988), 355.

6. Spence, *Search for Modern China*, 474.

7. Ibid., 482.

8. Larry Bland, ed., *The Papers of George Catlett Marshall*, vol. 5 (Baltimore: Johns Hopkins University Press, 2003), 276n1.

9. Ibid., 395.

10. "The Treaty Agreement between Chang Chih Chung, Chou En-lai, and George C. Marshall," 19 February 1946, Papers of Paul W. Caraway, 1946–1947, Military History Institute, Carlisle, Pennsylvania (hereafter cited as MHI).

11. Colonel Rothwell N. Brown, Chief, Conflict Control Group, "History of the Conflict Control Group, Manchuria, 1947," Folder History of the Conflict Control Group,

6 June 1946–31 January 1947, Box 3, Papers of Rothwell H. Brown (hereafter cited as Brown Papers), MHI.

12. Bland, *Marshall Papers*, 491–492.

13. Executive Headquarters Field Team to Chief, Conflict Control Group, Changchun, 18 January 1947, Folder History of the Conflict Control Group, 6 June 1946–31 January 1947, Box 3, Brown Papers, MHI; Marshall to Truman, 23 January 1946, *Foreign Relations of the United States* (hereafter cited as *FRUS*) 1946, vol. 9 (Washington, DC: Government Printing office, 1972), note 142 (hereafter cited as 9:142).

14. Vincent, "Summary of a Personal Letter from Mr. John Fairbank, 6 December 1945," *FRUS* 1946, 9:131–132.

15. Bland, *Marshall Papers*, 438; Sprouse, "Memorandum by the Second Secretary of Embassy in China," 1 January 1946, *FRUS* 1946, 9:132–133.

16. U.S. Department of State, *The China White Paper, August 1949*, vol. 1 (Stanford, CA: Stanford University Press, 1967), 138.

17. Spence, *Search for Modern China*, 487.

18. Ibid., 489; Sprouse, "Memorandum by the Second Secretary of Embassy in China," 13 January 1946, *FRUS* 1946, 9:137.

19. R. Keith Schoppa, *Revolution and Its Past* (Upper Saddle River, NJ: Pearson/Prentice Hall, 2006), 289.

20. Odd Arne Westad, *Decisive Encounters: The Chinese Civil War, 1946–1950* (Palo Alto, CA: Stanford University Press, 2003), 47–49.

21. Bland, *Marshall Papers*, 333n1.

22. JCS 1330/19, "Estimate of the USMAG to China," 9 February 1946, Box S-185, Records of the Joint U.S. Military Advisory Group to the Republic of China, RG 334 (hereafter cited as RG 334), National Archives, San Francisco, California (hereafter cited as NARA, San Francisco).

23. Wedemeyer to Marshall, 16 January 1946, *FRUS* 1946, 9:190; Bland, *Marshall Papers*, 544.

24. U.S. Department of State, *China White Paper*, 141.

25. "Treaty Agreement between Chang Chih Chung, Chou En-lai, and George C. Marshall," 19 February 1946, Caraway Papers, MHI; Draft Proposal by the Chinese Government, "Draft of Supplemental Methods to Real Application Regarding the Basic Plan of Army Reorganization and Integration of Communist Army into the National Army," 12 June 1946, *FRUS* 1946, 9:1035.

26. Bland, *Marshall Papers*, 334n3.

27. Office of the Chief, Military Advisory Group, "The Organization of the Military Advisory Groups," 5 October 1945, Box 1, RG 334, NARA, San Francisco.

28. U.S. Department of State, *China White Paper*, 143; Bland, *Marshall Papers*, 425n2.

29. Letter to General Wedemeyer, "Army Reorganization Plan," 21 October 1946, Box 56, RG 334, National Archives II, College Park, Maryland (hereafter NA II); Bland, *Marshall Papers*, 527.

30. "Minutes of Meeting between General Marshall and General Chou En-lai at 5 Ning Hai Road, Nanking," 21 June 1946, *FRUS* 1946, 9:1133.

31. Westad, *Decisive Encounters,* 44.

32. JCS 1330/19, "Estimate of the USMAG to China," 9 February 1946, Box S-185; "To Lt. Gen. Wang Yao-wu from M.G. David G. Barr, USA," Folder A 7–1, Box 136; both in RG 334, NARA, San Francisco.

33. Immanuel C. Y. Hsu, *The Rise of Modern China* (New York: Oxford University Press, 2000), 624.

34. Bland, *Marshall Papers,* 333.

35. Nanking Headquarters, AAG Plans, 24 June 1946, Folder Personnel and Administrative Advising Papers, Box 10, RG 334, NARA, San Francisco; Bland, *Marshall Papers,* 469n1.

36. Bland, *Marshall Papers,* 418.

37. JCS 1330/27, "Briefing of the Armed Forces Committee by R. Adm. S. S. Murray, USN," Enclosure C, 27 May 1948, Folder Murphey Briefing, Box S-185, RG 334, NARA, San Francisco.

38. Vincent to Acheson, "Memorandum by the Director of the Office of Far Eastern Affairs to the Under Secretary of State," 8 April 1946, *FRUS* 1946, 10:825.

39. Stuart to Marshall, "The Ambassador in China to the Secretary of State," 9 March 1947, *FRUS* 1946, 10:723.

40. Naval Advisory Division Headquarters, "Final Report, Naval Advisory Division," 16 February 1949, Folder Political Relations, Box 136, RG 334, NARA, San Francisco.

41. "Commander, USN Forces, Western Pacific to the CNC," 9 June 1948, Folder JUSMAG, 1947–1949, Chinese Training Group, Tsingtao Unit, RG 334, NARA, San Francisco; U.S. Department of State, *China White Paper,* 329.

42. Headquarters, Nanking Headquarters Command, United States Army Forces, China (USAFC), "Present Organization of the Chinese Military Council," 8 May 1946, Folder Political Relations, Box 136, RG 334, NARA, San Francisco.

43. Office of the Chief, MAG, "The Military Advisory Group in China," 29 June 1947, Folder Political Relations, Box 136, RG 334, NARA, San Francisco.

44. Headquarters, Nanking Headquarters Command, USAFC, "Present Organization of the Chinese Military Council," 8 May 1946, Folder Political Relations, Box 136, RG 334, NARA, San Francisco.

45. Headquarters, Nanking Headquarters Command, USAFC, "MAG: Combined and Joint Organizations," 17 September 1948, Folder 334.5.3, Box 56, RG 334, NARA, San Francisco.

46. Headquarters, Nanking Headquarters Command, USAFC, "Organization no. 1," 9 May 1946, Folder A-3-1, Box 173, RG 334, NARA, San Francisco.

47. JCS 1330/27, "Briefing of the Armed Forces Committee by R. Adm. S. S. Murray, USN," Enclosure B, 27 May 1948, Folder JUSMAG, Box S-185, RG 334, NARA, San Francisco; U.S. Department of State, *China White Paper,* 340.

48. Headquarters, Nanking Headquarters Command, USAFC, "MAG: Combined and Joint Organizations, 17 September 1948, Folder 334.5.3, Box 56, RG 334, NARA, San Francisco.

49. Headquarters, Nanking Headquarters Command, USAFC, "Kalgan Training

Center, Training and Organization, October 1946–December 1946," Folder A-3-1, Box 173, RG 334, NARA, San Francisco.

50. "Plans for Training Chinese Officers in U.S. Army Schools," 7 May 1946, Folder Political Relations, Box 136, RG 334, NARA, San Francisco.

51. Chinese Training Group, Tsingtao, 23 January 1948, Folder JUSMAG, 1947–1949, RG 334, NARA, San Francisco; Stuart to Marshall, "The Ambassador in China to the Secretary of State, 23 January 1948, *FRUS* 1948, 8:242–251.

52. Brigadier General F.C. Brink, "Standard Operating Procedure for Preparation of U.S. Manuals into Chinese," 25 September 1947, Folder Political Relations, Box 136, RG 334, NARA, San Francisco.

53. Office of the Chief, MAG, "The Military Advisory Group in China," 29 July 1947, Folder Political Relations, Box 136, RG 334, NARA, San Francisco.

54. Ibid.

55. Bland, *Marshall Papers,* 588.

56. Schoppa, *Revolution and Its Past,* 271; Office of the Director, JUSMAG, to the Republic of China, "Outline Armed Forces Reorganization," 19 April 1949, Folder Replacement and Training Program, Box 73, RG 334, NA II.

57. "Minutes of Meeting between General Marshall and General Chou En-lai, at 5 Ning Hai Road, Nanking," 21 June 1946, *FRUS* 1946, 9:1115.

58. Office of the Chief, MAG, "The Military Advisory Group in China," 29 June 1947, Folder Political Relations, Box 136, RG 334, NARA, San Francisco.

59. CINCFE G-2, "Minutes of the Third Joint Conference," 28 March 1945, Folder S-184, Box 61, RG 334, NA II.

60. Naval Advisory Department, "'A' Subjects," 29 November 1948, Folder 035-48, RG 334, NARA, San Francisco.

61. Office of the Chief, AAG, Nanking, "Observing Instructor Training at Tangshan," 1 February 1947, Folder 033-48, Box 173, RG 334, NARA, San Francisco.

62. Colonel Willis B. Scudder, "Chinese Civil War," Folder Chinese Civil War, 1948, Box 2, Willis B. Scudder Papers (Colonel, USA), MHI; Naval Advisory Group Survey Board, "Memorandum for R. Adm. Thurber," 10 July 1948, File A-3-1, Box S-186, RG 334, NARA, San Francisco; General Ku Chu-tung, Chinese Army (CA), "Memorandum to General Barr," 12 June 1948, Folder "P" Subjects, Box 4, RG 334, NA II.

63. U.S. Department of State, *China White Paper,* 324.

64. Ibid., 347–351.

65. Ibid., 347.

66. Ibid., 348.

67. Ibid., 349.

68. Ibid.

69. Ibid., 350.

70. Ibid.

71. "To the Chief of Staff, USA," 7 October 1948, Box 73, RG 334, NA II.

72. Major General David G. Barr, "To Lt. Gen Wang Yao-wu from MG David G. Barr, USA," 19 June 1948, Box 136, RG 334, NARA, San Francisco.

73. Naval Attaché's Office, "Memorandum: Political Affiliations, Chinese Government Officials, and Prominent Personages," Folder A-8, April 1946–August 1947, Box S-181, RG 334, NARA, San Francisco.

74. Stuart to Marshall, "The Ambassador in China to the Secretary of State," 23 January 1948, *FRUS* 1948, 8:242–251.

75. Edward L. Dreyer, *China at War, 1901–1949* (New York: Longman, 1995), 357.

76. U.S. Department of State, *China White Paper*, 329.

77. Colonel Scudder, "Memorandum on Local Defense Organization," 13 August 1948, Folder Chinese Civil War, Box 2, Scudder Papers, MHI.

78. AAG, Ground Division, "Report of the Achievements, Ground Division," 1 June 1946, Folder 1 June 1946–30 June 1948, Box 2, Scudder Papers, MHI.

79. Ibid.

80. JUSMAG to ROC, 23 December 1948, Folder Office of the Director, Box S-180, RG 334, NARA, San Francisco.

Bibliography

Primary Sources

Archives

Military History Institute, Carlisle, Pennsylvania
The Rothwell H. Brown Papers
The Paul W. Caraway Papers
The Willis B. Scudder Papers
National Archives and Record Administration
Record Group 334: College Park, Maryland; San Francisco, California

Government Publications

United States Department of State. *FRUS* (*Foreign Relations of the United States*)
—1946, vol. 9. *The Far East: China*. Washington, DC: Government Printing Office, 1972.
—1946, vol. 10. *The Far East: China*. Washington, DC: Government Printing Office, 1972.
—1948, vol. 8. *The Far East: China*. Washington, DC: Government Printing Office, 1973.

Edited Collections

The Papers of George Catlett Marshall. Vol. 5. Ed. Larry I. Bland. Baltimore: Johns Hopkins University Press, 2003.
U.S. Department of State. *The China White Paper, August 1949*. Vol. 1. Stanford, CA: Stanford University Press, 1967.

Secondary Sources

Dreyer, Edward L. *China at War, 1901–1949.* New York: Longman, 1995.

Hsu, Immanuel C. Y. *The Rise of Modern China.* New York: Oxford University Press, 2000.

Mitter, Rana. *Forgotten Ally: China's World War II, 1937–1945.* New York: Houghton Mifflin Harcourt, 2013.

Rahman, Shamseer. "United States Economic and Military Assistance Policy toward China and Its Immediate Aftermath." Ph.D. diss., University of Kansas, 1988.

Reist, Katherine K. "The American Military Advising Missions in China, 1945–1949." *Journal of Military History* 77 (October 2013): 1379–1398.

Schoppa, R. Keith. *Revolution and Its Past.* Upper Saddle River, NJ: Pearson/Prentice Hall, 2006.

Spence, Jonathan D. *The Search for Modern China.* New York: W. W. Norton and Co., 1990.

Westad, Odd Arne. *Decisive Encounters: The Chinese Civil War, 1946–1950.* Palo Alto, CA: Stanford University Press, 2003.

Yu, Maochun. *OSS in China: Prelude to the Cold War.* Annapolis: Naval Institute Press. 1996.

7

Hidden Island

Military-Media Relations on Okinawa, 1945–1972

Nicholas Evan Sarantakes

From 1 April 1945, when soldiers and Marines of the U.S. Tenth Army walked onto the beaches of Okinawa, until 15 May 1972, when Army Lieutenant General James B. Lampert, U.S. High Commissioner of the Ryukyu Islands, departed the island carrying the cased flag of the U.S. Civil Administration of the Ryukyu Islands, the United States ruled this archipelago as a colony in everything but name. Those twenty-seven years were the longest period of military government in the history of the U.S. Armed Forces. This fact raises an interesting question: how were the uniformed services able to initiate and maintain an undertaking that was so incompatible with such basic aims of U.S. foreign policy as self-determination and anti-colonialism? An answer to this problem can be found in a study of the relationship between the military and the press. The armed services on Okinawa adopted a press policy designed to reduce coverage of the island to an absolute minimum in an effort to keep the public unaware of how much U.S. actions in the Ryukyus ran counter to traditional American values.

This chapter is an effort to contribute to two historiographies. The first is the nature of the relationship between the military and the media. This subject has been a focus of intense debate among journalists and scholars since the end of the Vietnam War, when the cooperative relationship between the military and the media that had existed since World War II broke down. One group has emphasized the independence of the media and the conflict and disputes between reporters and generals that this autonomy produces.[1] The other has stressed the dependence of journalists on the military and the resulting cooperation and agreement.[2] Most studies examine this relationship in times of war. This account is unique in that it explores military-press relations during a military occupation. The second historiography is that of Okinawa during the American years. There are only a handful of scholarly accounts of life on Okinawa at this time. Political scientist Watanabe Akio is the only author who discusses the role of the media in the events concerning life on this island and whose examination includes the Japanese-language press.[3] With access to most government documents on Okinawa, it is possible to put press influence into its proper historical context. Given Watanabe's earlier work on the Japanese media, this study will focus primarily on American journalists. Although radio, newsreel, and later television reporters covered Okinawa, they played a secondary role to the traditional print media. "The most important part of the Okinawa news media was the press rather than the T.V. or radio," Army Lieutenant General Albert Watson II, High Commissioner of the Ryukyu Islands in the mid-1960s, remarked.[4] The technological innovations, such as satellite communications, that would move the electronic media to the forefront were not available or were nonexistent during most of the period under investigation.

Okinawa was a strategically well-placed island, which was the main reason the United States and Japan fought a battle for its control in 1945. Many military officers were unwilling to part with a piece of real estate that had been so costly to take.[5] Army Ground Forces Lieutenant General Simon Bolivar Buckner Jr., Commanding General, Tenth Army during the engagement, foresaw the postwar importance of the island. "Told Adm. [Chester] Nimitz that Okinawa should be retained by us as a means of access to the China sea, a flanking position against north and south movements along the China coast; a check against further aggression by Japan and as an outpost to prevent Russia from expansion into the Pacific from Chinese ports that she might acquire at the end of the war by occupying them under the pretext of helping us against Japan," he noted in his diary. He also told Nimitz that the United States should administer the island as a "'protectorate,' 'mandate' or some other name" to avoid complicated legal questions about Okinawans and their citizenship.[6]

During the battle to take control of this important island, units of the U.S. Army wanted media coverage. Army Ground Forces Major General John Hodge, Commanding General, Twenty-Fourth Corps, eventually complained about the lack of attention war correspondents were giving his men. In a four-page memo he wrote while combat still raged on the island, he informed Buckner's successor (the general had died in combat), Marine Corps Lieutenant General Roy Geiger, Commanding General, Third Amphibious Corps, that many news stories about Okinawa were slighting the efforts of U.S. soldiers. "I read many clippings giving outstanding exploits of the Marines on Okinawa, often crediting them with moves actually made by my divisions. These get back to soldiers from their families and it makes for bitterest feeling toward the Marine Corps." This situation had only grown worse as the battle progressed. "I have been able to find but little mention of Army troops fighting their hearts out in the last twelve days of the 82-day battle." Hodge believed his men deserved better.[7]

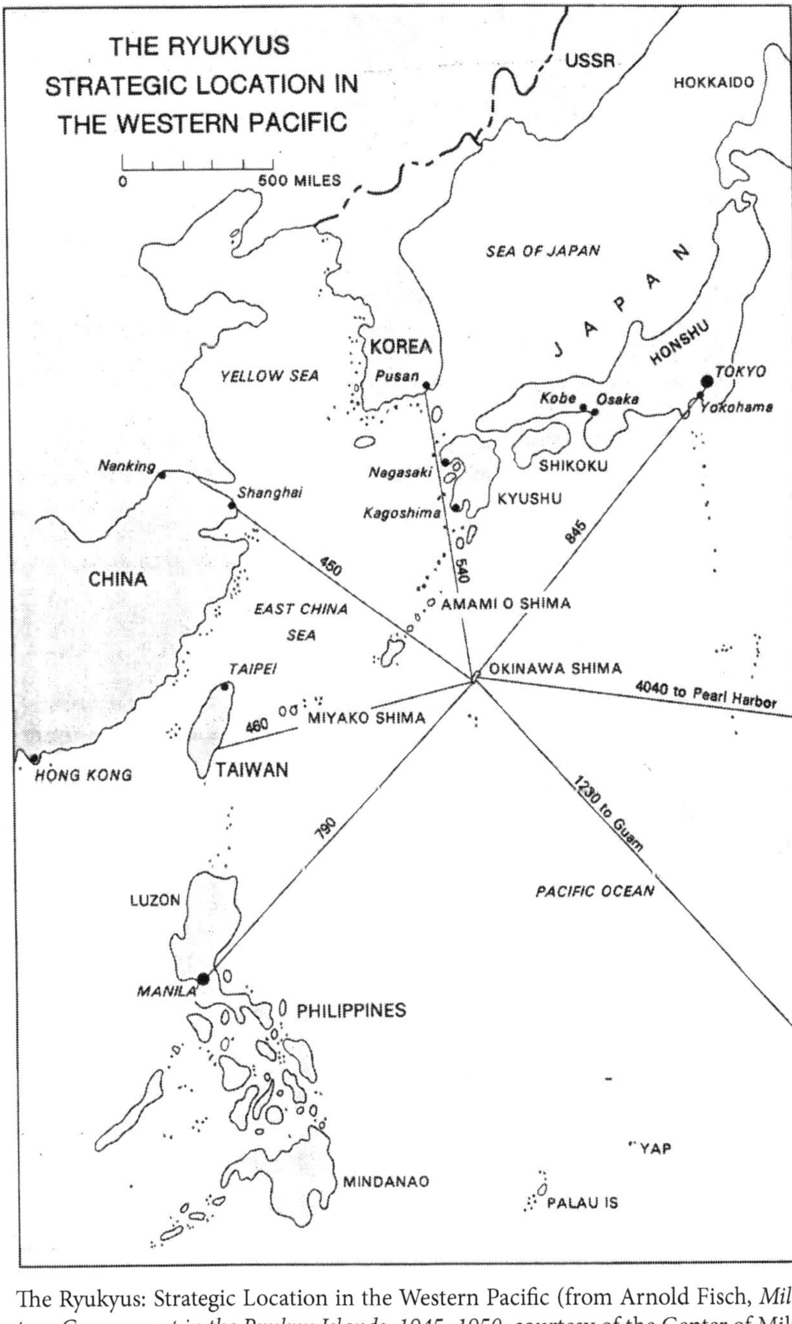

The Ryukyus: Strategic Location in the Western Pacific (from Arnold Fisch, *Military Government in the Ryukyu Islands, 1945–1950*, courtesy of the Center of Military History, Washington, DC)

After the battle ended, U.S. Army officers' attitudes on Okinawa's postwar status changed dramatically. Some officers wanted to develop it as a strategic base complex rather than just occupy the island. Much of this had to do with the uncertain status of the Ryukyus. General of the Army Douglas MacArthur, Commander-in-Chief, U.S. Army Forces, Pacific, wanted the United States to grant Japan a generous peace treaty. At the same time, he wanted to annex the Ryukyus and develop bases on the islands. The Department of State opposed this position throughout the second half of the 1940s. The State Department believed that there was no profit in keeping a heavily populated island of people who thought of themselves as Japanese. Debate on Okinawa's ultimate resolution only moved to the forefront of policy matters when it became part of the larger issue of a Japanese peace treaty. An important event in the resolution of Okinawa's fate came when George F. Kennan, Director, State Department Policy Planning Staff, led a mission to Japan where he met with MacArthur. Kennan listened to him explain the strategic significance of Okinawa's location and how the Japanese would have little complaint about losing the Ryukyus, since the area had always been a drain on the economic resources of the central government in Tokyo, costing more to administer than it produced in tax revenue. Kennan accepted the general's views on Okinawa. He, however, chose to disagree with the general on the immediate need for a settlement with Japan.[8]

The peace treaty would have to wait, and during the 1940s the island quickly developed a reputation as the worst assignment in East Asia. Press access to the island during this period of uncertainty about Okinawa's ultimate fate was limited. Few reporters wanted to visit Okinawa during this time, anyway. A correspondent from the *New York Herald Tribune* who did manage to visit the Ryukyus reported, "Very little has been done for the occupation personnel in the last four years beyond trying to keep war-time installations from blowing away in periodic typhoons, and little for the Okinawans beyond supplementing the local food supply." In 1949, a reporter from *Life* magazine, who accompanied Undersecretary of the Army Tracy Voorhees on an inspection of the island, found "an ugly, cluttered graveyard of rotting material" and American troops who were "depressed and sullen."[9] There was also an article that appeared in *Collier's* magazine that is an odd exception to this limited and generally negative portrayal of life on the island. The factual description of Okinawa is about the same as other journalistic accounts, but the author gives such a positive spin it is difficult to take this article seriously.[10]

The Japanese peace treaty that ultimately resolved Okinawa's fate came in 1951. The task of negotiating the treaty fell to John Foster Dulles. The leading foreign policy expert of the Republican Party, Dulles was the grandson and nephew of two former Secretaries of State. Most political observers expected he would hold that office should the Republicans ever regain control of the White House. He had served as a member of the official United States Peace Delegation at the Versailles Peace Conference, a position he obtained through the influence of his uncle, Secretary of State Robert Lansing. The experience in France had scarred Dulles, and he constantly projected his fears of another Versailles onto the negotiations of the Japanese treaty. On the matter of Okinawa, he had some significant reservations about postwar American administration. He was afraid that Japanese reactionaries would use the territorial issue to "crucify" Prime Minister Yoshida Shigeru and attack the agreement, just as had been the case in Weimar Germany. Dulles also worried that Okinawa might become "another Puerto Rico," creating a host of problems on matters such as citizenship, immigration, trade, and civil liberties.[11]

As a result, Dulles began formulating an idea that would handle these complications and objections. His answer was the legal concept of "residual sovereignty."[12] According to this theory, Okinawa would be just like the U.S. Panama Canal Zone in that the United States would administer the territory, but the inhabitants would keep their original citizenship. This solution seemed an ingenious, legalistic compromise that answered all the objections to the disposition of the Ryukyu Islands. Japan would still have legal claim to the islands, and Yoshida would be safe from the charge that he had sold out Japanese interests. This settlement would also satisfy the Senate and protect the United States from the charge of imperialism. In addition, the military would have the island, without international legal and political complications. Most of all, Dulles would have controlled the decision; he would appear generous, while keeping the Japanese in line. He discussed the issue with now–Secretary of Defense George Marshall and the Senate Foreign Relations Committee, obtaining the agreement of both. Only then did he announce the concept of "residual sovereignty" at the San Francisco Peace Conference, in September 1951.[13]

Although colonialism was in disrepute in the United States, the press in no way questioned the decision to keep Okinawa. The peace treaty and the accompanying conference were unqualified successes in the public's eye. The fact that the treaty came after a series of foreign policy disasters, including the fall of Eastern Europe to Communism, the "loss" of China, and the Korean War, made it all the more special. *Newsweek* magazine ran a front-cover article on Dulles and even ran a biographical article on his assistant, John Allison, an unknown midlevel Foreign Service Officer until then. Not to be outdone, *Time* magazine sponsored a television show on the American Broadcasting Company (ABC) and Columbia Broadcasting System (CBS) entitled "Your Stake in Japan." The conference was also the first event broadcast live on national television.[14]

Reports coming from Okinawa after the conference, especially compared to the accounts of the 1940s, made American retention of the Ryukyus seem like the right decision for all concerned. Several publications presented extremely flattering accounts of the American presence on the island. The reporters writing these stories focused on the strategic location of the island and the massive amount of military construction. An article that appeared in *Time* magazine examined the social impact of the construction, admitting: "Without anyone really intending it that way, the U.S. has been thrust into the colonial business." The story added that the American presence was a benign form of colonialism. Americans were helping the Okinawans rather than exploiting them.[15] This tepid admission of American colonialism was one of the few public acknowledgments of the issue at the time.

The military, however, wanted no such discussion in any way, shape, or form. The soldiers on Okinawa wanted no news coverage, be it positive or negative, at all. Any reporting, even an article as positive as the one in *Time,* made it clear that the United States of America had a colony on Okinawa, and that ran counter to U.S. ideals and public sentiment. Most Americans at the time believed the United States was different and unique from other nations in its conduct of world affairs. Few knew much about Okinawa, and the U.S. Army worried that if conditions on the island became common knowledge, the American people and their representatives in Congress would force the U.S. government to return the Ryukyus to Japan in a fit of anti-colonialism. As a result, the Army limited travel to the island. Controlling physical access limited the number of stories written about Okinawa. The military also insisted on briefing every journalist who managed to visit. This briefing stressed the strategic location of the island and the utility of the U.S. air bases in the Ryukyus. American planes based on Okinawa, for instance, could launch missions over China, Taiwan, Korea, the Soviet Union, Vietnam, and Japan. More importantly, the United States could deploy these units without having to seek prior approval from a foreign government, since it was the administering authority. The Public Relations Office of the U.S. Civil Administration also routinely controlled reporters, arranging safe interviews, which were often meaningless, and denying them support resources available to other civilians, such as access to the commissary and post-exchange (PX) systems. This control had a devastating effect on the news stories, particularly those of Robert Trumbull, Tokyo Bureau Chief of the *New York Times.* Trumbull was about the only journalist in the 1950s writing on Okinawa. His work was not a good example of excellence in journalism. His articles often had only one source, which he rarely identified, and usually ended up deep inside the paper.[16]

A number of other factors limited the local press residing on Okinawa. There were two Japanese-language newspapers on the island, the *Ryukyu Shimpo* and the *Okinawa Taimusu.* Both papers took editorial positions that favored the eventual reversion of the Ryukyus to Japan on a step-by-step basis. This position became known as gradual reversion, and its advocates viewed the presence of the U.S. bases and American rule as two separate issues. The papers accepted and supported U.S. foreign policy in East Asia and the presence of bases on the island. This position was significantly different from those of left-wing political activists, who wanted an immediate end to U.S. rule *and* a removal of all the bases. The editors of the papers said reversion was a process that would occur slowly and take time. As a result, the papers favored liberalization of travel restrictions; the use of Japanese passports; the flying of the Japanese national flag on fishing boats; the direct election of the Chief Executive, Ryukyu Islands; and the repeal of foreign investment laws, which prohibited the introduction of Japanese capital. All these changes were seen as preliminary steps to actual reversion.[17]

American officials had positive but qualified feelings about these newspapers. Although military administrators appreciated the editorial support of these publications, they also saw gradual reversion as a process that would only weaken U.S. control of the island. Reversion in any form was the last thing the military wanted to see happen, and Civil Administration officials looked at the papers warily at times. This ambiguity is readily apparent in the contradictory views of Army Lieutenant General Paul Caraway, High Commissioner, Ryukyu Islands in the early 1960s, who at one point said, "They [Okinawan and Japanese reporters] were really quite friendly to me, personally, and to the American administration in general" while also observing that "the Okinawan Press was, in general, at that time, very unfriendly to the military. That's what sold their tickets, they liked that part of it." His successor showed less confusion. "The local newspapers were controlled by individuals who were, I thought, generally friendly towards our administration," Lieutenant General Watson said. "I would say that the press was . . . really quite helpful and useful. I found that none of their coverage was adverse."[18]

The English-language press was more completely under the control of the U.S. Civil Administration than the Japanese-language periodicals. The *Okinawa Morning Star* was the main English-language publication on the island and the voice of the American expatriate community. Founded in 1954, the daily had editorial positions that were the exact opposite of those belonging to the Japanese-language papers. The *Morning Star* displayed a paternalistic attitude premised on the idea that Americans on the island knew better than the Okinawans what was best for Okinawa. The paper advocated measures that would make the separation from Japan permanent, such as the introduction of dollars on the island. On another occasion, the paper admitted that American rule of the island was colonial, but defended the practice, arguing it was necessary for national security and the revitalization of the island. The broadsheet enjoyed a symbiotic relationship with the Civil Administration. Retired and Reserve Army public relations officers found civilian employment with the *Morning Star.* Stringers for the Associated Press (AP), United Press International (UPI), and the *New York Times* normally held full-time jobs with the paper and were threatened with unemployment should they write stories critical of American rule. When *Washington Post* columnist Drew Pearson wrote an editorial blasting the Civil Administration for its control of the press, editor Robert M. Prosser fired back in defense of policies that censored his own paper.[19]

Although the military limited press coverage as best it could, preventing journalists from covering all developments on the island was simply impossible. The popular success of *The Teahouse of the August Moon* was one such development over which the Army had no control over. In its original form as a novel, *Teahouse* offered several gentle criticisms of the U.S. Civil Administration. The message was diluted and lost as the story became an award-winning Broadway play and then a motion picture.[20] Stories appeared in American publications about how popular *Teahouse* was on the real Okinawa.[21] The military got lucky, though. It appears that the popularity of *Teahouse* failed to inspire any reporters to write on the actual administration of Okinawa.

This luck failed to last. There were several other incidents when clumsy efforts to control the press backfired on the U.S. military. One such case was the election of Senaga Kamejiro as Mayor of Naha, the largest city on the island. On Christmas Day 1956, he won the office with a plurality of 40 percent. What made his electoral victory an issue was that he was President of the Okinawan People's Party, the communist party on the island. His election drew embarrassing attention to the fact that Okinawans had chosen a communist in a supposed showcase of American democracy.[22] Efforts to remove Senaga began almost immediately, but they only served to exaggerate his importance.[23] After repeated tries by the City Council to remove him through a vote of no confidence failed, the High Commissioner used his powers to revise a number of city ordinances and regulations that made this task easier. The next day, the Council removed Senaga on a 16-to-10 vote.[24] The ouster of Senaga unleashed a firestorm of criticism in the United States, Japan, and Okinawa. A businessman on the island remarked, "You say you are giving us the vote and if you don't like who we elect you change the laws—this is your wonderful democracy?"[25] Japanese commentators agreed, calling the action undemocratic and questioning America's commitment to its own principles and ideals.[26]

The Army's handling of the Senaga episode resulted in a fierce attack on its conduct in the press. Barton M. Biggs, a former Marine Corps officer who had served on Okinawa, wrote a devastating indictment of the U.S. Civil Administration that appeared in the December 1958 issue of *Harper's* magazine. "When I saw the election returns this spring," he explained later, "I knew what had happened. That's when I decided to tell the story."[27] The article, "The Outraged Okinawans," was primarily a memoir of Biggs's experiences while he was stationed on Okinawa. According to a later military analysis of the article, he made twenty-five different statements of fact. With this account, Biggs was trying to warn the American public that the actions and attitudes of service personnel on the island were backfiring. The military was creating an external environment among the Okinawans that was hostile, and an internal one among the troops that was detrimental to the U.S. presence on this key base. "We must realize that merely raising the standard of living will not create good will in an underdeveloped people if we insult their sense of personal dignity at the same time," he stated. The election of Senaga was only one expression of this hostile sentiment.[28] Officers in the Pentagon probably would have dismissed Biggs's argument were it not for his discussion of the internal military environment. He claimed that the American administration openly tolerated white slavery when Okinawan fathers sold their daughters into prostitution. He also wrote of venereal disease that was so rampant that it was affecting unit performance; low combat readiness; Marines living in hovels; and race riots that occasionally broke out among the troops.[29]

This reporting—particularly that on the sexual exploitation of Okinawan women—created many problems for the U.S. military on the island. Biggs reported that venereal disease incapacitated 10 to 15 percent of his Marine Corps company. His unit apparently was one of the luckier ones. A fourth of the Third Marine Division reported to sick bay with venereal disease in September 1957, the first month for which public health figures are available. The number of infected Marines grew steadily. A year later, the disease had infected and incapacitated 37 percent of the division.[30] These accusations were serious and warranted attention.

The military responded to these charges not with efforts to correct these problems, but with an attempt to keep the public relations disaster from becoming any worse. On 28 November, Admiral Harry D. Felt, Commander-in-Chief, U.S. Pacific Command (CINCPAC), directed Army Lieutenant General Donald P. Booth, High Commissioner, Ryukyu Islands, to appoint a commission to examine social conditions on the island and send him periodic reports on its progress. Booth followed orders to the letter on 3 December, appointing an interservice commission of eight officers. The chairman and all the members came from the same commands to undergo examination. The very composition of the task force limited the vigor and critical extent of the inquiry.[31]

The commission, however, spent a month taking testimony from twenty-seven witnesses and soliciting information from the various military units stationed on Okinawa. Much of what they uncovered supported the charges Biggs had made. In the official response of the Ninth Corps, a U.S. Army unit that existed primarily on paper, a captain wrote: "White slavery does exist. This is an age-old practice of the Orient." Housing was another issue the commission investigated. The task force found that Marines lived in Quonset huts, some of which were rotting; but none were housed in tents, as Biggs had claimed. In its final report, the board concluded some of the huts "do not meet acceptable standards of habitability."[32]

The commission avoided altogether an examination of the Third Marine Division and its declining efficiency. Poor maintenance, a sure sign of poor discipline and morale, was a real problem. Most major equipment was inoperable. Depending on the type of machinery in question, the amount of equipment that was out of commission ranged from 24 to 45 percent. Investigators from the General Accounting Office (GAO) found that 97 percent of the tanks in the division were in need of some type of repair, and 38 percent of them were out of service altogether. This trend continued well into the early 1960s. The GAO also found that many of the units in the division sent reports to higher commands that were vague, deceptive, or misleading. General Randolph Pate, Commandant, Marine Corps, went to Okinawa on an inspection visit and initiated a number of reforms, but even then it took another two years before he could tell the Senate that the division was ready for combat.[33] The commission mentioned none of this in its final report. The board declared, "Mr. Biggs' article, 'The Outraged Okinawans,' presents a grossly exaggerated picture of the military/civil environment on Okinawa." There were no race riots, discipline was high, and combat readiness was acceptable. The board agreed with Biggs that U.S.-Okinawan relations were key: "If we assume that the entire Ryukyuan labor force is in a position to bring about a major strike or slowdown, we do have a problem. However, all evidence indicates that such a possibility is extremely remote."[34]

Nothing came of the investigation. Preserving the status quo was the primary purpose of the commission. The board made some weak recommendations at the end of its twenty-one-page report. Booth agreed with the conclusions. Unit commanders took little action on any of these matters, and venereal disease remained the largest public health problem among Okinawans for another decade.[35]

A far more informative and influential journalistic effort to educate the American public about Okinawa came in 1961 from the *Honolulu Advertiser.* For two weeks in September, the paper ran a fourteen-part series on Okinawa that was a major breach of the military shroud that surrounded the Ryukyus. These articles received prominent play in the paper, appearing on the front page of both the morning and evening editions. The fate of the Ryukyus was an issue of some significance in Honolulu. Most Americans of Okinawan descent lived in Hawaii and were concerned about the fate of family members still living on the island. The *Honolulu Advertiser*'s coverage of Okinawa had even bested its crosstown rival, the *Honolulu Star-Bulletin*, on this topic.[36]

The series highlighted a number of problems on the island. Its author was Brian Casey, an experienced political reporter who traveled to the island and interviewed a wide range of American and Okinawan officials, businessmen, housewives, reporters, and politicians. Since Casey was reporting about Okinawa on a onetime basis, he was less dependent on the Civil Administration than reporters who covered the Ryukyus frequently, and he had no need to stay in the good graces of military officials on the island. He covered a number of topics in his articles: the strategic importance of the island; civil administration; military control of the press; economics; and Okinawan politics. He found that one of the reasons the U.S. public knew so little about the island was the policy the Civil Administration had for controlling access to information. "The brass is almost 100 percent successful in shielding VIP's from discontented elements in both the Okinawan and American civilian communities," one source told Casey. The reporter also wrote one article that was a profile of High Commissioner Caraway and another of the civil administrators, Army Brigadier General John G. Ondrick. Casey noted that Caraway was Commanding General, Ninth Corps, stationed on Okinawa and the representative of the Commander-in-Chief, U.S. Pacific Command. Failing to note that the Ninth Corps was a hollow organization without any combat units, he reported that Caraway spent 80 percent of his time tending to his military government duties. Casey attributed this disproportionate focus to Ondrick's inability to handle his own duties. "I don't think it makes any difference whether a man in a gray flannel suit or a khaki uniform runs this place," Caraway told Casey in effort to dismiss the reporter's suggestion that the Civil Administrator position should be designated for a civilian.[37]

Casey additionally covered the social conditions of the American community on the island. His articles are perhaps the single best contemporary accounts of American life on the island during the U.S. administration. "Few want to leave," he observed. An Army colonel explained why. "Where else could I drink Beefeaters' gin for a quarter, eat a lobster dinner for $1.75, get my car polished for $1.25, my shoes shined for a nickel? Tell me." Families could hire maids for $20 a month. "On Okinawa the livin' is easy, man. Real easy," the wife of an Air Force major remarked. Soldiers also found that vice was another major attraction. "Informed sources disagree whether it ranks before or after PX's in dollar volume," Casey wrote.[38]

The bulk of the articles, however, focused on the Okinawans. Casey wrote seven articles about Okinawan politics and the structure of the economy on the island. These articles were the first prominent presentation of Okinawan views in the American press. Casey interviewed a diverse group of people, representing a number of different political views, and it was clear that almost all Okinawans favored unification with Japan. "Our philosophy, our government policies and practices, the way we do things are similar to Japan's—quite different from the United States. No one can judge which way is better," Senaga Hiroshi, the Deputy Chief Executive, Ryukyu Islands, told him.[39]

As informative as the series was, it would have had little impact on U.S. policy were it not for the actions of Representative Daniel Inouye of Hawaii. On 26 September 1961 he entered all of the articles into the *Congressional Record.* The practice of including news articles and editorials from hometown newspapers in the *Record* was a common one in Congress. The *Record* was a journal that allowed members of Congress to communicate with one another even when they were not all in the chambers at the same time. The inclusion of articles from a regional or local publication gave these pieces a wider readership and more influence than would have otherwise been the case. When Inouye entered these stories into the *Congressional Record,* he gave them a national audience at a key moment in the history of the U.S. occupation of Okinawa. At the time, the White House was in the process of creating a special task force on the Ryukyus. The commission was the result of a promise President John F. Kennedy made to Japanese Prime Minister Ikeda Hayato to find ways to improve the economic and social conditions on Okinawa. The fourteen articles in the series made the assignment of an Army officer as the Civil Administrator an issue in Washington, D.C. Until that time, the military status of the Civil Administrator had never been a matter of contention. When the Presidential Task Force made its report in March 1962, one of its recommended reforms was that the position henceforth be an assignment for a civilian.[40] Military resistance to this initiative, however, diluted its impact. Caraway opposed any effort to loosen military control over the island. A talented bureaucrat with much experience in the ways of government—both his parents had been U.S. Senators, and he had served as military aide to Vice President Richard Nixon—he simply incorporated the duties of the Civil Administrator into his office, effectively scuttling efforts to loosen military control of the island.[41]

Other journalistic examinations of Caraway's administration came in 1964 and then again in 1965 when the *Washington Post* ran two different series on Okinawa. Given its location in the nation's capital, the *Post* enjoyed an influence that far exceeded its circulation. The paper was also in the process of becoming a national newspaper of the first rank along the lines of the *New York Times* and the *New York Herald Tribune.* The Okinawa articles were part of this effort. The *Post* had a capable reporter to write this series. Rafael Steinberg was a 1950 graduate of Harvard and, after finishing college, had been a war correspondent in Korea. After the war, he worked for *Time* in its New York and London Bureaus. In 1959, he became *Newsweek* Tokyo Bureau Chief, the magazine being owned by the Washington Post Company. Steinberg was married to a Japanese woman and spoke fluent Japanese.[42]

The five-part series, called "America's Unhappy Bastion," received prominent play in the *Post.* The first article appeared in the paper's Sunday "Outlook" section. Each day thereafter, the articles appeared on the front page.[43] The series had a strongly critical tone. The initial article stated: "Ruled by an American general who makes plain his feeling that he knows better than they do what is good for them, unprotected by any constitution and unable to carry on normal commerce and travel with Japan, which all of them consider their homeland, the people of Okinawa today are convinced that the United States has let them down." Steinberg, however, was a good journalist, and presented both sides of the issue. He noted that "almost every Okinawa complaint is earnestly refuted by the American Army administrators of this base, who point to economic growth, the roads, harbors and waterworks and the settlement of many vexing land claims as examples of progress."[44]

Given Steinberg's background and language abilities, the series had a heavy emphasis on Okinawan views and opinions. The main grievance these Japanese expressed was their lack of self-government. "Although there are a few points that have the look of progress, there has been no real advance commensurate with our hopes," Ota Seisaku, Chief Executive, Ryukyu Islands, told Steinberg. Caraway's view was simple: "They show no inclination to accept further responsibility." Steinberg, however, found that the desire for more control of public affairs cut across all divides in Okinawa. A teacher educated in the United States remarked, "It is poor tactics for the high commissioner to decide when the Ryukyu Government is responsible or not. Were the American people 'responsible' when they declared their independence? The Americans should encourage us to make our own decisions in accordance with our own customs and society, even if we make mistakes as long as it doesn't conflict with the security of the bases." Another sentiment that was almost universal was a desire for unification with Japan. "What we cannot endure," an opposition politician told the American reporter, "is that we have given up, have lost all these things which we would have as part of Japan—development of industry, a sense of nationality, freedom of travel, welfare benefits—just in order for the bases to be here to safeguard the peace and so forth."[45]

Steinberg also examined other issues. He clearly stated the strategic importance of a base only 400 miles from the coast of China and the loss of response flexibility that would be entailed in returning the island to Japan. The luxurious standard of living that Americans enjoyed on the island was another topic he investigated. Like Brian Casey in the *Honolulu Advertiser,* he found that military subsidization and the low cost of Okinawan labor gave Americans in the Ryukyus a level of economic prosperity that they never would have experienced back in the United States. The strengths and weaknesses of the Okinawan economy were other areas that Steinberg probed. He found that most Okinawan businesses serviced the U.S. military establishment and that there were huge parts of the island that lagged behind the cities near the bases.[46]

The *Post* ran an editorial calling for the return of the island to Japan. "However well American military commanders may deal with Okinawan problems, their efforts are not likely to find favor with their charges. Most people who have experienced any degree of democracy prefer bad self-government to good military government." The Editorial Board of the paper made it clear that it favored a settlement that would allow the United States to keep the bases on the island. "Our relations with Japan, infinitely more important to us than any single military base in the larger scheme of our Pacific defenses, will be damaged, sooner or later, if the discontents of Okinawa continue to roil Japanese politics." This position remained the editorial stance of the paper until President Richard Nixon agreed to return the Ryukyu Islands in 1969.[47]

These stories had no major impact on policy. Secretary of the Army Stephen Ailes wrote a lengthy response that appeared in the paper's "Outlook" section. Ailes said American rule was "firm and fair," and he disputed the contention that the Okinawan populace was unhappy with U.S. administration. He noted that the Army was successfully fulfilling its obligation to improve social welfare and enjoyed a reasonable acquiesce from the island residents. This second point was true, since the U.S. had no garrison troops. Had Ailes stressed this fact more, his response would have been stronger, but he chose to list the construction and physical improvements on the island, a trait Steinberg had noted among officials on Okinawa. While he did not challenge the legitimacy of Okinawan desires for home rule, Ailes said the Civil Administration was making an effort to give more responsibility to the resident population. The Okinawan government, "left to its own devices, would perhaps have learned the art of government and acquired responsibility in any event. But, in this unique situation, where military and civilian interests are deeply interwoven, the costs and risks involved in such a course have seemed excessive." He also disputed the intensity of reversion sentiment, questioning the ability of one reporter to accurately gauge public opinion. "It is my personal conviction," Ailes wrote, "that there is little sentiment for reversion," particularly if it required the "removal of the

American military establishment." Other than that essay, there was no other response or change in policy towards Okinawa.

Steinberg, for his part, claimed a victory of sorts a year later in another three-part series about Okinawa that also appeared in the *Post*. He emphasized the improvements that had taken place under the tenure of General Watson, the new High Commissioner, contrasting them to the autocratic methods of his predecessor. In this second series, Steinberg avoided mentioning Caraway by name. In an ironic twist, the tone of the first article was more positive and complimentary than the previous series, even though Steinberg was less restrained in his criticisms. In the other two articles, he examined the larger issues of direct election of the Chief Executive, Ryukyu Islands and the ultimate reversion of the island to Japanese administration.[48]

Even the *Post* cooled on the issue. The second series received far less prominence than the first, with the stories running inside the front section of the paper. "Nobody else gave a damn," Caraway said about these articles.[49] Casey and Steinberg had punched major holes in the Army's no-press-coverage policy. Both had written about the island on a onetime basis (in the case of Steinberg it was a two-time basis). As a result, both were less inclined to seek or need military support, and neither adopted the official line of the various services stationed on Okinawa. Both produced informative accounts that were impressive examples of good journalism, but neither led to the massive public reassessment of the U.S. presence in the Ryukyus that the Army feared.

There were other factors at work over which the Army had no control that caused media interest in Okinawa to grow in the late 1960s. The U.S.-Japan Mutual Security Treaty signed in 1960 had a ten-year term, after which either nation could terminate the alliance with a year's notice. Public interest in Japan about the status of Okinawa would create a number of political difficulties for those interested in preserving the alliance if the issue of Okinawa were still unresolved in 1970. As a result, President Lyndon Johnson met with Japanese Prime Minister Sato Eisaku in November 1967. During these meetings, Johnson agreed to return to Japan the Bonin Islands, which included Iwo Jima. Reaction to the summit was reserved. Editorials in several American newspapers expressed disappointment that the United States had not returned Okinawa.[50] One journalist privately warned the Johnson Administration to go further. Joseph Alsop, the syndicated columnist, met with White House staff member Alfred Jenkins and told him that American relations with Japan would be better served if the United States initiated Okinawan reversion rather than having the Japanese force them into such an effort.[51]

Sentiment in the press was hardly universally in favor of reversion, and one press baron challenged what he saw as movement in this direction in one of the few instances of the media challenging official strategic thinking about Okinawa. William Loeb, publisher of the Manchester, New Hampshire *Union Leader*, opposed reversion. He made a brief effort to make Okinawa a campaign issue during the 1968 New Hampshire primary. His position on Okinawa was summed up in the headline of an editorial he ran just before the actual agreement to return the island: "KEEP OKINAWA—BOUGHT WITH BLOOD." This effort had no impact on the presidential campaign; the American people were far more concerned about Vietnam. The war dominated all other foreign policy issues in that election.[52] Loeb's failure, however, is important. Had he succeeded in making Okinawa a political issue, it would have been along the lines of resisting reversion, making diplomatic negotiations much more difficult, if not impossible.

Despite the Johnson-Sato Agreement on Iwo Jima, Okinawa was at the forefront of U.S-Japanese relations when Richard Nixon became President of the United States in 1969. Suddenly, American journalists recognized that Okinawa was a major issue worth writing about. Reporters began producing more and more articles about the island, overwhelming the Army's no-publicity policy. Items about U.S. policy toward the island began receiving prominent play in news magazines, including *Time, The Reporter,* and *U.S. News and World Report;* and newspapers, such as the *New York Times,* the *Wall Street Journal,* and the *Christian Science Monitor.* A number of publications as diverse as political commentary magazines (*The Nation, Atlantic Monthly,* and *The New Republic*) and travel journals (*Travel* and *National Geographic*) ran features about the Ryukyus.[53]

Even though Nixon came into office with a firm idea of what he wanted to do about Okinawa, the military-press relationship had an impact on the negotiations that led to reversion. The new administration began discussing Okinawa the day after the inauguration. The military resisted, stressing a need to have nuclear storage rights and a Japanese commitment to allow the United States to use the bases on the island in the defense of South Korea, Taiwan, and South Vietnam. The President decided to compromise. If Japan would agree to allow the unrestricted use of Okinawa for the defense of these three countries, Nixon would drop the insistence on nuclear storage. The President, however, told the Joint Chiefs of Staff nothing about his decision. He worried that they might raise a political firestorm over the nuclear issue. Nevertheless, his decision became public when it appeared on the front page of the *New York Times.* White House Chief of Staff Bob Haldeman called the story "complete and accurate." The article infuriated the President. The only mention Nixon made of Okinawa in his memoirs was a complaint over this leak. He charged that the paper had revealed America's negotiating strategy, doing great damage. Undersecretary of State U.

Alexis Johnson worried that the Joint Chiefs of Staff would raise a ruckus about the nuclear storage issue. Despite these worries, the United States and Japan reached agreement, announcing the return of the island on 21 November 1969 during Prime Minister Sato Eisaku's visit to the White House.[54]

On the whole, American and Japanese reaction to the communiqué was positive. Most papers ran wire-service articles on the front page, and the bulk of editorial commentary was positive. The Senate's rejection of the nomination of Judge Clement F. Haynsworth Jr. to the Supreme Court and the funeral of Joseph Kennedy overshadowed the Okinawa communiqué in the American press.[55] The lingering influence of U.S. Army news policy on Okinawa, however, was still strong, and a few provincial papers made no mention of the event at all, seeing little of news value to their audience.[56]

After the Nixon-Sato Agreement, the United States and Japan held a long series of diplomatic negotiations on a variety of technical issues before the island reverted to Japanese control. It took two and a half years to convert a dollar-based economy to one based on the yen, change the road and traffic signs to a system that operated on the other side of the road, and institute Japanese subsidies for a number of food products. Many left-wing organizations on Okinawa, such as the Reversion Council, the Okinawa Teachers Association, and labor unions, were unhappy with the accord. These organizations, like many in Japan, had hoped to use the Okinawa issue to terminate the alliance with the United States and remove all U.S. bases from Okinawa and Japan. Nixon and Sato had negotiated a settlement that had preserved the alliance and allowed for the continued operation of all these bases. The technical negotiations offered the political left some time to try to undermine the agreement. As a result, several problems became crises, and the press played an important role in two of them. On 5 June 1969, several Okinawan organizations held a major rally outside the Second Logistical Command compound, the largest U.S. Army detachment stationed on the island, whose mission was to repair heavy equipment damaged in Vietnam. No interpreters were present during this demonstration. When the Military Police (MP) guarding the compound tried to force the crowd back, no one could communicate between the two groups. The guards fixed their bayonets, marched to edge of the crowd, and tried to push it back. In the process, the MP nicked Asato Tsumichiyo, a protest leader. Asato was also a member of the legislature. Lieutenant General Lampert, High Commissioner at the time, described him as a "leader of one of the non-Conservative parties, but a middle of the road party." A photographer captured the incident on film, which ended up in the *New York Times*. "That caused no end of trouble," the general remarked.[57]

Lampert immediately acted to keep the episode from exploding. He quickly expressed to Asato his regrets for the incident. Fortunately for the general, Asato had no interest in enflaming the situation and accepted the apology.[58] Other American efforts at crowd control improved after this incident. "We learned a lot from that particular experience," Lampert observed. Interpreters were present at future rallies. Guards were no longer given bayonets. The issue of live ammunition also required the High Commissioner's expressed authorization.[59]

The second crisis came a month later and was not so easy to resolve. In July 1969, a canister of nerve gas stored on Okinawa developed a leak. Lampert was sleeping when a phone call woke him. Army Major General Charles Horner, Commanding General of the 2d Logistical Command, was at the other end of the line. Speaking in guarded words, he told Lampert, "I just want to let you know that we've got a leaker." Some Americans had been exposed to the gas. No Okinawans were involved. Horner wanted to dump the faulty canister in the ocean. The High Commissioner decided to report the matter to Washington, and told Horner to wait. While messages traveled across the Pacific, a reporter for the *Wall Street Journal* learned of the leak and wrote a story that ended up on the front page. The presence and location of chemical weapons was a closely guarded secret, and the leak of one was a newsworthy item. Lampert described the article as "somewhat exaggerated." The story was actually quite weak, and the general could only blame himself and the Army for any deficiencies in the piece. The article contained no quotes or identified sources and said little that was new after the introductory paragraph. The body of the article was a history of chemical and biological weapons. "After the publication of this story, rather quickly the decision was made to publicly acknowledge the presence of the munitions on Okinawa," Lampert recalled.[60]

The issue of leaking chemical weapons offered political activists opposed to the alliance and the American bases the perfect issue to attack the Nixon-Sato Agreement. The assertion that the American bases clearly put the average Okinawan at risk now sounded extremely plausible. The American effort to remove the weapons had little calming influence, since it took over a year to find another storage facility. Riots broke out on 19–20 December 1970 after an anti-reversion, anti–nerve-gas protest rally in the city of Koza. An American driving near the rally hit an Okinawan pedestrian. The MP arrived at the scene and sent the driver to the hospital, leaving the pedestrian in the street. An account of this episode in the *Washington Post* called this act "the crowning symbol of an arrogant 'occupation' mentality." The accident caused a good deal of traffic congestion, which caused a second accident. Already angry and agitated, the Okinawan onlookers snapped and started to riot.[61] The crowd started burning an American-owned car and two MP vehicles. The mob then split in two. One group charged the gates of Kadena Air Force Base, throwing rocks and bottles. The crowd battled Air Police, breached the perimeter, and burned down a school before the Americans pushed them back. The other part of the mob tore through Koza, burning American cars. Two lines of Okinawan police and American MP in riot gear faced the mob as it approached a housing complex for military families. The police fired tear gas into the crowd to break it up. Lampert went on television and radio to calm the public and prevent the riot from spreading. The next day, the riot was front-page news in the United States.[62]

Americans downplayed the importance of the riots. An editorial in the *Honolulu Advertiser* asserted that the riots were not anti-American, but a protest against the polarized society on Okinawa, where a small foreign minority had most of the wealth and a different legal status. Lampert went even further, dismissing the riot as the result of the "anxieties and tension" accompanying reversion.[63] The riot, however, only increased interest in the island among the press. Reporters flocked to the island three weeks later, when the Army removed the first portion of the chemical weapons. Lampert reported briefing eighty-one reporters from a variety of American and foreign news agencies, such as the British Broadcasting Corporation (BBC), the American Broadcasting Corporation, the Columbia Broadcasting Corporation, the National Broadcasting Corporation (NBC), the Associated Press, United Press International, and Reuters. This big media contingent gave Okinawan political activists an even larger audience than they usually enjoyed, and the political activists canvassed a village on the removal route, telling the villagers that the Americans were putting them at great risk. It was reported that everyone in the village might die if a canister started to leak, or if one of the trucks transporting the nerve gas had an accident. This pitch was persuasive. The evening before the removal effort was to begin, the residents of the village threatened to block the travel of the trucks carrying the chemicals. Lampert thought the Okinawans wanted a confrontation for press attention. Yara Chobyo, Chief Executive, Ryukyu Islands, met with Lampert and suggested he postpone the shipment for forty-eight hours. Yara had organized the teachers' association, served as its first president, and owed his election to the work of the labor unions. He thought he could negotiate a settlement. Lampert agreed, and gave him the time to find a solution. Under Secretary of the Army Thaddeus Beal quickly approved the delay. The Reversion Council, unaware of this development, staged a rally at a spot along the convoy route that drew 2,000 people and waited for the trucks to arrive.[64]

Yara spent the next day meeting with representatives from the Reversion Council. "Situation fluid with increasingly encouraging indications as time for initiation of shipment approaches," Lampert told his superiors back in Washington. The general made it clear in his cables that he would hold off shipping the gas until he got a go-ahead signal from Yara.[65] Still, the two-day delay allowed tempers to cool. The villagers used the time to leave. Yara told Lampert the Okinawan police could handle the situation. Local law enforcement, however, had little to do. American drivers reported traveling through a ghost town of vacant houses and businesses with drawn shutters.[66] Nevertheless, Lampert drew wide praise in the press and from Washington for his handling of the episode. Columnists for the *Japan Times* wrote that the crisis over the gas shipments was "grossly overdone" and praised the general for his "cool and calm" judgment. With little conflict or story beyond trucks passing through empty villages, reporters left the island.[67]

This episode, however, was far from over. The Army had removed only 150 tons of the 100,000 tons stored on the island. Still, as media attention faded, removing the weapons became easier. Negotiations with the Japanese government on the matter began immediately after the first shipment. In order to avoid similar confrontations, the Japanese suggested that the U.S. Army build a special road away from any population center solely for the transport of the nerve gas. The Americans were willing to remove the weapons, but building a special road sounded a bit absurd to them, given the lethality of the gas and the length of time the United States had stored the weapons without incident. The Japanese responded, offering to pay for the road if the Americans would build it. Lampert accepted this compromise.[68] Construction on the road began in May and lasted throughout the summer. The Army finished removing the gas in mid-September.[69] Reversion took place less than a year later.

For twenty-seven years, the military on Okinawa adopted a press policy that was designed to keep coverage of the island to an absolute minimum in an effort to keep the American people and their representatives in Congress unaware that the Ryukyus were a U.S. colony in everything but name. Even though it was a time of peace on Okinawa, the soldiers had the advantage over the journalists. A few reporters covering Okinawa on a onetime basis were able to pierce the blanket of silence covering the American presence. For the most part, though, this policy of limiting press coverage worked for the military until international affairs in the Pacific region overwhelmed the efforts of the armed services to preserve their hold on this archipelago.

Notes

1. John F. Marszalek, *Sherman's Other War: The General and the Civil War Press* (Memphis, TN: Memphis State University Press, 1981); William Prochnau, *Once upon a Distant War: Young Correspondents and the Early Vietnam Battles* (New York: Random House, 1995); Bernard A. Weisberger, *Reporters for the Union* (Boston: Little, Brown,

1953); J. Cutler Andrews, *The North Reports the Civil War* (Pittsburgh, PA: University of Pittsburgh Press, 1955); Emmet Crozier, *American Reporters on the Western Front, 1914–1918* (New York: Oxford University Press, 1959); and Michael S. Sweeney, *The Military and the Press: An Uneasy Peace* (Evanston, IL: Northwestern University Press, 2006).

2. J. Cutler Andrews, *The South Reports the Civil War* (Princeton: Princeton University Press, 1970); Ford Risley, "The Confederate Press Association: Cooperative News Reporting of the War," *Civil War History* 47 (September 2001): 222–239; Charles H. Brown, *The Correspondents' War: Journalists and the Spanish-American War* (New York: Scribner's, 1967); John Seelye, *War Games: Richard Harding Davis and the New Imperialism* (Amherst: University of Massachusetts Press, 2003); Clarence Wyatt, *Paper Soldiers: The American Press and the Vietnam War* (New York: Norton, 1993); Peter Braestrup, *Big Story: How the American Press and TV Reported and Interpreted the Crisis of Tet in 1968 in Vietnam and Washington*, 2 vols. (Boulder, CO: Westview Press, 1977); Daniel C. Hallin, *The Uncensored War: The Media and Vietnam* (New York: Oxford University Press, 1986); William M. Hammond, *Reporting Vietnam: Media and Military at War* (Lawrence: University Press of Kansas, 1998); Joyce Milton, *Yellow Kids: Foreign Correspondents in the Heyday of Yellow Journalism* (New York: Harper and Row, 1989); Robert W. Desmond, *Tides of War: World News Reporting, 1931–1945* (Iowa City: University of Iowa Press, 1984); James Tobin, *Ernie Pyle's War: America's Eyewitness to World War II* (New York: Free Press, 1997); Phillip Knightly, *The First Casualty: From the Crimea to Vietnam: The War Correspondent as Hero, Propagandist, and Myth Maker* (New York: Harcourt Brace Jovanovich, 1975); and Peter Young and Peter Jesser, *The Media and the Military: From Crimea to Desert Strike* (New York: St. Martins' Press, 1997).

3. Akio Watanabe, *The Okinawa Problem: A Chapter in Japan-U.S. Relations.* (Carlton, Australia: Melbourne University Press, 1970); Frederick L. Shiels, *America, Okinawa, and Japan: Case Studies for Foreign Policy Theory* (Washington, DC: University Press of America, 1980); Arnold G. Fisch Jr., *Military Government in the Ryukyu Islands, 1945–50* (Washington, DC: U.S. Government Printing Office, 1987); L. Eve Armentrout Ma, "The Explosive Nature of Okinawa's 'Land Issue' or 'Base Issue,' 1945–1977: A Dilemma of United States Military Policy," *Journal of American-East Asian Relations* 1 (Winter 1992): 435–463; Nicholas Evan Sarantakes, "Continuity through Change: The Return of Okinawa and Iwo Jima, 1967–1972," *Journal of American East-Asian Relations* 3 (Spring 1994): 34–53; Sarantakes, *Keystone: The American Occupation of Okinawa and U.S.-Japanese Relations* (College Station: Texas A&M University Press, 2000); Christopher Aldous, "Achieving Reversion: Protest and Authority in Okinawa, 1952–70," *Modern Asian Studies* 37:2 (2003): 485–508; Laura Hein and Mark Selden, eds., *Islands of Discontent: Okinawan Responses to Japanese and American Power* (Lanham, MD: Rowman and Littlefield, 2003); and Robert D. Eldridge, *The Origins of the Bilateral Okinawa Problem: Okinawa in Postwar U. S.-Japan Relations, 1945–1952* (New York: Garland Publishing, 2001).

4. Lieutenant General Albert Watson II, Oral History, Senior Officers Debriefing Program, U.S. Army Military History Institute (hereafter MHI), Carlisle Barracks, Carlisle, Pennsylvania, 36.

5. Lester J. Foltos, "The New Pacific Barrier: America's Search for Security in the Pacific, 1945–47," *Diplomatic History* 13 (Summer 1989): 320, 323, 326, 336–337, 341. Okinawa was the bloodiest battle in U.S. Navy history. In addition, the Tenth Army suffered 39,000 casualties, which was approximately 22 percent of U.S. ground forces deployed on the island. For comparison, these numbers are similar to the casualties suffered by the two individual armies at the Battle of Gettysburg. Tenth Army figures are based on the numbers reported for total battle casualties and the number of assault troops unloaded, as found in Roy E. Appleman, James M. Burns, Russell A. Gugeler, and John Stevens, *United States Army in World War II: The War in the Pacific; The Last Battle* (Washington, DC: U.S. Government Printing Office, 1948), 490, 492. At Gettysburg, the Army of the Potomac suffered 23,000 casualties, about a quarter of its fighting force. The Army of Northern Virginia had 28,000 casualties, approximately a third of its strength. James M. McPherson, *Battle Cry of Freedom: The Civil War Era* (New York: Oxford University Press, 1988), 664.

6. Diary Entry, 23 April 1945, Box 1, Papers of Simon B. Buckner Jr., Dwight D. Eisenhower Presidential Library.

7. Hodge to Stilwell, 30 June 1945, Folder A-27, Box 28a, Career File, Papers of Joseph Stilwell, Hoover Institute, Stanford University.

8. Sarantakes, *Keystone,* 40–45.

9. *New York Herald Tribune,* November 2, 1949; Sarantakes, *Keystone,* 36–39, 46–47; *Life,* 19 December 1949, 19.

10. Weldon James, "How are Things on Okinawa?" *Collier's,* 12 July 1947, 18, 19, 64.

11. "Memorandum by Robert Fearey," 31 January 1951; "Memorandum of Conversation by Robert Fearey," 27 January 1951; "Memorandum by Robert Fearey," 19 March 1951, *FRUS 1951,* 6:1, 835–837, 818–822, 933.

12. "Memorandum of Conversation by the Second Secretary of the Embassy in the United Kingdom," 21 March 1951; "Memorandum on the Substance of Discussions at a Department of State-Joint Chiefs of Staff Meeting," 11 April 1951, *FRUS 1951,* 6:1, 937, 970; Johnson to Rusk, 22 March 1951, Folder Island, Box 6, Japanese Peace Treaty Files of John Foster Dulles, Lot File 54D423, Microfilm Reel 6, Record Group (hereafter RG) 59, National Archives II, College Park, Maryland (hereafter NA II).

13. "Memorandum by Dulles," 27 June 1951; "Memorandum of Conversation by Witman," 14 August 1951, *FRUS 1951,* 6:1, 1152–1153, 1269–1270; U.S. Department of State, *Conference for the Conclusion and Signature of the Treaty of Peace with Japan,* San Francisco, California, 4–8 September 1951, *Record of Proceedings* (Washington, DC: U.S. Government Printing Office, 1951), 78 and 277.

14. *Newsweek,* 10 September 1951; *Time,* 10 September 1951.

15. Enthusiastic presentations of the American presence in the early 1950s include the following: Peter Kalischer, "Our Gibraltar in the Pacific," *Collier's* 11 (October 1951): 22–25; George Barrett, "Report on Okinawa: A Rampart We Built," *New York Times Magazine,* 21 September 1952, 9, 62, 63, 65; Demaree Bess, "Okinawa—American Island," *Saturday Evening Post,* 11 July 1953, 26, 27, 86, 88; *Time,* 15 August 1955, 18–20.

16. The influence of the briefing is readily apparent in stories in the following pub-

lications: *New York World Telegram and Sun,* 15 March 1952; *New York Daily News,* 19 June 1960 and 19 June 1962; *U.S. News and World Report,* 22 June 1951, 26; *Christian Science Monitor,* 26 May 1955; and Denis Warner, "Our Fire Brigade on Okinawa," *Reporter,* October 13, 1960, 37–38. The control of reporters is discussed in David S. Grubnick to Caraway, 11 March 1965, Folder Selected letters from Okinawa *Morning Star* Reporters, Box 1968, Papers of Paul Caraway, MHI; and *Honolulu Advertiser,* 3 September 1961. For a sampling of Trumbull's articles, see the following: *New York Times,* 14 and 15 April 1956, 10 January 1957, 14 and 19 January 1958, and 14–15 November 1960; and "Okinawa: 'Sometimes Painful' Lesson for Us," *New York Times Magazine,* 7 April 1957, 29, 60, 62.

17. U.S. Civil Administration of the Ryukyu Islands, *The Newspapers of the Ryukyu Islands* (San Francisco: U.S. Government Printing Office, 1964), 1–3.

18. Lieutenant General Paul Caraway II, Oral History, 15, 61; Lieutenant General Albert Watson II, Oral History, 36, Senior Officers Debriefing Program, MHI.

19. *Okinawa Morning Star,* 11 April 1957, 12 April 1958, 15 August 1958, 13 January 1962; *Washington Post,* 7 January 1962; *Honolulu Advertiser,* 3 September 1961.

20. Vern Sneider, *The Teahouse of the August Moon* (New York: Putnam, 1951); John Patrick, *The Teahouse of the August Moon, a Play by John Patrick* (New York: G. P. Putnam's Sons, 1954); *The Teahouse of the August Moon,* Metro Golden Mayer Studios, dir. Daniel Mann, screenplay by John Patrick, 1956; *The Teahouse of the August Moon,* dir. George Schaefer, broadcast date 26 November 1962, National Broadcasting Company Television Network, Hallmark Hall of Fame Collection, Film and Television Archive, University of California at Los Angeles; John Patrick, Stan Freeman, and Franklin Underwood, *Lovely Ladies, Kind Gentlemen* (New York: French, 1971).

21. *New York Times,* 22 April 1954; *Life,* 14 June 1954, 101–102.

22. *New York Times,* 10 January 1957; *Christian Science Monitor,* 28 December 1956; *U.S. News and World Report,* 22 February 1957.

23. *Okinawa Taimusu,* 28 December 1956; *U.S. News and World Report,* 22 February 1957.

24. *U.S. News and World Report,* 16 August 1957; *Time,* 9 December 1957; "Memorandum of Conversation," 27 November 1957, 794c.00/1757, Box 3977, State Department Central Decimal File, 1955–59, RG 59, NA II; Robertson to Sprague, 11 December 1957, *FRUS, 1955–57,* vol. 23:1, 544–546.

25. Barton M. Biggs, "The Outraged Okinawans," *Harper's,* December 1958, 60.

26. *New York Times,* 26 November 1957; Martin to Parsons, 6 December 1957, Folder 1.3, Lot File 61 D69, Box 13, RG 59, NA II; Robertson to Sprague, 11 December 1957, *FRUS, 1955–57,* vol. 23:1, 544–546.

27. Biggs, "Outraged Okinawans," 56–60; *Washington Daily News,* 26 November 1958.

28. Biggs, "Outraged Okinawans," 56–60.

29. Ibid.

30. Risher to Booth, 12 January 1959, Commanding General 3rd Marine Division to Booth, 25 December 1958, 9147/8920-(59), Box 136, Central Decimal File, RG 218, NA II.

31. Risher to Booth, 12 January 1959; Booth to CINCPAC, 27 January 1959, 9147/8920-(59), Box 136, Central Decimal File, RG 218, NA II.

32. Steele to Risher, 23 December 1958, 9147/8920-(59), Box 136; Commanding General, 3rd Marine Division to Booth, 25 December 1958, 9147/8920-(59), Box 136, Central Decimal File, RG 218, NA II.

33. Senate Committee on Appropriations, *Foreign Assistance and Related Agencies Appropriations for 1964,* 88th Congress, 1st Session (Washington, DC: U.S. Government Printing Office, 1963), 107–110.

34. Risher to Booth, 12 January 1959, 147/8920-(59), Box 136, Central Decimal File, RG 218, NA II.

35. Risher to Booth, 12 January 1959, 147/8920-(59); Booth to CINCPAC, 27 January 1959, 9147/8920-(9 February 1959), Box 136, Central Decimal File, RG 218, NA II; Message of the High Commissioner to the Twenty-Third Session of the Legislature of the Government of the Ryukyu Islands, 1 February 1963, U.S. Civil Administration of the Ryukyu Islands, *Report for Period 1 July 1962 to 30 June 1963* (Washington, DC: U.S. Government Printing Office, 1963), 218; U.S. Civil Administration of the Ryukyu Islands, *Report for Period 1 July 1964 to 30 June 1965* (Washington, DC: U.S. Government Printing Office, 1965), 226; Camp Smedley D. Butler Command Chronology, July–December 1968, II-6; Camp Smedley D. Butler Command Chronology, July–December 1970, II-9, MCUA.

36. *Honolulu Advertiser,* 1–14 September 1961; *Honolulu Star-Bulletin,* 24 June, 6 July, 30 August, 16 October 1957, and 27 December 1959.

37. *Honolulu Advertiser*, 2, 4, 7, 8 September 1961.

38. Ibid., 2 and 6 September 1961.

39. Ibid., 8–14 September 1961.

40. *Congressional Record,* 1961, A7825–34.

41. Sarantakes, *Keystone,* 125–126.

42. *Washington Post,* 3 May 1964. The author would like to thank Leonard Downie, Executive Editor, *Washington Post,* for his assistance in finding these articles.

43. Ibid., 3–7 May 1964.

44. Ibid., 3 May 1964.

45. Ibid., 3, 5, and 7 May 1964.

46. Ibid., 3–7 May 1964.

47. Ibid., 5 May 1964.

48. Ibid., 26–28 December 1965.

49. Ibid., 10 May 1964; 26–28 December 1965.

50. *Washington Evening Star,* 23 November 1967; *New York Times,* 17 November 1967; *Pittsburgh Post-Gazette,* 16 November 1967.

51. Jenkins to Walt Rostow, 20 June 1968, Alfred Jenkins Memo Folder, Name File, National Security File, Lyndon Baines Johnson Presidential Library.

52. *Manchester Union Leader,* 5 January 1968; 19 November 1969.

53. *Progressive,* November 1969; *Reporter,* 2 November 1967; *Army,* November 1969; *Saturday Review,* 6 December 1969; *Atlantic Monthly,* October 1969; *New Republic,*

14 June 1969; *Nation,* 3 February 1969; *National Geographic,* September 1969; *Travel,* March 1969; *Wall Street Journal,* 5 June 1969; *Reader's Digest,* November 1969; *U.S. News and World Report,* 22 September 1969; *Time,* 13 June 1969; *Christian Science Monitor,* 2 and 14 February, 24 March, 2 and 31 May 1969; *New York Times,* 27 May 1969.

54. National Security Decision Memorandum 13, 28 May 1969, Box 1, RG 273, NA II; Henry A. Kissinger, *White House Years* (Boston: Little, Brown, 1979), 329; *New York Times,* 3 June 1969; Diary Entry, 3 June 1969, H. R. Haldeman, *The Haldeman Diaries: Inside the Nixon White House—the Complete Multimedia Edition* (Santa Monica, CA: Sony Imagesoft, 1994); Richard Nixon, *RN: The Memoirs of Richard Nixon* (New York: Grosset and Dunlap, 1978), 389; U. Alexis Johnson, *The Right Hand of Power: The Memoirs of an American Diplomat* (Englewood Cliffs, NJ: Prentice-Hall, 1984), 545.

55. *Atlanta Constitution,* 22 November 1969; *Christian Science Monitor,* 29–30 November 1969; *Chicago Tribune,* 22 November 1969; *Cleveland Plain Dealer,* 22 November 1969; *St. Louis Post Dispatch,* 21 November 1969; *New York Times,* 23 November 1969; *Los Angeles Times,* 22 November 1969; *Time,* 28 November 1969. A dissenting voice came from the *Columbia State,* 28 November 1969.

56. *Kansas City Star,* 22 November 1969; *Boston Globe,* 22 November 1969.

57. *New York Times,* 5, 7, 8, and 10 June 1969; Lieutenant General James B. Lampert, Oral History, 31–32, Senior Officers Debriefing Program, MHI.

58. Lieutenant General James B. Lampert, Oral History, 31–32, Senior Officers Debriefing Program, MHI.

59. Ibid.

60. *Wall Street Journal,* 18 July 1969; Lieutenant General James B. Lampert, Oral History, 36–43, Senior Officers Debriefing Program, MHI.

61. "Statement Delivered by High Commissioner James B. Lampert over Radio and Television Stations on Okinawa," U.S. Civil Administration of the Ryukyu Islands, *Report for Period 1 July 1970 to 30 June 1971* (Washington, DC: U.S. Government Printing Office, 1971), 264–265; *Washington Post,* 21 December 1970; Col. William G. Schless, Oral History, Part 2, 3–4, Senior Officers Debriefing Program, MHI.

62. "Statement Delivered by High Commissioner James B. Lampert over Radio and Television Stations on Okinawa," U.S. Civil Administration of the Ryukyu Islands, *Report for Period 1 July 1970 to 30 June 1971,* 264–5; *The Washington Post,* December 21, 1970.

63. *Honolulu Advertiser,* 14 January 1971; Remarks by High Commissioner James B. Lampert before the Fort Buckner Officer's Wives Club, 10 September 1971, U.S. Civil Administration of the Ryukyu Islands, *The Final Civil Affairs Report, 30 June 1971–15 May 1972* (Washington, DC: U.S. Government Printing Office, 1972), 152.

64. Lampert to CINCPAC, 11 January 1971, Lampert to Department of the Army, Folder: Chemical Weapons, Box 3, Papers of James Lampert, MHI.

65. Lampert to Department of the Army, 12 January 1971, Folder: Chemical Weapons, Box 3, Papers of James Lampert, MHI.

66. Lampert to Department of the Army, 13 January 1971, Folder: Chemical Weapons, Box 3, Papers of James Lampert, MHI.

67. *Japan Times,* 14 and 17 January 1971.

68. Col. William G. Schless, Oral History, Part 2, 6, Senior Officers Debriefing Program, MHI.

69. Lampert to CINCUSARPAC, 13 May 1971, Lampert to Secretary of Defense, 10 September 1971, Folder Chemical Weapons, Box 3, Papers of James Lampert, MHI.

Bibliography

Primary Sources

Archives

Dwight D. Eisenhower Presidential Library, Abilene, Kansas
Papers of Simon B. Buckner Jr.
Lyndon Baines Johnson Presidential Library, Austin, Texas
National Security File
Hoover Institute, Stanford University
Papers of Joseph Stilwell
U.S. Army Military History Institute, Carlisle Barracks, Carlisle, Pennsylvania
Papers of Paul Caraway
Papers of James Lampert
U.S. National Archives, College Park, Maryland
Record Group 59: Records of the Department of State
Record Group 218: Records of the Joint Chiefs of Staff
Record Group 273: Records of the National Security Council
U.S. Marine Corps Historical Center
Command Chronologies
Film and Television Archive, University of California at Los Angeles
The Teahouse of the August Moon

Oral Histories

U.S. Army Military History Institute, Senior Officers Debriefing Program
Lieutenant General Paul Caraway
Lieutenant General James B. Lampert
Colonel William G. Schless
Lieutenant General Albert Watson II

Magazines

Army
Atlantic Monthly
Collier's
Columbia State

Harper's
Life
The Nation
National Geographic
The New Republic
The New York Times Magazine
Newsweek
The Progressive
The Reader's Digest
The Reporter
Saturday Evening Post
Saturday Review
Time
Travel
U.S. News and World Report

Government Documents

U.S. Civil Administration of the Ryukyu Islands. *The Newspapers of the Ryukyu Islands,* San Francisco: U.S. Government Printing Office, 1964.

———. *Report for Period 1 July 1962 to 30 June 1963.* Washington, DC: U.S. Government Printing Office, 1963.

———. *Report for Period 1 July 1964 to 30 June 1965.* Washington, DC: U.S. Government Printing Office, 1965.

———. *Report for Period 1 July 1970 to 30 June 1971.* Washington, DC: U.S. Government Printing Office, 1971.

———. *The Final Civil Affairs Report, 30 June 1971–15 May 1972.* Washington, DC: U.S. Government Printing Office, 1972.

U.S. Department of State. *Conference for the Conclusion and Signature of the Treaty of Peace with Japan.* San Francisco, California, 4–8 September 1951. *Record of Proceedings.* Washington, DC: U.S. Government Printing Office, 1951.

United States Department of State. *FRUS* (*Foreign Relations of the United States*)

—1951, vol. 6:1. *Asia and the Pacific.* Washington, DC: U.S. Government Printing Office, 1977.

—1955–1957, vol. 23:1. *Japan.* Washington, DC: U.S. Government Printing Office, 1991.

Congressional Records

U.S. Senate. Senate Committee on Appropriations. *Foreign Assistance and Related Agencies Appropriations for 1964.* 88th Congress, 1st Session. Washington, DC: U.S. Government Printing Office, 1963.

CD/ROM

Haldeman, H. R. *The Haldeman Diaries: Inside the Nixon White House—the Complete Multimedia Edition.* Santa Monica, CA: Sony Imagesoft, 1994.

Film

The Teahouse of the August Moon. Hollywood: MGM Studios, 1956.

Plays

Patrick, John. *The Teahouse of the August Moon, a Play by John Patrick.* New York: G. P. Putnam's Sons, 1954.

Secondary Sources

Books

Andrews, J. Cutler. *The North Reports the Civil War.* Pittsburgh, PA: University of Pittsburgh Press, 1955.

———. *The South Reports the Civil War.* Princeton: Princeton University Press, 1970.

Braestrup, Peter. *Big Story: How the American Press and TV Reported and Interpreted the Crisis of Tet in 1968 in Vietnam and Washington.* 2 vols. Boulder, CO: Westview Press, 1977.

Brown, Charles H. *The Correspondents' War: Journalists and the Spanish-American War.* New York: Scribner's, 1967.

Crozier, Emmet. *American Reporters on the Western Front, 1914–1918.* New York: Oxford University Press, 1959.

Desmond, Robert W. *Tides of War: World News Reporting, 1931–1945.* Iowa City: University of Iowa Press, 1984.

Eldridge, Robert D. *The Origins of the Bilateral Okinawa Problem: Okinawa in Postwar U. S.-Japan Relations, 1945–1952.* New York: Garland Publishing, 2001.

Hallin, Daniel C. *The Uncensored War: The Media and Vietnam.* New York: Oxford University Press, 1986.

Hammond, William M. *Reporting Vietnam: Media and Military at War.* Lawrence: University Press of Kansas, 1998.

Hein, Laura, and Mark Selden, eds. *Islands of Discontent: Okinawan Responses to Japanese and American Power.* Lanham, MD: Rowman and Littlefield, 2003.

Johnson, U. Alexis. *The Right Hand of Power: The Memoirs of an American Diplomat.* Englewood Cliffs, NJ: Prentice-Hall, 1984.

Kissinger, Henry A. *White House Years.* Boston: Little, Brown, 1979.

Knightly, Phillip. *The First Casualty: From the Crimea to Vietnam; The War Correspondent as Hero, Propagandist, and Myth Maker.* New York: Harcourt Brace Jovanovich, 1975.

Marszalek, John F. *Sherman's Other War: The General and the Civil War Press.* Memphis, TN: Memphis State University Press, 1981.

McPherson, James M. *Battle Cry of Freedom: The Civil War Era.* New York: Oxford University Press, 1988.

Milton, Joyce. *Yellow Kids: Foreign Correspondents in the Heyday of Yellow Journalism.* New York: Harper and Row, 1989.

Nixon, Richard. *RN: The Memoirs of Richard Nixon.* New York: Grosset and Dunlap, 1978.

Patrick, John, Stan Freeman, and Franklin Underwood, *Lovely Ladies, Kind Gentlemen.* New York: French, 1971.

Prochnau, William. *Once upon a Distant War: Young Correspondents and the Early Vietnam Battles.* New York: Random House, 1995.

Sarantakes, Nicholas Evan. *Keystone: The American Occupation of Okinawa and U.S.-Japanese Relations.* College Station: Texas A&M University Press, 2000.

Seelye, John. *War Games: Richard Harding Davis and the New Imperialism.* Amherst: University of Massachusetts Press, 2003.

Shiels, Frederick L. *America, Okinawa, and Japan: Case Studies for Foreign Policy Theory.* Washington, DC: University Press of America, 1980.

Sneider, Vern. *The Teahouse of the August Moon.* New York: Putnam, 1951.

Sweeney, Michael S. *The Military and the Press: An Uneasy Peace.* Evanston, IL: Northwestern University Press, 2006.

Tobin, James. *Ernie Pyle's War: America's Eyewitness to World War II.* New York: Free Press, 1997.

Watanabe, Akio. *The Okinawa Problem: A Chapter in Japan-U.S. Relations.* Carlton, Australia: Melbourne University Press, 1970.

Weisberger, Bernard A. *Reporters for the Union.* Boston: Little, Brown, 1953.

Wyatt, Clarence. *Paper Soldiers: The American Press and the Vietnam War.* New York: Norton, 1993.

Young, Peter, and Peter Jesser. *The Media and the Military: From Crimea to Desert Strike.* New York: St. Martins' Press, 1997.

Official Histories

Appleman, Roy E., James M. Burns, Russell A. Gugeler, and John Stevens. *United States Army in World War II: The War in the Pacific; The Last Battle.* Washington, DC: U.S. Government Printing Office, 1948.

Fisch, Arnold G., Jr., *Military Government in the Ryukyu Islands, 1945–50.* Washington, DC: U.S. Government Printing Office, 1987.

Articles

Aldous, Christopher. "Achieving Reversion: Protest and Authority in Okinawa, 1952–70." *Modern Asian Studies* 37:2 (2003): 485–508.

Foltos, Lester J. "The New Pacific Barrier: America's Search for Security in the Pacific, 1945–47." *Diplomatic History* 13 (Summer 1989): 320–341.

Ma, L. Eve Armentrout. "The Explosive Nature of Okinawa's 'Land Issue' or 'Base Issue,' 1945–1977: A Dilemma of United States Military Policy." *Journal of American-East Asian Relations* 1 (Winter 1992): 435–463.

Risley, Ford. "The Confederate Press Association: Cooperative News Reporting of the War." *Civil War History* 47 (September 2001): 222–239.

Sarantakes, Nicholas Evan. "Continuity through Change: The Return of Okinawa and Iwo Jima, 1967–1972." *Journal of American–East Asian Relations* 3 (Spring 1994): 34–53.

Conclusion

Sarandis "Randy" Papadopoulos

This book in part owes its title to Carl von Clausewitz's often-cited dictum "War is a continuation of politics by other means." The nineteenth-century German thinker sought not to normalize armed conflict, but rather to show how a war's nature, logic, and grammar are inextricably resident in a broader political or cultural context for each side involved. Just as Clausewitz posited nearly two hundred years ago, the Pacific's unique geography imposes a discrete context for the logic of how people occupy, transit across, and struggle over its expanse. These essays show how living and fighting across the Pacific—before, during, and after World War II—have proven distinctive indeed.

Vast geography is the hallmark of the Pacific Ocean region, the largest single segment of the globe, encompassing more area than all of Earth's landmass, or four times the surface of the moon. Overwhelmingly, the region is empty save for water and marine life, compelling people to master its expanse. Yet it is an integral part of human space, as well: the recent failed trade agreement for a "Trans-Pacific Partnership" treaty would have more closely integrated the economic lives of 11 percent of the world's population and over a quarter of the planetary economy, including more than a third of its trade.[1] And that economic arrangement did not include nearly two billion more people who live in other countries on the ocean's periphery. American naval theorist Alfred Thayer Mahan seems correct in his century-old anticipation that the Pacific would become the main focus of human activity.[2]

The half century after Mahan saw radical change in America's Pacific presence. In 1890, when Frederick Jackson Turner declared the continental frontier closed, perhaps 25,000 Americans lived west of California; by 1941, the number had risen tenfold, mostly in Hawai'i, the Philippines, and China. Five years later, that number had grown into the millions, making the Pacific a successor to the domestic frontier.[3] Perhaps surprisingly, that scale has not dropped in seventy years, despite the Philippines gaining its independence, the end of U.S. military occupations in East Asia, and the conclusion of the Korean and Vietnam Wars. Indeed, the 1959 admission to statehood of Alaska and Hawai'i has made the Pacific more American. It is unsurprising, then, that the 2012 U.S. "Defense

Strategic Guidance" stated, "*we will of necessity rebalance toward the Asia-Pacific region.*"[4]

With such a broad presence, transmitting information mattered seventy-five years ago, much as it does today, and that reality mandated creating a reliable communication network. Academic audiences may bristle at the term "command and control," with its subtexts of hierarchy and subordination, but as Rebecca Raines illustrates in Chapter 1, distributing information was essential not only to issue orders but to supply forces and respond to changing circumstances in the World War II theatre. Doing so over an area ranging from Alaska to Australia meant an immense infrastructure, and by the mid-twentieth century the relative mobility of units meant using radio. Telegraph messages and hand-delivered mail could only fill in so much; the last warning sent to Pearl Harbor before the 7 December attack got to Honolulu's RCA telegraph office—using a private company, in other words—just after 7:30 a.m., less than half an hour before the attack began. It was not delivered to the military for over four hours—that is, after both attacking aircraft waves had wreaked their havoc.[5]

Mid-twentieth-century communications differed from what we know today. Typed text, not voice, dominated communications, and the influence of radioteletype comes through clearly in Raines's chapter. The equivalent German system, the Lorenz Cypher, was broken in 1942 by Allied codebreakers, allowing the reading of thousands of secret military dispatches.[6] Given the American requirement for hundreds of thousands of wireless messages daily to and from stations across the world, any vulnerability in this system would have been crucial. The Pacific's vital node in Hawai'i, which alone handled half the volume of traffic managed by the Pentagon itself, meant the crucial station could be vulnerable to attack or intercepted signals. Had the Japanese known of its existence and compromised the station, the blow would have been crippling.

To fully grasp the impact of communications, consider the Philippines invasion example cited by Raines. Executing the Leyte Gulf landing sixty days earlier than planned—due to intelligence uncovered about Japanese weakness—took the repeated relay of questions and reports across the Pacific from Washington to New Guinea and back. This U.S. military information moved securely across ten time zones and in high volume; it also moved quickly. Later, when Associated Press photographer Joe Rosenthal snapped his iconic picture of the flag raising atop Mt. Suribachi on 23 February 1945, a runner took the film down the volcano, it was developed on board a ship, and it was then wired to New York, all in less than eighteen hours. Without the sophisticated wartime networks of the U.S. military, this responsive command and control system would not have existed, making the Pacific War bloodier and longer. By war's end, advanced communications had reduced the perceived separation of Pacific locations from the United States. With that capability in place, Americans could try to widen their regional role after the defeat of Imperial Japan.

The Pacific's continuities bridge these chapters with one another, and Steve Call's melding of popular culture with air power evokes the portrayals of air power in wartime as responsive and precise, while also destructive on a large scale. Given the searing wartime images and newsreels showing Americans what Japanese naval aircraft did to the U.S. Fleet at Pearl Harbor, perhaps such arguments could only be expected. Ironically, prewar Navy publicists had noted, "despite the claims of air enthusiasts no battleship has yet been sunk by bombs" next to an image of the battleship USS *Arizona*: that ship was sunk one week later in Hawai'i with over 1,100 of its crew.[7] Air power was new and clearly had disrupted military conventions. Such a caesura compelled military advocates to show both the capability and the capacity of the airplane's potency in American hands.

The popular media emphases that Call shows of speedy and unified responses by American and Allied aircraft being on target portrayed land-based air power acting as a literal "bolt from the blue." His chapter, therefore, establishes the arc of destructive aerial attack and its impact as privileging *offensive* air power, not its defensive counterpart. This conclusion came despite media outlets' portrayal of the prowess of the American Volunteer Group, the "Flying Tigers." Instead, the Flying Tigers' seeming success—their protection of Rangoon—was negated by the Japanese conquest of that capital. Allied air power, therefore, would have to be shown surmounting the expanse of the Pacific and negating Japan's island- and sea-based defenses.[8] To expand on Call's point linking Alexander de Seversky to the post-1945 atomic era, the condition applies into the early twenty-first century, where air power seems best advertised by catchphrases such as "shock and awe"—that is, attacks enabled by precision-guided weapons rather than by homeland defense missions.

The thornier World War II question was how to portray aviation above a water-dominated PTO. For European image-makers, Battle of Britain pictures of *Balkankreuz*-bearing aircraft crashed in the Kentish countryside or photographs of German cities burning below sticks of just-dropped bombs showed air power successes. The diffuse Pacific War was different, broader and indistinct; islands looked relatively identical to media consumers at home. Even newsreels of the Doolittle Raid, showing the crews and aircraft beforehand as well as a prewar Tokyo air raid drill, left too much to the imagination, forcing use of simulations showing the attackers' targets in Japan.[9] Such reconstructions set the stage for the use by Disney of animation in *Victory through Air Power.* To demonstrate the influence of Pacific air power, creative artistry was needed, and the leap to show effect meant licensing portrayals of mass destruction of a cartoonish, non-human enemy. Here, then, was the technological subject to support the creation of a media-shaped understanding of World War II in the Pacific.

Incorporating special units into the U.S. Marine Corps, a service self-consciously tailored for Pacific warfare, fundamentally challenged its cultural underpinnings—and image—as a tough, self-reliant infantry force. Stephen Housknecht's examination of the Marine Corps Raiders uncovers questions of specialization in an already selective military. Small in numbers before World War II, the Marine Corps settled on a complex role—amphibious assault—as its core proficiency in the Pacific war. That role would demand grit and sophisticated problem solving, lending the Corps a mystique. Created just before American entry into World War II, the Raider Battalions were made up of volunteers singled out in training to perform unique, highly dangerous missions—usually with minimal outside support—and to tackle the most vital targets. Alongside so-called Para-Marines, a similarly-sized Marine Corps parachute formation, the Raiders would provide a highly mobile, specialized edge in the Pacific War.[10] With politically connected advocates in Colonel Merritt Edson and especially Colonel Evans Carlson, the Raiders were meant to master the isolated Pacific outposts of a relatively unknown Japanese enemy.

In practice, the special units proved only somewhat useful. The high quality of their personnel meant commanders needed to employ them sparingly, lest they be quickly decimated. Consequently, Edson's battalion fulfilled a subsidiary role taking Tulagi when the First Marine Division was busy on Guadalcanal. Carlson's force performed as expected on Makin Island, making a surreptitious approach by landing from the submarines USS *Argonaut* and *Nautilus,* and annihilating the defenders at acceptable cost. But amphibious operations became more routine and less specialized, something all Marine Corps infantry had to adapt to. After these initial successes, tougher Japanese defenses negated the local maneuvering room of the Pacific needed by the Raiders.

As Houseknecht notes, ending the Marine Corps experiment with special units reflected fewer opportunities for their use. Simply put, the Marine Corps solution to overcome dense Japanese positions—making coastal landings under cover of naval gunfire matched by inland advances supported by heavy weapons—contradicted the Raiders' ethic and equipment. Landing a battalion of Raiders at Tarawa or Peleliu would have quickly consumed the highly trained troops. The Marine Corps of 1944 and the new Commandant, General Alexander A. Vandegrift, who knew the Raiders from the Guadalcanal campaign, could not accept this "elite within an elite" and therefore disbanded the units.[11] Paradoxically, in the twenty-first century, three Marine Corps Raider Battalions have returned, intended to become what their predecessors were. But these modern Raiders do so under the pattern of "You're Marines first, and then your special operations is what you do. And we try to live by that."[12] The argument has been settled.

The Raiders were a Marine Corps innovation to manage the anticipated nature of island combat in the Pacific and create a sort of punctuated equilibrium to disturb static Japanese defenders. The post-1945 U.S. military occupation of the Pacific Islands marked a discontinuity of a different sort, bringing American service members into regular contact with other cultures on an even greater scale than was the case with the prewar American occupations of islands such as Guam.[13]

The island of Pohnpei may have suffered little physical damage during World War II, but the U.S. Navy occupation after the conflict renewed a lengthy imperial attempt at remaking its 5,000 residents' diet and their cultural approach toward food. In Chapter 4, Josh Levy describes how postwar Americans entered the remote insular Pacific to maintain its strategic integrity to threats from without as well as to introduce their vision of public health to the islanders. To make the islands safe meant making them American, at least in part. Previous German and Japanese administrators and colonists had left their mark on Pohnpei's society, especially in terms of food. Despite being present in small numbers—with just forty sailors aided by public health workers replacing 8,000 wartime Japanese military personnel—after 1945 the Americans would try to do the same.[14]

Americanization failed to extend to one seemingly interchangeable commodity for Navy personnel, rice, a good that the Pohnpeians deemed was best provided from Japan. The islanders rejected American white or brown rice, showing that a generation of Japanese colonial rule had durably reshaped tastes and diets. In the same light, newly available American food became important to the islanders in a manner similar to the changed palates among first-generation immigrants in the United States.[15] The crucial distinction was that exogenous food items continued to be added into diets on Pohnpei, a trend reinforced by their incorporation into tribute distribution. That shift stood in defiance of the price of imported items; valued foods began to be measured by their cost rather than their rarity or difficult harvesting, and therefore prized when given as a gift, even though they did not come from a local farm and could over the long term hurt the health of a consumer.

What is most surprising to read in Levy's essay is the longevity of the U.S. impact, despite both the relatively small numbers of sailors and health workers on the island and the agency Pohnpeians apparently exercised in their tribute uses of food. Americans successfully reshaped consumption in a relatively short period, although not necessarily in ways they had planned or even hoped. To be sure, the wrecking of the island's economy by blockade magnified the immediate impact of American arrival in 1945, but they had only six years in which to make changes. For good or ill, Japan had reshaped Pohnpeian lives over a generation and by stationing thousands of more people on the island. The subsequent and smaller American entry onto a medium-sized Pacific island, regardless of its local intention, was truly striking in the genuine and fast reshaping of the patterns of the people who lived there. This last point suggests that the post–World War II era was different, with changed resources granting small numbers of Americans more influence than European or Japanese colonists could have imagined a decade earlier. Problems could also arise, however, when Americans disagreed with one another on the impact that changing technology could make.

As the Pearl Harbor attack stunned many Americans at the opening of the Pacific War, the atomic bombs dropped on Hiroshima and Nagasaki proved similarly startling at the conflict's end. Military members saw things no differently, though they held opposing viewpoints in perceiving the new weapons' utility, as Hal Friedman notes. The U.S. Navy, however, had for fifty years seen the Pacific as its strategic preserve. The new weapon promised reevaluation of that status and a potential cut in funding.[16] For a service now possessing the world's foremost fleet, such a reduction would be a hard pill to swallow. The public messages derived from the Bikini atomic bomb tests would need modulation, as Vice Admiral William H. P. Blandy understood. Blandy, as wartime Chief of the Navy's Bureau of Ordnance, had faced service criticism three years earlier for unsolved problems in his office's torpedo designs; for him, there would be no public criticism of the Navy after the Crossroads tests.[17]

As Professor Friedman rightly notes, the services' struggle to define aviation and the resources it commanded dated back a generation. What was new in 1945, however, was the Navy's lack of an oceangoing opponent in the Pacific or anywhere else. Having tailored forces to operate at what would later be termed "transoceanic" distances and projecting strength into and across nine time zones' breadth, the Fleet was in the midst of reinventing its approach to war.[18] Despite winning its most important conflict in the Pacific in 1945, by 1946, the Navy held greater strength than ever before in history, but without a major sea power opponent. The U.S. Navy's leaders, therefore, believed their service's position was actually more vulnerable than at any time in the previous generation. Arguably, so did the U.S. Army and the U.S. Army Air Forces.[19]

Given that self-perceived technological vulnerability, a seam opened between the U.S. Navy and Army, the latter including the soon-to-be-independent AAF. Neither one trusted the other during the budget battles of the day. The sole means Blandy possessed to control the consequences of the Bikini Atoll tests was to admit the press to the remote atoll and make the explosions semi-public events while coordinating and limiting the commentaries made by the military staffs involved. Managing information in peacetime from then on assumed greater importance for the U.S. armed services in the Pacific, emerging as a new "front line." That pattern recurred throughout the period described in this book and beyond. Largely lost in the equation were the evicted island's residents, who had no choice in the matter until later paid restitution.[20] Here was a military service, the U.S. Navy, ideally suited to the Pacific, but after 1945 confronting a technical challenge that undermined its raison d'être.

Another shift of the postwar world stemmed from the possibility of revolution in a major power. Just as during the Russian Revolution, America crossed the Pacific to intervene on the Asian mainland, this time more broadly in China. Stretching American influence to the other side of the Pacific Ocean at the end of World War II meant a greater role in China. For Katherine Reist, the consequent American approach was to reform the Guomindang Army, forestall a renewed civil war, disarm millions of Japanese troops, and resist Soviet influence. The custom of using American military means to address China's internal instability extended back to the suppression of the 1900 Boxer Rebellion, through the 1912 arrival of the Army's 15th Infantry Regiment in North China, and to the garrisoning of the Shanghai by the 4th Marine Regiment after 1927. Six Navy gunboats patrolled the Yangtze River as well.[21] Wartime advisors and equipment, plus the American Volunteer Group, backed Chiang Kai-shek in the war with Japan. But the American military presence was intended to do far more after 1945. Given all its challenges, the training mission became a form of what was later termed "nation-building."

Here were members of the U.S. military, aided by the State Department, in 1946 trying to establish a friendly counterpart in the world's most populous nation. If successful, American defense would have an outpost in China, and no less a personage than General George C. Marshall arrived to smooth relations between the Guomindang and the Communists and make it possible.[22] The military training mission of just over 1,000 personnel would create a trio of modern services by reforming staffs and schools as well as improving China's recruiting, pay, procurement, communications, and supply system. The personnel of the services would come from the amalgamation of the Nationalist and Communist forces to build a national army. There was no shortage of ambition in the plan, Professor Reist explains, but reforming a nation by first building its army was difficult. The process simply came off the rails during China's Civil War, the world's largest armed conflict after 1945.

The broad American goal for China was defensive, to establish a reliable and capable military ally. But the contrast with previous experience in creating an Asian military could not have been more stark. In the Philippines, the colonialist United States spent a generation building an insular constabulary, only mobilizing a larger, mostly untrained army just before the Pearl Harbor attack.[23]

China was a vastly more complex problem, as the American diplomatic mission to the Guomindang had already discovered during the war with Japan. Stacked up against the local issues in China—including widespread corruption by Chiang Kai-shek's own officers; autonomous, even freelance militias; Mao Zedong's unwillingness to accept a subordinate role; and a Nationalist Army unwilling to fight the Communists—and with little time to make changes, the Joint U.S. Military Advisory Group stood no chance of success. The parallels to ultimately unsuccessful American attempts to create a South Vietnamese Army between 1950 and 1972 are prominent indeed.[24]

If continental East Asia frustrated the most ambitious American goals for China, Korea, and Vietnam, locations in the Pacific itself have been kinder to U.S. interests. Whether serving as a springboard to influence events on the mainland or to steer societies into sympathy with American goals, the U.S. occupation remade places such as Okinawa. Nicholas Sarantakes focuses on the lengthy occupation of Okinawa and the U.S. Army's control of news reporting from the Western Pacific island. In a period seeing Japan stripped of overseas holdings, Great Britain, France, and the Netherlands liquidating their empires, and the United States divesting itself of the Philippines, colonial occupiers no longer enjoyed their previously acceptable, open imperatives. The terms on the ground had changed, and potent American figures such as Representative Daniel Inouye of Hawai'i could ensure the standard was different. Foreign armies needed justification to remain in the insular or Western Pacific.[25] For Okinawa, however, neither most local residents nor the wider archipelagic populace wanted the Americans to leave; fear of Soviet Communism meant that U.S. military bases stayed. Still, the terms of remaining there—for a longer period and with a larger force than the post-1865 Reconstruction of the American Confederacy—needed mediation.

Those unique circumstances meant the Okinawa occupation required management of press reporting for a duration unmatched in postwar Austria, Germany, Italy, Japan, or South Korea. As the target of two atomic bomb attacks, Japanese citizens would not grant as broad a license as contemporary Germans permitted their subjugating armies. Conversely, West Germans signed on to accepting intrusive occupiers and confronted scrutiny of their society, perceiving that a monstrosity—the Soviet Army—sat just across a barbed wire fence and, later, the concrete of the Berlin Wall.[26] American occupiers walked a different line in East Asia, with collective security or economic development the sole positive messages they could employ and messages that demanded the regulated use of "soft power." One suspects the linguistic challenge did not help, with incomprehension perhaps prompting the U.S. Military Government to influence Okinawan local politics and, for example, have Mayor Senaga Kamejiro removed.

The fracturing of support for the occupation during the 1960s partly stemmed from outside the island and beyond Japan. The basing of U.S. military forces on Okinawa could be ignored or abstracted until a KC-135 crashed at Kadena Air Force Base in May 1966, killing an islander.[27] Subsequently, a B-52 bomber, armed for a bombing mission over South Vietnam, skidded and crashed while taking off in November 1968.[28] No Okinawans were hurt in the latter case, but such events could not be kept out of the press, and media commentary grew in volume. These events and news of them also brought home the meaning of hosting the American military, and the need to constrain that meaning. Hosting the U.S. military as it waged war in Southeast Asia—whether for Okinawans, all Japanese, or the broader world—became less palatable. As Sarantakes concludes, the gradual opening of the press in that context sped the end of the Military Government, making the American Pacific presence strictly one by invitation and with more conditions attached. These circumstances are still raising questions in American relations with Okinawa and Japan during the twenty-first century.

The Pacific world of the early to mid-twentieth century—where between them Europe, Japan, and the United States could dominate its peoples largely unimpeded—is gone. That regional condition has been replaced today by increasing economic importance, broader political negotiation, and wider cultural acceptance as well as the potential for the next confrontation between the leading nations of the world.[29] How the questions of Asia and the Pacific are resolved cannot be foreseen. But the essays in *War in the American Pacific and East Asia, 1941–1972* connect that mid-twentieth-century world to our own, offering important way points for navigating between then and now. One of the principal values of studying history is to gain clues from the past, obtain insights about the current day, and perceive how events might unfold in the future. The essays presented in this volume offer us much to ponder as we do so.

Notes

I would like to thank my mentors, Eugenia Kiesling, Leo Ribuffo, and Ronald Spector, for their past efforts to inject greater rigor and clearer writing into my work as well as for their celebrating original thought. For the confidence Hal Friedman placed in me, I extend my thanks. And to my family, thank you for granting me the time needed to make scholarly contributions.

The opinions expressed here are solely those of the author and do not reflect those of the Department of the Navy, the Department of Defense, or the United States government.

1. For a description, see http://dfat.gov.au/trade/agreements/tpp/pages/trans-

pacific-partnership-agreement-tpp.aspx, accessed 28 May 2016. This agreement was canceled on 23 January 2017 by President Donald J. Trump; see https://www.whitehouse.gov/the-press-office/2017/01/23/presidential-memorandum-regarding-withdrawal-united-states-trans-pacific, accessed 4 August 2017.

2. Alfred Thayer Mahan, *The Problem of Asia and Its Effect upon International Policies* (Boston: Little, Brown and Co., 1900), 162–164, 192, at https://books.google.com/books?id=cshlc277vBEC&printsec=frontcover&dq=Alfred+Thayer+Mahan%22+the+problem+of+asia&hl=en&sa=X&ved=0ahUKEwj9s-i80_3MAhUFXD4KHb6NArwQ6AEIHDAA#v=onepage&q&f=false, accessed 28 May 2016.

3. Making these estimates was prompted by Ricky W. Law, "Knowledge Is Power: The Interwar German and Japanese Mass Media in the Making of the Axis," *GHI Bulletin* 54 (Spring 2014) at http://www.ghi-dc.org/fileadmin/user_upload/GHI_Washington/Publications/Bulletin54/bu54_027.pdf, accessed 29 May 2016.

4. U.S. Department of Defense, *Sustaining U.S. Global Leadership: Priorities for 21st Century Defense* (Washington, DC: U.S. Government Printing Office, 3 January 2012): 2, at http://archive.defense.gov/news/Defense_Strategic_Guidance.pdf, accessed 29 May 2016. Emphasis in original. This is the so-called pivot to Asia, although the Defense Department describes it as a "rebalance."

5. U.S. Congress, *Report of the Joint Committee on the Investigation of the Pearl Harbor Attack* (Washington, DC: U.S. Government Printing Office, 1946), 225, at https://archive.org/stream/investigationofp00unit#page/n7/mode/2up, accessed 30 May 2016.

6. Tony Sale, "The Lorenz Cipher and How Bletchley Park Broke It," at http://www.codesandciphers.org.uk/lorenz/fish.htm, accessed 30 May 2016.

7. See the page excerpted from the 1941 Army-Navy Football Game program at http://www.navy.mil/navydata/people/secnav/danzig/speeches/arizona3.jpg, accessed 28 May 2016.

8. David C. Evans and Mark R. Peattie, *Kaigun: Strategy, Tactics and Technology in the Imperial Japanese Navy, 1887–1941* (Annapolis: Naval Institute Press, 1997), 464–467, 489.

9. "Yanks Bomb Tokyo!" Castle News Parade (film MP 71–8:99, circa 1942), at https://www.youtube.com/watch?v=-yXzYxUC93A, accessed 29 May 2016.

10. Including Corporals Ira H. Hayes and Harlon H. Block, who helped raise the Iwo Jima flag. See Jon T. Hoffman, *Silk Chutes and Hard Fighting: U.S. Marine Corps Parachute Units in World War II* (Washington, DC: Marine Corps History and Museums Division, 1999), 38, at http://www.marines.mil/Portals/59/Publications/Silk%20Chutes%20and%20Hard%20Fighting%20-%20U.S.%20Marine%20Corps%20Parachute%20Units%20in%20WWII%20%20PCN%2019000314700.pdf, accessed 29 May 2016. Another of the flag raisers, Sergeant Michael Strank, had been in the Third Raider Battalion.

11. Ibid.

12. Colonel Craig Kozeniesky, quoted in Jay Price, "Marine Raiders Keep Low Profile among U.S. Special Operations Forces," National Public Radio, *All Things Considered*, 16 May 2016, at http://www.npr.org/2016/05/16/478272716/marine-raiders-keep-low-profile-among-u-s-special-operations-forces, accessed 29 May 2016.

13. Anne Hattori, *Colonial Dis-Ease: U.S. Navy Health Policies and the Chamorros of Guam, 1898–1941* (Honolulu: University of Hawaii Press, 2004).

14. One-quarter of the forces came from the Imperial Japanese Navy, while the balance were Army soldiers. See Ponape entry in "Japanese Garrisons on the By-Passed Pacific Islands, 1944–1945," at http://www.dutcheastindies.webs.com/japan_garrison.html, accessed 30 May 2016.

15. Louis E. Grivetti and Marie B. Paquette, "Food Choices among First Generation Chinese in California," *California Agriculture* (December 1978), 7–8, at https://ucanr.edu/repositoryfiles/ca3212p6-62595.pdf, accessed 30 May 2016.

16. Edward Miller, *War Plan Orange: The U.S. Strategy to Beat Japan, 1897–1945* (Annapolis: Naval Institute Press, 1991).

17. Buford Rowland and William R. Boyd, *U.S. Navy Bureau of Ordnance in World War II* (Washington, DC: Department of the Navy, 1953), 95–109.

18. The most recent works are Hal M. Friedman, *Blue versus Purple: The U.S. Naval War College, the Soviet Union, and the New Enemy in the Pacific, 1946* (Newport, RI: Naval War College Press, 2017); and Jeffrey G. Barlow, *From Hot War to Cold: The U.S. Navy and National Security Affairs, 1945–1955* (Palo Alto, CA: Stanford University Press, 2009). The term *transoceanic* originated in Samuel P. Huntington, "National Policy and the Transoceanic Navy," *USNI Proceedings* 80 (May 1954), at https://blog.usni.org/2009/03/09/from-our-archive-national-policy-and-the-transoceanic-navy-by-samuel-p-huntington, accessed 29 May 2016.

19. I am indebted to Hal Friedman's point of rising American insecurity by drawing my attention to George Kennan's 1950 first Chicago lecture. See John J. Mearsheimer, "Introduction" to George F. Kennan, *American Diplomacy* (Chicago: University of Chicago Press, 2012) ix, at http://mearsheimer.uchicago.edu/pdfs/Kennan.pdf, accessed 29 May 2016.

20. William M. Hammond, *Public Affairs: The Military and the Media*, 2 vols. (Washington, DC: Center of Military History, United States Army, 1990, 1996), at http://www.history.army.mil/html/bookshelves/collect/usavn.html, accessed 31 May 2016. For the Bikini Islanders, see Jonathan Weisgall, *Operation Crossroads: The Atomic Bomb Tests at Bikini Atoll* (Annapolis: Naval Institute Press, 1994).

21. For three years, the Fifteenth Infantry was commanded by then-Colonel George C. Marshall, while Fourth Marine Regiment units were led by then-Major Alexander Vandegrift. See Bernard D. Cole, *Gunboats and Marines: The United States Navy in China, 1925–1928* (Newark: University of Delaware Press, 1982).

22. See Michael Hunt, *Frontier Defense and the Open Door: Manchuria in Chinese-American Relations, 1895–1911* (New Haven, CT: Yale University Press, 1973). Again, I am indebted to Hal Friedman for reminding me of this work.

23. Louis Morton, *The Fall of the Philippines* (Washington, DC: Office of the Chief of Military History, Department of the Army, 1953), Chapter 2, at http://www.history.army.mil/html/books/005/5-2-1/CMH_Pub_5-2-1.pdf, accessed 30 May 2016.

24. Ronald H. Spector, *Advice and Support: The Early Years* (Washington, DC: U.S. Army Center of Military History, 1985) at http://www.history.army.mil/html/

books/091/91-1/CMH_Pub_91-1-B.pdf; and James L. Collins Jr., *The Development and Training of the South Vietnamese Army, 1950–1972* (Washington, DC: U.S. Army Center of Military History, 1975), at http://www.history.army.mil/html/books/090/90-10/cmh-Pub_90-10.pdf, both accessed 31 May 2016.

25. Ronald H. Spector, *In the Ruins of Empire: The Japanese Surrender and the Battle for Postwar Asia* (New York: Random House, 2007). The contrast with the U.S. presence in South Korea before and after the Korean War is apposite; see Allan R. Millett, *The War for Korea, 1945–1950: A House Burning* (Lawrence: University Press of Kansas, 2005).

26. Donald A. Carter, *Forging the Shield: The U.S. Army in Europe, 1951–1962* (Washington, DC: Center of Military History, 2015), 375–385.

27. See http://aviation-safety.net/database/record.php?id=19660519-0, accessed 31 May 2016.

28. See https://aviation-safety.net/wikibase/wiki.php?id=48320, accessed 29 May 2016, and Thomas R. H. Havens, *Fire across the Sea: The Vietnam War and Japan, 1965–1975* (Princeton: Princeton University Press, 1987).

29. Joseph A. Gagliano, *Congressional Policymaking in Sino-U.S. Relations during the Post–Cold War Era* (London: Routledge, 2015).

Bibliography

Primary Sources

U.S. Congress. *Report of the Joint Committee on the Investigation of the Pearl Harbor Attack.* Washington, DC: U.S. Government Printing Office, 1946. At https://archive.org/stream/investigationofp00unit#page/n7/mode/2up, accessed 30 May 2016.

U.S. Department of Defense. *Sustaining U.S. Global Leadership: Priorities for 21st Century Defense.* Washington, DC: U.S. Government Printing Office, 3 January 2012. At http://archive.defense.gov/news/Defense_Strategic_Guidance.pdf, accessed 29 May 2016.

"Yanks Bomb Tokyo!" Castle News Parade (film MP 71-8:99, circa 1942). At https://www.youtube.com/watch?v=-yXzYxUC93A, accessed 29 May 2016.

Secondary Sources

Books

Barlow, Jeffrey G. *From Hot War to Cold: The U.S. Navy and National Security Affairs, 1945–1955.* Palo Alto, CA: Stanford University Press, 2009.

Bradley, James, and Ron Powers. *Flags of Our Fathers.* New York: Bantam, 2000.

Cole, Bernard D. *Gunboats and Marines: The United States Navy in China, 1925–1928.* Newark: University of Delaware Press, 1982.

Evans, David C., and Mark R. Peattie. *Kaigun: Strategy, Tactics, and Technology in the Imperial Japanese Navy, 1887–1941.* Annapolis: Naval Institute Press, 1997.

Friedman, Hal M. *Blue versus Purple: The U.S. Naval War College, the Soviet Union, and the New Enemy in the Pacific, 1946.* Newport, RI: Naval War College Press, 2017.

Gagliano, Joseph A. *Congressional Policymaking in Sino-U.S. Relations during the Post–Cold War Era.* London: Routledge, 2015.

Hattori, Anne. *Colonial Dis-Ease: U.S. Navy Health Policies and the Chamorros of Guam, 1898–1941.* Honolulu: University of Hawaii Press, 2004.

Havens, Thomas R. H. *Fire across the Sea: The Vietnam War and Japan, 1965–1975.* Princeton: Princeton University Press, 1987.

Hunt, Michael. *Frontier Defense and the Open Door: Manchuria in Chinese-American Relations, 1895–1911.* New Haven, CT: Yale University Press, 1973.

Kennan, George F. *American Diplomacy.* Chicago: University of Chicago Press, 2012.

Mahan, Alfred Thayer. *The Problem of Asia and Its Effect upon International Policies.* Boston: Little, Brown and Co., 1900.

Miller, Edward. *War Plan Orange: The U.S. Strategy to Beat Japan, 1897–1945.* Annapolis: Naval Institute Press, 1991.

Millett, Allan R. *The War for Korea, 1945–1950: A House Burning.* Lawrence: University Press of Kansas, 2005.

Spector, Ronald H. *In the Ruins of Empire: The Japanese Surrender and the Battle for Postwar Asia.* New York: Random House, 2007.

Official Histories

Carter, Donald A. *Forging the Shield: The U.S. Army in Europe, 1951–1962.* Washington, DC: Center of Military History, 2015.

Collins, James L., Jr. *Development and Training of the South Vietnamese Army, 1950–1972.* Washington, DC: U.S. Army Center of Military History, 1975.

Hammond, William M. *Public Affairs: The Military and the Media.* 2 vols. Washington, DC: Center of Military History, United States Army, 1990, 1996.

Hoffman, Jon T. *Silk Chutes and Hard Fighting: U.S. Marine Corps Parachute Units in World War II.* Washington, DC: U.S. Marine Corps History Division, 1999.

Morton, Louis. *The Fall of the Philippines.* Washington, DC: Office of the Chief of Military History, Department of the Army, 1953.

Rowland, Buford, and William R. Boyd. *U.S. Navy Bureau of Ordnance in World War II.* Washington, DC: U.S. Department of the Navy, 1953.

Spector, Ronald H. *Advice and Support: The Early Years.* Washington, DC: U.S. Army Center of Military History, 1985.

Articles

Danzig, Richard. Annual Secretary of the Navy Forrestal Lecture delivered at the U.S. Naval Academy, Annapolis, Maryland, 17 April 2000. At http://www.navy.mil/navydata/people/secnav/danzig/speeches/forrestal0417.html, accessed 28 May 2016.

Grivetti, Louis E., and Marie B. Paquette. "Food Choices among First Generation Chinese in California." *California Agriculture* 32:12 (December 1978): 6–8. At https://ucanr.edu/repositoryfiles/ca3212p6–62595.pdf, accessed 30 May 2016.

Huntington, Samuel P. "National Policy and the Transoceanic Navy." *USNI Proceedings* 80:5 (May 1954). At https://blog.usni.org/2009/03/09/from-our-archive-national-policy-and-the-transoceanic-navy-by-samuel-p-huntington, accessed 29 May 2016.

Law, Ricky W. "Knowledge Is Power: The Interwar German and Japanese Mass Media in the Making of the Axis." *GHI Bulletin* 54 (Spring 2014). At http://www.ghidc.org/fileadmin/user_upload/GHI_Washington/Publications/Bulletin54/bu54_027.pdf, accessed 29 May 2016.

Price, Jay. "Marine Raiders Keep Low Profile among U.S. Special Operations Forces." National Public Radio, *All Things Considered*, 16 May 2016, at http://www.npr.org/2016/05/16/478272716/marine-raiders-keep-low-profile-among-u-s-special-operations-forces, accessed 29 May 2016.

Websites

Aviation Flight Safety Network Wikibase. At https://aviation-safety.net/wikibase/, accessed 29 May 2016.

Forgotten Campaign: The Dutch East Indies Campaign 1941–1942. At http://www.dutcheastindies.webs.com/japan_garrison.html, accessed 30 May 2016.

The Lorenz Cipher and How Bletchley Park Broke It. At http://www.codesandciphers.org.uk/lorenz/fish.htm, accessed 29 May 2016.

Acknowledgments

This project has been a long time in creation. From inception to publication has taken over a decade and a half, in part because some contributors left the project for one reason or another and since a myriad of other logistical and career factors interceded. Along those lines, the contributors and I would like to thank the individuals who assisted us in the process, though readers should understand that any errors in this work are ultimately our responsibility.

As Editor, I would like to thank the staffs of the Air Force Historical Research Agency, the Douglas MacArthur Memorial Archives and Library, the Defense Technical Intelligence Center, the Department of Energy, the Dwight D. Eisenhower Library, the Harry S. Truman Library, the Library of Congress, National Archives II, and the Navy Operational Archives (now part of the Naval History and Heritage Command). I would also like to thank Chris Hamel of Heritage Hall School in Oklahoma City and Michael Unsworth, Michigan State University History Bibliographer, for assistance with this project a long time ago. In fact, it was long conversations about American military interservice rivalry with Chris and Mike that got me thinking about the role of bureaucratic factors in the creation of U.S. national security policy and what would eventually become the chapter I have contributed here.

Joe Fitzharris, Professor Emeritus of History at the University of St. Thomas in Minneapolis, was also key in the creation of this volume. As the Great Plains Regional Coordinator for the Society for Military History and as the longtime organizer of the Northern Great Plains History Conference, Joe was, to a great extent, the "founder of the feast." It was the Northern Great Plains History Conference at which I met most of the authors who would eventually contribute to the volume. It was in the process of presenting numerous papers at Northern Great Plains, as well as interaction with people over many congenial meals associated with the Conference, that I first got the idea for this collection of essays. Joe cannot be thanked enough for literally providing the venue by which all of this germinated, but also in encouraging the process and standing by to give essential advice along the way about the project, careers, family, perspective, and everything else that makes us what we are.

I would also like to thank the staff at the University Press of Kentucky for their patience and flexibility with an editor who looks on this project like a parent looks on a child. I particularly thank Melissa Hammer, Senior Acquisitions Editor; Ila McEntire, Senior Editing Supervisor; Natalie O'Neal, Editorial Assistant; Jackie Wilson, Marketing Assistant; and Donna Bouvier, Freelance Manuscript Editor.

I would especially like to thank the contributors to the collection for persevering in the completion of the volume and assisting in the process throughout the endeavor.

Contributors

Steve Call is Professor of History at SUNY-Broome Community College. He holds a PhD from Ohio State University (1997). His publications include *Danger Close: Tactical Air Controllers in Afghanistan and Iraq* (2007) and *Selling Air Power: Military Aviation and American Popular Culture after World War II* (2009).

Hal M. Friedman is Associate Chair of History and Professor of Modern History in the History Program of the Department of Social Sciences within the School of Liberal Arts at Henry Ford College in Dearborn, Michigan. Educated at Eastern Michigan University with a BS in Political Science and History (magna cum laude) in 1987, Professor Friedman took his MA and PhD degrees in the History of International Relations at Michigan State University in 1991 and 1995, respectively. He has taught as an Adjunct Faculty Member of the Command and Staff College Distance Education Program within the U.S. Marine Corps University's College of Continuing Education. Professor Friedman has published a trilogy on U.S. national security policy toward the Pacific Basin between 1945 and 1947, as well as a trilogy on the U.S. Naval War College's transition from the Pacific War to the Cold War in the Pacific. He has also published numerous articles and book reviews in journals, and has been honored a number of times, including with the Major General Thomas S. Jones USMC Distance Learning Instructor of the Year Award for the Fort Worth Region from the Command and Staff College Distance Education Program, Marine Corps College of Continuing Education. He is also a Graduate Senior Instructor in Norwich University's online Master of Arts in History Program, an Adjunct Lecturer of Strategy and Policy in the U.S. Naval War College's Non-Resident Fleet Seminar Program, and both the Recording Secretary and Midwest Regional Coordinator for the Society for Military History.

Stephen Houseknecht holds a BA in History from Evangel University and an MA in History from Missouri State University, with an emphasis in American military history. His master's thesis focuses on the creation of the U.S. Marine Raider Battalions in 1942, the forces that led to their eventual decline in 1944, and the nature of elite military cultures. He is currently the Director of Academic Support in the Center for Student Success at Evangel University in Springfield, Missouri, where he also serves as an Adjunct Professor of History.

Josh Levy is a PhD Candidate in History at the University of Illinois at Urbana-Champaign. His dissertation is entitled "Eating Empire, Going Local: Food, Health, and Sovereignty on Pohnpei, 1898–1986." His publications include *Micronesian Government: Yesterday, Today, and Tomorrow*, a high school level civics textbook currently in use in Micronesian schools. He holds a BA from Amherst College and a Master of Theological Studies degree from Harvard Divinity School.

Sarandis "Randy" Papadopoulos received his BA from the University of Toronto, an MA from the University of Alabama, and a PhD from the George Washington University. His dissertation was entitled "Feeding the Sharks: The Logistics of Submarine Warfare, 1935–1945," comparing the German and U.S. Navies. He has been a Lecturer in History at George Washington University, the University of Maryland–College Park, and Norwich University, and is currently the Secretariat Historian for the Department of the Navy. His publications include numerous articles, especially those in the book *You Cannot Surge Trust: Combined Naval Operations of the Royal Australian Navy, Canadian Navy, Royal Navy, and United States Navy, 1991–2003* (2013). Papadopoulos has also served as principal coauthor of the book *Pentagon 9/11* (2007), which was published under the auspices of the Historian, Office of the Secretary of Defense. A former Society for Military History Regional Coordinator, he is a trustee for the Society and since 2015 he has served as President of the U.S. Commission on Military History and helps organize the Military Classics Seminar, a monthly program of the Commission. Papadopoulos is also a recipient of the U.S. Department of the Navy Superior and Distinguished Civilian Service Awards.

Rebecca Robbins Raines is a retired historian with the U.S. Army Center of Military History in Washington, DC. She received a BA in History from the University of Maine and an MA in American History from Georgetown University. She was Chief of the Center's Force Structure and Unit History Branch, which is responsible for maintaining the history of the Army's units. During her tenure with the Center, she became an expert on the Signal Corps. She is the author of *Getting the Message Through: A Branch History of the U.S. Army Signal Corps* (1996) in the Army Historical Series as well as the volume *Signal Corps* in the Army Lineage Series (2006), and has presented papers and written numerous articles on various aspects of the Corps' history. She is currently writing a biography of the Signal Corps' founder, Brigadier General Albert J. Myer, for whom Fort Myer, Virginia, is named. She and her husband, Edgar, reside in Alexandria, Virginia.

Katherine K. Reist specializes in East Asian History, with a particular interest in the American military in China from the Boxers to the People's Republic of China. She is a graduate of Muskingum College and the Ohio State University. Presently Head of the History Department at the University of Pittsburgh at Johnstown, she is an Associate Professor in the Department. Recent articles appeared in *New Interpretations in Naval History* and *The Encyclopedia of War*, as well as in *The Journal of Military History* ("The American Military Advising Mission to China, 1945–1949").

Nicholas Evan Sarantakes is an Associate Professor of Strategy and Policy at the U.S. Naval War College. He earned a BA from the University of Texas, an MA from the University of Kentucky, and a PhD from the University of Southern California; all three degrees are in History. His first two books looked at the battle and occupation of Okinawa: *Keystone: The American Occupation of Okinawa and U.S.-Japanese Relations* (2000), followed by *Seven Stars: The Okinawa Battle Diaries of Simon Bolivar Buckner, Jr. and Joseph Stilwell* (2004). His next book looked at coalition warfare: *Allies against the Rising Sun: The United States, the British Nations, and the Defeat of Imperial Japan* (2009). His fourth book, *Dropping the Torch: Jimmy Carter, the Olympic Boycott, and the Cold War* (2010), is a diplomatic history of the 1980 Olympic Boycott. His most recent book is *Making* Patton: *A Classic War Film's Epic Journey to the Silver Screen* (2012). He is currently writing a book on the Battle of Manila, and another on the home front in World War II. He has written a number of articles that have appeared in publications including *Diplomatic History, English Historical Review, Journal of Military History, Joint Forces Quarterly,* and ESPN.com. He is a Fellow of the Royal Historical Society and has received five writing awards. He previously taught at Texas A&M University–Commerce, the U.S. Air War College, the University of Southern Mississippi, and the U.S. Army Command and General Staff College. He is also a Book Review Editor for *Presidential Studies Quarterly.*

David J. Ulbrich is currently Associate Professor and Program Director of Norwich University's online MA Programs in History and Military History. He received his doctorate in History from Temple University in 2007. The Naval Institute Press published his first book, *Preparing for Victory: Thomas Holcomb and the Making of the Marine Corps, 1936–1943*, which won the 2012 General Wallace M. Greene Jr. Prize for the Outstanding Book on Marine Corps History and earned an Honorable Mention for the 2012 Rear Admiral Samuel Eliot Morison Award for Naval Literature. More recently, Ulbrich and Matthew S. Muehlbauer published the textbook *Ways of War: American Military History* *from the Colonial Period to the Twenty-First Century* (2nd ed., 2017). Ulbrich and Muehlbauer also coedited *The Routledge Global History of War and Society* (2018).

Index

Page numbers in italics refer to illustrations.